Advances in Experimental Philosophy of Law

Advances in Experimental Philosophy

Series Editor:

Justin Sytsma, Associate Professor in Philosophy, Victoria University of Wellington, New Zealand

Editorial Board:

Empirical and experimental philosophy is generating tremendous excitement, producing unexpected results that are challenging traditional philosophical methods. *Advances in Experimental Philosophy* responds to this trend, bringing together some of the most exciting voices in the field to understand the approach and measure its impact in contemporary philosophy. The result is a series that captures past and present developments and anticipates future research directions.

To provide in-depth examinations, each volume links experimental philosophy to a key philosophical area. They provide historical overviews alongside case studies, reviews of current problems and discussions of new directions. For upper-level undergraduates, postgraduates and professionals actively pursuing research in experimental philosophy these are essential resources.

Titles in the series include:

Advances in Experimental Epistemology, edited by James R. Beebe
Advances in Experimental Moral Psychology, edited by Hagop Sarkissian and Jennifer Cole Wright
Advances in Experimental Philosophy and Philosophical Methodology, edited by Jennifer Nado

Advances in Experimental Philosophy of Law

Edited by
Karolina Prochownik and Stefan Magen

BLOOMSBURY ACADEMIC
LONDON • NEW YORK • OXFORD • NEW DELHI • SYDNEY

BLOOMSBURY ACADEMIC
Bloomsbury Publishing Plc
50 Bedford Square, London, WC1B 3DP, UK
1385 Broadway, New York, NY 10018, USA
29 Earlsfort Terrace, Dublin 2, Ireland

BLOOMSBURY, BLOOMSBURY ACADEMIC and the Diana logo are trademarks of
Bloomsbury Publishing Plc

First published in Great Britain 2023

Copyright © Karolina Prochownik, Stefan Magen and Contributors, 2023

Karolina Prochownik and Stefan Magen have asserted their right under the Copyright,
Designs and Patents Act, 1988, to be identified as Editors of this work.

For legal purposes the Acknowledgments on p. xi constitute an extension of this
copyright page.

Series design by Catherine Wood
Cover image © Dieter Leistner / Gallerystock

A catalog record for this book is available from the British Library.

A catalog record for this book is available from the Library of Congress.

ISBN: HB: 978-1-3502-6016-0
ePDF: 978-1-3502-6017-7
eBook: 978-1-3502-6018-4

Series: Advances in Experimental Philosophy

Typeset by Deanta Global Publishing Services, Chennai, India

To find out more about our authors and books visit www.bloomsbury.com and
sign up for our newsletters.

Contents

Figures

Tables

Acknowledgments

We are immensely grateful to all who have enabled this volume to come into being. First of all, we are thankful to the former editor of the *Advances in Experimental Philosophy* series, James Beebe, for the trust that he showed in inviting us to co-edit the volume on *Advances in Experimental Philosophy of Law* and for his invaluable guidance. We are also grateful to the current editor of the series, Justin Sytsma, for his feedback and guidance at the later stages of the book production. We sincerely thank the editorial board (Joshua Alexander, James Andow, Florian Cova, Joshua Knobe, Edouard Machery, Thomas Nadelhoffer, Jennifer Nado, Eddy Nahmias, Noel Struchiner, Pascale Willemsen, Jennifer Cole Wright) for their constructive feedback regarding the book's outline and list of contributors. We would also like to thank the anonymous reviewers, who generously dedicated their time and talent in reviewing the chapters in the current collection and who substantially contributed to the work's exceptional quality.

Most of all, we are grateful to all of the volume's contributors, who delivered outstanding, original chapters that meaningfully integrate previous research and stimulate future exploration in experimental jurisprudence—especially since producing such exemplary research was particularly challenging during the Covid-19 pandemic.

We are also thankful to the editorial team of Bloomsbury Publishing, especially Suzie Nash and Colleen Coalter, for their kindness and collaboration at different stages of manuscript preparation.

Finally, our work in co-editing this volume was supported by a generous DFG-CAPES grant, "Experimental Legal Philosophy: The Concept of Law Revisited" (project number 434400506).

Introduction

The Past and Future of the Experimental Philosophy of Law

Karolina Prochownik

The experimental philosophy of law (also called experimental jurisprudence or XJur[1]) is a relatively recent field of interdisciplinary research[2] that uses empirical data and methods to inform questions of jurisprudence (Knobe & Shapiro, 2021, p. 165; Prochownik, 2021, p. 1; see also Donelson; Hoeft; this volume). XJur researchers have been mainly concerned with using experimental studies conducted on ordinary people's intuitions about concepts of legal and legal-philosophical significance and underpinning psychological mechanisms to inform (conceptual) debates in legal theory and legal philosophy (e.g., Tobia, 2022; Prochownik, 2021).

The two main lines of XJur research differ by the type of questions they aim to inform and/or the type of concepts they investigate. On the one hand, some research has addressed *particular* jurisprudential questions concerning specific concepts of legal theory and practice, such as intentionality, causation, reasonableness, and consent (see Sommers, 2021; Prochownik, 2021; Tobia, 2022; for reviews). Many of these studies have investigated lay people's (and, occasionally, legal experts') concepts and their congruence with their counterparts in the legal system (e.g., Sommers, 2020; Tobia, 2018; Kneer & Bourgeois-Gironde, 2017; Prochownik, 2022).

On the other hand, more recent empirical studies have addressed *general* jurisprudential questions concerning concepts of broader legal and philosophical significance (Prochownik, 2021; see also Donelson; this volume). For instance, several empirical studies have investigated people's concept of a legal rule (Struchiner, Hannikainen, & Almeida, 2020; Almeida, Struchiner, & Hannikainen, 2022; Flanagan, Almeida, Struchiner, & Hannikainen, 2022) and the concept of law itself[3] (Donelson & Hannikainen, 2020; Hannikainen, Tobia et al., 2021; Flanagan & Hannikainen, 2022; Hannikainen, Flanagan, & Prochownik, 2022).[4]

This volume extends these two main lines of XJur research by presenting novel empirical findings, elaborating on previous studies, and indicating future research directions in general and particular jurisprudence, and beyond. Finally, the current collection opens avenues for diversification of empirical research methods and, by doing so, paves the way for more methodologically inclusive XJur. This last point is important because XJur, like the entire experimental philosophy movement, has historically relied on vignette studies and questionnaires. Accordingly, I summarize the ten chapters in this collection, classified into three topical groups: "Topics in Experimental General Jurisprudence," "Topics in Experimental Particular Jurisprudence," and "(New) Methods and Topics in Jurisprudence."

I.1 Topics in Experimental General Jurisprudence

General jurisprudence includes the most significant debates in legal philosophy, concerning what is law and the law's connection to moral values. These types of questions were historically undertaken by scholars in analytical jurisprudence, who often used conceptual analysis to formulate theories of the sufficient and necessary conditions for something to be a law (e.g., whether formally legislated rules must align with moral standards to count as law). Since there have been only a handful of studies in XJur examining the concepts of general significance for jurisprudence, there are many issues open for debate regarding whether (and if so, which) empirical research methods can be used to inform debates in this domain, the scope of such investigations, and their legal-philosophical implications. Two chapters in this collection directly speak to these questions.

In Chapter 1, "Experimental Approaches to General Jurisprudence," Raff Donelson argues that empirical studies can advance debates in traditional analytical jurisprudence, both with regard to meta-debates about this field and specific issues within it. He envisages three projects within experimental general jurisprudence that could help shed light on these problems, following a typology for research projects in experimental philosophy proposed by Nadelhoffer and Nahmias (2007). The first project of Experimental Analysis would focus on examining people's intuitions concerning philosophically significant matters (Nadelhoffer & Nahmias, 2007, p. 126). As specifically applied to general legal philosophy, it may primarily provide insights into people's intuitions concerning the concept of law. Donelson argues that this line of research is relevant, insofar as many scholars in analytical jurisprudence treat premises regarding what counts as law as common ground. Therefore, Experimental Analysis, in general experimental jurisprudence, can examine if such premises truly are commonly shared.[5] For instance, in this vein, Donelson cites his work with Hannikainen (2020), finding that laypeople's intuitions do not unequivocally align with Lon Fuller's (1964) theory that only a system of rules constrained by eight procedural principles of "inner morality" can count as law. Thus, Donelson concludes, Fullerian intuitions are not common ground.

The second project of Experimental Descriptivism would examine the psychological mechanisms underpinning people's intuitions about philosophically relevant questions (Nadelhoffer & Nahmias, 2007). According to Donelson, this project, when applied to general jurisprudence, may help to assess whether Experimental Analysis legitimately treats folk intuitions as sources of insight about the concept of law. For instance, the aforementioned Donelson and Hannikainen (2020) found that people endorse Fullerian principles as necessary truths about the law, at the same time believing that actual laws violate these principles. Such contradictory intuitions about Fuller's theory may result from the susceptibility of folk judgments to error. But these seemingly inconsistent judgments may also arise because law is a dual-character concept. Specifically, there may be two independent criteria for categorizing something as an instance of law (i.e., a system of rules may count as a "law" when it satisfies one set of criteria, but must satisfy a set of extra normative criteria to count as "true law").[6] Under the former interpretation, folk intuitions would not be reliable sources of insight in legal philosophizing; under the latter interpretation, they would be.

The third project of Experimental Restrictionism would examine the reliability and diversity of people's intuitions (Nadelhoffer & Nahmias, 2007). According to Donelson, this project, when applied to general jurisprudence, may help to illuminate whether there is a univocal or pluralist concept of law. This could be tested, for instance, by comparing intuitions about the law held by people from different countries.

Finally, Donelson responds to two potential criticisms of XJur concerning the expertise defense argument[7] and the limitations of survey methodology. First, XJur is sometimes criticized for concerning itself with lay intuitions instead of expert intuitions. According to Donelson, these critics need to establish first why expert judgments are preferred over lay judgments and, second, must identify the relevant experts. Second, although survey methodology has been recently criticized (e.g., Moss, 2017), it is not the only method of conducting research in experimental jurisprudence. To overcome this criticism, Donelson argues for greater methodological diversity within XJur.[8]

Another related question in general jurisprudence concerns the nature of legal rules. In Chapter 2, "The Experimental Jurisprudence of the Concept of Rule: Implications for the Hart-Fuller Debate," Guilherme de Almeida, Noel Struchiner, and Ivar Hannikainen use their experimental findings to inform another influential debate in legal philosophy, which took place between Hart and Fuller in 1958. The Hart-Fuller debate concerned ordinary meaning and legal interpretation of legal rules, among other problems. One of its important aspects involved the "no vehicles in the park" rule and focused on whether it is the rule's text or purpose that is crucial for deciding whether the rule was violated. Hart claimed the rule's text alone suffices in many cases to determine whether the rule was violated. Fuller argued that such decisions can be made only after considering the rule's moral purpose.

Almeida and colleagues argue that both Hart and Fuller based their claims on their intuitions and assumed that other people (laymen or lawyers) shared those intuitions. Because the validity of the underlying assumption can be empirically tested, experimental jurisprudence offers a fruitful methodology to inform this discussion. In Chapter 2, the researchers discuss their previous original findings on the concept of rule (Struchiner et al., 2020) in terms of their three alternative explanations and potential implications for the Hart-Fuller debate.[9]

Importantly, Almeida and colleagues point out that empirical data do not clearly indicate whether people are Hartians or Fullerians. Instead, people seem to favor one set of intuitions or another depending on circumstances. For example, when asked to decide whether the "no vehicle in the park" rule was violated, as well as whether the rule's text and purpose were violated, people based their rule violation decisions more on the violation of the rule's text. However, when asked simply whether the rule was violated, they privileged the breach of the rule's purpose over its text (Struchiner et al., 2020).

Almeida and colleagues offer three possible explanations for these findings that have different implications for the Hart-Fuller debate. The first is that people's judgments about whether the rule was violated are descriptive and made based on the rule's text alone. In contrast, the impact of moral purpose on people's decisions reflects whether people evaluate the norm violator as blameworthy or blameless. This interpretation supports Hart's theory over Fuller's.

The second possible explanation treats the rule as a hybrid concept with both descriptive and normative content. Therefore, people find the rule is violated only when both the rule's text and its purpose were violated. In light of this interpretation, the moral purpose is always essential for interpreting rules, supporting Fuller's theory and weakening Hart's.

The third possible explanation is that "rule" is a dual-character concept, meaning it has two independent criteria for categorization, one descriptive, another normative. This account supports both positions in some way: Hart is correct as far as the descriptive sense of the rule is concerned, while Fuller would be correct regarding its normative sense. Overall, Almeida and colleagues' findings suggest a more sophisticated view than either of these accounts and, by doing so, may help to break the stalemate over the Hart-Fuller debate.

I.2 Topics in Experimental Particular Jurisprudence

In contrast to experimental general jurisprudence, research in experimental particular jurisprudence makes use of empirical data to inform jurisprudential questions concerning basic concepts in specific domains of law (e.g., criminal and tort law); typically, as those concepts are constructed in the theory and practice of specifically defined legal system(s) (e.g., common law or continental legal system) (see also, Prochownik, 2021). Most previous research in this group investigated ordinary intuitions concerning the application of certain legal concepts and the psychological mechanisms underpinning such intuitions. Such research may inform both legal theory and legal practice by determining whether these concepts are or should be congruent with their ordinary counterparts,[10] whether they are applied in a competent or biased way by the folk and legal experts,[11] and the legal interpretation of their ordinary meanings.[12]

Four chapters in this volume contribute to this line of research by presenting and discussing novel experimental findings on folk intuitions surrounding particular legal concepts essential in several domains of law, such as criminal, tort, and environmental law. Specifically, these chapters examine folk intuitions concerning the ascription of legally relevant *mental states* (e.g., intent, intentional action, knowledge, and its special case of willful ignorance) and folk intuitions about the concepts of *causation, culpability,* and *liability*. Notably, all the novel experiments presented in this part adhere closely to Anglo-American legal tradition.

Three chapters examine folk concepts of mental states that are of legal significance as topics of investigation. In Chapter 3, "Legislative Intent and Acting Intentionally," Kevin Tobia examines laypeople's judgments of intentional action by building upon one of the most influential studies in experimental philosophy on the so-called "side-effect effect" (e.g., Knobe, 2003; see Cova, 2016 for a review). The "side-effect effect" concerns a specific asymmetry observed in people's ascriptions of intentional action. When asked to evaluate the intentions of a chairman who starts a new program to increase his company's profits, but which also brings about either harmful or helpful side effects for the environment, study participants were significantly more likely to think that the chairman intentionally harmed than helped the environment. In other words, although the chairman did not specifically intend the side effects to occur, his knowledge that they would occur was sufficient for ascribing intentionality when harmful side effects occurred than when the side effects were helpful. Crucially, both laypeople (e.g., Knobe, 2003, 2004) and legal experts (Kneer & Bourgeois-Gironde, 2017) showed the tendency to perceive bad side effects as more intentional than good side effects.

Based on these findings, one could predict that the same "side-effect effect" should generalize to the judgments of intent, including those of *legislative intent*. Against this prediction, Tobia reports findings of three novel experiments that show that laypeople's concept of legislative intent is not the same as their idea of what legislators do intentionally. In the first study, he presented lay participants with scenarios in which legislators passed a "no vehicles in the park" bill, foreseeing it would have both positive (e.g., improving safety) and negative (e.g., worsening cleanliness) effects in the park. Participants were then asked to indicate which of the two was the bill's legislative intent. The majority perceived the legislative intent to be morally good, regardless of what kinds of positive or negative side effects legislators foresaw.

In the second study, lay participants evaluated vignettes modeled on the original chairman scenario described earlier (Knobe, 2003). The vignettes described a new law aimed at improving business profits, but that would also have harmful or helpful side effects for the environment. Also in this case, more participants thought that the law's intent was to help than to harm the environment. At the same time, they were more likely to think that legislators intentionally harmed than intentionally helped the environment (replicating the "side-effect effect").

A similar result emerged in the third study using a slightly different formulation: participants were requested to assess "legislative intent" instead of "the law's intent," as in the second study. In this third study, the "side-effect effect" was present for judgments of intentional action of legislators but not for judgments of legislative intent. Overall, these novel findings suggest that people judge legislative intent more positively because they believe that laws have (morally) good purposes.[13]

Another chapter in this collection sheds further light on folk concepts of legally relevant mental states. In Chapter 4, "Why Blame the Ostrich? Understanding Culpability for Willful Ignorance," Lara Kirfel and Ivar Hannikainen apply an experimental-jurisprudential approach to the doctrine of willful ignorance, especially popular in the Anglo-American legal system and others. According to this doctrine, a defendant who intentionally decided to remain unaware of the fact that his actions violate the law is culpable to the same extent as a person who genuinely knows she is violating the law. In other words, the doctrine assumes that one can assign to the willfully ignorant agent the mens rea of knowledge. In its basic form, willful ignorance requires (1) that the defendant be sufficiently suspicious of the illegal character of her actions and (2) that the defendant intentionally fail to inquire whether the action in question actually is illegal (Sarch, 2018).

Kirfel and Hannikainen present novel findings of two experiments that shed light on how the different components of this legal doctrine map into ordinary people's judgments. Their two studies manipulated the following factors: (1) whether an agent had knowledge or only a suspicion about the illegal character of their actions, (2) whether this suspicion was reasonable, (3) whether it was difficult or easy for the agent to inquire whether the action was illegal, and (4) whether their knowledge of the circumstances was general (i.e., that their action was illegal) or specific (i.e., that they were trafficking drugs).

The researchers found that ordinary people's judgments were only partially consistent with the legal doctrine of willful ignorance. First, acting with willful ignorance was not perceived as culpable to the same extent as having genuine knowledge, although it was perceived as more culpable than acting with no suspicion. Second, whether it was possible for an agent to inquire whether his actions were illegal played no role in people's judgments. Third, general knowledge was more important than specific knowledge in willful ignorance cases. In a general discussion, the authors address the potential implications of these findings for legal theory and for philosophy more generally.

In Chapter 5, "Culpability and Liability in the Law of Homicide: Do Lay Moral Intuitions Accord with Legal Distinctions?," Sousa and Lavery examine whether lay concepts of culpability and liability (and the associated concept of intentional action) are congruent with their legal counterparts in the Anglo-American law of homicide. The authors first delineate different components of the law of homicide in the common-law system (i.e., distinct types of homicides: murder, voluntary and involuntary manslaughter; mental state components of these offenses: purpose, knowledge, recklessness, and negligence; and possible legal defenses such as those related to self-defense). They then empirically investigate whether the distinctions drawn in the Anglo-American law of homicide are also reflected in the judgments of laypeople coming from this legal system (specifically, the UK). In particular, Sousa and Lavery presented participants with pairs of vignettes contrasting various features relevant to the law of homicide (e.g., whether the agent committed the crime purposefully or knowingly and whether specific defenses applied to the case), who then made judgments of culpability and liability.

The researchers predicted that across different scenarios, lay judgments of culpability and liability would follow the pattern of *immunitivism* (that persons who are not culpable would not be punished) and *retributivism* (that culpable persons would be punished proportionately to their degree of culpability), as both of these principles permeate the Anglo-American legal tradition. Their results confirmed this hypothesis. Moreover, the results demonstrated a surprising degree of similarity among several more specific criteria governing the attribution of culpability and liability (and intentional action) in the law and laypeople's judgments. Notably, Sousa and Lavery adopt a fine-grained approach to connecting language and concepts in their chapter. They consider polysemy of words related to culpability and liability as a potential factor explaining some of their (otherwise puzzling) findings.

In Chapter 6, "Causation and the Silly Norm Effect," Güver and Kneer set out to empirically investigate the "norm effect," which states that violations of norms influence laypeople's attribution of causation (e.g., Knobe & Fraser, 2008; Hitchcock & Knobe, 2009). Their goal was twofold. On the one hand, they sought to inform the debate on the psychological mechanisms underlying the norm effect. On the other hand, they sought to expand the psychological debate to the law, where it is oftentimes assumed that the *legal* concept of causation corresponds to its equivalent in *ordinary* language (a phenomenon they term the correspondence assumption).

Psychological accounts of the norm effect vary (see Willemsen & Kirfel, 2019). Güver and Kneer focus chiefly on two: the Bias View and the Responsibility View. According to the Bias View (e.g., Alicke, 2000), the impact of normative considerations on causation amounts to bias. The Bias View holds that although laypeople are capable of purely descriptive judgments of causation, their judgment often falls prey to a blame-driven bias and, in an act of backward rationalization, they exaggerate their causal ascriptions. Under the Bias View, any violation of norms—be it a pertinent (e.g., don't drink and drive) or a silly (e.g., wear blue shoes while driving) norm that is apt to elicit a desire to blame the agent—is also capable of distorting laypeople's judgment. Under the Responsibility View (e.g., Sytsma, 2021), people's judgments of causation are inherently normative, meaning that only factors pertinent to moral responsibility (e.g., an agent's intentions) impact folk judgments of causation; factors that do not pertain to moral responsibility (e.g., the agent's race or gender) have no such impact. These two psychological views are mirrored in the Anglophone legal analysis of proximate causation: although legal formalists hold proximate causation to be a descriptive notion, legal realists contend that it tracks normative features of responsibility judgments.

Güver and Kneer set out to disentangle these competing psychological accounts in two novel experiments. They confront lay participants with vignettes in which different types of norms—ranging from pertinent to nonpertinent to silly as regards the agent's moral culpability—are violated. Surprisingly, they find that participants' causal judgments are sensitive to norm violations even when they were in no way related to the agent's moral culpability ("the silly norm effect"), thus lending strong support to the Bias View.

Finally, Güver and Kneer discuss the legal implications of their findings, noting that the results are troubling for a multitude of formalist and realist positions and that the law cannot properly situate the correspondence assumption as is. After all, the correspondence assumption requires that the law delegate the assessment of legal causation to the intuitions of lay jurors—intuitions which, as Güver and Kneer point out, are riddled with biases.

I.3 (New) Methods and Topics in Experimental Jurisprudence

Questionnaires and vignette studies have been the most commonly used research tools to this point in both experimental philosophy and experimental jurisprudence, but they do not exhaust all possible methodological approaches in these areas of research. In fact, the use of such research methods in experimental philosophy has been under attack due to their significant limitations (e.g., Deutsch, 2009; Huebner, 2015; Kauppinen, 2007; Moss, 2017). Moreover, it is questionable whether any uniform methodology can be appropriate for investigating *all* different types of jurisprudential questions.[14] Three chapters in our volume represent a call for greater *methodological inclusivism and diversification.* Namely, they broaden the current methodological landscape of XJur by combining different methods, such as corpus methods and questionnaires,[15] or employing novel methods, such as behavioral methods,[16] to inform traditional and new questions in jurisprudence.[17]

Two chapters in this part of the collection make a case for a greater *thematic inclusivism and diversification* of XJur. One chapter postulates a new research subfield of "longtermist" experimental jurisprudence, which employs empirical research methods to inform legal and philosophical debates concerning, among others, the rights of future generations. This is an important extension of the scope of research in experimental particular jurisprudence, which is typically focused on actual concepts of legal theory and practice (mainly of criminal law and, to a lesser degree, tort law) in the Anglo-American legal system. Specifically, applying an experimental perspective to investigate the rights of future generations extends the thematic scope of XJur to include human rights and international law.[18] Another chapter applies an original corpus-linguistic approach to shed light on a new question of potential jurisprudential interest of whether legal concepts are used more descriptively or evaluatively. These two lines of innovative research demonstrate that the XJur of the future is not limited to traditional questions of general and particular jurisprudence. In the following, I summarize four chapters that pave the way for the XJur of the future, methodologically and/or thematically.

In Chapter 7, "Ordinary Meaning and Consilience of Evidence," Justin Sytsma argues that consilience of evidence in XJur can be better achieved when a single jurisprudential question concerning the ordinary meaning of legally relevant concepts is investigated using more than one method. He begins by observing two trends in recent research into ordinary meaning in experimental philosophy and experimental jurisprudence. On the one hand, some experimental philosophers, whose research has largely relied on questionnaires, have recently argued for greater reliance on corpus methods, extending the empirical methods toolset of the field. On the other hand, some researchers in experimental jurisprudence have lately argued against exclusive reliance on linguistic sources, including corpora, and in favor of greater reliance on questionnaires as a research method. Sytsma proposes to overcome this seeming tension by arguing that both types of methods (corpus linguistics and questionnaire methods) can (and should) supplement each other in investigating complex questions, like those concerning ordinary concepts and their meaning, and contribute to the consilience of evidence on these questions. In particular, since each of these methods has its limitations (e.g., corpus methods are context-independent; questionnaires are context-dependent when determining the ordinary usage of terms), one method may overcome the limitations of the other. To make this point clear, Sytsma analyzes empirical evidence concerning the ordinary meaning of the term "vehicle" as it occurs in the "no vehicles in the park" rule, widely discussed in both armchair and experimental legal philosophy (e.g., Hart, 1958; see also Almeida, Struchiner, Hannikainen, this volume;

Tobia, this volume). He investigates the available empirical evidence regarding the ordinary usage of the term "vehicle" using both linguistic corpora and questionnaires and demonstrates that both sources lead to remarkably similar conclusions regarding the acceptable uses of this term.

Similarly, in Chapter 8, "Examining Evaluativity in Legal Discourse: A Comparative Corpus Linguistic Study of Thick Concepts," Willemsen, Baumgartner, Frohofer, and Reuter make use of corpus linguistics to empirically examine the evaluativity of legal discourse compared to ordinary language. For that purpose, they initially created two corpora: legal professional corpus (based on opinions from US appellate courts) and public corpus (based on the online forum Reddit). Subsequently, they compared the degree of evaluativity of a variety of adjectives that occurred in both of these corpora. Notably, in the present study, Willemsen and colleagues focused on a selection of ethical, epistemic, and legal adjectives (e.g., "honest," "logical," and "legal") that belong to *thick concepts* in philosophy. Thick concepts have both evaluative and descriptive components (e.g., the thick concept "rude" expresses a negative evaluation of behavior that descriptively involves a violation of good manners) and thus were appropriate for testing the comparative hypothesis of the researchers concerning the evaluativity of legal and public discourse.

To examine the degree of evaluativity of thick adjectives as they are used in the legal and public corpora, the researchers first referred to the Sentiment Analysis and ranked each adjective on two dimensions: (1) whether it is negative or positive and (2) the degree of negativity or positivity.[19] Second, they analyzed the sentiment value of the connective adjectives (i.e., the adjectives that co-occurred with their target thick adjectives) across two corpora. For instance, when the thick adjective "unfair" was used with another evaluative adjective (e.g., "rude"), the researchers inferred that usage was more evaluative. However, when the same thick adjective co-occurred with a more descriptive adjective (e.g., "difficult"), they inferred that usage was more descriptive.

Willemsen and colleagues demonstrated that the average sentiment value was overall lower for the legal corpus than the public corpus. More importantly, they found that legal professionals used the same adjectives more descriptively than laypeople. Overall, the study provides initial empirical findings, suggesting that lawyers use thick adjectives more neutrally than laypeople.[20]

However, combining vignette and corpus studies and applying novel corpus linguistics approaches to the old and new jurisprudential questions are not the only possible ways to make XJur more methodologically inclusive. In Chapter 9, "A Case for Behavioral Studies in Experimental Jurisprudence," Leonard Hoeft makes the case for even greater methodological diversification of experimental jurisprudence. He points out that although this young field aims to address jurisprudential questions empirically, its thematic and methodological scope have been relatively narrow: legally relevant concepts of ordinary people and their underpinning cognitive mechanisms have been approached mainly using vignette studies. In vignette studies, people answer questions concerning short hypothetical scenarios. According to Hoeft, although this line of research may provide insights into people's concepts as manifested in their linguistic applications, it has some significant drawbacks. Among the most important drawbacks, traditional inquiries in general jurisprudence consider the nature of the law as it is, not just as people perceive it. To fully account for law as a social phenomenon that includes social practices and institutions, one must adopt a broader methodological approach. XJur should not be focused only on an empirically oriented conceptual analysis and on people's cognition, as is the case in the majority of studies so far. Rather, different methodological avenues should be explored within XJur. Case in point, behavioral game theory could be a fruitful methodological avenue for making the results of previous (vignette) studies more robust and for extending the thematic scope of the field to investigating both laypeople's compliance with the law and its application by legal officials. Behavioral game theory studies have already been used (and can be used in the future) to study prototypical legal institutions (e.g., sanctioning mechanisms), normative institutions that may confer legitimacy (e.g., voting and authority), and other influences on legal behavior via framing effects or signaling.

For the most part, experimental legal philosophy has focused on examining people's intuitions about *actual* particular legal concepts. In Chapter 10, "Experimental Longtermist Jurisprudence," Martínez and Winter make an innovative step forward and investigate the issue of rights of future generations from the perspective of what they call "experimental longtermist jurisprudence" (XLJ)—a subfield within XJur that focuses on conducting empirical research to inform philosophical and legal questions pertaining to the distant future.

Although philosophically speaking, the interests of future generations seem equally important to the interests of present generations, legal systems offer few mechanisms to protect the interests of future generations. According to Martínez and Winter, this creates room for empirical studies into the causes of this state of affairs (e.g., by using surveys and controlled vignette studies) in people's beliefs and on how their minds work, to address philosophical, legal, and policy-related questions that affect future generations.

Martínez and Winter propose to discuss these questions at three related levels of abstraction. At the *philosophical* level, XLJ descriptively examines people's beliefs about legal longtermism (i.e., concerning whether future generations ought to be granted legal protection), the proximate causes of these beliefs (cognitive mechanisms and biases underpinning such beliefs), and the ultimate causes of these beliefs (their potential evolutionary function or lack thereof). At the *doctrinal* level, XLJ descriptively examines the overlap between people's beliefs about longtermist jurisprudence and their understanding of the corresponding legal concepts (if applicable). Finally, at the *application of law* level, XLJ examines people's beliefs regarding potential legal mechanisms that could protect future generations.

Throughout the chapter, Martínez and Winter discuss fascinating results of their own empirical research with both laypeople and legal experts informing these debates. For instance, they report that legal experts desire much more legal protection for future generations than is provided by current laws and explain this discrepancy in terms of cognitive biases governing people's (normally, short-term oriented) thinking. Although research questions considered at these three levels involve *descriptive* examination of people's (laypeople or legal experts) intuitions, they have import for corresponding *normative* questions concerning how and to what extent we should legally protect future generations, and which legal mechanisms we should use to reach this goal.

I.4 Experimental Jurisprudence of the Future: Research Directions and Challenges

The chapters in this volume contribute to previous research in experimental general and particular jurisprudence and expand XJur research both thematically and methodologically. Based on this collection, one may foresee at least three directions for future research and associated challenges for XJur.

I.4.1 The Need for Greater Thematic Inclusivism and Diversification of Research Areas

Several chapters in this volume call for opening XJur to new research topics that may be classified as either general or particular jurisprudence (and beyond). In the following, I briefly consider the possibilities of further applying experimental jurisprudence to the new topics and research areas in these two subfields.

General questions concerning the concept of law or legal rules have been at the heart of traditional analytical jurisprudence (e.g., Hart, 1961). Several experimental studies have been recently conducted to inform such core debates, especially by testing whether intuitions underpinning general legal-philosophical positions are commonly shared.[21] This research is currently in its infancy, and there is a need for much more empirical data to enable researchers to inform questions in general jurisprudence more thoroughly and conclusively.

In particular, studies in experimental general jurisprudence have been selective, focusing on several specific debates and theories in general jurisprudence: (1) the debate between legal positivism and natural law theories, specifically whether morality is a necessary or a contingent component of the concept of a law (Flanagan & Hannikainen, 2022; Flanagan et al., 2022); (2) Lon Fuller's procedural natural law theory (Donelson & Hannikainen, 2020; Hannikainen et al., 2021);[22] and (3) the Hart-Fuller debate over the nature of rules (Struchiner, Hannikainen, & Almeida, 2020; Almeida, Struchiner, & Hannikainen, 2022; Almeida et al., this volume). This leaves many other theories and discussions in traditional (armchair) legal philosophy beyond the scope of experimental-jurisprudential investigations.[23] At the same time, there is a need for more in-depth theoretical reflection and methodological awareness concerning the implications[24] of empirical studies, and their potential advantages and limitations, for the fundamental debates in legal philosophy. The route from theory to empirical findings and back is not straight: a theory must be made operational to be empirically tested; the process of operationalizing it may impact the empirical data gathered; the empirical data gathered may then constrain possible theoretical conclusions (see also Prochownik, 2021, p. 9). This raises several important questions. For instance, how do we reach consilience of evidence in XJur (e.g., Sytsma, this volume)? When (if at all) can we speak of majority support for a legal-philosophical theory?[25] When (if at all) can we say that one legal-philosophical theory of law is correct and the other is incorrect?[26] More theoretical work is needed to address such questions, which arise at the intersection of general and experimental jurisprudence.

Although there have been many more empirical studies in particular than in general experimental jurisprudence, the scope of such studies has also been relatively narrow. Research in experimental particular jurisprudence has been focused on examining folk concepts related to criminal and (to a lesser extent) tort law in the Anglo-American legal tradition (e.g., Knobe & Shapiro, 2021; Kobick & Knobe, 2009; Macleod, 2019; Sommers, 2020; Solan, 2009; Tobia, 2018, 2020a; Robinson & Darley, 1995). Such research has mainly investigated whether certain ordinary concepts (e.g., causation, intent, reasonableness, and consent) are congruent with their legal counterparts in particular branches of law in the common-law system and drawing potential implications for legal theory and practice.

We foresee at least two lines of potential future research directions in this area. First, more research in experimental particular jurisprudence is needed to investigate basic concepts in other branches of law, such as constitutional law, civil law, administrative law, international law, and human rights (e.g., Martínez and Winter, this volume). Second, such research should go beyond the basic concepts and principles of the common law (Anglo-American) legal system to include fundamental concepts and principles of other legal systems (e.g., the civil law system). On a related note, future XJur research should be extended in the direction of comparative legal scholarship, that is, cross-cultural empirical research comparing people's legally relevant concepts across different legal systems and cultures.

Cross-cultural XJur research seems relevant for both subfields of jurisprudence.[27] It is crucial for theories in general jurisprudence, which seek to describe the necessary features of the concept of law (and related concepts like a legal rule). Because many legal philosophers simply assume the congruence of their theoretical positions with common views (e.g., Hart, 1961; Fuller, 1964), cross-cultural experimental general jurisprudence may provide the best test of such empirical assumptions (see, for instance, Hannikainen, Tobia et al., 2021; see also Donelson, this volume; Almeida et al., this volume).[28] Ultimately, further empirical research may help to establish if there is a univocal folk concept of law or whether there are many such concepts.

In addition, cross-cultural research in experimental particular jurisprudence may investigate whether folk intuitions underpinning specific legal concepts (e.g., intent, causation, and culpability) are universally shared or vary across legal systems and cultures. Such future empirical findings may have interesting descriptive implications: they may explain similarities and/or variations in legal concepts and related principles across legal systems (e.g., Prochownik, 2021). For instance, if folk intuitions concerning a particular legal concept are universal, such universality might explain similarities in the corresponding legal concepts across cultures and legal systems. On the other hand, if folk intuitions concerning a particular legal concept vary, such variation might explain the variation in the corresponding legal concepts across cultures and legal systems.[29] Moreover, comparative XJur may help verify the empirical adequacy of frequent assumptions in legal theory and practice that certain legal concepts are modeled on ordinary concepts. In other words, it may test whether particular legal concepts are actually supported by common views, either universally or locally.[30]

Finally, as convincingly argued by Hoeft (this volume), experimental jurisprudence should be open to empirical approaches that move beyond examining the psychological underpinnings of legally relevant *concepts* to include legally relevant *behaviors* and their psychological underpinnings. This point is closely connected with the need for greater methodological diversification of XJur.

I.4.2 The Need for More Methodological Inclusivism and Diversification of Research Tools

Experimental jurisprudence is, in principle, methodologically open. For instance, it has been broadly characterized as relying on empirical methods (broadly speaking) to inform questions of jurisprudence (Knobe & Shapiro, 2021, p. 165; Tobia, 2022, p. 735). Indeed, in recent years there have been attempts to apply various methods to inform jurisprudential questions, such as corpus methods (e.g., Tobia, 2018; Sytsma, this volume; Willemsen et al., this volume), neuroscientific methods (fMRI studies, e.g., Vilares et al., 2017), behavioral and experimental economics (e.g., Hoeft, 2019, this volume; Winter, 2020), psychological questionnaires, and vignette studies (e.g., Tobia, this volume; Sousa & Lavery, this volume; Güver & Kneer, this volume; Kirfel & Hannikainen, this volume). However, in practice, most studies conducted so far have used vignettes and questionnaires. This trend is reflected in the current collection.

In vignette studies, participants are asked questions about some features of short hypothetical scenarios. Depending on the specific research questions and hypotheses, participants are sometimes requested to provide demographic information and answer psychological questionnaires. However, as indicated earlier, vignette studies and questionnaires are subject to limitations (see, especially Hoeft, this volume). They may not always be a sufficient or adequate research tool for investigating questions of jurisprudence. Instead, some research questions may require combining the vignette approach with other methods or applying an entirely distinct methodological approach. For instance, questions concerning ordinary concepts and meaning are quite complex and therefore require different sources of evidence, such as questionnaires *and* corpus methods (Sytsma, this volume).

The current research status quo seems to have its roots in the fact that many projects within experimental jurisprudence, similarly to projects within experimental philosophy, are aimed at informing conceptual analyses (e.g., Alexander, Mallon, & Weinberg, 2010; Nadelhoffer & Nahmias, 2007; Stich & Tobia, 2016; Sommers, 2021; Tobia, 2022). Consider general analytical jurisprudence which is largely concerned with providing sufficient and necessary conditions for something being a law (Donelson, this volume). Many legal philosophers in this tradition appeal to their own intuitions and assume that these intuitions are commonly shared (e.g., Almeida et al., this volume). XJur researchers aim to contribute to this tradition by empirically testing people's intuitions underpinning their thinking about the law (e.g., Donelson & Hannikainen, 2020; Flanagan & Hannikainen, 2022). Because hypothetical scenarios manipulating features relevant to such legal-philosophical theories provide a straightforward way of testing people's intuitions, it is not surprising that they have been widely used in experimental general jurisprudence.

However, together with the growing thematic diversification of XJur, researchers need to be open to different and novel research avenues. In particular, distinct and new methods may be more appropriate for studying jurisprudential questions beyond conceptual analysis. For example, the social phenomenon of law consists of both people's beliefs and people's norm-compliant behavior. Therefore, a full-fledged account of the law as a social phenomenon requires supplementing vignette studies with behavioral game-theory experiments, which seem better fitted for studying how the law affects people's conduct (Hoeft, this volume).[31]

I.4.3 The Need for More Descriptive Inclusivism and Diversification of the Explanatory Framework

Many XJur research studies have descriptive implications for jurisprudential debates (Prochownik, 2021). Specifically, such studies aim to describe psychological mechanisms and processes involved in people's intuitions concerning general and particular legal concepts and/or to explain recurrent jurisprudential themes in terms of these intuitions and their underpinning psychological mechanisms and processes. For instance, Almeida and colleagues (this volume) examine three alternative psychological explanations of their previous findings concerning the nature of rules and discuss implications of each of these explanations for the Hart-Fuller debate. Assume that one of these accounts, stating that rule is a dual-character concept, is the correct one. (For some recent evidence in this direction, see Almeida et al., 2022.)[32] If a rule has two independent criteria for categorization (one descriptive or textualist, another normative or purposivist), that could explain why the Hart-Fuller debate in legal philosophy is so robust and difficult to resolve: people may endorse both the Hartian and Fullerian intuitions but in different circumstances, which may fuel and contribute to the vitality of these two legal-philosophical positions.

These explanations are known as proximate explanations in contemporary behavioral sciences and are aimed at accounting for *how* a certain trait or behavior works (e.g., Scott-Phillips, Dickins, & West, 2011; Baumard, André, & Sperber, 2013). For instance, in the foregoing example, people's inclination to endorse both types of intuitions in the Hart-Fuller debate is explained in terms of the dual-character structure of the concept of the rule.

However, full-fledged explanations in human behavioral sciences require both proximate and ultimate explanations. The latter are aimed at accounting for *why* people have a certain trait of behavior in the first place. Specifically, "ultimate explanations are concerned with the fitness consequences of a trait or behavior and whether it is (or is not) selected" (Scott-Phillips, Dickins, & West, 2011, p. 38) or "the possible origin and adaptive basis of various proximate social psychological phenomena" (Mesoudi, 2009, p. 933). Noteworthy, ultimate explanations may account for the origin of a given trait or behavior in terms of *natural* and *cultural* evolutionary processes (e.g., Mesoudi, 2009; Laland, Sterelny, Odling-Smee, Hoppitt, & Uller, 2011).[33] For instance, in the foregoing example, one could ask why certain legal concepts, such as rules, have an inherent dual character (i.e., whether this can be explained in terms of the fitness consequences of such a trait).[34]

Because proximate explanations (concerning psychological mechanisms underpinning traits or behaviors) are the core domain of psychological and cognitive sciences, it is not surprising that experimental philosophy and jurisprudence that largely draw from these disciplines have focused on them.[35] However, it is arguable that combining proximate and ultimate explanations provide a fuller picture of the phenomenon in question: together they offer a multidimensional account of a trait or behavior in question in terms of both proximate psychological mechanisms and a potential evolutionary origin.[36] Therefore, future experimental jurisprudence should integrate ultimate explanations into its explanatory framework.

In fact, some preliminary attempts in this direction have already been made in different subfields of experimental jurisprudence. For instance, Martínez and Winter (this volume) examine people's attitudes concerning the legal protection of future generations. They investigate more than the content of such beliefs. They also address the "how" question, concerning the cognitive underpinnings of these beliefs, and the "why" question, concerning their origin. As they point out, "philosophical-level XLJ [experimental longtermist jurisprudence] is concerned with understanding both the *proximate cause* of longtermism-related beliefs (cognitively, what leads people to hold certain longtermist-related beliefs and/or engage in longtermist-related behavior) and [the] *ultimate cause* of those beliefs (what evolutionary or adaptive forces gave rise to them in the first place) (p. 247)." For example, scholars examine potential cognitive biases that may underpin people's preference for current or near-term future generations as well as the potentially adaptive character of such choices (over the inclination to care and act for long-term future generations). These two factors contribute to our understanding of why people (and legal systems) seem to downplay the importance of legal protection for future generations.

Some preliminary steps have also been made to supplement existing proximate explanations in experimental general jurisprudence with ultimate explanations. Several recent studies find that people's views of natural law and legal positivism are contextual (e.g., Donelson & Hannikainen, 2020; Hannikainen, Tobia et al., 2021; Struchiner, Hannikainen, & Almeida, 2020). Therefore, some researchers have suggested that laypeople have an intrinsic (albeit rudimentary) connection between law and morality (Flanagan & Hannikainen, 2022; Hannikainen et al., 2021; Flanagan et al., 2022). This implies that the folk concept of law is consistent with at least some variants of natural law theory.

If this view is correct, one may ask why people's legal determinations are intertwined with moral evaluations (or, in other words, why they manifest natural law intuitions in at least some circumstances). In this vein, Hannikainen, Flanagan, and Prochownik (2022) considered several potential evolutionary scenarios (including a cultural evolutionary scenario), which could lead to the emergence of such a connection in the human mind. One possibility is that the link between moral and legal norms was formed during gene and culture co-evolution (e.g., Boyd & Richerson, 2005; Richerson & Boyd, 2005).[37] For instance, the connection between fairness norms and legal norms could have first emerged in the cultural group selection process: social groups with fair legal systems may have been more cooperative, thus outcompeting other less cooperative groups (Richerson et al., 2016, p. 15).[38] Consequently, legal norms and institutions that satisfied the requirements of justice spread culturally. In other words, cumulative cultural evolutionary processes that shaped legal institutions to accommodate moral standards may have led humans to incorporate moral considerations into their legal determinations (Flanagan et al., 2022).[39]

This scenario is consistent with research in the cognitive science of religion. The role of enhancing cooperation among large groups of strangers, originally played by religions with moralistic Big Gods, is now in recent times played by efficient, secure, rule-of-law institutions, bringing about the cultural decline of such beliefs in countries with a strong rule of law (see Norenzayan, 2013; Norenzayan et al., 2016). In other words, supernatural monitoring and punishment were eventually outsourced to secular monitoring and punishment, which proved more efficient (at least in some modern states) for enhancing large-scale cooperation over time. As hypothesized by Norenzayan (2013, p. 73), "where there are strong institutions that govern public life—that is, where people are reassured that contracts are enforced, competition is fair, and cheaters will be punished—levels of trust and cooperation are high for everyone, believers and nonbelievers alike."[40]

Overall, one can argue that, because fair legal systems and institutions are potentially more efficient than unfair legal systems at enhancing cooperation and trust within social groups, they may have been culturally selected over time via the intergroup competition process (Richerson et al., 2016) to replace the function of moralistic religions (Norenzayan et al., 2016). Future XJur research should more thoroughly investigate this and other potential (cultural) evolutionary scenarios that account for the moralistic nature of the rudimentary folks' concept of law.

Acknowledgments

I am grateful to Stefan Magen for his very constructive feedback on the previous version of this chapter. I would also like to thank Levin Güver for helpful suggestions. This work was supported by the DFG-CAPES research grant "Experimental Legal Philosophy: The Concept of Law Revisited" (project number 434400506).

Notes

1 See Tobia (2022).
2 Experimental jurisprudence involves research projects at the intersection of legal theory, experimental and legal philosophy, and cognitive and social science.
3 Donelson (in this volume, p. 27) characterizes general jurisprudence as the study of "law at its most general."
4 The notions of particular and general jurisprudence have a long tradition in legal philosophy, although their exact definitions and scope have been subject to debate. For instance, according to John Austin, one of the first legal philosophers to have made this distinction, general jurisprudence studies notions and principles common to many legal systems. He claims, "it is concerned directly with principles and distinctions which are common to various systems of particular and positive law; and

which each of those various systems inevitably involves," and that "it is concerned with law as it necessarily *is*" or "with law as it must be" (Austin, 1832, p. iii, A2). On the other hand, particular jurisprudence examines notions and principles of specific legal systems. Austin indicates that particular jurisprudence is "the science of any such system of positive law as now actually obtains, or once actually obtained, in a specifically determined nation or specifically determined nations" (Austin, 1832, p. iii, A2). Although this research does not delve into the definitional issues concerning these two kinds of jurisprudence, the distinction between experimental general and particular jurisprudence, followed in this volume, reflects and nods to this tradition in legal philosophy.

5 That certain legal-philosophical premises are not commonly shared does not automatically imply that theories making such assumptions are false. According to Donelson (this volume), it may shift the burden of proof to such theories.

6 According to Donelson, this shows that understanding a psychological mechanism behind given folk intuitions may have a bearing on assessing the Experimental Analysis as a method of general jurisprudence.

7 Simply put, the expertise defense argument states that experimentalists mainly examine lay people's intuitions, while it is the relevant experts' intuitions that should matter to inform theoretical debates.

8 See also Hoeft, this volume; Sytsma, this volume.

9 Thus, the research presented in this chapter would fall under Experimental Analysis and Experimental Descriptivism in experimental general jurisprudence, according to the typology presented in Chapter 1 (Donelson, this volume).

10 For instance, Tobia (2020b).

11 For example, Kneer and Bourgeois-Gironde (2017); Prochownik, Krebs, Wiegmann, and Horvath (2020).

12 For instance, Macleod (2019).

13 In this respect, this study elaborates on previous work by De Freitas, Tobia, Newman, and Knobe (2017) and Flanagan and Hannikainen (2022). Note that this research provides insights about the legally relevant concepts of intentional action and intent (as applied to legislative bodies), but has implications for general jurisprudence as well. For instance, it raises the possibility that lay people assign morally good purposes to laws because they are intuitive natural law theorists (i.e., they consider a law to be a valid law if it satisfies certain moral criteria: in this particular case, if it aims to achieve morally valuable purposes). This hypothesis should be examined in more detail and tested in future research.

14 See, especially, Hoeft, this volume, and Donelson, this volume.

15 See Sytsma, this volume.

16 See Hoeft, this volume.

17 Note that corpus methods in experimental jurisprudence are not new (see, especially, Tobia, 2020a). The present chapters concerning these methods are innovative in combining corpus analysis with other tools for more robust methodological findings (see Sytsma, this volume) or applying it in a novel way to address a new research question in XJur (see Willemsen et al., this volume).

18 Note that research in experimental particular jurisprudence has focused on investigating legal concepts relevant to the specifically defined legal system, either broadly (e.g., Anglo-American legal system; see, for example, Sousa and Lavery, this volume; Kirfel and Hannikainen, this volume) or narrowly defined (e.g., German law; see, for instance, Prochownik et al., 2020). Therefore, XJur research into the

basic concepts pertaining to human rights and international law may be classified as either a new type of XJur (in a similar vein, see Martínez & Winter, this volume) or a special subtype of experimental particular jurisprudence (providing that the existing law being investigated is specified to include the laws of the entire international community). The classification will also depend on the relevant distinctions in the philosophy of law. For instance, according to a more conservative understanding of "particular jurisprudence" (e.g., Austin, 1832), concepts and principles of international law would not belong to its area of investigation. Since this is ultimately a definitional matter concerning the understanding and scope of "particular jurisprudence," investigating it goes beyond my primary goal of introducing this collection.

19 The researchers relied on the SentiWords dictionary, which encodes each adjective according to these both dimensions.

20 Although the chapter does not discuss potential legal-philosophical implications of these findings directly, note that they may be indirectly relevant for some debates in general jurisprudence and may also stimulate future research directions in XJur. In particular, as indicated previously, one of the fundamental debates in legal philosophy concerns the concept of law and whether satisfying certain moral standards is one of the law's necessary components. On the one hand, if legal experts use legal concepts more descriptively than evaluatively overall, this may be more compatible with legal positivism (a view that morality does not play an essential role in the concept of law). On the other hand, if laypeople use legal concepts more evaluatively than descriptively overall, this makes natural law (a view that morality plays an essential role in the concept of law) more plausible. Therefore, future XJur findings of this kind may shed some light on the common grounds of these two legal-philosophical positions (see Donelson, this volume).

21 The approach is justified insofar as many legal philosophers assume that their intuitions are commonly shared by people. XJur provides a method to test such assumptions (see, for instance, Prochownik, 2021; Donelson, this volume; Almeida et al., this volume).

22 Note that this research could be considered a subproject within the first category.

23 See, for example, Alexy (2010, pp. 35–8), arguing for the dual nature of the concept of law.

24 Especially normative, but also descriptive, implications (see Prochownik, 2021).

25 See, also, Prochownik (2021).

26 For related questions concerning implications of XJur for particular jurisprudence, see, for instance, Tobia (2020b, 2022); Prochownik (2021). Since these issues have already been discussed in the literature concerning the experimental particular jurisprudence, I do not address them here.

27 See, Hannikainen, Kneer et al. (2021) for the first attempt at the cross-cultural replication of studies in experimental general and particular jurisprudence.

28 Cross-cultural XJur may help assess whether a given legal-philosophical position regarding the concept of a law is universally shared by testing people's intuitions concerning the necessary components of a law across different legal systems and cultures.

29 Moreover, comparative XJur research may assess the extent to which particular ordinary concepts accord with their legal counterparts in different legal systems.

30 See, for instance, Prochownik (2022) for a more detailed discussion of the potential implications of the cross-cultural XJur research on the concept of causation.

31 Since several chapters in this volume (especially, Hoeft's and Sytsma's) discuss these methodological issues, I do not discuss them here in greater detail and simply refer the reader to these chapters.

32 See also Knobe, Prasada, and Newman (2013) and Reuter (2018) for general discussions of dual-character concepts.

33 Note that cultural evolutionary theories assume that changes in cultural variants over time can be, to some extent, modeled on Darwinian evolution (e.g., Claidière, Scott-Phillips, & Sperber, 2014). For instance, some theories assume that this process manifests features such as variation, competition, and inheritance (e.g., Mesoudi, 2009, 2011; Richerson et al., 2016). However, some researchers believe that culture should be rather considered at the proximate rather than ultimate level of explanation (e.g., Scott-Phillips, Dickins, & West, 2011).

34 Although, the question of abstract dual-character concepts such as "law" (Flanagan & Hannikainen, 2022) or "rule" (Almeida et al., 2022) is yet to be investigated, an initial step in this direction has been made regarding dual-character concepts of social roles (such as "scientist," "father," and "friend"). Del Pinal and Reuter (2015, 2017) proposed that normative dimension of such dual-character concepts encode the commitment to performing social roles or functions. For instance, a true scientist is committed to performing the role of the scientist (satisfies normative criteria for being a scientist such as impartial pursuit of knowledge) regardless of whether she also collects data and writes up scientific papers (satisfies descriptive criteria for being a scientist). Del Pinal and Reuter (2017) also consider the "why" question and argue that concepts that encode information about commitment of others to performing certain social roles or functions allow for better predicting of their future behavior. That would explain why social role concepts, but not other concepts, have a dual-character structure. Although, the researchers do not directly consider potential adaptive consequences of having such conceptual systems, making this extra step could be considered by future researchers. For instance, perhaps human disposition to develop concepts with two independent categorization criteria was shaped by evolutionary forces because having such concepts is adaptive (i.e., it allows for better predicting the future behaviors of others). Still, as indicated earlier, whether this ultimate explanation could extend to abstract dual-character concepts that do not encode information about social roles is an important subject for further investigation.

35 In fact, some prominent scholars in these fields (Knobe, 2016) have argued that experimental philosophy *is* cognitive science.

36 It is no surprise that combining proximate and ultimate explanations is a standard in other related fields, such as the cognitive science of religion (e.g., Mercier, Kramer, & Shariff, 2018).

37 This theory assumes that once humans evolved the propensity to acquire and transmit culture, it became possible for them to work out cultural solutions to adaptive problems. In turn, cultural-level adaptations had an impact on shaping human psychology. For instance, when human groups started to transmit the social norms and institutions that enhanced cooperation in the Pleistocene era, human psychology was further adapted to be more tuned to social norms (e.g., Richerson & Boyd, 2005).

38 Richerson et al. (2016, p. 15) hypothesized, "CGS [cultural group selection] will tend to favor societies that produce public goods like defense, transportation infrastructure, and a fair legal system."

39 Note that this explanation does not require that natural selection shaped human psychology to be predisposed to connecting legal and moral considerations. Instead,

it may be that when fair legal systems, their legal norms, and institutions emerged and were transmitted as cultural adaptations to large-scale cooperation, they began to actively impact how the evolved human psychology functioned. A similar scenario has been proposed with regard to the cultural evolution of moralistic religions with Big Gods (e.g., Norenzayan, 2013; Norenzayan et al., 2016): they could have emerged as cultural-level adaptations to large-scale cooperation by connecting specific kinds of religious beliefs (in moralistically involved supernatural agents) with the psychological mechanisms for cooperation (reputation monitoring and punishment).

40   Notably, several lines of empirical evidence are compatible with this view: religious and law-related primes positively affected people's prosocial behavior (Shariff & Norenzayan, 2007), belief in an interventionist and powerful god decreased people's support for earthly punishments (Laurin, Shariff, Henrich, & Kay, 2012), people primed with secular authority concepts showed less distrust toward atheists (Gervais & Norenzayan, 2012), and religious individuals in countries with strong secular rule of law manifested lower intolerance of atheists (Norenzayan & Gervais, 2015).

References

Alexander, J., Mallon, R., & Weinberg, J. M. (2010). Accentuate the negative. *Review of Philosophy and Psychology, 1*(2), 297–314. doi: https://doi.org/10.1007/s13164-009 -0015-2.

Alexy, R. (2010). *The argument from injustice: A reply to legal positivism* (B. L. Paulson and S. L. Paulson, Trans.). Oxford: Oxford University Press. (Original work published 1992)

Alicke, M. D. (2000). Culpable control and the psychology of blame. *Psychological Bulletin, 126*(4), 556–74. doi: https://doi.org/10.1037/0033-2909.126.4.556.

Almeida, G. F. C. F., Struchiner, N., & Hannikainen, I. R. (2023). Rule is a dual character concept. *Cognition. 230*, 105259.

Austin, J. (1832). *The province of jurisprudence determined* (incl. *An outline of a course of lectures on general jurisprudence or the philosophy of positive law*). London: John Murray, Albemarle Street.

Baumard, N., André, J. B., & Sperber, D. (2013). A mutualistic approach to morality: The evolution of fairness by partner choice. *Behavioral and Brain Sciences, 36*(1), 59–78. doi: 10.1017/S0140525X11002202.

Boyd, R., & Richerson, P. J. (2005). *The origin and evolution of cultures*. Oxford: Oxford University Press.

Claidière, N., Scott-Phillips, T. C., & Sperber, D. (2014). How Darwinian is cultural evolution?. *Philosophical Transactions of the Royal Society B: Biological Sciences, 369*(1642), 20130368. doi: https://doi.org/10.1098/rstb.2013.0368.

Cova, F. (2016). The folk concept of intentional action: Empirical approaches. In J. Sytsma & W. Buckwalter (Eds.), *A companion to experimental philosophy* (pp. 117–41). Oxford: Wiley-Blackwell. doi: https://doi.org/10.1002/9781118661666 .ch8.

De Freitas, J. Tobia, K. P., Newman, G. E., & Knobe, J. (2017). Normative judgments and individual essence. *Cognitive Science, 41*, 382–402. doi: https://doi.org/10.1111/cogs .12364.

Del Pinal, G., & Reuter, K. (2015). Jack is a true scientist: On the content of dual character concepts. Zurich Open Repository and Archive. Retrieved from https://www.zora.uzh .ch/id/eprint/175832/1/paper0104.pdf.

Del Pinal, G., & Reuter, K. (2017). Dual character concepts in social cognition: Commitments and the normative dimension of conceptual representation. *Cognitive Science, 41*, 477–501. doi: https://doi.org/10.1111/cogs.12456.

Deutsch, M. (2009). Experimental philosophy and the theory of reference. *Mind & Language, 24*(4), 445–66. doi: https://doi.org/10.1111/j.1468-0017.2009.01370.x.

Donelson, R., & Hannikainen, I. (2020). Fuller and the folk: The inner morality of law revisited. In T. Lombrozo, J. Knobe, & S. Nichols (Eds.), *Oxford studies in experimental philosophy* (Vol. 3, pp. 6–28). Oxford: Oxford University Press. doi: 10.1093/ oso/9780198852407.003.0002.

Flanagan, B., Almeida, G. F. C. F., Struchiner, N., & Hannikainen, I. R. (2022). *Moral appraisals guide intuitive legal determinations*. Manuscript in preparation.

Flanagan, B., & Hannikainen, I. R. (2022). The folk concept of law: Law is intrinsically moral. *Australasian Journal of Philosophy, 100*(1): 165–79. doi: 10.1080/00048402.2020.1833953.

Fuller, L. L. (1958). Positivism and fidelity to law—A reply to professor Hart. *Harvard Law Review, 71*(4), 630–72. doi: 10.2307/1338226.

Fuller, L. L. (2000). Eight ways to fail to make law. In J. Feinberg & J. Coleman (Eds.), *Philosophy of law* (6th ed., pp. 91–4). Belmont: Thomson/Wadsworth. (Original work published 1964)

Gervais, W. M., & Norenzayan, A. (2012). Reminders of secular authority reduce believers' distrust of atheists. *Psychological Science, 23*(5), 483–91. doi: https://doi.org/10.1177 %2F0956797611429711.

Hannikainen, I. R., Kneer, M., Tobia, K., Dranseika, V., Almeida, G. d F. C. F., Poama, A., . . . Güver, L. (2021, August 24). Experimental jurisprudence cross-cultural study swap. doi: https://doi.org/10.17605/OSF.IO/SK7R3.

Hannikainen, I. R., Flanagan, B., & Prochownik, K. (2022). The natural law thesis under empirical scrutiny. In H. Viciana, A. Gaitán, & F. Aguiar (Eds.), *Issues in experimental moral philosophy*. Routledge. Manuscript in press.

Hannikainen, I. R., Tobia, K., Almeida, G., Donelson, R., Dranseika, V., Kneer, M., . . . & Struchiner, N. (2021). Are there cross-cultural legal principles? Modal reasoning uncovers procedural constraints on law. *Cognitive Science, 45*. doi: https://doi.org/10 .1111/cogs.13024.

Hart, H. L. A. (1958). Positivism and the separation of law and morals. *Harvard Law Review, 71*(4), 593–629. doi:10.2307/1338225.

Hart, H. L. A. (1994). The concept of law (P. Bullock & J. Raz, eds., 2nd ed.). Oxford: Calderon Press. (Original work published 1961)

Hitchcock, C., & Knobe, J. (2009). Cause and norm. *The Journal of Philosophy, 106*(11), 587–612. doi: https://doi.org/10.5840/jphil20091061128.

Hoeft, L. (2019). The force of norms? The internal point of view in light of experimental economics. *Ratio Juris, 32*(3), 339–62. doi: https://doi.org/10.1111/raju.12250.

Huebner, B. (2015). What is a philosophical effect? Models of data in experimental philosophy. *Philosophical Studies: An International Journal for Philosophy in the Analytic Tradition, 172*(12): 3273–92. https://doi.org/10.1007/s11098-015-0469-2.

Kauppinen, A. (2007). The rise and fall of experimental philosophy. *Philosophical Explorations, 10*(2), 95–118. https://doi.org/10.1080/13869790701305871.

Kneer, M., & Bourgeois-Gironde, S. (2017). Mens rea ascription, expertise and outcome effects: Professional judges surveyed. *Cognition, 169,* 139–46. doi: https://doi.org/10.1016/j.cognition.2017.08.008.

Knobe, J. (2003). Intentional action and side effects in ordinary language. *Analysis, 63*(3), 190–4. doi: https://doi.org/10.1111/1467-8284.00419.

Knobe, J. (2004). Intention, intentional action and moral considerations. *Analysis, 64,* 181–7. doi: https://doi.org/10.1093/analys/64.2.181.

Knobe, J. (2016). Experimental philosophy is cognitive science. In J. Sytsma & W. Buckwalter (Eds.), *A companion to experimental philosophy* (pp. 37–52). Oxford: Wiley-Blackwell.

Knobe, J., & Fraser, B. (2008). Causal judgment and moral judgment: Two experiments. In W. Sinnott-Armstrong (Ed.), *Moral psychology* (Vol. 2, pp. 441–7). Cambridge, MA: MIT Press.

Knobe, J., Prasada, S., & Newman, G. E. (2013). Dual character concepts and the normative dimension of conceptual representation, *Cognition, 127*(2), 242–57. doi: https://doi.org/10.1016/j.cognition.2013.01.005.

Knobe, J., & Shapiro, S. J. (2021). Proximate cause explained: An essay in experimental jurisprudence. *University of Chicago Law Review, 88,* 165–236.

Kobick, J., & Knobe, J. (2009). Interpreting intent: How research on folk judgments of intentionality can inform statutory analysis. *Brooklyn Law Review, 75,* 409–31.

Laland, K. N., Sterelny, K., Odling-Smee, J., Hoppitt, W., & Uller, T. (2011). Cause and effect in biology revisited: Is Mayr's proximate-ultimate dichotomy still useful?. *Science, 334*(6062), 1512–16. doi: https://doi.org/10.1126/science.1210879.

Laurin, K., Shariff, A. F., Henrich, J., & Kay, A. C. (2012). Outsourcing punishment to God: Beliefs in divine control reduce earthly punishment. *Proceedings of the Royal Society B: Biological Sciences, 279*(1741), 3272–81. doi: https://doi.org/10.1098/rspb.2012.0615.

Macleod, J. A. (2019). Ordinary causation: A study in experimental statutory interpretation. *Indiana Law Journal, 94,* 957–1029.

Mercier, B., Kramer, S. R., & Shariff, A. F. (2018). Belief in God: Why people believe, and why they don't. *Current Directions in Psychological Science, 27*(4), 263–8. doi: https://doi.org/10.1177%2F0963721418754491.

Mesoudi, A. (2009). How cultural evolutionary theory can inform social psychology and vice versa. *Psychological Review, 116*(4), 929. doi: https://doi.org/10.1037/a0017062.

Mesoudi, A. (2011). *Cultural evolution: How Darwinian theory can explain human culture and synthesize the social sciences.* Chicago and London: University of Chicago Press.

Moss, D. (2017). Experimental philosophy, folk metaethics and qualitative methods. *Teorema: Revista Internacional De Filosofía, 36*(3): 185–203.

Nadelhoffer, T., & Nahmias, E. (2007). The past and future of experimental philosophy. *Philosophical Explorations, 10*(2), 123–49. doi: https://doi.org/10.1080/13869790701305921.

Norenzayan, A. (2013). *Big Gods: How religion transformed cooperation and conflict.* Princeton: Princeton University Press.

Norenzayan, A., & Gervais, W. M. (2015). Secular rule of law erodes believers' political intolerance of atheists. *Religion, Brain & Behavior, 5*(1), 3–14. doi: https://doi.org/10.1080/2153599X.2013.794749.

Norenzayan, A., Shariff, A. F., Gervais, W. M., Willard, A. K., McNamara, R. A., Slingerland, E., & Henrich, J. (2016). The cultural evolution of prosocial religions. *Behavioral and Brain Sciences, 39.* doi: 10.1017/S0140525X14001356.

Prochownik, K (2022). Causation in the law, and experimental philosophy. In P. Willemsen & A. Wiegmann (Eds.), *Advances in experimental philosophy of causation* (pp. 165–88). London: Bloomsbury Publishing.

Prochownik, K., Krebs, M., Wiegmann, A., & Horvath, J. (2020). Not as bad as painted? Legal expertise, intentionality ascription, and outcome effects revisited. In S. Denison, M. Mack, Y. Xu, & B. C. Armstrong (Eds.), *Proceedings of the 42nd annual meeting of the Cognitive Science Society* (pp. 1930–6). Cognitive Science Society.

Prochownik, K. M. (2021). The experimental philosophy of law: New ways, old questions, and how not to get lost. *Philosophy Compass, 16*(12), e12791. doi: https://doi.org/10.1111/phc3.12791.

Reuter, K. (2018). Dual character concepts. *Philosophy Compass, 14*(1), e12557. doi: https://doi.org/10.1111/phc3.12557.

Richerson, P., Baldini, R., Bell, A. V., Demps, K., Frost, K., Hillis, V., . . . Zefferman, M. (2016). Cultural group selection plays an essential role in explaining human cooperation: A sketch of the evidence. *Behavioral and Brain Sciences, 39.* doi:10.1017/S0140525X1400106X.

Richerson, P. J., & Boyd, R. (2005). *Not by genes alone: How culture transformed human evolution.* Chicago: University of Chicago Press.

Robinson, P. H., & Darley, J. M. (1995). *Justice, liability, and blame: Community views and the criminal law.* Boulder: Westview Press.

Sarch, A. (2018). Willful ignorance in law and morality. *Philosophy Compass, 13*(5), e12490. doi: https://doi.org/10.1111/phc3.12490.

Scott-Phillips, T. C., Dickins, T. E., & West, S. A. (2011). Evolutionary theory and the ultimate–proximate distinction in the human behavioral sciences. *Perspectives on Psychological Science, 6*(1), 38–47.doi: https://doi.org/10.1177%2F1745691610393528.

Shariff, A. F., & Norenzayan, A. (2007). God is watching you: Priming God concepts increases prosocial behavior in an anonymous economic game. *Psychological Science, 18*(9), 803–9. doi: https://doi.org/10.1111%2Fj.1467-9280.2007.01983.x.

Solan, L. M. (2009). Blame, praise, and the structure of legal rules. *Brooklyn Law Review, 75*, 517–44.

Sommers, R. (2020). Commonsense consent. *Yale Law Journal, 129*, 2232–605.

Sommers, R. (2021). Experimental jurisprudence. *Science, 373*(6553), 394–5. doi: https://doi.org/10.1126/science.abf0711.

Stich, S., & Tobia, K. (2016). Experimental philosophy and the philosophical tradition. In J. Sytsma & W. Buckwalter (Eds.), *A companion to experimental philosophy* (pp. 5–21). Oxford: Wiley-Blackwell.

Struchiner, N., Hannikainen, I., & Almeida, G. (2020). An experimental guide to vehicles in the park. *Judgment and Decision Making, 15*(3), 312–29.

Sytsma, J. (2021). The responsibility account. In P. Willemsen & A. Wiegmann (Eds.), *Advances in experimental philosophy of causation* (pp. 145–64). London: Bloomsbury Publishing.

Tobia, K. P. (2018). How people judge what is reasonable. *Alabama Law Review, 70*, 293–359.

Tobia, K. P. (2020a), Testing ordinary meaning: An experimental assessment of what dictionary definitions and linguistic usage data tell legal interpreters. *Harvard Law Review, 134*(2): 726–806.

Tobia, K. P. (2020b). Legal concepts and legal expertise. Manuscript in preparation. Retrieved from https://ssrn.com/abstract=3536564.

Tobia, K. (2022). Experimental jurisprudence. *University of Chicago Law Review*, 89, 735. Retrieved from https://ssrn.com/abstract=3680107.

Vilares, I., Wesley, M. J., Ahn, W. Y., Bonnie, R. J., Hoffman, M., Jones, O. D., . . . Montague, P. R. (2017). Predicting the knowledge–recklessness distinction in the human brain. *Proceedings of the National Academy of Sciences*, *114*(12), 3222–7. doi: https://doi.org/10.1073/pnas.1619385114.

Willemsen, P., & Kirfel, L. (2019). Recent empirical work on the relationship between causal judgements and norms. *Philosophy Compass*, *14*(1), e12562. doi: https://doi.org/10.1111/phc3.12562.

Winter, C. K. (2020). The value of behavioral economics for EU judicial decision-making. *German Law Journal*, *21*(2), 240–64. doi: https://doi.org/10.1017/glj.2020.3.

Part I

Topics in Experimental General Jurisprudence

Experimental Approaches to General Jurisprudence

Raff Donelson

Experimental jurisprudence is a big tent. Scholars working within this tradition investigate a collection of questions surrounding legal causation,[1] legal consent,[2] the meaning of legal texts,[3] law itself,[4] and many other legal topics. One thing uniting all of these is a shared hope that we might come to a better understanding of these vexing legal concepts (and sometimes also the stuff to which the concepts refer) by employing empirical techniques of the social sciences, particularly those of experimental cognitive psychology.

While there is a way to neatly join these varied projects under a single heading, this chapter proceeds from making a distinction among the projects. I distinguish *general jurisprudence* from other jurisprudential projects. *General jurisprudence* names the set of jurisprudential projects that seek to investigate law at its most general. When general jurisprudence scholars focus on analyzing concepts, they typically seek to investigate concepts such as *legal system*, *legal norm*, and *law*. Of course, there are plenty of other legal topics that one could investigate. One could want to know how to predict judicial conduct, how best to interpret constitutional text (generally or in some specific jurisdiction), or how people employ concepts from certain legal traditions, like that of *the reasonable person* used in common-law nations. These latter three inquiries, though very important for legal practice and for enriching our knowledge of the world, do not address the broader questions of general jurisprudence. That is, by treating those questions, we do not gain much traction on what legal systems generally are or what distinguishes legal norms from other sorts of norms.

This chapter focuses squarely on general jurisprudence and seeks to illustrate how experimental techniques and empirical findings can lead to progress on the kinds of questions raised by general jurisprudence scholars. To be sure, general jurisprudence is not the most common concern of empirically minded legal scholars, so my narrow focus requires some explanation. Communities of legal scholars differ in how much they accept the notion that empirical work can inform discussion in their subfields. By my estimation, general jurisprudence scholars are among the most hostile. This owes, in large measure, to the fact that general jurisprudence is usually understood as a branch of legal philosophy, and, traditionally, philosophers hold that the theses they discuss can be neither supported nor rebutted by empirical evidence. Knowing how general jurisprudence scholars understand their own field, it should be clear that an experimental general jurisprudence—a general jurisprudence informed by empirical evidence—is a radical departure and of great theoretical consequence.

Because the chapter has the goal of demonstrating that there can be experimental general jurisprudence, its primary audience are philosophers, particularly those legal philosophers who doubt that experimental work can be relevant to their field. There will be readers who share none of the skepticism of such legal philosophers, but the chapter may still hold some value for them. The chapter also seeks to speak to legal scholars and social scientists who either know a bit about general jurisprudence or know a bit about the study of cognition but who fail to see how the two subjects can be usefully connected.

For those less familiar with the finer details of general jurisprudence scholarship, Section 1.1 offers a systematic definition of general jurisprudence and surveys the questions within its ambit. This section aims to offer the background and vocabulary to help all readers appreciate the arguments to come. In Section 1.2, I outline several ways that experimental work might support particular theses or projects within general jurisprudence. In Section 1.3, I consider two important criticisms of the experimentalist methodology. Section 1.4 concludes and charts possible paths for future research.

1.1 Further Defining General Jurisprudence

Here begins a more careful definition of general jurisprudence. I begin by thinking through a suggestion made by Plunkett and Shapiro (2017), who contend that one can usefully analogize general jurisprudence to *metaethics*, the field of philosophical study on the foundations of morality. After drawing out this analogy, I turn to talking about an important subfield of general jurisprudence and the "modes" by which it is pursued.

1.1.1 Metaethics, General Jurisprudence, and Analogies

Just as metaethics is a theoretical conversation about first-order moral discourse and practice, general jurisprudence is largely a theoretical conversation about first-order legal discourse and practice. In first-order moral discourse, we make claims like "stealing is immoral," and, in the metaethical arena, we ask (and hopefully answer) questions about that claim, questions like the following.

(1) For the claim "stealing is immoral," what does that predicate (*is immoral*) mean?
(2) Is immorality a genuine feature of our world?
(3) What would make such moral claims true?
(4) How do we learn which first-order moral claims are true?
(5) What follows practically from the truth of a first-order moral claim?[5]

In first-order legal discourse, we make claims, like "stealing is illegal (in such-and-so jurisdiction)," and, in the general jurisprudence arena, we again ask questions about that claim, questions like the following.

(1') For the claim "stealing is illegal," what does that predicate (*is illegal*) mean?[6]
(2') Is illegality a genuine feature of our world?[7]
(3') What would make such legal claims true in any jurisdiction?[8]
(4') How do we learn which first-order legal claims are true?[9]
(5') What follows practically from the truth of a first-order legal claim?

In addition to treating questions like (1)–(5), metaethics also turns in on itself, asking about its own claims—what do *they* mean[10] and how do we come to know whether *they* are correct.[11] General jurisprudence is similar on this score too, as one finds work about the meaning of jurisprudential claims[12] and about how they are known.[13] General jurisprudence, then, like metaethics, is concerned with a broad array of questions—metaphysical, semantic, epistemological, practical, and more.

Despite the aforementioned similarities, there is a big disanalogy between metaethics and general jurisprudence. General jurisprudence is dominated by a single question that is largely absent in moral inquiry. General jurisprudence is dominated by the "what is law?" question. The dominance is so complete that commentators often define general jurisprudence as being concerned with answering that question alone.[14] This makes general jurisprudence pretty different from metaethics. I doubt that metaethics is dominated by any of its various concerns, and certainly not the analogue question, "What is morality?" That question crops up rarely and obliquely.

1.1.2　Enter Analytic Jurisprudence and Its Modes

Before moving forward, here is a fitting place to take stock of the conversation and our various distinctions. I began the chapter by distinguishing general jurisprudence from theoretical reflection on particular aspects of law. General jurisprudence differs from those other conversations in that it focuses on law at its broadest. Nested within general jurisprudence is a wide array of conversations, conversations about what legal claims mean, about whether we have a general reason to follow something simply in virtue of its lawfulness, about what law is, and so on. This portion of the chapter aims to bring one of these conversations into sharper focus, the "what is law?" question.

Inquiry that seeks to answer the "what is law?" question is *analytic general jurisprudence*, or just *analytic jurisprudence*. The modifier *analytic* is le mot juste because in answering the "what is law?" question, scholars attempt to *analyze* law or break law down into its component parts. Scholars accordingly assume that law is not basic or fundamental; it is made of elements which scholars can find. The task is similar to analyzing a square. Analysis reveals that a square is a polygon with exactly four equal sides and exactly four right angles. Ideally, perhaps, analysis of law would follow the same pattern, but analyzing law is difficult, and many scholars are content to take on just part of the task, to offer a partial answer to the "what is law?" question. Instead of offering the full set of components or the full set of necessary and sufficient conditions, scholars often argue, sometimes vociferously, over a particular component.

One of the more prominent conversations in all of legal philosophy is the debate between legal positivists and legal anti-positivists. This is just one of many debates within analytic jurisprudence, and it is a debate between two sides that offer partial answers to the "what is law?" question. Specifically, the debate concerns one supposedly necessary feature of a legal norm. One side—the anti-positivist—contends that some norm can be a legal norm (in the fullest sense) only if it comports with (some of) the strictures of morality, while the opposing side—the positivist—denies this, claiming that something's status as a legal norm does not depend on comporting with morality.

So far, I have maintained that analytic jurisprudence is concerned with the "what is law?" question, but that question itself is ambiguous. We better understand the subfield when we further distinguish different projects that scholars investigate. The "what is law?" question can be understood as asking about our shared *concept* of law or as asking about the extra-conceptual *object* that is law. For lack of better terms, we might say analytic jurisprudence can be pursued in the *conceptual mode* (as concerned with the concept of law) or in the *objectual mode* (as concerned with the object, law). To be clear, depending on one's views about concepts, the conceptual mode might wholly overlap with the objectual mode.[15]

A final thing to note concerns an important meta-debate about analytic jurisprudence. The meta-debate concerns how one should go about answering the "what is law?" question. A major part of the controversy in this meta-debate lies between those who contend that one cannot answer the "what is law?" question without recourse to first-order normative inquiry (so-called methodological legal anti-positivists) and those who deny that (so-called methodological legal positivists).[16] Methodological legal anti-positivists and methodological legal positivists typically agree that answering the "what is law?" question is an attempt to accurately represent or describe something (be it a concept or a thing); their disagreement is about whether such description requires prior evaluation, usually moral or political evaluation. This shared premise is disputed by another camp, the pragmatists. These thinkers contend that we should, at least sometimes, appraise (and offer) answers to the "what is law?" question based on the practical consequences of those answers (or the widespread acceptance of those answers).[17] For our purposes, a thoroughgoing understanding of the meta-debate is not necessary, but it is important to know that there is such a debate.

1.2 Ways That Experiments Can Benefit Projects in General Jurisprudence

Having offered some general background on general jurisprudence, I now turn to making a case that experimental work can advance conversations in this field. One way that experimentalists usefully contribute is by having conversations such as the present one. Experimental general jurisprudence scholars do not simply report on the results of experiments; instead, they offer arguments about why the results of their experiments are relevant to conversations had by their nonexperimentalist colleagues. In other words, experimental general jurisprudence scholarship participates in the meta-debate about analytic jurisprudence. This participation is helpful to general jurisprudence even if it were to turn out, after much debate, that empirical work is not relevant to debates within analytic jurisprudence. It would be helpful because increased discussion about this methodological question would help general jurisprudence scholars move from merely *assuming* that nonexperimental (or *armchair*) methods are uniquely appropriate to actually *knowing* that these methods are uniquely appropriate.

Of course, I doubt that armchair methods are uniquely appropriate. As explained in the following, experiments—and empirical findings more generally—can make a direct impact on projects in analytic jurisprudence and not just as a contribution to meta-debates. I proceed by drawing on a three-part typology of projects in experimental philosophy offered by Thomas Nadelhoffer and Eddy Nahmias.[18] Arguably, experimental general jurisprudence is just a species of experimental philosophy, so this typology should be apt. For each type, I both explain how this can be useful for analytic jurisprudence and offer an example of recent work that attempts to make this kind of contribution.

1.2.1　Experimental Analysis

The first kind of endeavor outlined by Nadelhoffer and Nahmias is what they call Experimental Analysis. This type of work seeks to discover "in a controlled and systematic manner what intuitions ordinary people tend to express" about some philosophical concept or question (Nadelhoffer & Nahmias, 2007, p. 126). For reasons that become clear in Section 1.3, I would broaden the category to also include work attempting to elicit the intuitions of *expert* respondents like other philosophers[19] or, in the case of law, legal experts such as practicing lawyers or judges.[20]

To develop one way that Experimental Analysis can help move philosophical conversations forward, I draw on a picture of philosophical debate that Maynes (2017) uses to vindicate experimental philosophy (x-phi). All philosophical arguments have to start somewhere. Presuppositionless philosophy is not possible. Thus, philosophy, of necessity, relies on *unproven* premises. Which unproven premises should we include in our arguments? Logic requires that we include at least a set of premises that, when combined, allow one to validly reach the conclusion we aim to demonstrate. But this requirement is a little too flexible since it does not rule out circular arguments or arguments that everyone takes to be unsound. Beyond the rules of logical inference, we generally must obey another rule for philosophical debates, namely that we only rely on those initial[21] premises that are part of the common ground, or as Maynes puts it, "the set of premises that, in this particular context, all interlocutors agree to accept" (2017, p. 48). Construing the common ground constraint as I just have—as a categorical ban on non-common-ground premises—might be implausibly strong. On a more modest version, *ceteris paribus*, we have more reason to accept a valid argument composed solely of common ground initial premises than a valid argument with non-common-ground initial premises. Whether one prefers the stronger or weaker iteration, the root idea behind such a constraint is reasonable. The common ground constraint is reasonable, not because common ground propositions are more likely to be true, but rather because adopting it is necessary if we are going to inquire *together* as a community. If we should accept this constraint, we have to know what is, and is not, common ground. Experimental Analysis can answer such questions.

In my own experimental work, I have tried to determine what is common ground for arguments put forward in analytic jurisprudence. In "Fuller and the Folk: The Inner Morality of Law Revisited," Ivar Hannikainen and I explore Lon Fuller's procedural natural law theory. On Fuller's view, some norm cannot be a legal norm unless it meets certain procedural criteria. Those criteria are what he calls "the inner morality of law" (Fuller, 1969, p. 4). For instance, Fuller thinks that something cannot be a law if it is not a general norm, if it is not understandable by those it purports to govern, or if it changes too often.

As Hannikainen and I note, it is unclear whether Fuller's project proceeds in the conceptual or objectual mode (Donelson & Hannikainen, 2020, pp. 10–1). If it is a conceptual project, Fuller's claims about these particular procedural criteria are, more or less, predictions of what "we" think. As such, an experiment could directly prove or disprove such claims. One could alternatively read Fuller as engaging on the objectual mode. As such, what the folk think about the particular procedural criteria is not direct, dispositive evidence. An armchair scholar might contend that the folk intuitions are not evidence at all. I suggest that thinking about the common ground constraint shows why folk intuitions are indirectly relevant.

Fuller's argument, understood as objectual, can be reconstructed along the following lines. It begins with premises like this:

(a) If a norm flouts criterion 1, it is not law.
(b) If a norm flouts criterion 2, it is not law.
(c) If a norm flouts criterion 3, it is not law.

Then, Fuller draws a general conclusion of what follows about law (and not just our concept thereof) from premises (a)–(c). That general conclusion is procedural natural law theory, construed as an objectual claim. What permits Fuller to rely on (a)–(c)? That they are common ground. Fuller's use of a good old-fashioned intuition pump supports this reading. Fuller develops a thought experiment with a king named Rex who flouts all of these procedural criteria (1969, pp. 33–9). In each of the cases where Rex violates a Fullerian criterion, we are supposed to think that he fails to make genuine law, and Fuller relies on this thought we supposedly have as one of his premises.

Now, if it turns out that ordinary people—and legal experts too, like seasoned attorneys—do not agree that flouting the Fullerian criteria means that the norm is not law, Fuller's case is weakened. This is because he would be relying on premises that are not common ground. As fate would have it, this is precisely what Hannikainen and I show. For many of the Fullerian criteria, respondents were not inclined to agree that a norm fails to be law when it contravenes the criterion in question. Our findings do not show that Fuller's theory is false, if construed as an objectual project, but the findings do shift the burden of proof, and that is important work too.

To be clear, Hannikainen and I may be wrong in several ways that would not undermine the probative value of such experiments. For instance, further research might show that folks and experts do agree with Fuller. That can bolster his case, which again would show the value of Experimental Analysis. Maybe further research will show that the folk agree, but experts disagree, or vice versa. These sorts of results would be harder to interpret, but the work of interpreting them would go some ways to establishing whether Fuller's claims are common ground. If Fuller's project is objectual, to undermine the probative value of experiments, one would need to reject the common ground constraint. This common-sense constraint would not be easy to reject, if understood just in a burden-shifting way, and even if one did, there are other possible arguments which might support the claim that Experimental Analysis would be helpful.[22]

1.2.2 Experimental Descriptivism

The second kind of endeavor outlined by Nadelhoffer and Nahmias is what they call Experimental Descriptivism. This type of work seeks "to better understand the nature of the underlying psychological processes and cognitive mechanisms that produce our intuitions [about philosophical questions]" (Nadelhoffer & Nahmias, 2007, p. 127). In other terms, Experimental Descriptivism looks for the causal, as opposed to normative, reasons why people (seem to) have certain intuitions.

This type of work appears to be of greater significance for psychologists than for philosophers, and, at first blush, it may not be clear why this is philosophically relevant at all. Exploring an important set of criticisms of *x*-phi, however, reveals why Experimental Descriptivism is crucial for certain philosophical projects.

Antti Kauppinen (2007) offers a frontal attack on Experimental Analysis or what he calls the positive experimental project. The heart of the attack is the claim that experimental philosophers working in that vein do not know enough about what leads survey respondents to respond as they do. If the respondents are incompetent users of the concepts in question, if respondents are not answering under ideal circumstances, or if pragmatic, rather than semantic, considerations are swaying the respondents, their responses may be of little epistemic value (Kauppinen, 2007, pp. 101–5). In a later attack, Kauppinen also throws in the possibility that respondents are using loose talk when they answer (2014, p. 284), a possibility which, if true, would also endanger the epistemic value of the responses. Kauppinen is surely right that, if experimental philosophers are wholly in the dark about the processes from which respondents' intuitions emerge, philosophers' findings may not be entirely convincing. This criticism, though, is precisely the vindication of Experimental Descriptivism.

Interestingly, Kauppinen recognizes that Experimental Descriptivism "may in principle help identify which responses are good sources of evidence about concepts" (2014, p. 285); however, he still denies that this answers his worries about the probative value of Experimental Analysis. He simply asserts, "On the whole, the likelihood that surveys provide useful evidence of folk concepts is low. The odds are that either the outcome is easily anticipated from the armchair, or one or another distorting factor intervenes to produce results that merit no weight in conceptual analysis" (Kauppinen, 2014, p. 285). The problem with such bald assertions is obvious: when there are several live possibilities, we cannot know the truth without investigating. Perhaps there are occasions on which it is perfectly fine to speculatively opine with "odds are . . ." but this is not how we make progress on difficult theoretical questions.

As an example of Experimental Descriptivism in jurisprudence, one needs to look no further than to a very recent effort to understand why folk respondents, at least sometimes, seem inclined to claim something that looks like a contradiction: that legal norms must meet certain criteria in order to be legal norms *and* that actual legal norms do not meet those criteria.[23] One possibility is that respondents do not understand that something cannot fail to have its essential characteristics. If survey respondents make this error, it might imply that folk beliefs here are not useful data. They should just be ignored. There is, however, another possibility, which could save the usefulness of folk beliefs: the folk might think of law as a dual-character concept.

To understand how this suggestion works, first, we must understand dual-character concepts. For dual-character concepts, a token can be an instance of a kind without being a *full* or *true* instance of the kind because the token fails to meet extra conditions which are necessary for full membership.[24] To give an example, contrast a political leader with a *true* political leader. Arguably, to be a political leader only requires that one hold political office, but the *true* political leader holds political office with the aim of improving the lives of the people. Membership in the class of political leaders is one thing, but membership in the class of true political leaders requires that one meet extra conditions.

With this idea borne in mind, we can return to Experimental Descriptivism and the law. If the folk hold the contradictory beliefs, that is, that laws must obey Fullerian principles and that laws actually fail to obey Fullerian principles, Kauppinen is probably right that folk responses are not helpful, and Experimental Analysis, at least when it elicits folk intuitions on this question, is doomed. However, if the folk think of law as dual character, there is no contradiction. The folk, on this interpretation, hold that laws need not obey Fullerian principles, but *true* laws must obey Fullerian principles. If this reading were right, as a first matter, that would mean that a reason for ignoring the folk responses, namely their seeming inconsistency, would dissipate. As a second matter, it would also mean that we have some additional reason to think that law might be the kind of thing that is dual character. Some scholars have suggested that while some laws fail to comport with morality, law in its fullest sense must comport with morality. This is sometimes called *weak natural law theory*,[25] and this view arguably gains plausibility points if it turns out that it reflects the folk conception of law. Of course, to determine whether the folk responses are irrelevant or a boon for weak natural law theory, one needs to understand the psychological process that best explains the response pattern. Experimental Descriptivism purports to offer such explanations.

1.2.3 Experimental Restrictionism

The third and final kind of endeavor outlined by Nadelhoffer and Nahmias is what they call Experimental Restrictionism. This type of work seeks to prove "that some of the methods and techniques that philosophers working in the analytic tradition have taken for granted are threatened by . . . empirical evidence concerning both the diversity and the unreliability of folk intuitions" (Nadelhoffer & Nahmias, 2007, p. 128). As with the other two categories, I would broaden this to include expert intuitions as well, as there is important empirical work, purporting to show that philosophers' intuitions are diverse and unreliable.[26]

As a program, Experimental Restrictionism begins with the fact that some philosophical arguments seem to rely on a shared intuition as a major premise. Paradigm examples of this include the Gettier (1963) argument against the justified-true-belief analysis of knowledge or the Nozick (1974, pp. 42–5) experience machine argument against hedonic accounts of well-being. Such arguments may be challenged by empirical findings that the intuition in question is only shared by a narrow group who is not epistemically privileged[27] or by findings that whether someone holds the given intuition on a particular occasion seems to be affected by irrelevant factors.[28]

In the world of analytic jurisprudence, there is relatively little work of this kind. Priel (2013) perhaps comes closest. Priel's interesting thesis is that there is no *single* thing that is law. The thesis hinges on two fairly controversial claims. The first is an empirical claim that people from the United States and people from the United Kingdom hold different conceptions of law. In other words, there is an American conception of law and a British conception of law. (The difference between these conceptions lies in the connection between law and politics, but exploring this is not relevant for our purposes.) The second premise in Priel's argument is a controversial metaphysical claim, namely that law depends, ontologically speaking, on a people's conception of it. Putting these together, we get Priel's startling conclusion: legal pluralism is true.

Priel's work approximates Experimental Restrictionism. I class it as Restrictionist for two reasons. First, he clearly casts aspersions on "methods and techniques that philosophers working in the analytic tradition have taken for granted." His claim is that an entire project, that of contemporary analytic jurisprudence, is largely premised on the thought that researchers around the world are all researching the same thing and trying to determine its nature, when, in fact, there are *many* different analysanda, all incidentally called "law" or some cognate thereof.[29] Second, Priel's project is Restrictionist insofar as he casts his aspersions precisely by drawing on the diversity of intuitions. Arguably, Priel lies outside the main camp of Restrictionists because, as far as I know, he does not condemn wholesale the use of philosophers' intuitions as premises in arguments;[30] instead, he merely suggests that such intuitions might, at best, be giving glimpses of different objects. Another reason to exclude Priel from the camp of Experimental Restrictionism is due to the fact that his work is not experimental. Even though he is not an experimentalist, Priel is not content merely to assert his empirical premise or to say, without support, "odds are . . . ." His approach, instead, is broadly empirical insofar as he relies on historical and other social-scientific data to make inferences about what his target groups believe.

One can easily imagine an experimentalist version of Priel's project that surveys people from the two countries and reports the degree of difference in their intuitions. If experimental results vindicated his suspicions, it would go some way toward establishing his version of legal pluralism. Of course, if results suggest that Yanks and Brits see the law exactly the same, Priel's view would be less plausible. To be clear, his view would not be entirely undermined. There are obvious ways to explain away the worrisome empirical result, but the thought that certain results would be unfortunate for Priel's thesis already assumes that experimental results do matter.

Moreover, such results matter well beyond vindicating Priel's own legal pluralist view. Others have argued that there is no univocal concept of law and, on that basis, have suggested that the project of accurately describing the concept of law should be replaced by a search for a concept of law that would yield the best political consequences (Murphy, 2001, 2005). This is the pragmatist approach mentioned earlier. This means that experiments meant to test Priel's claim could also have ramifications in the meta-debate about how to answer the "what is law?" question.

1.3 Responding to Objections

Experimental general jurisprudence is very new, and, as such, there are few published critiques of this scholarship. For that reason, this "objections and replies" section focuses on raising and responding to worries raised to experimental philosophy more generally. In the little criticism that has surfaced, one finds armchair general jurisprudence scholars mimicking some of the moves made by other armchair philosophers.[31] In this section, I discuss two sets of worries. One set of worries concerns expertise. The other concerns the survey method of gathering information.

1.3.1 The Expertise Defense

A certain dialectic is familiar in conversations about experimental philosophy. The experimentalist reports findings that the folk have the intuition that p or that the folk's propensity to intuit that p is affected by irrelevant factors x, y, and z. The experimentalist then draws some important conclusions based on those findings. The armchair philosopher, in turn, says that the folks' intuitions or propensities to intuit are irrelevant, for what should really interest philosophers are the intuitions of those with sufficient expertise on the topic, usually professional philosophers. This is an assertion of the expertise defense. After the expertise defense is asserted, the experimentalist usually goes out to find experimental evidence that philosophers also intuit that p or (more commonly) that philosophers' propensity to intuit that p is also affected by irrelevant factors.[32]

If something like this dialectic re-emerges when the conversation shifts to general jurisprudence, I hope both sides pay attention to what is specific about law. Law may be importantly different from the kinds of things that x-phi and armchair philosophers have heretofore discussed, and thus, it may take more thoughtfulness to mount a challenging version of the expertise defense. Here, I make two observations about the dialectic if it is to apply to experimental general jurisprudence.

First, if armchair philosophers wish to assert the expertise defense, we need to figure out whether and why the questions under scrutiny are those in which expertise should make any difference. To give an idea of how one's theory of the relevance of expertise matters, consider two very different theories. Perhaps experts' intuitions should be preferred because their intuitions are more likely to be formed by reliable processes than those of the folk (Kauppinen, 2007). If that were the proffered theory of relevance, experimentalists could proceed in the normal way—that is, begin figuring out whether the purported experts really have that expertise—but they might also figure out whether the experimental setting can be designed such that the folk can form their intuitions using the reliable methods too. Those are the paths of research on one theory of the relevance of expert opinion, but there are alternative theories. One might think that, for certain concepts, reference is in part fixed by expert opinion, sometimes because of their cognitive prowess and sometimes for practical reasons (Engelhardt, 2019).[33] If that were true, whatever expert opinion happened to be is automatically more relevant than folk opinion, but the immediate task for those who raise an expertise defense like that would be to show that law really is a concept fixed by expert opinion. (As an aside, I tend to doubt that latter theory, for law is not a rarefied scientific concept, like epistemic justification or RNA.) To sum up this observation, before experimentalists start devising tests to rebut the expertise defense, their intellectual opponents need to offer a theory about why the opinions of experts is to be preferred to the folk when it comes to law.

Second, supposing one has a theory about why expertise should make a difference, one needs to specify the sort of expertise required and to think about who has that expertise. When the expertise defense is mounted with respect to inquiry in metaethics or metaphysics, it makes some sense to believe that expertise lies in familiarity with the questions and further that professional philosophers are the relevant experts. It is less obvious that philosophers are our experts when it comes to law. A little anecdote demonstrates why. I once attended a general philosophy conference, and at this conference, during his presentation, a philosopher casually asserted that, necessarily, law only applies in the jurisdiction in which it is made. Of course, this may well be a necessary truth, but I asked the philosopher if it would affect his view to learn that the country where we presently were talking asserts that many of its criminal statutes apply extra-territorially and that scores of people are prosecuted for such offenses annually. The philosopher was ignorant of this, which I suspected given his casualness, and, judging by some murmurs in the room, many of the other philosophers present were ignorant of this as well.[34] This is just one anecdote, and it was just one room, but the lesson is likely generalizable. Philosophers as a group are unlikely to have special expertise about law because they have no special familiarity with law.

If philosophers as a group are not the experts, who are the experts and what does their expertise consist in? Here are two candidate answers for experts: legal philosophers and practicing attorneys. These two candidates will bring different kinds of expertise. Attorneys will have several years of training about the law, but many attorneys do not think specifically about the questions of general jurisprudence in their day-to-day working lives, and some jurisdictions and law schools fail to require aspiring attorneys to learn anything about such questions. Also, attorneys may internalize the rules of their own legal system to such a degree that they can no longer imagine alternative kinds of legal systems, which might mean that their legal expertise has distorting effects.[35] Legal philosophers, on the other hand, are much more likely to have read something in general jurisprudence, but reading H. L. A. Hart does not guarantee a capacious understanding of contemporary legal systems, and plenty of well-regarded legal philosophers have not attended law school, which would provide this more capacious understanding (ideally). In mentioning that there are things to be said in favor of, and against, both attorneys and legal philosophers as legal experts, my point is not that there no legal experts. Rather, I aim to show that one needs an argument to establish who the relevant experts are about law.

1.3.2 Survey Methods

A number of scholars have raised technical issues with experimental philosophy.[36] Some of the worries concern the fact that many experimentalists rely on survey data,[37] and there are pressing problems about whether the respondents' answers really track the object of inquiry. Some of the worries concern the fact that experimental science generally has a replication problem,[38] a problem that may be no less at home in x-phi (but see, Cova et al., 2021). I have a very brief suggestion for x-phi critics to bear in mind.

While these are genuine problems, we must remember what they problematize. These are problems with particular tools for finding certain information; these worries do not suggest that the information, if found, would be irrelevant. X-phi is not endangered if it turns out that quantitative surveys are unreliable or less reliable than something else. If there are more reliable methods for finding out what people believe and how they form judgments—for example, qualitative surveys, case studies, brain imaging and behavioral studies—these should be employed instead. The quantitative survey does not define x-phi and should not define experimental jurisprudence. Let a hundred flowers blossom.

1.4 Concluding Remarks

Experimental jurisprudence is a broad field, composed of work in general jurisprudence, which treats law at its most general, and lots of other work on other legal topics. While there are not many articles in experimental general jurisprudence at present, making the case for such work is an important step because it will cause many general jurisprudence scholars to rethink the field. This chapter urged this rethinking by arguing that experimental work can be helpful for several questions within general jurisprudence.

Experimentalists can contribute to important meta-debates about the best or unique way to answer questions in analytic jurisprudence. In particular, experimentalists, in defending their own experimental analyses, demonstrate that analytic jurisprudence has room for other methods of finding truths, and experimentalists of a more Restrictionist variety might bolster the pragmatist approach to analytic jurisprudence insofar as some of those pragmatist scholars rely on empirical claims about the proliferation of concepts of law.

In addition to contributing to meta-debates *about* analytic jurisprudence, experimentalists have already pursued, or may well pursue, work that makes a contribution *within* analytic jurisprudence. Some scholars, experimental analysts, have evaluated prominent theories of law and have shown that, depending on one's understanding of the *mode* of jurisprudence, folk and expert intuitions are either directly or indirectly relevant. Other scholars, the Experimental Descriptivists, have undertaken projects that serve to bolster the relevance of experimental analyses. Finally, there is also room for other scholars, pursuing Restrictionist strategies; such work may explain whether analytic jurisprudence is misguided in its assumption that law is a single thing which can be the subject for analysis.

At present, experimental general jurisprudence is without much specific criticism, but one can imagine the course critique may take. Critics may urge that experimentalists abandon projects, which center on ascertaining folk intuitions, and critics may caution the use of surveys as the primary means by which experimentalist projects proceed. These criticisms, depending on the precise circumstances, can be fair. There may be occasions on which experts, rather than the folk, should be the focus. There may be particular experiments for which surveys are unreliable and other methods, empirical and nonempirical, are superior for studying the specific thing under investigation. With that said, much more work is needed to better understand when and where these criticisms work with particular ventures in experimental general jurisprudence.

Having outlined three kinds of experimentalist projects, Analytical, Descriptivist, and Restrictionist, there is room for much more of all of these going forward, especially Experimental Analysis of law. Legal scholars have spent centuries trying to provide a general account of law, and, for centuries, they have used the same tools. It is time to expand the toolkit.

Acknowledgments

For feedback on earlier drafts of this chapter, I thank participants in the USC Legal Theory Seminar, especially Felipe Jiménez and Gregory Keating, participants in a workshop at the University of Arizona College of Law, the editors of this collection, and an anonymous reviewer. Finally, I thank Nicholas Gonano for excellent research assistance.

Notes

1 For example, Macleod (2019), Knobe and Shapiro (2020).
2 For example, Sommers (2020).
3 For example, Tobia (2020).
4 For example, Donelson and Hannikainen (2020), Flanagan and Hannikainen (2022).
5 For an argument that nothing should follow practically from the truth of a moral proposition, see Donelson (2017).

6   See, for example, Kevin Toh's work on expressivism about first-order legal discourse (Toh, 2011).

7   For remarks about the plausibility of legal eliminativism, see Donelson (2020, pp. 96–7).

8   As Ronald Dworkin famously put this question, what are the *grounds* of law? (1986, p. 4).

9   Many classic discussions in general jurisprudence that are primarily metaphysical have pretty immediate epistemic consequences. For instance, the debate between inclusive legal positivists and exclusive legal positivists is a conversation about whether a jurisdiction can make law in such a way that it incorporates genuine moral values (not just what somebody thinks is morally valuable). Of course, one's answer to that question supplies part of the answer to "how do we come to know the true first-order legal claims in a given jurisdiction?" If one is an inclusive legal positivist and in a jurisdiction that appears to incorporate moral value, one will contend that knowing the law requires knowing what morality requires. The exclusive legal positivist will deny that.

10   For an example of such a debate, consider Dworkin (1996) who argues that metaethical claims are just first-order moral claims.

11   For a fascinating new paper on this topic, see Compaijen and Meijer (2021).

12   Donelson (2020).

13   The methodological positivism and methodological non-positivism debate is one such debate. For some limited discussion, see *infra*Section 1.1.2.

14   Plunkett and Shapiro point this out (2017, p. 37).

15   One might think that the content of LAW is fixed by the nature of law, which is fully in line with content externalism. Alternatively, one might think that the nature of law is circumscribed by how we think of it because it is a non-natural kind.

16   As Perry puts it, "Methodological legal positivism is the view that legal theory can and should offer a normatively neutral description of . . . law," and the methodological anti-positivists deny this (1998, p. 427).

17   For example, Murphy (2001); Stoljar (2012); Donelson (2020). For an overview of this work, see Donelson (2021).

18   Nadelhoffer and Nahmias (2007). There are other typologies of experimental philosophy. Some prefer a simple two-part typology, distinguishing the positive project from the negative project. The negative project will be what Nadelhoffer and Nahmias call Experimental Restrictionism, while the positive project will be what Nadelhoffer and Nahmias call Experimental Analysis. That typology is fine for certain purposes, but it leaves out a category of work that is important for talking about experimental general jurisprudence in particular. That category is what Nadelhoffer and Nahmias call Experimental Descriptivism.

19   See Mizrahi (2015, pp. 54–6) for a summary of some of the work looking at philosophers.

20   Donelson and Hannikainen (2020, pp. 22–3).

21   By *initial premises*, I mean premises that are introduced in an argument as assumptions, rather than premises that themselves are the conclusions of other arguments. For instance, consider the following argument.

     (1)   If P, then Q
     (2)   P
     (3)   Q
     (4)   If Q, then R
     (5)   R

In this argument (3) is a premise used to support (5); however, it is not an initial premise for our purposes because it is a conclusion reached on the basis of (1) and (2). The common ground constraint only applies to initial premises. I thank participants at the Legal Theory Seminar at the University of Southern California for urging me to clarify here.

22 In Donelson and Hannikainen (2020), we rely on a "presumption against error theories" argument. Roughly, the argument contends that proponents of an error theory—an argument that suggests that most people falsely believe that *p* when *–p* is true—have an explanatory burden not borne by those whose arguments do not suggest such an error. Of course, an error theory can be true, but there is a defeasible presumption against them, and as such, it is epistemically valuable to know which views are error theories.

23 This finding is first reported in Donelson and Hannikainen (2020). The result was replicated in Hannikainen et al. (2021).

24 For this suggestion, see Hannikainen et al. (2021).

25 Murphy (2011).

26 For example, Schwitzgebel and Cushman (2012).

27 For a study contending that the Gettier argument is not widely shared, see Nichols, Stich, and Weinberg (2003). This has been disputed, however (Machery et al., 2017).

28 For a study contending that the Nozick argument tracks unreliable intuitions, see Weijers (2014).

29 Why *many* and not just two? Well, if the nature of law differs between two extremely similar polities (the United States and the United Kingdom), it surely differs among other polities which have far less in common.

30 Seyedsayamdost, for instance, defines Restrictionists as "those who are in favor of restricting the method of intuitions to a minimum in philosophy" (2019, p. 121).

31 For instance, see Jiménez (2021).

32 See Moti Mizrahi (2015, pp. 54–6) for summary of some of the rebuttals of the expertise defense.

33 As an aside, this might be the best way to read the Jiménez (2021) critique of experimental general jurisprudence.

34 Or maybe some were wondering if they had incurred criminal liability somewhere!

35 This might explain an effect found in Donelson and Hannikainen (2020), namely that American attorneys were slightly more likely than the folk to think that a norm fails to be law if it flouts Fullerian criteria. Many of those criteria are also conditions of legal validity under the US Constitution.

36 For example, Huebner (2015).

37 For example, Moss (2017).

38 Baker (2016).

References

Baker, M. (2016). 1,500 scientists lift the lid on reproducibility. *Nature*, *533*, 452–4. https://doi.org/10.1038/533452a.

Compaijen, R., & Meijer, M. (2021). The reification of value: Robust realism and alienation. *International Journal of Philosophical Studies*. https://doi.org/10.1080/09672559.2021.1923779.

Cova, F., Strickland, B., Abatista, A., Allard, A., Andow, J., Attie, M., . . . Zhou, X. (2021). Estimating the reproducibility of experimental philosophy. *Review of Philosophy and Psychology, 12*(1), 9–44. https://doi.org/10.1007/s13164-018-0400-9.

Donelson, R. (2017). Ethical pragmatism. *Metaphilosophy, 48*(4), 383–403. https://doi.org /10.1111/meta.12253.

Donelson, R. (2020). Describing law. *Canadian Journal of Law & Jurisprudence, 33*(1), 85–106. https://doi.org/10.1017/cjlj.2019.31.

Donelson, R. (2021). The pragmatist school in analytic jurisprudence. *Philosophical Issues, 31*(1), 65–84. https://doi.org/10.1111/phis.12204.

Donelson, R., & Hannikainen, I. R. (2020). Fuller and the folk: The inner morality of law revisited. In T. Lombrozo, J. Knobe, & S. Nichols (Eds.), *Oxford studies in experimental philosophy* (vol. 3, pp. 6–28). Oxford: Oxford University Press.

Dworkin, R. (1986). *Law's empire*, Cambridge, MA: Harvard University Press.

Dworkin, R. (1996). Objectivity and truth: You'd better believe it. *Philosophy and Public Affairs, 25*(2), 87–139. https://doi.org/10.1111/j.1088-4963.1996.tb00036.x.

Engelhardt, J. (2019). Linguistic labor and its division. *Philosophical Studies: An International Journal for Philosophy in the Analytic Tradition, 176*(7), 1855–71. https:// doi.org/10.1007/s11098-018-1099-2.

Flanagan, B., & Hannikainen, I. R. (2022). The folk concept of law: Law is intrinsically moral. *Australasian Journal of Philosophy, 100*(1), 165–79. https://doi.org/10.1080 /00048402.2020.1833953.

Fuller, L. L. (1969). *The Morality of Law* (rev. ed). New Haven: Yale University Press.

Gettier, E. L. (1963). Is justified true belief knowledge? *Analysis, 23*(6), 121–3. https://doi .org/10.2307/3326922.

Hannikainen, I. R., Tobia, K. P., de Almeida, G. F. C. F., Donelson, R., Dranseika, V., Kneer, M., . . . Struchiner, N. (2021). Are there cross-cultural legal principles? Modal reasoning uncovers procedural constraints on law. *Cognitive Science, 45*(8), e13024. https://doi.org/10.1111/cogs.13024.

Huebner, B. (2015). What is a philosophical effect? Models of data in experimental philosophy. *Philosophical Studies: An International Journal for Philosophy in the Analytic Tradition, 172*(12), 3273–92. https://doi.org/10.1007/s11098-015-0469-2.

Jimenez, F. (2021). Some doubts about folk jurisprudence: The case of proximate cause. *The University of Chicago Law Review Online*. https://lawreviewblog.uchicago.edu/2021 /08/23/jimenez-jurisprudence/.

Kauppinen, A. (2007). The rise and fall of experimental philosophy. *Philosophical Explorations, 10*(2), 95–118. https://doi.org/10.1080/13869790701305871.

Kauppinen, A. (2014). Ethics and empirical psychology—Critical remarks to empirically informed ethics. In M. Christen, C. van Schaik, J. Fischer, M. Huppenbauer, & C. Tanner (Eds.), *Empirically informed ethics: Morality between facts and norms. Library of ethics and applied philosophy* (vol. 32). Cham: Springer. https://doi.org/10.1007/978-3 -319-01369-5_16.

Knobe, J., & Shapiro, S. J. (2020). Proximate cause explained: An essay in experimental jurisprudence. *The University of Chicago Law Review, 88*(1), 165–236.

Machery, E., Stich, S., Rose, D., Chatterjee, A., Karasawa, K., Struchiner, N., . . . Hashimoto, T. (2017). Gettier across cultures. *Noûs, 51*(3), 645–64. https://doi.org/10.1111/nous .12110.

Macleod, J. A. (2019). Ordinary causation: A study in experimental statutory interpretation. *Indiana Law Journal, 94*(3), 957–1029.

Maynes, J. (2017). On the stakes of experimental philosophy. *Teorema: Revista Internacional De Filosofía, 36*(3), 45–60.

Mizrahi, M. (2015). Three arguments against the expertise defense. *Metaphilosophy, 46*(1), 52–64. https://doi.org/10.1111/meta.12115.

Moss, D. (2017). Experimental philosophy, folk metaethics and qualitative methods. *Teorema: Revista Internacional De Filosofía, 36*(3), 185–203.

Murphy, L. (2001). The political question of the concept of law. In J. Coleman (Ed.), *Hart's postscript* (pp. 371–409). Oxford: Oxford University Press.

Murphy, L. (2005). Concepts of law. *Australian Journal of Legal Philosophy, 30*(1), 1–19.

Murphy, M. (2011). The explanatory role of the weak natural law thesis. In *Philosophical foundations of the nature of law* (pp. 3–21), edited by Wil Waluchow and Stefan Sciaraffa. Oxford: Oxford University Press.

Nadelhoffer, T., & Nahmias, E. (2007). The past and future of experimental philosophy. *Philosophical Explorations, 10*(2), 123–49. https://doi.org/10.1080/13869790701305921.

Nichols, S., Stich, S., & Weinberg, J. ([2003] 2012). Meta-skepticism: Meditations in ethno-epistemology. In S. Stich (Ed.), *Collected papers, volume 2: Knowledge, rationality, and morality, 1978–2010* (pp. 224–46). Oxford: Oxford University Press.

Nozick, R. (1974). *Anarchy, state, and Utopia*. New York: Basic Books.

Perry, S. R. (1998). Hart's methodological positivism. *Legal Theory, 4*(4), 427–67. https://doi.org/10.1017/S1352325200001105.

Plunkett, D., & Shapiro, S. (2017). Law, morality, and everything else: General jurisprudence as a branch of metanormative inquiry. *Ethics, 128*(1), 37–68. https://doi.org/10.1086/692941.

Priel, D. (2013). Is there one right answer to the question of the nature of law? In W. Waluchow and S. Sciaraffa (Eds.), *Philosophical foundations of the nature of law* (pp. 322–50). Oxford: Oxford University Press.

Schwitzgebel, E., & Cushman, F. (2012). Expertise in moral reasoning? Order effects on moral judgment in professional philosophers and non-philosophers. *Mind & Language, 27*(2), 135–53. https://doi.org/10.1111/j.1468-0017.2012.01438.x.

Seyedsayamdost, H. (2019). Philosophical expertise and philosophical methodology. *Metaphilosophy, 50*(1–2), 110–29. https://doi.org/10.1111/meta.12349.

Sommers, R. (2020). Commonsense consent. *Yale Law Journal, 129*(8), 2232–324.

Stoljar, N. (2012). In praise of wishful thinking: A critique of descriptive/explanatory theories of law. *Problema: Anuario de Filosofía y Teoría del Derecho, 6*, 51–79.

Tobia, K. P. (2020). Testing ordinary meaning: An experimental assessment of what dictionary definitions and linguistic usage data tell legal interpreters. *Harvard Law Review, 134*(2), 726–806.

Toh, K. (2011). Legal judgments as plural acceptances of norms. In B. Leiter (Ed.), *Oxford studies in philosophy of law: Volume 1*. Oxford: Oxford University Press. https://doi.org/10.1093/acprof:oso/9780199606443.003.0003.

Weijers, D. (2014). Nozick's experience machine is dead, long live the experience machine! *Philosophical Psychology, 27*(4), 513–35. https://doi.org/10.1080/09515089.2012.757889.

The Experimental Jurisprudence of the Concept of Rule: Implications for the Hart-Fuller Debate

Guilherme da F. C. F. de Almeida, Noel Struchiner and
Ivar R. Hannikainen

2.1 Introduction

The Hart-Fuller debate occupies a prestigious place within contemporary jurisprudence. Since its opening rounds in the late 1950s, there has been unwaning academic interest in its meaning and implications. However, one of the core questions explored by the debate—the precise roles played by text and purpose in the concept of rule—remains unsettled sixty years later. Why is that so? One possible explanation lies on incompatibilities between the intuitions of Hartians and Fullerians.

One of the main thought experiments that divided Hart and Fuller concerned a rule prohibiting vehicles in the park. According to Hart, the rule is indecisive with regard to "bicycles, roller skates, [and] toy automobiles," but it always prohibits regular cars, even when other considerations, such as purpose, would recommend a different result (Hart, 1958).

Fuller—who "paced up and down at the back of the room 'like a hungry lion'" (Lacey, 2010, pp. 1–2) while Hart delivered his talk—pushed back. In his view, even cases lying at the very core of a rule's text required resort to purposes. He came up with the following counterexample to Hart's view:

> What would Professor Hart say if some local patriots wanted to mount on a pedestal in the park a truck used in World War II, while other citizens, regarding the proposed memorial as an eyesore, support their stand by the "no vehicle" rule? Does this truck, in perfect working order, fall within the core or the penumbra? (Fuller, 1958, p. 663)

For Fuller, the rule clearly allowed the memorial truck. Since Hart would probably say that the truck *did* violate the rule, this example seems to extract incompatible responses from the two scholars.

Crucially, Hart and Fuller's broader arguments about rules and about the law went on *assuming* that others would share their own intuitions regarding this central case. In other words, they may have assumed something along the lines: "Surely, people will share my intuition," assumed Hart; "surely they will not," thought Fuller. Based on these initial assumptions, each philosopher went on to develop his own highly sophisticated theory.

Over the years, these theories have gathered support and criticism from different groups of legal scholars. We suspect that people who tend to agree with Hart's response regarding the memorial truck example end up sympathetic to positivistic theories like Hart's own, while those who share Fuller's intuition are drawn to natural law theories in the same vein as his. Everyone seems to be relying on the assumption that their own intuitions are representative of how people in general, or at least of how lawyers and legal scholars, think about the law. But how could one be sure about this without actually checking *other people's* intuitions?

If that account of the dispute is accurate, a systematic empirical investigation of people's intuitions might help move the debate forward. Here, we will be discussing not only whose intuitions the experimental evidence vindicates but also, and more importantly, *why* and under *which conditions* people have different intuitions.

We begin with a brief recount of the arguments involved in the Hart-Fuller debate and its impact in legal academia (Section 2.2). In Section 2.3, we will argue that part of the reason why the debate ended in deadlock is the existence of conflicting intuitions at the heart of each side's arguments. We will further suggest that this deadlock—and possibly others like it—might be overcome by experimentally investigating people's intuitions. How can empirical data about people's intuitions adjudicate between competing philosophical theses about law? Section 2.4 answers this question by distilling the relevant portion of the Hart-Fuller debate into two empirical theses. Section 2.5 then describes how Schauer's analysis of the concept of rule might be leveraged to test them.

In Section 2.6, we turn to the evidence we gathered regarding the concept of rule (Struchiner, Hannikainen, & Almeida, 2020). It shows that both text and purpose matter for judgments of rule violation. Under certain circumstances, text matters more than purpose, but under a different presentation, purpose becomes the dominant factor.

Section 2.7 turns to possible interpretations of these basic findings. One possible account suggests that whenever someone breaks a rule's text unintentionally, we feel pressured to say that they did not violate the rule itself, a phenomenon the authors call "excuse validation" (Turri & Blouw, 2015). On the other hand, whenever someone complies with a rule's text, but intended to do something bad, we might want to say that they did violate the rule, as a form of "blame validation" (Alicke, 2000). Under that interpretation, rules are identical with their texts, but saying something like "Jane broke the rule" implies a further speech act that is moral in nature and that interferes with rule violation judgments. However, when people are given the opportunity to disentangle rule violation judgments from moral judgments, they reveal their commitment to a purely textual concept of rule. Thus, this way to account for the results is perfectly compatible with Hart's side of the debate, while leaving very little room for the Fullerian side.

An alternative reading proposes that the folk concept of rule is partly descriptive, since rule violation judgments are partly defined by whether a behavior straightforwardly falls within the scope of a rule's text, and also partly normative, since morally loaded purposes play an important role in judgments of rule violation. This explanation would lead to a largely Fullerian picture where purpose is pervasively important, an idea that might cast doubt upon the central tenets of legal positivism, a theory highly associated with Hart's work.

Finally, one last possible reading proposes that the concept of rule has a dual character. Dual character concepts have two different senses, one whose application is determined solely by descriptive features, and another whose application is determined solely by normative features (Reuter, 2019; Knobe, 2022; Knobe, Prasada, & Newman, 2013). According to that view, what explains our findings is that some people default to the descriptive sense, while others default to the normative one, with cues such as the questions that are asked alongside the rule violation question serving to disambiguate between senses. The implications of this last explanation are more ecumenical: they allow us to see that both Hart and Fuller were right about the concept of rule, but that they were each pursuing a different sense in which the concept might be used.

We conclude by emphasizing the need for further experimentation and by highlighting the philosophical progress made possible by empirical data (however incomplete it might be). This suggests that other issues in jurisprudence might also benefit from an experimental approach.

2.2 A Brief History of the Hart-Fuller Debate

The Hart-Fuller debate began with Hart's Oliver Wendell Holmes Lecture at Harvard Law School (Hart, 1958). In it, Hart proposed the aforementioned example of a rule prohibiting vehicles in a park. Against legal realists, he intended the example to show that, even though legal language might be indeterminate in certain cases, rules are still able to regulate some situations exclusively by means of their texts, without recourse to moral judgments. Thus, we can conclude that a rule's text is at least sometimes sufficient to determine whether the rule itself was violated.[1]

Fuller immediately responded with the memorial truck example. His takeaway from the intuition that a memorial truck doesn't violate the "no vehicles" rule was that assessing rule violations was *never* solely about text. We always need to take purpose into account. What makes Hart's example an easy case is that purpose, not text, is clear:

> If the rule excluding vehicles from parks seems easy to apply in some cases, I submit this is because we can see clearly enough what the rule "is aiming at in general" so that we know there is no need to worry about the difference between Fords and Cadillacs. If in some cases we seem to be able to apply the rule without asking what its purpose is, this is not because we can treat a directive arrangement as if

it had no purpose. It is rather because, for example, whether the rule be intended to preserve quiet in the park, or to save carefree strollers from injury, we know, "without thinking," that a noisy automobile must be excluded. (Fuller, 1958, p. 663)

In addition to that, Fuller thought that we *morally* evaluate the rule in assigning a purpose to it: we must take into account not simply what the legislature intended, but what reasonableness requires.[2] As Vega Gomez would put it "[. . .] we ask questions of 'ought' to determine what the rule 'is'" (2014, p. 48).

Later rounds of the debate centered on the status of Fuller's inner morality of law,[3] but the dispute around legal interpretation kept its importance throughout. Today, over sixty years separates us from the debate's beginning. In the intervening period, there was no lack of academic interest regarding the theme.[4] In 2008, to celebrate the debate's fiftieth anniversary, two symposia were held. One of them resulted in a collection of essays edited in 2010 by Peter Cane titled "The Hart-Fuller Debate in the Twenty-First Century."[5] Cane states in the preface that the essays "demonstrate that this debate between two of the twentieth century's greatest legal theorists continues to present a rich, and by no means exhausted, seam of jurisprudential ideas waiting to be mined in the years to come" (2010, p. vi).

Despite the large literature discussing the "no vehicles in the park" rule and its implications for legal theory, there is no consensus about who was right. After all, can rules be applied without reference to their underlying purposes? Or is the application of rules unavoidably moral? How often are rule violation judgments informed by morality? Even though Hart's textualist view seems to be more popular among contemporary legal philosophers,[6] there are still those who support Fuller's side, even if they are not always ready to give him the due credit. For instance, some have characterized Dworkin's highly influential views about the nature of law in very Fullerian terms: "[Dworkin] believes that the interpretation of legal sources inevitably involves moral deliberation (and that is where he departs from positivism)" (Shecaira, 2015, p. 26).[7]

Neither side is ready to concede. As a result, this venue of philosophical investigation into the nature of law might seem to be—in contrast to Peter Cane's thoughts—a dead end. But we believe that this is only the case if we limit ourselves to the traditional methods of philosophy.

2.3 Experimental Philosophy as a Way Out of the Deadlock

Many philosophers and jurisprudents claim to use a distinctive method: conceptual analysis. But what exactly is conceptual analysis? Shapiro describes the method as "a kind of detective work." Just as detectives trying to solve a murder find some clues and use them to come up with a theory to identify the killer, philosophers start with some truisms and use them to develop their own theory about a given concept or idea (Shapiro, 2011, p. 13).

Where are we to find the truisms Shapiro refers to? One prominent strategy is to think about some hypothetical cases involving the concept and probe our intuitions about it. For instance, when considering Hart's original example, we might instantly agree that the regular cars violate the rule solely because of the rule's text. Moreover, we believe that almost everyone in our audience would share that reaction.[8] If this is indeed the case—if our audience shares our intuition—then it is a truism that sometimes rules are just a function of their text. After all, we didn't need any fancy theory to arrive at that conclusion. Hart's example alone was enough to show that this is the case, and further reflection doesn't seem to suggest any knockdown argument against it. Any theory or concept of rule should hence accommodate that fact.

We might call this strategy for finding truisms "the appeal to intuitions." When appealing to intuition:

> A philosopher describes a situation, sometimes real but more often imaginary, and asks whether some of the people or objects or events in the situation described have some philosophically interesting property or relation [. . .]. When things go well, both the philosopher and her audience will agree on an answer, with little or no conscious reflection, and they will take the answer to be *obvious*. The answer will then be used as evidence for or against some philosophical thesis. (Stich & Tobia, 2016, p. 6)

It is easy to see how Hart, Fuller, and at least some of their heirs are conceptual analysts who appeal to intuitions.[9] Hart [Fuller] describes a situation (a regular car enters the park [a group mounts a functioning truck as a monument in the park] under the "no vehicles in the park" rule) about which people have clear intuitions (text is [isn't] sufficient). These presumptively shared intuitions are then taken to reveal a truism (rule violation judgments can [cannot] be a purely factual matter), which any successful theory of rules—and, consequently, law—must account for. Starting from the realization that text is sometimes sufficient, a core feature of Hart's concept of law is the separability of law and morals. Similarly, a defining attribute of Fuller's theory is a conceptual connection between law and morality, tracking Fuller's intuition that purposes are always necessary.

By now, the reader might have noted a problem: Hart and Fuller (and their respective followers) appeal to different and incompatible intuitions. Hart himself seemed to acknowledge this when, in the first page of his review of Fuller's *The Morality of Law*, he reports to be "haunted by the fear that our starting-points and interests in jurisprudence are so different that [Fuller] and I are fated never to understand each other's work" (1983, p. 343). No amount of theoretical work might resolve the fact that each side feels differently about the examples that incited the debate. This might help explain why so much work devoted to the Hart-Fuller debate led to so little progress. But if the deadlock is actually the result of conflicting appeals to intuitions, experimental evidence might help us move forward. After all, appeals to intuition rely not only on the intuitions of the arguer, but crucially, those of their audiences. If we can show that the intended audiences favor one, but not the other, intuition, we might remove one of the roadblocks hindering philosophical progress.

Experimental philosophy suggests that the best way to investigate philosophical concepts is to uncover people's *actual* intuitions. We can turn to the methods traditionally employed by psychologists in order to do so in a systematic and quantitative way.[10]

Legal philosophy is a field especially apt to be advanced by psychological experiments, as demonstrated by the recent surge in works in experimental jurisprudence (for recent reviews, see Prochownik, 2021; Sommers, 2021; Tobia, 2022). Under mainstream views in both positivism and natural law, law is at least partly determined by social facts that include in some way people's beliefs and attitudes about law. Even though legal philosophers disagree about whether the existence of law can also depend on moral facts, there is some agreement about the importance of human attitudes for establishing the content and overall structure of law.[11]

Hart and Fuller are no exceptions. Hart's theory emphasizes that the attitudes and beliefs of at least some members of a society are a necessary condition for the existence of law, meaning that mere behavioral regularity isn't enough (1994, p. 116). Fuller, by his turn, urged legal philosophers to put aside the task of "building 'conceptual models' to represent legal phenomena [. . .] and [. . .] turn instead to an analysis of the social processes that constitute the reality of law" (1969, p. 242). Presumably, as implied by Rundle (2012), a focus on "social processes" should be sensitive to the beliefs and attitudes that all people in a society actually have.

An important question remains: *whose* beliefs and attitudes matter for legal philosophy? There is serious disagreement about this issue, so much so that Matthew Adler coined the expression "recognitional community" to refer to the appropriate group and the polemics surrounding whose acceptance matter (Adler, 2006).

Hart famously held that only the beliefs and attitudes of officials (lawyers included) are a necessary condition for law (see Adler, 2006; Shapiro, 2009). Many other answers are possible. It could be that only judges belong to the recognitional community, or, going in the opposite direction, it could be that the recognitional community includes all citizens of a given country.[12]

Fuller would disagree with Hart in this issue. At several points, Fuller emphasizes the perspective of subjects, complaining about the positivists' focus on legal authorities.[13] Thus, in this chapter, we will report the results of experiments run with both lawyers[14] and lay people. After all, even Hart granted that "in a healthy society," citizens' attitudes and beliefs would coincide with those of the authorities (1994, p. 116).[15]

2.4 The Empirical Theses of the Hart-Fuller Debate

Is it possible to draw testable hypotheses from the controversy between Hart and Fuller? We believe that it is, at least if we construe the task of legal philosophy in a sufficiently broad fashion. If we take legal philosophy—and Hart and Fuller specifically—to be in the business of investigating interesting, even if not metaphysically necessary, features of law, then philosophical claims might be translated into empirical theses.[16] In any event, this section should not be read as the attribution of an overtly empirical agenda to either Hart or Fuller. After all, neither had anything experimental in mind in 1957. However, the appeals to intuition on each side hint that their respective claims hinged upon important empirical presuppositions. Specifically, their claims turn on whether or not their assumptions that their own intuitions are shared among the recognitional community are true or not. Here, we offer an attempt to work out which testable claims these intuitions entail, stating the disagreement between Hart and Fuller with regard to the concept of rule in two theses. We then proceed to consider the kind of evidence that could bear on each of them. Doing so demands an interpretation of Hart and Fuller's exchange. Apart from the expansive view of the task of jurisprudence, we take our interpretation of the debate to be fairly orthodox,[17] though by no means unanimous.[18] But we hope that the theses we explore, inspired by these authors, are sufficiently interesting in themselves to merit discussion even if we misconstrued their personal predictions.

Hart's concept of rule makes room for both text and purpose but distinguishes the roles they play in legal interpretation. As discussed in the Introduction, he is concerned with marking out a distinction between a core of settled meaning, where we know that a rule's text unambiguously applies (for instance, a regular car under the "no vehicles in the park" rule), and the penumbra, where we need to resort to purposes (social aims) in order to make legal decisions. Nonetheless, Hart emphasizes that "the hard core of settled meaning is law in some centrally important sense and that even if there are borderlines, there must first be lines" (1958, p. 614).

If there is something "centrally important" to law regarding judgments based on the core of settled meaning, we should expect that textual compliance should *often* be enough to determine rule violation judgments. In contrast, Fuller can be read as making the contrasting claim that text is often not enough, but that purpose, on the other hand, might be. As Schauer puts it:

> Fuller is arguing not only that his purpose-focused approach is a necessary feature of law properly so called, but also that it is an accurate description of what most judges and other legal actors would actually do in most common law jurisdictions. On this point Hart might well be read as being agnostic, but there is still a tone in Hart of believing that Fuller not only overestimates the role of purpose in understanding the concept of law, but may well also be overestimating the role of purpose and underestimating the role of plain language in explaining the behavior of lawyers and judges. (2008, p. 1130)[19]

Using this as a starting point, we might state Hart's position as the Textual Prevalence thesis (TP).

> Textual Prevalence thesis (TP): most people privilege text over purpose when assessing rule violation.

We understand TP as making two empirical claims: one, that most legal issues do not fall at the penumbra, but at the core (the core is larger than the penumbra); and, two, that, in these circumstances, most people, most of the time, take textual violation to be a sufficient condition for rule violation.[20] Both claims seem plausible, but we will focus on the second one for its role within the Hart-Fuller debate. For this claim to be true, it must be the case that, most of the time, most people take text violations to be sufficient for declaring or recognizing rule violations. If, on the contrary, people seldom take textual violation to be sufficient, TP is false.

By his turn, Fuller's memorial truck counterexample was meant to resist the idea that text is the most important element in legal interpretation. While it is possible to read him as making strong statements to the effect that violating purpose is a necessary condition for rule violation judgments,[21] a charitable interpretation reads his purposivism in a weaker fashion, one that simply contrasts with TP.[22] We might restate this interpretation as the Purposive Prevalence thesis:

Purposive Prevalence thesis (PP): most people privilege purpose over text when assessing rule violation.

PP is very much in the spirit of *The Morality of Law*. It respects the insights that law is an essentially purposeful activity and that interpretation is of "basic significance [. . .] for every aspect of the legal enterprise" (Fuller, 1969, p. 224). It is also empirically testable: if we show that Fuller is wrong about the prevalence of purposivism in interpretation—because textual interpretation is more prevalent than purpose[23]—we can discard it.

2.5 Testing the Theses

What sort of experiment can adjudicate between the two theses? Consider the following example.[24] Imagine that John, a restaurant owner, has a bad experience involving a dog named Angus. The dog barks, jumps, and behaves badly, irritating the restaurant's customers. With the purpose of avoiding nuisances to his customers in the future, John establishes the "no dogs" rule by fixing a sign on the restaurant door that reads: "No dogs allowed."

Now, imagine that a man wants to enter the restaurant with his pet bear. What does the rule have to say about it? The rule's text doesn't prohibit entrance: bears aren't dogs. On the other hand, the rule's purpose emphatically prohibits the bear: if pet dogs can cause distress to the restaurant's customers, pet bears can cause much graver trouble. What goes for bears also goes for tigers, lions, eagles, and drunk men. The rule's text would allow each of those cases, but the rule's purpose would prohibit them. These cases, where the text allows for things that the purpose would not, are labeled as *underinclusion* cases.

Consider now the following scenario: "a child enters the restaurant carrying a purse containing what seems to be a teddy bear. Actually, it's her dog, which doesn't bark and barely moves, being easily mistaken for a toy" (Struchiner, Hannikainen, & Almeida, 2020). In this case, it's the rule's text that clearly forbids the dog's entry, while the rule's purpose would allow it. This happens in *overinclusion* cases.

There are two other classes of cases defined by the relations between text and purpose: *core* cases, where both text and purpose agree that something should be included within the rule's scope (for instance, loud, misbehaving dogs like Angus), and *off-topic* cases, where neither text nor purpose applies (a woman enters the restaurant with her quiet child).

Looking at core, overinclusion, underinclusion, and off-topic cases, what would Hart and Fuller predict? They would surely agree that everyone should deem *core* cases to be rule violations (hence, the inappropriateness of Hart's original "regular car" example) and that no one should ever think that an off-topic case is in violation of the rule. Their theories, however, make very different predictions about overinclusion and underinclusion cases.

If TP is correct, it follows that agreement with rule violation judgments should be *greater* in cases of overinclusion than in cases of underinclusion. In contrast, PP states that people resort to purposes more often than they do to text when judging rule violations. Thus, cases of underinclusion should be treated as rule violations more often than cases of overinclusion.

2.6 The Evidence

We sought to probe people's intuitions about the roles played by text and purpose in rule violation judgments (Struchiner, Hannikainen, & Almeida, 2020). In this section, we report the results of three out of the four studies reported in that earlier paper, exploring the relationship between them and the theses that define the Hart-Fuller debate about rules. Table 2.1 summarizes the results for all reported studies.[25]

In the first of those studies, we employed a core case, an overinclusion case, an underinclusion case, and an off-topic case under each of four different rules.[26] For instance, one of the rules established "no wearing shoes in the house" so that the

Table 2.1 Summary Results for Selected Studies from Struchiner, Hannikainen, and Almeida (2020)

	N (# lay people)	Condition/Case type		Result	Favors
First study	200 (101)	Core		94%	TP
(% rule violation		Overinclusion		56%	
judgments)		Underinclusion		22%	
		Off-topic		11%	
Second study	175 (40)	Text × Rule		.55	PP
(Pearson correlation)				$p = 0.005$	
		Moral × Rule		.61	
				$p = 0.002$	
Third study	364 (125)	Only rule	Over	3.46	PP
(Mean ratings of rule			Under	3.54	
violation in a 7-point		Textual probe	Over	3.42	
scale)			Under	3.57	
		Moral probe	Over	4.48	TP
			Under	3.74	
		Both probes	Over	4.69	
			Under	3.14	

apartment would be kept clean. The core case described a man walking inside with dirty boots; the overinclusion case described someone trying on a brand-new pair of pristine shoes; the underinclusion case described a barefoot guest with muddy feet; and, lastly, the off-topic case described a barefoot guest whose feet were clean. Participants were asked whether they thought each case violated the rule. They also answered questions probing whether they thought that text and purpose were violated in that case.

In total, 200 volunteers (101 reported no legal training) completed our survey. The results were that 94 percent of responses on core cases said that the rule was broken, while only 11 percent of the answers given to off-topic cases were to that effect. So far, so obvious. Importantly, overinclusion cases were judged to be in violation of the rule by 56 percent of study participants, in contrast to a mere 22 percent for underinclusion cases. The results were similar—and still statistically significant—when the analysis was restricted to the ninety-nine participants who reported at least some legal training.[27]

This data clearly supports Hart's side of the debate: TP is vindicated by this experiment, since agreement with rule violation judgments was higher for overinclusion cases than underinclusion cases. This suggests that purposive interpretation is not as widespread as PP claims.

One limitation of this study was that participants made several judgments in sequence: they judged whether text, purpose, and the rule itself were violated. Plausibly, the reminders to consider text and purpose while reflecting on the rule might have had some effect on rule violation judgments. Given that, rule violation judgments in isolation might reflect a different balance of text and purpose. To address this limitation, we devised a new study where we asked each participant to consider a single question. As such, we recruited 175 volunteers (40 reported no legal training). Out of those, some were asked to assess only textual compliance, another group assessed only to which extent the described action was a moral violation, and a third group judged solely whether the rule was violated or not.

It turns out that, under such conditions, moral considerations are slightly more important in determining rule violation judgments. Again, the pattern is the same— and still statistically significant—when we restrict the analysis to participants who reported at least some legal training.

This result is consonant with PP, which goes to show that Fuller's appeals to intuitions were not completely off the mark. To confirm whether intuitions about rules are really that sensitive to contextual factors, we ran a final study with 364 volunteers (125 reported no legal training), this time manipulating which questions were asked to each participant. Take, for instance, the "no shoes" rule discussed earlier. If we describe the case of Tim, a visitor who enters John's house with either perfectly clean shoes (overinclusion) or very dirty feet (underinclusion), we can ask three questions according to the proposed framework: "Did Tim break the 'no shoes' rule?" (rule violation assessment), "Did Tim wear shoes in the house?" (textual probe), and "Is Tim morally blameworthy for what he did?" (moral probe). Participants always assessed rule violation, but could either receive no probes, one of them separately, or both probes jointly. In conditions where multiple questions were asked, the order of the questions was randomized, but answers were collected in a single screen, such that participants could change their ratings after reading all questions.

This experiment replicated the contrast between the two previous studies: when both probes were present, participants showed a tendency toward textualism, but when the only question related to rule violation judgments, this tendency disappeared, with a slight preference for purposivism. Moreover, textualism was driven by the introduction of the moral probe and not by the introduction of the textual probe.

2.7 Explaining the Evidence

How should we make sense of the evidence reviewed in the previous section and what can it teach us about the Hart-Fuller debate and the concept of rule? Given that the results do not univocally support either TP or PP, some more sophisticated framework must be employed to account for them. Even if a framework emphasizes text or purpose, it must also offer some explanation for why intuitions sometimes diverge from this element in a systematic way. This section considers three alternative explanations that are compatible with the data and explore their implications.

The first theory we want to consider starts from the assumption that the concept of rule is purely textual and that TP is true. It then explains away the finding that purposes are often significant to rule violation judgments by discounting it as a by-product of an indirect speech act. According to this view, a single rule violation judgment entails two different speech acts. The first one is descriptive in nature: to see whether the rule was broken or not, it suffices to verify whether the described behavior conformed to the rule's text. The other speech act, however, is evaluative and involves either blaming or excusing someone morally for their actions (Turri & Blouw, 2015).

When those two speech acts are conflated into a single question, people don't have a vehicle to show that they are not wrongly attributing blame. Thus, rule violation judgments become moralized. However, when a richer answer is possible, such that participants are able to disentangle the descriptive and normative aspects of the situation at hand, people should be able to express their purely textual concept of rule.

The predictions of this explanation fit the data quite well: rule violation judgments are indeed much more textualist when participants answer a separate question about moral blame than in other conditions. Purpose matters much more when rule violation judgments are probed using a single question that does not allow for separate judgments of blame. Thus, although some circumstances might elicit judgments that *seem* to support PP, they really don't. The reason purpose influences judgments under those circumstances is completely unrelated to people's linguistic competence regarding the concept of rule.

If this theory turns out to be correct, that will spell good news for Hart's empirical assumption. After all, this would indicate that the most precise ways of measuring intuitions about rule violation judgments reveal widespread textualism. Given widespread textualism, Hart's theory would have started out from a true assumption and would require no revision whatsoever. On the other hand, Fuller's assumption would fail completely. According to the pragmatic interpretation, Fuller either mistook his conversational sensitivity for conceptual competence or had idiosyncratic intuitions that are not widely shared. In any event, Fuller's theory would rest on mistaken assumptions.

That, however, is not the only way to interpret the data. A second reading vindicates Fuller's assumption. Instead of discounting the influence of purpose as a result of indirect speech acts, this view sees this influence as evidence that the concept of rule is a hybrid of text and purpose, so that you can only *fully* violate a rule once you violate both elements.

This explanation might also account for the discrepancies between the conditions of the third study by reference to the part-whole relationship between the questions. Earlier work (Schwarz, Strack, & Mai, 1991) found that when participants were first asked about the quality of their marital or dating life and then asked about their overall life quality, two different things could happen. When the questions were presented as a sequence, without any introduction explicitly connecting them, participants tended to show what the authors call an assimilation effect: answers to the two questions tended to be highly correlated, which means that ratings about life quality were *assimilated* to ratings about marital life such that those with a good marital life tended to report good life quality and those with a poor marital life were more likely to report poor life quality. The explanation is that marital life is a part of overall life quality and asking about it brings attention to its importance to life in general. On the other hand, when both questions were introduced as part of a single context (through a statement that the participant would be asked about a number of aspects of her life, which could be relevant to overall well-being), participants showed what the authors called a contrast effect: whereas assimilation means that answers to the general question tend to follow the specific one, contrast means that there is no such relationship; when a contrast effect is present, participants treat the specific judgments as irrelevant to the general judgment. The suggested explanation invokes the Gricean maxim of non-redundancy. In a conversation, we assume that people won't ask two redundant questions. Hence, we take the second question (e.g., about overall life quality) to refer to the remaining aspects of the composite concept (e.g., everything that matters to life quality except marital happiness).[28]

This might explain the effect of the moral probe: since the concept of rule contains a morally laden component (purpose), asking simultaneously about moral blame and rule violation in the context of a single case might lead participants to employ the maxim of non-redundancy and answer rule violation questions more textually.

If this account turns out to be correct, it will vindicate Fuller's assumption that purpose matters throughout. If people sometimes privilege text, that tells us more about part-whole dynamics than about the concept of rule, which is nonetheless thoroughly sensitive to violations of purpose. Thus, the Fullerian theory that develops based on that assumption would be safe and sound, while Hart might need to revise several aspects of his own theory.

Finally, we wish to consider one last explanation. Recent research has shown that several concepts have a dual character, meaning that they have two different senses, each applied according to its own criteria. Usually, one sense is purely descriptive, while the other is normative. Moreover, these two senses are independent in that violating the descriptive criteria is sufficient to violate the descriptive sense and violating the normative criteria is sufficient to violate the normative sense (Reuter, 2019; Knobe, Prasada, & Newman, 2013; Knobe, 2022). For instance, someone is a father *in one sense* if the said person is the biological father, but that person might not be a father *in another sense*, according to which fathers are caring and supporting of their offspring. Crucially, some studies suggest that the concept of law has such a structure (Almeida, Struchiner, & Hannikainen 2023; Flanagan & Hannikainen, 2020).

A dual character concept of rule establishes that rules have a descriptive sense about which TP is true, and a normative sense about which PP is true. Additional questions would then serve as cues that guide participants into one of the two different senses. Specifically, introducing a separate moral question would lead participants to interpret the rule violation question as pertaining to the descriptive sense. Thus, this last explanation can also fit the data.

If this final theory is correct, it will mean that both Hart and Fuller were right, each in a different sense. Hart's assumption would be correct with regard to the *descriptive* sense in which people apply the concept of rule, while Fuller's assumption would be right about the *normative* sense. This would mean that neither ensuing theory would need drastic revision. Instead, what would need drastic revision is our understanding of the relationship between both theories. A dual character concept of rule would require us to conceptualize Hart's and Fuller's legal theories as complementary, and not in competition; isolated, each would only account for an aspect of ordinary intuitions about rules, but in conjunction, they could offer a much more elegant and all-encompassing explanation for the legal phenomenon.

2.8 Conclusion

Experiments might help move jurisprudence past some roadblocks. In this chapter, we argued that the road leading the Hart-Fuller debate to philosophical progress was blocked by conflicting appeals to people's intuitions. We sought to overcome this barrier by investigating the intuitions of laypeople and lawyers about the concept of rule.

One possible outcome that this strategy could have delivered was a clear verdict about which side was right. If almost everyone showed a textualist pattern of intuitions under diverse circumstances, we would have concluded quite clearly that Hart's assumption was right, while Fuller's was wrong. In contrast, were all people purposivists, no matter how we probed their intuitions, Fuller's own take would have been vindicated, while Hart's would not.

This was not at all what we found. Instead of finding univocal textualism or purposivism, we found that different circumstances prompted different intuitions in people. Some of these circumstances supported the Fullerian intuition, while others suggested Hart might be right. Thus, any empirically informed theory that seeks to explain people's intuitions about rules needs to offer some explanation of why and when people privilege each component.

We saw three different explanations that fit the data. The pragmatic interpretation discounts the influence of purpose as a result of indirect speech acts, suggesting that Hart was right all along. The hybrid interpretation takes the opposite approach, explaining away the influence of the moral probe in terms of part-whole dynamics and suggesting that Fuller's assumption was the one vindicated. Finally, the dual character conception takes an ecumenical view, suggesting that the concept of rule is not applied according to a single criterion but has two independent senses, each related to a different aspect. About the descriptive sense associated with the concept of rule, Hart's assumption was right, but about the normative sense, Fuller was correct.

As we have seen, each of these three interpretations carries completely different implications for the issues at stake in the Hart-Fuller debate. Moreover, the experimental data is unable to adjudicate between them.

A skeptic could (wrongly) conclude that our experiments amounted to no significant results, bringing us to a dead end. We started up with a deadlock between Hartians and Fullerians and instead of resolving the deadlock, we added one more deadlocked option (the dual character view). Under this account, experimental jurisprudence would mean failure with extra steps.

This skeptical outlook must be rejected. While the experiments weren't able to provide a definitive answer to the question about the concept of rule, they did tell us a lot about people's intuitions regarding rule violations. First, they helped us reject certain options that would otherwise seem plausible. Given the results, simplistic readings that state that one of the two assumptions was completely right, while the other was completely wrong, are no longer on the table. Second, they allow us to develop more sophisticated accounts, such as the three views discussed earlier. Finally, these more sophisticated accounts make predictions of their own. For instance: if the pragmatic interpretation is right, cases where blame is not applicable should lead to textualism. New experiments might then test these new predictions, leading to ever more refined views about the folk concept of rule. Thus, experimental jurisprudence might advance (and already has advanced) important debates in legal philosophy.

Acknowledgments

The authors would like to thank Piotr Bystranowski, Brian Flanagan, Joshua Knobe, Fábio Leite, Lucas Miotto Lopes, Fábio Shecaira, Walter Sinnott-Armstrong, and Kevin Tobia for their comments on earlier versions of this chapter. This research was made possible through support from the National Council of Scientific and Technological Development (CNPq; grant number: 309735/2019-0), the Carlos Chagas Filho Research Support Foundation (FAPERJ; grant number: E-26/201.071/2021), the Coordenação de Aperfeiçoamento de Pessoal de Nível Superior (CAPES; grant number: 001), the DFG-CAPES research grant "Experimental Legal Philosophy: The Concept of Law Revisited" (project number 434400506), and the Spanish Ministry of Science, Innovation and Universities (MICINN; grant number: PID2020-119791RA-I00).

Notes

1 Bix (1995) reads Hart differently. According to him, in *The Concept of Law*, Hart's claims were limited to *legal* interpretation and, as such, emphasized the central cases the legislator *had in mind*. To work out whether cases in the penumbra fall under the purview of the rule or not, we should compare the features of penumbral cases with the features of the central cases actually anticipated by the legislator. Thus, under Bix's reading, Hart had the idea of speaker meaning as one of his chief concerns. Hart himself saw problems with Bix's interpretation, as disclosed by Bix's postscript to the relevant section of his book. We believe that our reading, in line with Schauer (2008), is a better representation of Hart's work. Regardless, we're much more interested in discussing the philosophical ideas of textualism and purposivism than in attributing them to specific authors.

2 The intentions of rule makers are often reasonable and moral. Thus, many cases conflate intentions and purposes, but, at least for Fuller, there is a clear distinction between both. See (Fuller, 1969, p. 229).

3 Especially Fuller (1969) and Hart's review of it (1983, chapter 16).

4 A brief and non-exhaustive list of works that discuss the "no vehicles in the park" rule and its connections to legal interpretation and jurisprudence includes Bix (1991), Fish (2005), Hurd (2015), Marmor (2005, pp. 99–118), Schlag (1999), Shecaira (2015), Soames (2012), Slocum (2016, pp. 213–76), Tobia (2020), Gomez (2014).

5 The other symposium, held at NYU, resulted in a special issue of the New York University Law Review that includes contributions such as (Schauer, 2008).

6 In that sense, Lacey remarked that "a fair-minded observer of the jurisprudential scene would have to conclude that Hart, as it were, won the war" (2010, p. 4).

7 Shecaira, *supra*, note 14, at 26. Schauer offers a similar reading: "One way of understanding Fuller, and possibly theorists such as Ronald Dworkin and Michael Moore as well, is believing that the good judge is one who sets aside the plain language of the most directly applicable legal rule in the service of purpose, or of reasonableness, or of making law the best it can be, or of integrity, or simply of doing the right thing. Dworkin's sympathy with the outcome in *Riggs* makes this clear for him, and Fuller's only slightly less overt sympathy for his mythical Justice Foster in *The Case of the Speluncean Explorers* is in the same vein" (2008, pp. 1130–1). Vega Gomez also agrees: "One cannot avoid here bringing Ronald Dworkin into the debate. Fuller's claims constitute a preliminary analysis of Dworkin's idea that there is a right answer in legal disputes and that it is misleading to say that judges create new law or legislate. For Fuller and also for Dworkin, we discover what the law is through an analysis of an 'ought' question" (2014, p. 49).

8 As we will see, philosophers appeal or refer to the intuitions of many different audiences. Shapiro's desired answer is, undoubtedly, lawyers: "[answering interesting philosophical questions about law] does not however mean identifying what the layperson would recognize as obvious truths about the law. It means identifying those truths that those who have a good understanding of how legal institutions operate [. . .] take to be self-evident, or at least would take to be so on due reflection" (2011, p. 15).

9 Regarding the interactions between conceptual analysis in jurisprudence and empirical presuppositions, see Bix: "Legal philosophy, like many forms of philosophy, is a hybrid of conceptual analysis and empirical description. [. . .] The conceptual analysis is usually meant to reflect, or at least be constrained by, the empirical

observations, and the empirical observations usually support, explicitly or implicitly, some conceptual point. Nonetheless, the two types of investigation should not be confused" (1995, p. 4).

10 This kind of experimental philosophy is sometimes called its "positive program" (Stich & Tobia, 2016, p. 10).

11 See Bix (2000). See also Himma: "Each of the major conceptual theories of law— positivism, natural law theory, and Dworkin's interpretivism—begin from the assumption that law is, in part, manufactured by contingent social practices, including those involved in legislation and adjudication. This means that the content of legal norms, including those that define the contours of the legal system to which those norms belong, can vary from one legal system to the next" (2015, p. 86).

12 For a more thorough review of the different possibilities, see Adler (2006).

13 See, for instance, Rundle, arguing that Fuller's disagreement with positivism "[. . .] is not that it looks to and takes its cues from the source of lawgiving power. The problem, rather, is how positivism privileges that perspective *exclusively*, with no meaningful regard for the way that law's distinctive mode of interacting with *the legal subject*, as an agent, provides the basis for distinguishing law from other modes of rule" (2012, p. 726).

14 Two clarifications are in order. First, Hart (1994) used the term "officials" more broadly than that, but he often referred to lawyers as being officials of the system. So, when we are investigating the intuitions of lawyers, we are investigating the intuitions of at least some of the relevant officials. Future work should try other definitions of officials (such as judges or executive officers) to see whether they can all be lumped together under a single category, or if we need finer distinctions. Second, we included law students in our definition of lawyer for the analysis reported later. Future work should aim at investigating whether there are systematic differences between law students and practicing lawyers with regard to the concept of rule.

15 Moreover, there is an emerging body of evidence indicating that legal concepts often have significant overlap with their ordinary counterparts, so the investigation of lay intuitions might illuminate the structure of legal concepts regardless (Tobia, 2021).

16 For arguments in favor of this broader understanding of legal philosophy, see Schauer (2013, 2015, 2020), Priel (2007).

17 We are in complete agreement with Vega Gomez's (2014) and Schauer's (2008) readings, which are the most thorough examinations we could find of the points of the debate we want to investigate.

18 For instance, Bix (1995), as discussed in the Introduction.

19 Even though, on this passage, Schauer limits the claim to the beliefs of lawyers and judges, we believe that we can extend these claims to lay people who take the internal point of view.

20 TP is not meant to downplay the role that purpose inevitably plays at the penumbra. When we are unsure about whether or not the rule's textual formulation covers a given case, it is hard to maintain that we should follow text and not purpose—after all, text is by definition not enough to guide us here.

21 Fuller asks in his original 1958 essay whether it is "really ever possible to interpret a word in a statute without knowing the aim of the statute" (p. 664). Drawing on excerpts such as this, Schauer remarks that Fuller "meant to insist that it was *never* possible to determine whether a rule applied without understanding the purpose that the rule was supposed to serve" (2008, p. 1111).

22 After all, in a book reclaiming Fuller's jurisprudence, Rundle stated that "numerous instances of hyperbole [infected] some of his claims" (2012, p. 6). The most charitable way to understand the apparently universal claims Fuller makes about the role of purpose in legal interpretation is to interpret them as hyperbolic and investigate weaker and more plausible versions of his professed purposivism.

23 Alternatively, PP could be read as a purely normative thesis stating that, no matter how frequently people invoke purposes in making rule violation judgments, purposes *should* count at least as much toward those as the rule's text does. We believe that Fuller would subscribe to this normative version of PP, but we do not believe this version is relevant to his debate with Hart. Inasmuch as Hart and Fuller were really debating with each other—as opposed to talking past each other—, they were debating about theses that are in some sense descriptive, as is the case with our versions of TP and PP.

24 The entire section draws heavily from Schauer (2002).

25 In the original paper, we reported the estimated marginal means outputted by linear models for both the first and the third study. This explains differences between the precise numbers. Regardless of the differences in presentation, the overall message is still the same.

26 Study 2 in the original paper.

27 All differences discussed here are statistically significant at $p < 0.05$. For more details, see Struchiner, Hannikainen, and Almeida (2020). All code, data, and stimuli were also made available at: https://osf.io/7ft6e/

28 Subsequent research has suggested that assimilation and contrast happened in an unpredictable way in part-whole question sequences (Carlson, Mason, Saltiel, & Sangster, 1995). This literature has eventually developed highly complex theories that includes roles for conversational pragmatics and availability filters to try to explain under which circumstances assimilation or contrast should be expected (Bless & Schwarz, 2010).

References

Adler, M. (2006). Popular constitutionalism and the rule of recognition: Whose practices ground U.S. law? *Northwestern University Law Review, 100*(2), 719–806.

Alicke, M. D. (2000). Culpable control and the psychology of blame. *Psychological Bulletin, 126*(4), 556–74. https://doi.org/10.1037/0033-2909.126.4.556.

Almeida, G. F. C. F., Struchiner, N., & Hannikainen, I. R. (2023). Rule is a dual character concept. *Cognition 230*, 105259.

Austin, J. (1832). *The province of jurisprudence determined*. Cambridge: Cambridge University Press.

Bix, B. (1991). H. L. A. Hart and the 'Open Texture' of language. *Law and Philosophy, 10*(1), 51. https://doi.org/10.2307/3504835.

Bix, B. (1995). *Law, language, and legal determinacy*. Oxford University Press. https://doi.org/10.1093/acprof:oso/9780198260509.001.0001.

Bix, B. (2000). On the dividing line between natural law theory and legal positivism. *Notre Dame Law Review, 75*(5), 1613–24.

Bless, H., & Schwarz, N. (2010). Mental construal and the emergence of assimilation and contrast effects. In *Advances in experimental social psychology* (Vol. 42, pp. 319–73). Elsevier. https://doi.org/10.1016/S0065-2601(10)42006-7.

Cane, P. (Ed.). (2010). *The Hart-Fuller debate in the twenty-first century*. Oxford: Hart Publishing.

Carlson, J. E., Mason, R., Saltiel, J., & Sangster, R. (1995). Assimilation and contrast effects in general/specific questions. *Rural Sociology, 60*(4), 666–73. https://doi.org/10.1111/j .1549-0831.1995.tb00599.x.

Fish, S. (2005). There is no textualist position. *San Diego Law Review, 42*(2), 629–50.

Flanagan, B., & Hannikainen, I. R. (2020). The folk concept of law: Law is intrinsically moral. *Australasian Journal of Philosophy*, 1–15. https://doi.org/10.1080/00048402.2020 .1833953.

Fuller, L. L. (1958). Positivism and fidelity to law: A reply to professor Hart. *Harvard Law Review, 71*(4), 630–72.

Fuller, L. L. (1969). *The morality of law*. New Haven: Yale University Press.

Gomez, J. V. (2014). The Hart-Fuller debate. *Philosophy Compass, 9*(1), 45–53. https://doi .org/10.1111/phc3.12096.

Hart, H. L. A. (1958). Positivism and the separation of law and morals. *Harvard Law Review, 71*(4), 593–629.

Hart, H. L. A. (1983). *Essays in jurisprudence and philosophy*. Oxford: Oxford University Press. https://doi.org/10.1093/acprof:oso/9780198253884.001.0001.

Hart, H. L. A. (1994). *The concept of law* (2nd ed.). Clarendon Press.

Himma, K. E. (2015). Conceptual jurisprudence: An introduction to conceptual analysis and methodology in legal theory. *Revus, 26*, 6592. https://doi.org/10.4000/revus.3351.

Hurd, H. M. (2015). Interpretation without intentions. In G. Pavlakos & V. Rodriguez-Blanco (Eds.), *Reasons and intentions in law and practical agency* (pp. 52–71). Cambridge University Press. https://doi.org/10.1017/CBO9781107707573.005.

Knobe, J. (2022). Personal identity and dual character concepts. In K. P. Tobia (Ed.), *Experimental philosophy of identity and the self* (pp. 49–70). London: Bloomsbury.

Knobe, J., Prasada, S., & Newman, G. E. (2013). Dual character concepts and the normative dimension of conceptual representation. *Cognition, 127*(2), 242–57.

Lacey, N. (2010). Out of the 'Witches' Cauldron'? Reinterpreting the context and reassessing the significance of the Hart-Fuller debate. In P. Cane (Ed.), *The Hart-Fuller debate in the twenty-first century* (pp. 1–42). Oxford: Hart Publishing.

Marmor, A. (2005). *Interpretation and legal theory* (2nd ed.). Oxford: Hart Publishing.

Priel, D. (2007). Jurisprudence and necessity. *Canadian Journal of Law & Jurisprudence, 20*(1), 173–200. https://doi.org/10.1017/S0841820900005749.

Prochownik, K. M. (2021). The experimental philosophy of law: New ways, old questions, and how not to get lost. *Philosophy Compass, 16*(12). https://doi.org/10.1111/phc3 .12791.

Reuter, K. (2019). Dual character concepts. *Philosophy Compass, 14*(1), e12557.

Rundle, K. (2012). *Forms liberate: Reclaiming the jurisprudence of Lon L. Fuller*. Oxford: Hart Publishing.

Schauer, F. (2002). *Playing by the rules: A philosophical examination of rule-based decision-making in law and in life*. Oxford: Clarendon Press.

Schauer, F. (2008). A critical guide to vehicles in the park. *New York University Law Review, 83*(4), 1109–34.

Schauer, F. (2013). Hart's anti-essentialism. In L. Duarte d'Almeida, J. Edwards, & A. Dolcetti (Eds.), *Reading HLA Hart's the concept of law* (pp. 424–43). Oxford: Hart Publishing.

Schauer, F. (2015). *The force of law*. Cambridge, MA: Harvard University Press.

Schauer, F. (2020). Social science and the philosophy of law. In J. Tasioulas (Ed.), *The Cambridge companion to the philosophy of law* (1st ed., pp. 95–114). Cambridge: Cambridge University Press. https://doi.org/10.1017/9781316104439.006.

Schlag, P. (1999). No vehicles in the park. *Seattle University Law Review, 23*(2), 381–9.

Schwarz, N., Strack, F., & Mai, H.-P. (1991). Assimilation and contrast effects in part-whole question sequences: A conversational logic analysis. *Public Opinion Quarterly, 55*(1), 3. https://doi.org/10.1086/269239.

Shapiro, S. J. (2009). What is the rule of recognition (and does it exist)? In M. Adler & K. E. Himma (Eds.), *The rule of recognition and the U.S. constitution* (pp. 235–68). Oxford: Oxford University Press. https://doi.org/10.1093/acprof:oso/9780195343298.003.0009.

Shapiro, S. J. (2011). *Legality*. Cambridge, MA: Harvard University Press.

Shecaira, F. P. (2015). Sources of law are not legal norms. *Ratio Juris, 28*(1), 15–30.

Slocum, B. G. (2016). *Ordinary meaning: A theory of the most fundamental principle of legal interpretation*. Chicago: University of Chicago Press. https://doi.org/10.7208/chicago/9780226304991.001.0001.

Soames, S. (2012). Vagueness and the law. In A. Marmor (Ed.), *The Routledge companion to philosophy of law* (pp. 95–108). New York: Routledge.

Sommers, R. (2021). Experimental jurisprudence. *Science, 373*(6553), 394–5. https://doi.org/10.1126/science.abf0711.

Stich, S., & Tobia, K. P. (2016). Experimental philosophy and the philosophical tradition. In J. Sytsma & W. Buckwalter (Eds.), *A companion to experimental philosophy* (pp. 3–21). Chichester: John Wiley & Sons, Ltd. https://doi.org/10.1002/9781118661666.ch1.

Struchiner, N., Hannikainen, I. R., & Almeida, G. F. (2020). An experimental guide to vehicles in the park. *Judgment and Decision Making, 15*(3), 312–29.

Tobia, K. P. (2020). Testing ordinary meaning. *Harvard Law Review, 134*(2), 726–806.

Tobia, K. P. (2021). Law and the cognitive science of ordinary concepts. In *Law and mind: A survey of law and the cognitive sciences* (pp. 86–96). Cambridge: Cambridge University Press.

Tobia, K. P. (2022). Experimental jurisprudence. *The University of Chicago Law Review, 89*(3), 735–802.

Turri, J., & Blouw, P. (2015). Excuse validation: A study in rule-breaking. *Philosophical Studies, 172*(3), 615–34. https://doi.org/10.1007/s11098-014-0322-z.

Part II

Topics in Experimental Particular Jurisprudence

Legislative Intent and Acting Intentionally

Kevin Tobia

3.1 Introduction: An Intuition about Legislative Intent

Suppose that the legislators of a small nation unanimously passed a bill stipulating that "no vehicles are allowed in the park" (cf. Hart, 1958). The legislators contemplated exactly two foreseeable effects:

(a) The bill would improve safety, by eliminating any risk of car accidents in the park.
(b) The bill would worsen cleanliness, by prohibiting garbage-trucks and automated sweeper trucks from the park.

Which, if either, is the bill's *legislative intent*? Seemingly (a).

But suppose instead that the legislators foresaw these two effects:

(a) The bill would worsen safety, by eliminating ambulance-car access to the park.
(b) The bill would improve cleanliness, by prohibiting high-emission trucks from the park.

Here the legislative intent would seem to be (b).

3.2 Study 1: Testing the Intuition

In an experimental jurisprudence study (see generally Prochownik, 2021; Tobia, 2022), I presented two groups of laypeople with the scenarios described earlier and asked "which, if either is the bill's legislative intent?" The choices were (a), (b), both, or neither. All materials and data, for every study presented in this chapter, are available at https://osf.io/yvgqt/.

In the first case, 92 percent said (a) was the legislative intent; in the second case, 83 percent said (b) was the legislative intent (Figure 3.1).[1]

$$\chi^2_{\text{Pearson}}(3) = 66.13, \, p = \, < 0.001, \, \widehat{V}_{\text{Cramer}} = 0.94, \, CI_{95\%} \, [0.89, 0.97], \, n_{\text{obs}} = 73$$

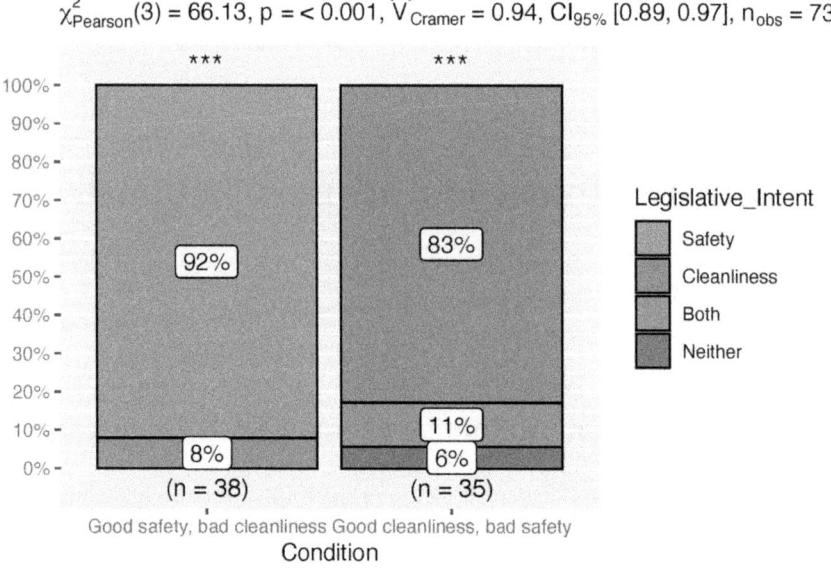

In favor of null: $\log_e(BF_{01}) = -38.75$, a $= 1.00$

Figure 3.1 Evaluation of the legislative intent of a rule stating "no vehicles are allowed in the park," with two foreseeable effects contemplated by the legislature: In condition 1, the rule would improve safety and worsen cleanliness; in condition 2, the rule would improve cleanliness and worsen safety. While 92 percent chose safety in condition 1 (left bar), 83 percent chose cleanliness in condition 2 (right bar). © Kevin Tobia.

In each case the legislators foresaw one safety effect and one cleanliness effect and drafted the same text: "no vehicles are allowed in the park." But judgment of legislative intent differs between the cases. In the first (the bill will improve safety and worsen cleanliness), participants overwhelmingly evaluated the legislative intent of "no vehicles are allowed in the park" to be to improve safety. However in the second (the bill will improve cleanliness and worsen safety), participants overwhelmingly evaluated the legislative intent of that bill to be to improve cleanliness.

How can the same text be understood to reflect a legislative intent about (only) safety in one case and (only) cleanliness in the other? A simple explanation is that laypeople intuitively understand *good* effects to be more (legislatively) intended than bad effects, all else equal.

3.3 Study 2: Legislative Intent and Intentional Action

This is a straightforward hypothesis about lay judgments of *legislative intent*, but it seems to be in tension with the well-known "side-effect effect," concerning judgment of what people do *intentionally*. Countless studies have found that people are more inclined to judge that an actor produced a foreseeable side effect intentionally when that effect is *bad* (e.g., Knobe, 2003, 2004). In the seminal case, participants evaluate a chairman who either foreseeably helps or harms the environment by starting a new program to increase business profits:

> The vice president of a company went to the chairman of the board and said, "We are thinking of starting a new program. It will help us increase profits, but it will also harm [and it will also help] the environment."

> The chairman of the board answered, "I don't care at all about harming [helping] the environment. I just want to make as much profit as I can. Let's start the new program." They started the new program. Sure enough, the environment was harmed [helped].

In the original study, 82 percent said the chairman *intentionally* harmed the environment, while only 33 percent said the chairman *intentionally* helped. The asymmetry is smaller when participants evaluate the chairman's *intention* to harm or help (McCann, 2005). But the effect's direction is ineliminable: Bad outcomes are evaluated as *more* intentional than good ones.

This same asymmetry arises in assessments of *group* intentionality (Michael & Szigeti, 2019). For example, when assessing what a company did intentionally, bad side effects are evaluated to be more intentional (all else equal). If ordinary judgment of *legislative intent* simply reflected beliefs about the intentions of a group (e.g., a legislature), one might expect a similar pattern of ordinary intuitions concerning the legislative intent of laws that produce good and bad outcomes. That is, one would expect seemingly bad outcomes to be more legislatively intended than seemingly good ones.

However, this is not what the data suggest. Consider a second "legislative intent" experiment based on the seminal "chairman cases."[2] Differences between the two vignette versions are **bolded and underlined** here (but not in the original survey):

> A group of legislators from the country of "Guilder" went to the full legislature and said, "We are thinking of passing a new law. The law will help increase business profits, **but it will also harm the environment**."

> None of the legislators cared at all about **harming** the environment. They all just wanted to increase business profits as much as they could. They voted to pass the bill into law. Sure enough, the environment was **harmed.**

> Now, thirty years later, a Guilder court is deciding a legal case about how that law should be interpreted. The precise legal issue is complicated, but the court's decision depends only on determining the law's "*intent*."

> Was part of the law's *intent* to harm the environment?

In a "help" version, there were three small changes:

> A group of legislators from the country of "Guilder" went to the full legislature and said, "We are thinking of passing a new law. The law will help increase business profits, **and it will also help the environment**."

None of the legislators cared at all about **helping** the environment. They all just wanted to increase business profits as much as they could. They voted to pass the bill into law. Sure enough, the environment was **helped**.

Now, thirty years later, a Guilder court is deciding a legal case about how that law should be interpreted. The precise legal issue is complicated, but the court's decision depends only on determining the law's *"intent."*

In the "harm" version, 38 percent said part of the law's intent was to harm the environment; in the help version, 50 percent agreed that part of the law's intent was to help the environment, $X^2(1, N = 470) = 7.46, p = 0.006$.

After the law's intent question, participants evaluated whether the legislators helped or harmed the environment "intentionally." There was a side-effect effect: fewer (20%) said the legislators intentionally helped than said they intentionally harmed (61%), $X^2(1, N = 470) = 80.72, p < 0.001$.

To be sure, this study found only a very small difference between conditions concerning legislative intent (12%). But the broader pattern of results suggests that ordinary judgment of *legislative intent* differs importantly from judgment of what legislators do *intentionally* (Figure 3.2).

What explains this difference in judgments about the law's "intent" and what its lawmakers did "intentionally"? One possible explanation is that ordinary judgments of legislative intent are influenced by or reflect judgments about the law's perceived *purpose*. Legal scholars have long noted that there are two senses of "intent"—one of which is "'intent' as 'purpose'" (MacCallum, 1966).

Recent experimental work suggests that people tend to attribute good purposes to individuals and collective entities (e.g., bands or nations). As De Freitas et al. put it, "[p]erhaps people believe that there is some sense in which the purpose of bands is to make meaningful music, the purpose of physics papers is to make valuable scientific contributions, and the purpose of human beings is to be morally good" (De Freitas, Tobia, Newman, & Knobe, 2017; see also Rose, Schaffer, & Tobia, 2020). So too, perhaps people tend to believe that a law's purpose is to realize good (Flanagan & Hannikainen, 2020), and this informs the evaluation of legislative intent.

After answering the two questions about the law's *intent* and what the legislators did *intentionally*, participants answered two final questions, on scales from 1 to 7:

Are the legislators who wrote the law blameworthy or praiseworthy for the law's effect on the environment? (1 = praiseworthy; 7 = blameworthy)

Was part of the law's purpose to help [harm] the environment? (1 = no; 7 = yes)

Participants blamed more in Harm ($M = 6.28$, $SD = 1.07$) and praised more in Help ($M = 3.55$, $SD = 1.32$), mirroring the pattern of attributions of acting *intentionally*. Consistent with the purpose hypothesis, participants were more inclined to evaluate the law's purpose to be helping ($M = 4.15$, $SD = 2.36$) than to be harming ($M = 3.11$, $SD = 2.17$). This mirrors the pattern of results concerning the law's *intent* (Figure 3.3).

$\chi^2_{Pearson}(1) = 7.46, p = 0.006, \widehat{V}_{Cramer} = 0.12, CI_{95\%} [0.02, 0.22], n_{obs} = 470$

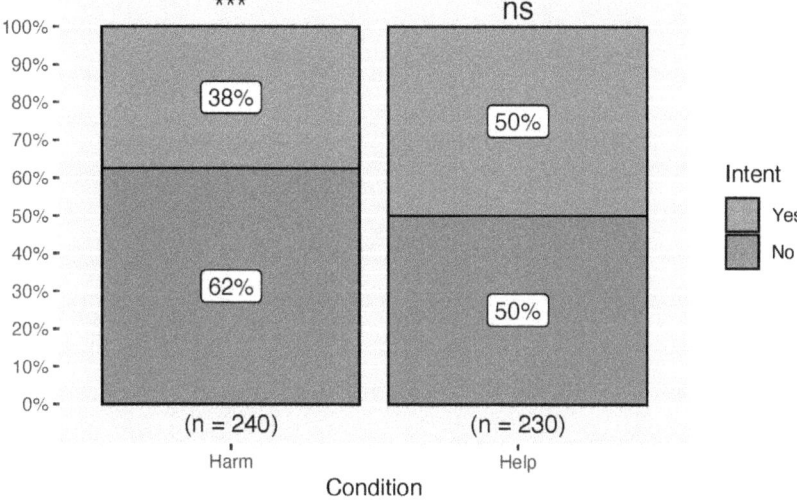

In favor of null: $\log_e(BF_{01}) = -1.57, a = 1.00$

$\chi^2_{Pearson}(1) = 80.72, p = < 0.001, \widehat{V}_{Cramer} = 0.41, CI_{95\%} [0.34, 0.49], n_{obs} = 47$

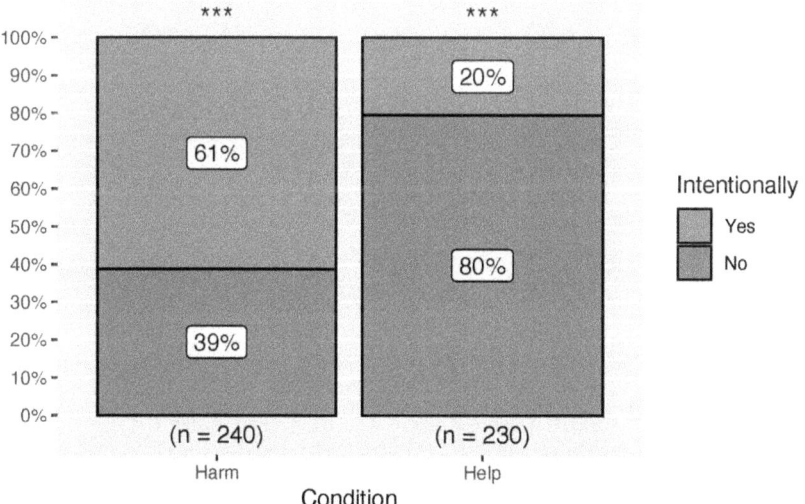

In favor of null: $\log_e(BF_{01}) = -39.54, a = 1.00$

Figure 3.2 Judgments of legislative intent (top) and intentional action (bottom), by condition. © Kevin Tobia.

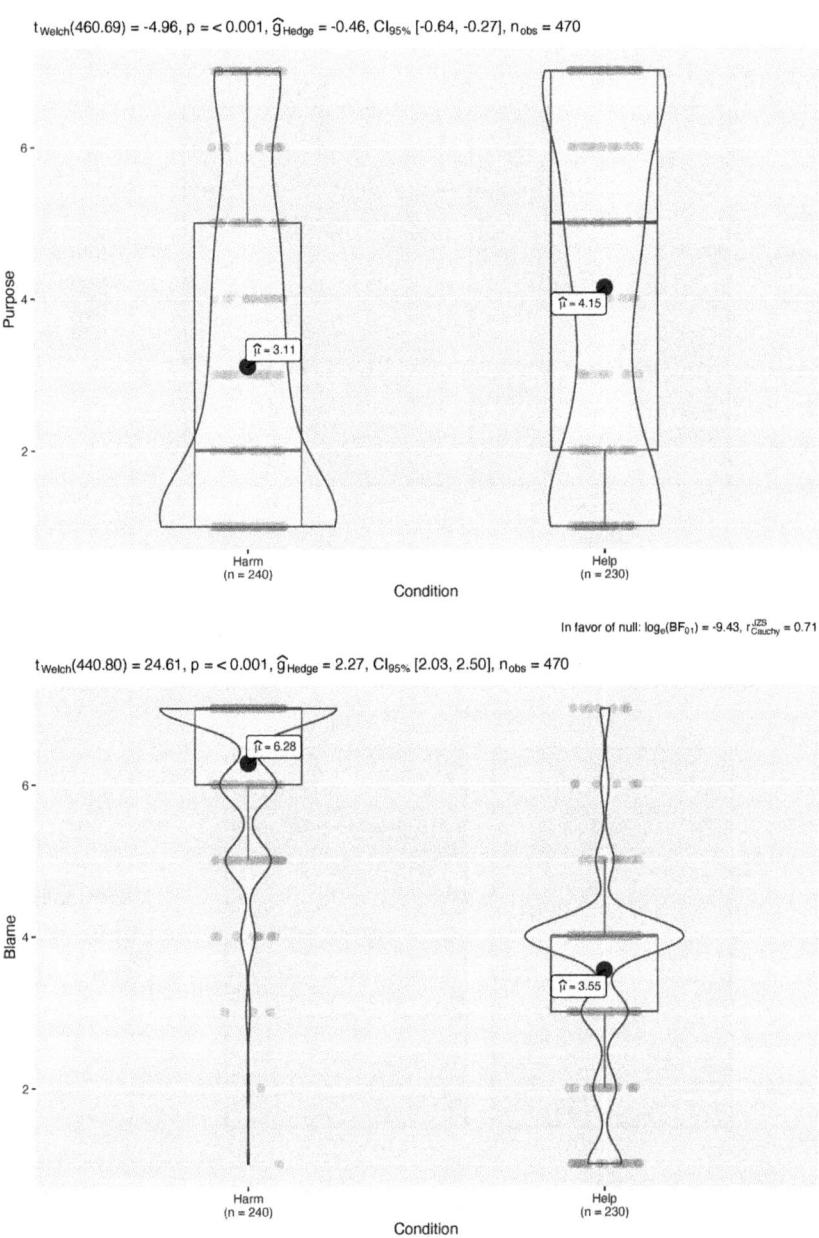

Figure 3.3 Mean ratings for Praise-Blame and Purpose questions. © Kevin Tobia.

3.4　Study 3: Assessing the Robustness of the Effect

A third study was conducted to assess the possibility that Study 2's results were driven by something peculiar about the phrase "law's intent" rather than a phrase like "legislative intent." The third study followed the design of Study 2, but used the phrase "legislative intent." In total, 250 participants were recruited and 196 correctly answered a check question.

There was no significant difference in the legislative intent judgments: 57 percent agreed that the legislative intent was to help and 50 percent agreed that the intent was to harm. There was a side-effect effect: fewer (38%) said the legislators intentionally helped than said they intentionally harmed (56%). Participants blamed more in Harm ($M = 5.90$ $SD = 1.31$) and praised more in Help ($M = 3.55$, $SD = 1.61$, $t(194) = 11.26$, $p < 0.00001$. Participants were not significantly more inclined to evaluate the law's purpose to be helping ($M = 4.25$, $SD = 2.28$) than to be harming ($M = 3.78$, $SD = 2.33$), $t(194) = -1.43$, $p = 0.155$ (Figure 3.4).

3.5　Legislative Intent Is Not (Merely) What Legislators Do Intentionally

These experimental results suggest a puzzling pair of ordinary intuitions: the legislative intent of a law is not simply what the law's legislators did intentionally.

Should we conceive of legislative intent (or intent) in this ordinary way? This question is illuminated by considering whether the side-effect effect itself reflects bias or conceptual competence. Broadly speaking, one view is that the side-effect effect is ultimately a bias. For example, perhaps ordinary people are mistaken in judging that the chairman *intentionally* harms. The true concept of intent, a "bias account" theorist might hold, only applies to effects that are desired. If the chairman knew of the harm but did not desire it, it is simply a mistake to evaluate that effect as one produced intentionally. Alternatively, one might treat the side-effect effect as a reflection of conceptual competence; the ordinary concept of intent is one that allows for (or even predicts) such an asymmetry.

One argument in favor of the bias account is that people might disagree about which side effects are good or bad; in such cases, we would expect disagreement in attributions of intentional action. Insofar as there is a fact of the matter about what acts were performed intentionally—and one that does not depend on the moral views of the particular judge—one of those intuitions would be false.

If the effect of good/bad valence is reversed in attributions of a law's intent, a parallel argument might be offered: Seemingly, a law's legislative intent cannot depend on the moral or political preferences of whichever individual happens to assess it. This seems to count against conceiving of legislative intent in a way that is consistent with the experimental results here.

Consider next "competence" accounts of the side-effect effect. Many of these accounts suggest that attributions of acting intentionally (correctly) reflect our

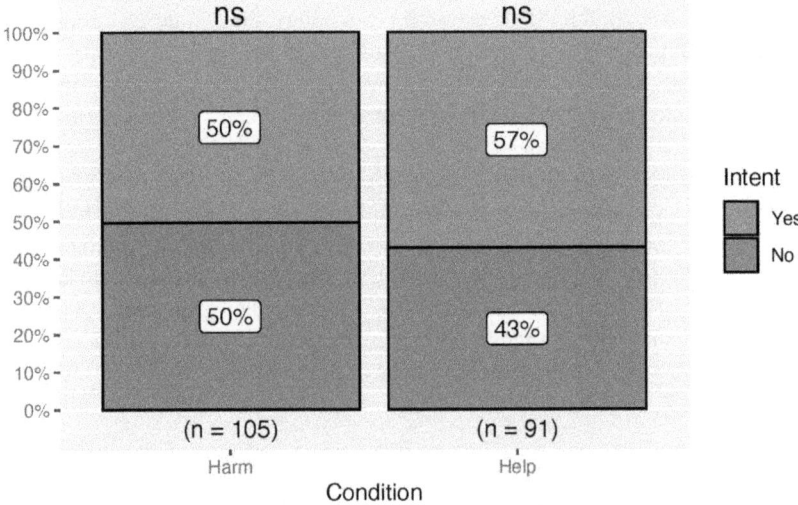

$$\chi^2_{Pearson}(1) = 0.87, p = 0.351, \widehat{V}_{Cramer} = 0.00, CI_{95\%} [-0.17, 0.07], n_{obs} = 196$$

In favor of null: $\log_e(BF_{01}) = 1.30$, a = 1.00

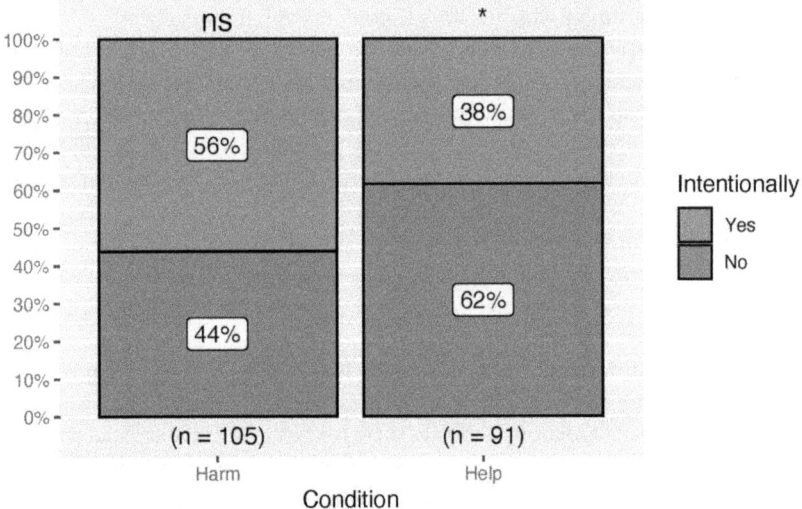

$$\chi^2_{Pearson}(1) = 6.14, p = 0.013, \widehat{V}_{Cramer} = 0.16, CI_{95\%} [0.00, 0.34], n_{obs} = 196$$

In favor of null: $\log_e(BF_{01}) = -1.32$, a = 1.00

Figure 3.4 Judgments of legislative intent (top) and intentional action (bottom), by condition. © Kevin Tobia.

normative evaluation of the agent's attitudes with respect to the side effects. For example, we take the harmful action to be intentional because it is blameworthy. Or the asymmetry between harm and help cases reflects our evaluation of what conduct is normal: To be indifferent to environmental aid is not the same (normatively) as to be indifferent to environmental harm.

These "competence" accounts about the concept of *intent* seem less helpful when evaluating the concept of legislative intent. In legal interpretation, the aim of assessing "legislative intent" is not usually to hold legislators to account for their acts. When courts evaluate the legislative intent of older statutes, the original authors may no longer be legislators at all. Rather, the focus is to determine the legal effect of the law, with reference to what *the law* was intended to do. As such, perhaps the ordinary notion of "legislative intent" is appropriately reflecting considerations of the law's purpose, rather than who is blameworthy or what constitutes normal action for a legislator in this context.

An implication of this "competence" account is that legislative intent is rightly informed by the normative status of a law's foreseeable effects. There are many foreseeable effects of laws that are not commonly considered part of the "legislative intent." A law's passage might help lawmakers win their next election, but this is not commonly understood as the law's "legislative intent." So it is not that *any* good effect would be seen as part of the legislative intent. The goodness of promoting animal welfare does not make it appear to be part of the intent of any given tax bill. There must be some nexus between the law's content and the effect.

On this view, consistent with the ordinary intuitions, legislative intent should be understood with reference to the law's purpose. And laws are generally seen to have good purposes—even when those were not brought about "intentionally" by its legislative authors. This is not to suggest an overly rosy picture of laws, or an overly pallid picture of legislators. Rather, it is to suggest that the ordinary distinction between *intentional action* and *legislative intent* facilitates evaluation of groups for what they did and laws for what they do.

Acknowledgments

Great thanks to Karolina Prochownik and Stefan Magen for very helpful feedback and the invitation to contribute this chapter. This research was funded by the Swiss National Science Foundation Spark Grant for "The Ordinary Meaning of Law," CRSK-1_190713.

Notes

1   Ninety-nine participants were recruited from Amazon's Mechanical Turk (44% female; M_{age} = 35.4). Seventy-three correctly answered a reading comprehension question and were included in the analysis (37% female; M_{age} = 35.9). In the first case, 92 percent identified the safety effect as the legislative intent, 0 percent said the cleanliness effect,

8 percent said both, and 0 percent said neither, $X^2(3, 38) = 94.9, p < 0.001$. In the second case, 0 percent said the safety effect, 83 percent said the cleanliness effect, 11 percent both, and 6 percent neither, $X^2(3, 36) = 63.4, p < 0.001$.

2   Five hundred participants were recruited from Amazon's Mechanical Turk (46% female; $M_{age} = 38.7$). Four hundred and sixty-seven correctly answered a reading comprehension question and were included in the analysis (47% female; $M_{age} = 38.9$). The full text, exclusion criterion, and analyses were preregistered. The comprehension question presented at the study's end was: What did the new law actually do (increase business profits and help the environment, increase business profits and harm the environment, decrease business profits and help the environment, or decrease business profits and harm the environment)?

References

De Freitas, J. Tobia, K. P., Newman, G. E., & Knobe, J. (2017). Normative judgments and individual essence. *Cognitive Science, 41*, 382–402.

Flanagan, B., & Hannikainen, I. (2020). The folk concept of law: Law is intrinsically moral. *Australasian Journal of Philosophy*. https://doi.org/10.1080/00048402.2020.1833953.

Hart, H. L. A. (1958). Positivism and the separation of law and morals. *Harvard Law Review, 71*, 606–15.

Knobe, J. (2003). Intentional action and side effects in ordinary language. *Analysis, 63*, 190–3.

Knobe, J. (2004). Intention, intentional action and moral considerations. *Analysis, 64*, 181–7.

MacCallum, G. C. (1966). Legislative intent. *Yale Law Journal, 75*, 754.

McCann, H. (2005). Intentional action and intending: Recent empirical studies. *Philosophical Psychology, 18*, 737–48.

Michael, J. A., & Szigeti, A. (2019). 'The group Knobe effect': Evidence that people intuitively attribute agency and responsibility to groups. *Philosophical Explorations, 22*, 44.

Prochownik, K. (2021). The experimental philosophy of law: New ways, old questions, and how not to get lost. *Philosophy Compass*, https://doi.org/10.1111/phc3.12791.

Radin, M. (1930). Statutory interpretation. *Harvard Law Review 43*.

Rose, D., Schaffer, J., & Tobia, K. (2020). Folk teleology drives persistence judgments. *Synthese, 119*, 1–19.

Tobia, K. (2022). Experimental jurisprudence. *University of Chicago Law Review, 89*, 735.

4

Why Blame the Ostrich?:
Understanding Culpability for Willful Ignorance

Lara Kirfel[*] and
Ivar R. Hannikainen

4.1 Introduction

Imagine the following scenario: John Ostrich tests positive for Covid-19 and isolates for five days, the mandatory period established by the Center for Disease Control and Prevention (CDC). During this period, his symptoms are mild, and by day 6, John feels perfectly fine. His friend Anne is hosting a birthday party which John is eager to attend. He could take one of the rapid antigen tests he has at home to find out whether he is still positive and therefore could infect others. But he's not *obligated* to: The CDC has eliminated this requirement for leaving isolation. John prefers not to know whether he is still infectious, so he leaves the house without taking a test and heads to the party. Sure enough, a couple of days later, Anne texts John that she has tested positive for Covid-19 along with several other attendees at the party.

As it happens, John was still positive and was the cause of the outbreak at Anne's party. How blameworthy is John for spreading Covid, even though he did not technically *know* that he still was infectious? In ordinary legal contexts, a defendant's ignorance is treated as grounds for reduced culpability relative to knowledge. Meanwhile, in cases like Mr. Ostrich's, legal theorists have advocated for a specific willful ignorance doctrine to apply. According to this doctrine, deliberate ignorance of certain incriminating facts suffices to satisfy the knowledge element of crime. Furthermore, jury instructions often specifically request that a jury equate deliberate ignorance with knowledge of the incriminating facts. As a result, a defendant who deliberately avoids gathering knowledge of their own misconduct is *as culpable* as a defendant who knows about the illegal status of their behavior (Charlow, 1991). However, within legal theory, there have been ongoing debates about when to apply the willful ignorance doctrine and whether the substitution of knowledge can be legally justified. In this study, we approximate the legal concept of willful ignorance by empirically

[*] Corresponding author: Lara Kirfel, l.kirfel@stanford.edu, Stanford University, 450 Jane Stanford Way, Stanford, CA 94305

investigating people's judgments of culpability, their knowledge attributions, and even broader character inferences from willfully ignorant misconduct. Finally, we aim to situate our findings in the broader legal-theoretical debate around the normative status of the willful ignorance doctrine.

4.2 *United States v. Jewell* or the Ostrich Instruction

The legal concept of willful ignorance (also referred to as willful blindness, deliberate ignorance, or intentional ignorance) (Sarch, 2014) prevents a person from evading civil or criminal liability by intentionally remaining unaware of facts that would otherwise render them liable. The so-called "Ostrich instruction" was first given to a jury in 1967 in *United States v. Jewell*, when the concept of willful ignorance was invoked for the first time to uphold a conviction. In this criminal case, defendant Jewell was arrested after driving a car in which packs of marijuana had been concealed in a secret compartment between the trunk and rear seat. Beforehand, Jewell had been approached at a bar in northern Mexico. After being offered marijuana (which he declined to buy), Jewell was asked to drive a car across the US-Mexican border for $100. On a narrow view of liability, the defendant would need to have knowingly (i.e., the element of mens rea) brought the drugs into the country (i.e., the element of actus reus). So, Jewell contested he did not in fact know that the car contained contraband.

The court, however, ratified the defendant's conviction and upheld the following jury instruction:

> The Government can complete their burden of proof [of knowledge] by proving, beyond a reasonable doubt, that if the defendant was not actually aware that there was marijuana in the vehicle he was driving when he entered the United States his ignorance in that regard was solely and entirely a result of his having made a conscious purpose to disregard the nature of that which was in the vehicle, with a conscious purpose to avoid learning the truth. (Kaplan, Weisberg, & Binder, 2014, p. 229)

In this regard, willful ignorance constitutes a striking departure from the ordinary way in which criminal conviction is established. Criminal liability usually rests on some form of *knowledge* of one's misconduct, but the willful ignorance doctrine establishes that courts may treat self-inflicted ignorance as satisfying the knowledge requirement of criminal conviction (Edwards, 1954). The rationale for this doctrine is that willfully ignorant misconduct is just as culpable as intentional misconduct (equal culpability thesis) (Hellman, 2009; Luban, 1998; Sarch, 2016). But under what circumstances is ignorance willful? What exactly qualifies as willful ignorance? Notwithstanding ongoing debates among legal theorists about the legal notion of willful ignorance, two basic requirements are widely agreed upon: a willfully ignorant defendant must be sufficiently suspicious of the illegal status of their action and at the same time fail to learn about it (Sarch, 2018; Williams, 1961).

Following Sarch's (2018) definition of a basic legal account of willful ignorance, a defendant is willfully ignorant of an incriminating fact p if . . .

Basic Legal Account of Willful Ignorance: (Sarch, 2018)

(i) . . . they have sufficiently serious suspicions of p, and

(ii) . . . they deliberately fail to take reasonably available steps to ascertain whether p actually is true.

Among legal theorists, there has been some discussion about whether this two-part definition of willful ignorance is adequate or calls for further refinement (Sarch, 2017). For instance, in addition to (i) and (ii), it has been suggested that the defendant is required to remain willfully ignorant with the specific *motive* of supporting their defense in case of prosecution (Hellman, 2009; Husak & Callender, 2019; Wieland, 2019). Other scholars have advocated limiting criterion (ii) to ignorance-preserving *actions* but not omissions: The defendant must undertake affirmative steps to avoid learning about p (e.g., actively rejecting an offer to be informed about the content of the suitcase), rather than simply omitting or failing to investigate p (Husak & Callender, 2019; Sarch, 2019).

In this chapter, we approach the WI concept by adopting the basic, two-part account. The ongoing discussion regarding its use in the law, however, highlights unresolved legal and theoretical issues (Husak & Callender, 2019): namely, whether and why deliberately ignorant perpetrators should be seen as satisfying the mens rea requirement for conviction.

4.3 Substituting Knowledge: What Does a Willfully Ignorant Person "Know"?

What is Jewell's culpable mental state in *United States v. Jewell*? Or, put differently, what did Jewell know about the nature of his actions? While knowledge is notoriously difficult to define (Gettier, 1963), the Model Penal Code requires that a defendant "is aware that his conduct is of that [illegal] nature or that the circumstances exist . . . , or practically certain that the result will occur" (Marcus, 1993). A reasonable person in Jewell's shoes would have been suspicious of their involvement in illegal conduct. As such, Jewell—and, by extension, willfully ignorant agents in general—qualify at least as "reckless." However, given the availability of incriminating information that they deliberately ignore (Alexander & Ferzan, 2009), the mens rea state of willfully ignorant defendants might be thought of as *exceeding* the level of recklessness. They are not merely aware of a substantial risk but also purposely avoid confirming the incriminating facts.

Yet, at the same time, willfully ignorant agents arguably fall short of the knowledge requirement for criminal conviction. That is, by most definitions, it cannot be established that they really knew what they were doing. So what exactly is the culpable mental state in WI? Why are willfully ignorant agents treated in court as though they had acted knowingly? We now elaborate on two qualitatively distinct explanations that legal theorists have advanced on this question (Husak & Callender, 2019).

4.3.1 Suspicion as a Knowledge State

Some theorists claim that the mental state of a willfully ignorant person is indeed a species or *kind* of genuine knowledge (Ashworth & Horder, 2013; Williams, 1978). This view, however, raises complex questions about how to conceptualize willful ignorance as knowledge (Husak & Callender, 2019): Which of the elements traditionally taken to indicate knowledge, that is, "justified true belief," does a willfully ignorant agent need to meet in order to possess some kind of knowledge? Is being suspicious of p akin to believing that p? Would Jewell be justified in believing that the car contains drugs even without inspecting it? Or does the fact that he intentionally refrained from searching the car indicate that he had sufficient evidence of the illegal substance in his vehicle? And, moreover, how specific must his suspicion be in order to qualify as equivalent to *knowledge* of the presence of marijuana in his car? There is a prolific disagreement among moral philosophers about whether moral responsibility requires a detailed understanding of one's involvement (e.g., of aiding an international marijuana trafficking operation in the role of a courier) (Vargas, 2005) or whether a broader knowledge state (such as a non-specific recognition of one's wrongdoing) suffices (Nelkin & Rickless, 2017).

We will not go into this discussion in great detail, but legal commentators have raised the concern that the mental state of many defendants who allege willful ignorance does not amount to genuine knowledge (Husak & Callender, 2019). Legal texts do not specify how strongly and how specifically a defendant must suspect that the incriminating fact exists. While some make references to beliefs with "high probability" of p, the exact threshold remains vague or underspecified in legal scholarship (Simons, 2021).

4.3.2 Deliberate Ignorance as Ill Will

Alternatively, WI has been argued to be equivalent to a knowing offense on the grounds that both epistemic states reflect the same degree of antisociality or ill will. According to Yaffe (2018), willful ignorance manifests the agent's failure to grant sufficient weight to other people's interests. In this regard, Yaffe argues that it shows a quality of "ill will" (Strawson, 2018) in much the same way as a knowing agent. By remaining ignorant, the willfully ignorant perpetrator puts his own interests first. An inquiry into the nature of their actions might lead to a bad conscience, for example, learning about the harmful effect on others, and this as a result might interfere with their plan to proceed with that action. Sarch (2018) argues that willful ignorance involves a breach of the pro tanto duty to inform oneself, and therefore manifests a disregard to values and interests protected by the law (Alexander & Ferzan, 2009). Husak and Callender (2019) have, however, raised the concern that such an argument might risk violating the "principle of legality": that is, the principle that, when a statute clearly requires the mental state of knowledge, the ordinary moral disapproval of knowing and willfully ignorant wrongdoers cannot form the basis for their equal conviction.

4.4 Willful Ignorance: An Empirical Approximation

Despite the fact that the willful ignorance doctrine is frequently employed in courts, the concept of willful ignorance continues to be heavily debated among legal theorists (Child, 2021; Sarch, 2019; Simons, 2021). The vague definition of what kind of behavior counts as deliberate ignorance has led to discrepancies in jury instructions and reasoning in judicial opinions. As a consequence, some have argued in favor of lowering the mens rea standard to recklessness in cases that require proof of willful ignorance (Husak & Callender, 2019; Sherrin, 2014). Others have concluded that courts should refrain from employing the WI doctrine until agreement on a more precise and palatable definition of WI is reached (Simons, 2021). As Husak and Callender (2019) note, unlike other legal or mens rea terms, the concept of willful ignorance is not commonly used in ordinary language: "[It] is more of a technical, stipulative term of legal art with no precise analogue in everyday speech. This concept has not been borrowed from ordinary language; attributions of willful ignorance are extremely rare outside of legal contexts" (p. 205).

How to resolve the theoretical and—in consequence—practical problems around the WI doctrine in court? As a way forward, Simons (2021) suggests that "an empirical analysis of how ordinary people and legal actors understand the mens rea term (here, knowledge) would go some way toward addressing the concern, especially if we were to employ that analysis to improve the comprehensibility of jury instructions explaining the mens rea term" (pp. 22–3). Assessing ordinary judgments might shed light on the question whether the definitional decoupling of this term from mens rea like "knowledge" and "recklessness" maps onto people's ordinary judgments about WI behavior (see Kneer & Skoczeń, 2023; Mikhail, 2009). In particular, empirical research may advance the debate around WI in two important respects. First, experimental evidence can uncover whether willfully ignorant and knowing perpetrators are considered equally culpable, in line with the equal culpability hypothesis. Second, empirical studies can, in principle, identify the factors that promote people's judgments of culpability in the context of WI. Are people's assessments of the culpability of WI driven by the degree of knowledge they attribute to a WI defendants? If so, is it the same degree and kind of knowledge as in the case of "true" knowledge? What inferences do people make from willfully ignorant behavior?

4.5 Study 1

Empirical studies show that people's categorization of legal mental states roughly corresponds to the Model Penal Code's hierarchy of mens rea (Ginther et al., 2014; Jones et al., 2018; Jones, Montague, & Yaffe, 2020; Shen, Hoffman, Jones, & Greene, 2011). The present study aims to extend this line of research on mens rea to the concept of willful ignorance. Following the basic account of WI, we will assess people's perception of WI by decomposing it into its two main components: (i) the state of suspicion and (ii) the opportunity for inquiry.

First, we vary whether an agent is suspicious of the harmful consequences of their action or not. Suspicion constitutes a key component of willful ignorance. Without suspicion, the fact that an agent does not pursue further investigation of a certain matter is not culpable. In order to link WI to the mens rea of *recklessness* and *negligence*, we included an additional manipulation of "suspicion": whether *a reasonable person* would suspect or not. Recklessness is loosely defined as "willingly taking an initial action that a reasonable person would know will likely lead to the actus reus being committed" (Stark, 2016; Williams, 1981). If a reasonable person would not believe their action may yield harmful consequences, the defendant should not be considered reckless (Stark, 2020). In Study 1, we therefore manipulated whether a reasonable person would be wary of the action they were about to engage in, as well as whether the agent in question in fact held suspicion. While there is a current legal debate around what actually constitutes *reasonableness* (Alicke & Weigel, 2021; Jaeger, 2020; Tobia, 2018), we instrumentalized the reasonableness of suspicion in terms of "common knowledge." In other words, suspicion would be reasonable when most fellow citizens in the defendant's position would have suspected and unreasonable otherwise (Valverde, 2009).

We also experimentally manipulated the second component in the basic account of WI: namely, the opportunity to acquire incriminating knowledge about one's action. Sarch (2018) argues that the difficulty or risk involved in acquiring knowledge determines whether WI agents are required to pursue it. When acquiring the incriminating knowledge is too burdensome, costly, or potentially harmful, the WI doctrine might be justifiably waived (Sarch, 2017). In our study, we vary the defendant's opportunity to inquire about the suspicious state of affairs, that is, whether there are "reasonably available steps" toward acquiring knowledge. By varying the ease of inquiry, we ask whether people take the difficulty or ease with which knowledge could have been acquired into account (Kirfel & Lagnado, 2021).

Crossing these two factors, suspicion and opportunity for inquiry, formed the basis for Study 1. As our primary dependent measure, we assessed people's judgments of culpability. To evaluate the equal culpability thesis, we will compare these variations on WI to a standard case of intentional illegal conduct (in which we stipulate the defendant's knowledge). In addition, we examined participants' attributions of knowledge as well as their inferences regarding the defendant's social preferences. These additional measures provided the opportunity to evaluate the two primary accounts of WI laid out in the introduction.

4.5.1 Participants and Design

In total, 406 (162 women) participants (M_{age} = 40.61, SD_{age} = 11.95) took part in Study 1. Participants were assigned to one of seven conditions, in a 3 ("Suspicion," "Reasonable," "Unreasonable") × 2 (Inquiry: "Possible," "Impossible") + 1 (Knowledge) between-subjects design. Condition *ns* ranged between fifty-five and sixty-one participants.

4.5.2 Materials and Procedure

4.5.2.1 Scenario: Part I

We employed a variation on the original *United States v. Jewell* (1967) criminal case as the experimental scenario in our study. In this scenario, John is crossing a national border that is frequently used for drug trafficking. Drug trafficking over the border causes instability and crime in both neighboring countries.

First, we varied whether the illegal activities over the border crossing are common knowledge or not. In the *reasonable vs. unreasonable* condition, the fact that the route is a drug-trafficking route is either widely known or unknown to most people. Varying the commonality of this knowledge allows us to manipulate how reasonable it would be for someone to be concerned when asked to transport a suitcase on that route.

> **Reasonable vs. Unreasonable:** "He plans to travel to a border crossing that is commonly known for being a drug trafficking route [*unbeknownst to everyone, is being used as a drug trafficking route*]. In fact, the route is known to be one of the major trafficking routes in Europe [. . . *is assumed to be one of the safest travel routes in Europe*]. Travel brochures and media have often [*never*] reported the criminal trafficking activities along this route such that they are common knowledge among [*completely unknown to*] locals as well as travellers."

Next, we manipulated what John actually knows. More precisely, we manipulated whether John's background knowledge would inspire suspicion when asked to transport a suitcase across the border. To this end, we stated that John either knows or does not know about the drug trafficking on his travel route.

> **Suspicion vs. No Suspicion:** "John knows [*does not know*] that the route he is about to take is frequently used for drug trafficking."

At a gas station near the border, John is approached by a group of travellers who ask him if he would do them a favor and transport some luggage to a friend across the border. John would be rewarded with $100 for his help. Here, the "Knowledge" condition differed from the willful ignorance condition. In the Knowledge condition, John agrees to transport the luggage and knows about its illegal content. John acquires this knowledge through various means: The group tells him about the content of the suitcase; but it is also easy to open the suitcase ("Easy inquiry") so John looks inside and ascertain that there are drugs ("Inquiry").

> **"Knowledge" Scenario:** "The group also tells him that the luggage contains illegal drugs. [**Knowledge**]

John agrees to transport the luggage.

> The suitcase contains white powder packed into transparent plastic bags. The suitcase is not locked so John could easily open the suitcase to see what is inside. In fact, the suitcase is closed only with a simple zipper [**Easy Inquiry**]. Knowing how easy it would be to open the suitcase, John takes a look into the suitcase and sees that the suitcase indeed contains illegal drugs. [**Inquires**]"

In the willful ignorance condition, however, John is not informed by the group that the suitcase contains drugs ("Ignorance"), and he agrees to transport the suitcase. Here, his epistemic state regarding the content of the suitcase (at the time of his decision to cooperate) depends to some extent on his background knowledge about the illegal activities along the route (i.e., on our experimental manipulations; *Suspicion Reasonable vs. No Suspicion Reasonable vs. No Suspicion Unreasonable*). In the willful ignorance condition, John does not inspect the suitcase ("No Inquiry"). We manipulated whether it would have been easy for him to do so ("Easy Inquiry," see section in the scenario already mentioned) or whether opening the suitcase would have been extremely effortful ("Difficult Inquiry," see the following scenario).

> **"Willful Ignorance" Scenario: Difficult Inquiry":** "However, the group does not tell him that the luggage contains illegal drugs [**Ignorance**]. John agrees to transport the luggage.
>
> The suitcase contains white powder packed into transparent plastic bags. The suitcase is sealed such that it is impossible for John to open it himself and see what's inside. In fact, he would have to drive two hours back to the nearest mechanic who could saw the suitcase open for him [**Difficult Inquiry**]. Knowinghow difficult it would be to open the suitcase, John deliberately decides not to take the steps that would allow him to check what's inside the suitcase. [**No Inquiry**]"

For an overview of the 3 ("Suspicion," "Reasonable," "Unreasonable") × 2 (Inquiry: "Possible," "Impossible") + 1 (Knowledge) design, see Table 4.1. After having read up to this point of the scenario, participants were asked a series of comprehension check questions (see Appendix A).

4.5.2.2 Scenario: Part II and Dependent Measures

The middle part of the scenario describes the outcome of John's actions. A few hours later John is at the border control. The transport police patrols across the cars and their detection dog starts to bark when they approach John's car. After searching the car and breaking up the suitcase, the police finds that the suitcase contains illegal drugs. This part was the same for all scenario conditions. Participants were then asked to indicate their agreement with three different statements on a 7-point Likert scale. One statement about the agent's *liability*, "John is culpable of illegal drug smuggling." (1—"strongly disagree," 7—"strongly agree"), one statement about the agent's *blameworthiness*, "How much blame does John deserve for illegally smuggling drugs?" (1—"None at all,"

Table 4.1 Experimental Conditions of Study 1

Knowledge	Willful Ignorance				
Knowledge	**Ignorance**				
	Suspicion		**No Suspicion**		
(Suspicion reasonable)	*Suspicion reasonable*		*Suspicion reasonable*		*Suspicion unreasonable*
Inquiry	**No Inquiry**				
(Easy inquiry)	*Easy inquiry*	*Difficult inquiry*	*Easy inquiry*	*Difficult inquiry*	*Easy inquiry*	*Difficult inquiry*

People were allocated to either a "Knowledge" or a "Willful Ignorance" condition. In the "Willful Ignorance" condition, we varied whether the agent actually suspected of the illegal nature of their action or not. When the agent had no suspicion (in the "No Suspicion" condition), we also varied whether it would be reasonable for the defendant to entertain this suspicion, or whether such a suspicion would have been unreasonable according to the reasonable person standard. In the "Willful Ignorance" condition, the defendant never undertakes the effort to inquire about the circumstances that they are in (No inquiry). We manipulated whether the relevant inquiry would have been easy or difficult to carry out. © Lara Kirfel and Ivar R. Hannikainen.

7—"Very much"). We formed a single index of *culpability* by averaging the liability and blameworthiness items (Cronbach's $\alpha = 0.89$). Participants also rated a statement about the agent's *knowledge* state, "John *knowingly* transported drugs across the border" (1—"strongly disagree," 7—"strongly agree").

4.5.2.3 Scenario: Part III and Social Preference

The final part of the scenario jumps ahead to a situation in John's life a few years later. In this scenario, John faces a real-life dictator game (Guala & Mittone, 2010) that would allow him to act prosocially (and share) or antisocially (and steal).

> A few years later, John is back in his hometown where he works as a graphic designer in a visual design studio. Over the past year, he has been working together with his colleague Brad on a huge ad campaign for an influential company. Both John and Brad have contributed an equal amount to this project.
>
> The customer has been so pleased with their work that they have decided to pay the team an extra bonus of $1000 for their work. Since John has been the point of contact for the team, the cheque of $1000 has been issued on his name, and only he can cash it in. Brad was on holiday at that time and does not know about the bonus.
>
> It would be easy for John to transfer money to Brad since John has access to all bank details of all employees.

Based on what they had learned about John, participants were asked to predict the amount of money that John would allocate to Brad, on a sliding scale from 0 USD to 1000 USD. This measure enabled us to examine whether participants draw general inferences about an agent's prosocial or antisocial orientation on the basis of their degree of involvement in crime. Predictions on the lower half of the scale (i.e., stealing) indicate an antisocial impression of John, while values at or above the midpoint (i.e., sharing) would indicate a prosocial impression.

4.5.3 Results

The results are organized into four sections. In the first three sections, we examine each of three dependent variables in sequence. Lastly, in the fourth section, we propose a causal model according to which the effects of suspicion are causally mediated by the ascription of varying degrees of knowledge. In each section, we present a sequence of two analyses. The first analysis assesses the effect of suspicion and inquiry relative to knowledge through one-way ANOVAs. In the second analysis, we examine the effects of suspicion and inquiry relative to the absence of suspicion and the impossibility of inquiry in two-way ANOVAs. *P* values are adjusted using the Tukey method for the correction of family-wise error.

4.5.3.1 *Knowledge Attributions*

In the one-way ANOVA, condition affected knowledge attributions, $F(2, 173) = 80.46$, $p < 0.001, \eta^2_p = 0.93$. Suspicion elicited lower knowledge attributions than did knowledge, whether inquiry was easy, $B = -3.39$, $t = -10.91$, Cohen's $d = -2.33$, 95% $CI[-1.86, -2.81]$, or difficult, $B = -3.33$, $t = -10.99$, Cohen's $d = -2.31$, 95% $CI[-1.84, -2.77]$, $ps < 0.001$. The pairwise comparison between suspicion conditions revealed no effect of opportunity for inquiry, $p = 0.98$ (see Figure 4.1 *x*-axis.).

In the two-way ANOVA, suspicion affected knowledge attributions, $F(2, 340) = 65.28$, $p < 0.001$, $\eta^2_p = 0.38$, while inquiry once again did not (Inquiry: $F[1, 340] = 0.04$, $p = 0.86$; Suspicion × Inquiry: $F[2, 340] = 0.03$, $p = 0.97$). Suspecting agents were ascribed greater knowledge than were unsuspecting agents across various conditions: when inquiry was possible and impossible, and whether suspicion would have been reasonable or not, $1.87 < Bs < 2.02, 6.70 < ts < 7.36, 1.11 < $ Cohen's $ds < 1.26$. Meanwhile, knowledge attributions to unsuspecting agents did not depend on whether suspicion was described as reasonable or not, $ps > 0.89$. In sum, suspicion promoted knowledge attributions. Suspecting agents were ascribed some degree of knowledge, higher than unsuspecting agents yet lower than knowledgeable agents.

4.5.3.2 *Culpability*

Condition affected culpability judgments, $F(2, 173) = 13.67, p < 0.001, \eta^2_p = 0.16$. Namely, suspecting agents were seen as less culpable than knowing agents, whether inquiry would have been easy, $B = -1.04$, $t = -5.23$, Cohen's $d = -0.93$, 95% $CI[-1.32, -0.54]$, or difficult, $B = -0.82$, $t = -3.73$, Cohen's $d = -0.91$, 95% $CI[-1.28, -0.53]$, $ps < 0.001$. The pairwise comparison between suspicion conditions assessing the effect of inquiry was not significant, $p = 0.57$ (see Figure 4.1 top panel). In the two-way ANOVA, suspicion affected culpability judgments, $F(2, 340) = 22.13$, $p < 0.001$, $\eta^2_p = 0.16$, whereas inquiry did not (Inquiry: $F[1, 340] = 0.04$, $p = 0.83$; Suspicion × Inquiry: $F[2, 340] = 1.50$, $p = 0.22$). The effect of suspicion indicated that, across various conditions, suspecting agents were more culpable than unsuspecting agents. This pattern held true when inquiry

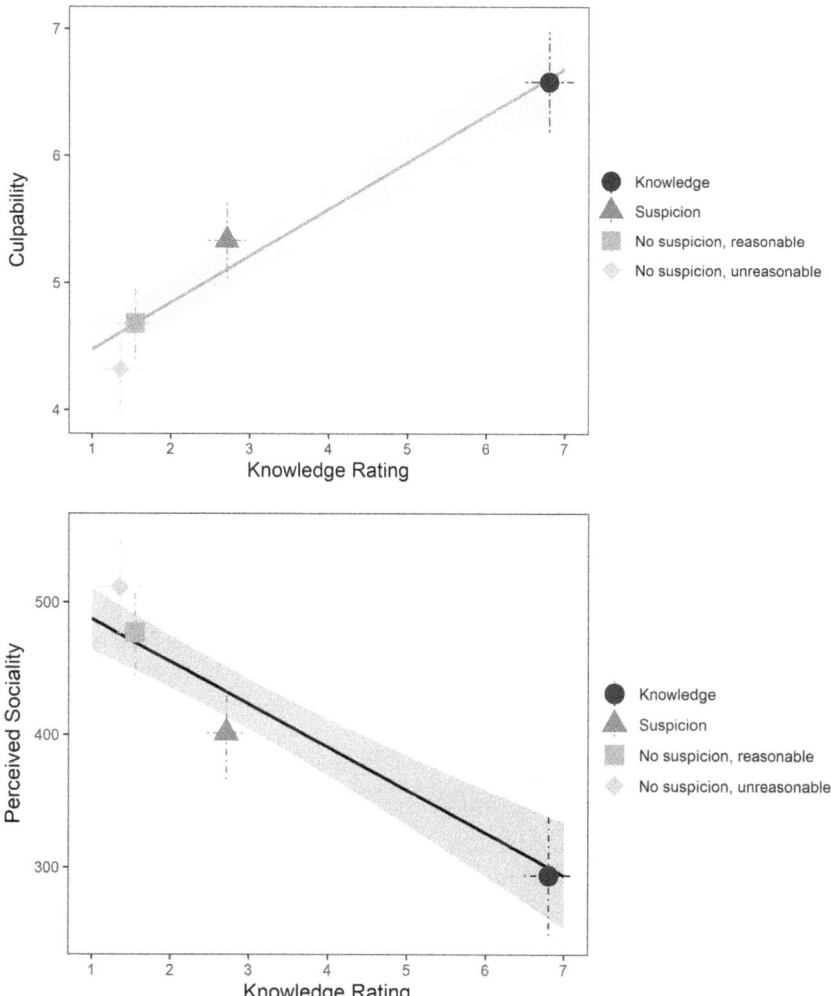

Figures 4.1 and 4.2 Results of Study 1. The figure displays culpability ratings (*y*-axis, top panel) and allocation predictions (*y*-axis, bottom panel) against knowledge ascriptions (*x*-axis). Mean ratings for each experimental condition are overlaid along with their 95 percent confidence intervals. © Lara Kirfel and Ivar R. Hannikainen.

was easy, whether suspicion was normal, $B = 1.63$, $t = 5.20$, or abnormal, $B = 1.20$, $t = 3.84$, $ps < 0.001$. The pattern also held true when inquiry would have been difficult, whether suspicion was reasonable, $B = 1.01$, $t = 3.20$, $p = 0.004$, or not, $B = 1.29$, $t = 4.03$, $p < 0.001$. Meanwhile, the culpability of unsuspecting agents was unaffected by whether cognisance of the drug-trafficking operations was described as common or rare, $ps > 0.36$.

Paralleling the results with knowledge, in both analyses, suspicion influenced culpability-promoting culpability relative to the absence of suspicion, but reducing it relative to knowledge. In contrast, we observed no effects of either inquiry or reasonableness.

4.5.3.3 Social Preference

In the one-way ANOVA, condition affected predicted allocations in a dictator game, F $(2, 173) = 5.41, p = 0.005, \eta^2_p = 0.06$. Suspecting agents were predicted to steal significantly less than knowing agents when inquiry was easy, $B = -124.8, t = -3.2$, Cohen's $d = -0.56$, 95% $CI[-0.92, -0.20]$, $p = 0.004$, and non-significantly less when inquiry was difficult, $B = -85.9, t = -2.16$, Cohen's $d = -0.37$, 95% $CI[-0.74, 0.00]$, $p = 0.081$. The pairwise comparison between suspicion conditions revealed no effect of the opportunity for inquiry, $p = 0.59$ (see Figure 4.1 bottom panel).

In the two-way ANOVA, suspicion affected predicted allocations in the dictator game, $F(2, 340) = 5.45, p = 0.005, \eta^2_p = 0.03$, while inquiry once again did not (Inquiry: $F[1, 340] = 1.80, p = 0.18$; Suspicion × Inquiry: $F[2, 340] = 0.23, p = 0.80$). Suspecting agents were predicted to steal a larger sum than unsuspecting agents whether suspicion was reasonable, $B = 60.74, t = 2.92$, Cohen's $d = 0.35$, 95% $CI[0.74, 0.61]$, $p = 0.010$, or unreasonable, $B = 58.93, t = 2.82$, Cohen's $d = 0.37$, 95% $CI[0.11, 0.63]$, $p = 0.014$. Meanwhile, predicted antisocial behavior among unsuspecting agents did not depend on whether suspicion was described as reasonable, $p = 1$.

In line with the previous results, suspicion also affected the agent's perceived social preference. Suspecting agents were seen as more antisocial (i.e., likely to steal in a dictator game) than unsuspecting agents, yet more prosocial than knowing agents (see Figure 4.1 bottom panel).

4.5.3.4 Multiple Regression Analyses

Entering knowledge attributions into the culpability model substantially weakened the effect of suspicion relative to both knowledge, $F(1, 172) = 0.54, p = 0.58, \eta^2_p = 0.01$, and the absence of suspicion, $F(2, 339) = 4.04, p = 0.018, \eta^2_p = 0.02$. In those same models, the effects of knowledge attribution on culpability were strong: $F(1, 172) = 37.15, \eta^2_p = 0.22, F(1, 339) = 33.94, \eta^2_p = 0.10, ps < 0.001$. Knowledge attributions also accounted for the effect of suspicion on participants' social inferences, both relative to knowledge, $F(1, 172) = 0.60, p = 0.55, \eta^2_p = 0.01$, and the absence of suspicion, $F(2, 339) = 0.82, p = 0.44, \eta^2_p = 0.00$. In those same models, the effect of knowledge attributions on allocation predictions was highly significant: $F(1, 172) = 8.35, \eta^2_p = 0.05, p = 0.004; F(1, 339) = 8.77, \eta^2_p = 0.03, p = 0.003$.

Thus, the impact of our suspicion manipulation on the agent's culpability and perceived social preferences was partly accounted for by differences in the ascription of knowledge across conditions.

4.5.4 Summary

In sum, a deliberately ignorant accomplice in a criminal offense is viewed as more innocent than another who knowingly commits the same crime. This pattern holds regardless of whether the course of action that could grant knowledge would have been easy or difficult to undertake. Willfully ignorant agents are, however, attributed a greater degree of knowledge than agents who lack any suspicion that they are involved in crime. Participants' knowledge ascriptions also supported a broader inference about the agent's moral character: Namely, willfully ignorant agents were perceived as more antisocial than unsuspecting agents, but not as antisocial as knowing agents. Crucially, however, the extent to which knowledge was ascribed to the perpetrator explained differences in culpability and social preference across conditions: that is, why willfully ignorant agents are seen as both more culpable and generally more antisocial than unsuspecting agents, but less so than knowing agents.

4.6 Study 2

The degree of knowledge ascribed to an agent proved to be a crucial factor in people's verdicts of culpability, and even shaped broader inferences about their moral character. At the same time, Study 1 documented substantial variation in knowledge attributions in the context of willful ignorance (i.e., the "Suspicion" condition). This inspired the prediction that people could have interpreted the knowledge prompt in disparate ways. Specifically, we reasoned that participants may have considered different epistemic states that vary in their precise *content*. For instance, participants could be asking themselves: Did John know that the suitcase contained drugs? Or, alternatively, did John know that he was complicit in an unlawful activity? These differences in scope could help explain variability in people's knowledge attributions and also yield insight into whether culpability is determined by a broader or narrower epistemic state.

Therefore, in Study 2, we examined the role of general versus specific knowledge (Nelkin & Rickless, 2017; Vargas, 2005; Wieland & Robichaud, 2017) in judgments about willfully ignorant misconduct. To this end, we drew on a comparison between two agents who, while sharing a general suspicion that they are involved in illicit activity, differ in whether their suspicion is true or false of their specific circumstances. In the "(True) Suspicion" condition, John suspects that he might be aiding a drug-trafficking operation. Meanwhile, in the "False Suspicion" condition, John suspects that he might be involved in the smuggling of gold. In reality, John is involved in drug trafficking (just as in Study 1). Therefore, on the *specific* level, John's suspicion is true in one condition and false in the other. At the same time, at a *general* level, they share a certain epistemic state: i.e., the suspicion that they are engaged in crime. A further ambition of Study 2 was to understand which of these epistemic states, the specific or the general, undergirds people's verdicts of culpability. Lastly, since the opportunity for inquiry did not affect any of our results in Study 1, we dropped this manipulation in Study 2.

4.6.1 Participants and Design

In total, 609 (243 women, 2 non-binary, and 1 undisclosed) participants (M_{age} = 40.34, SD_{age} = 12.03) took part in the study. Participants were assigned to one of seven conditions, in × a 4 ("Suspicion," "False Suspicion," "No Suspicion") × 2 (Knowledge:

"General," "Specific") × 2 (Knowledge Rating Condition: "Between-subject," "Within-subject") + 1 (Knowledge) mixed design. Condition *ns* ranged between 139 and 164 participants (aggregated over between/within condition).

4.6.2 Materials and Procedure

We re-used the "Knowledge," "Suspicion," and "No Suspicion" scenarios from Study 1 (in the "Easy Inquiry" condition). In the "Knowledge" condition, the agent carried out the inquiry (i.e., "Inquiry") while in the "Suspicion" and "No Suspicion" conditions he did not (i.e., "No Inquiry"). Given that our manipulation of reasonableness did not reveal an effect in Study 1, we removed the description of the agent's suspicion as either reasonable or unreasonable. In all three experimental conditions, the agent either knows, suspects, or does not suspect that the route he is about to travel on is used for drug trafficking. The relevant content of the agent's respective epistemic state hence concerns illegal drug trafficking, that is, the agent is to a varying extent aware of both the immoral significance of the activities on his route ("unlawful trade") and the exact nature of the activity ("trafficking of *drugs*"). In order to contrast the role of general knowledge of moral significance versus more specific knowledge of the exact wrongdoing, we created a new condition. In this new condition ("False Suspicion"), the agent is aware of the illegal nature of the activities over the border crossing, but is mistaken about the exact activity in which he could be involved: he believes, on reasonable grounds, that the route is used for gold smuggling.

4.6.3 Scenario: "False Suspicion"

John is travelling with his camper across Europe. He plans to travel to a border crossing that is commonly used as a gold smuggling route. In fact, the route is one of the major gold smuggling routes in Europe. Gold smuggling generally leads to a significant increase in instability and crime in the affected areas.

John knows that the route he is about to take is frequently used for smuggling of gold.

When he stops at a gas station just before the border, he is approached by a group of travellers. They ask him whether he would do them a favor and transport some luggage over the border to a friend who is awaiting the luggage. John would be rewarded with $100 for his help. However, the group does not tell him that the luggage contains illegal marijuana.

John agrees to transport the luggage.

The suitcase contains marijuana buds packed into transparent plastic bags. The suitcase is not locked such that John could easily open the suitcase to see what is inside. In fact, the suitcase is closed only by a simple zipper. Knowing how easy it would be to open the suitcase, John however deliberately decides not to take the steps that would allow him to check what's inside the suitcase.

4.6.4 Measures

After reading the scenario and answering a series of comprehension questions (see Study 1), participants rated John's *knowledge* on two separate matters: One rating concerned the agent's general knowledge about the illegality of his actions, that is, "John *knew* that he was aiding an unlawful activity" (1—"strongly disagree," 7—"strongly agree"). Another rating concerned the agent's specific knowledge of the circumstances, that is, "John *knew* that there are drugs in the suitcase" (1—"strongly disagree," 7—"strongly agree"). Depending on whether subjects participated in the between or within-subjects version of the study, they provided one of the knowledge ratings only, or both knowledge ratings.

In addition, participants evaluated the agent's *culpability* (through the pair of items) and *social preference* (through the dictator game), just as in Study 1.

4.6.5 Results

4.6.5.1 General and Specific Knowledge Attributions

In separate one-way ANOVAs, both specific, F (3, 412) = 465.0, and general, F (3, 409) = 145.8, knowledge ascriptions varied significantly across conditions, $ps < 0.001$. Participants ascribed both knowledge states in the Knowledge condition and denied both knowledge states in the No Suspicion condition (see Table 4.2).

Relative to the No Suspicion condition, in the False Suspicion condition John was ascribed more general knowledge of his involvement in an unlawful activity, $B = 1.70$, $t = 7.18$, $p < 0.001$, but no more specific knowledge about the contents of the suitcase, $B = 0.30$, $t = 1.80$, $p = 0.28$. Relative to the False Suspicion condition, in the True Suspicion condition John was ascribed more specific knowledge about the contents of the suitcase, $B = 1.05$, $t = 6.27$, $p < 0.001$, but no more knowledge of his involvement in illicit activities, $B = 0.15$, $t = 0.67$, $p = 0.91$.

4.6.5.2 Culpability

Next, we examined whether culpability (Cronbach's $\alpha = 0.91$) varied across conditions. We were primarily interested in understanding whether a False Suspicion (of one's involvement in gold smuggling instead of drug trafficking) would constitute grounds for absolution relative to True Suspicion, and/or conviction relative to no suspicion at all. If specific knowledge about the circumstances of one's involvement (in this

Table 4.2 Means and *SD*s of All Ratings in the Four experimental Conditions of Study 2. © Lara Kirfel and Ivar R. Hannikainen

	No Suspicion, $n = 139$	False Suspicion, $n = 161$	True Suspicion, $n = 146$	Knowledge $n = 164$
Specific Knowledge	1.46 (0.99)	1.71 (1.25)	3.20 (2.04)	6.79 (0.49)
General Knowledge	2.20 (1.83)	3.53 (2.11)	4.14 (2.13)	6.72 (0.70)
Culpability	4.14 (2.03)	4.73 (1.77)	5.08 (1.66)	6.64 (0.71)
Allocation	515 (158)	445 (230)	430 (217)	338 (245)

case, the actual content of the suitcase) promotes culpability, one would expect to find a difference in culpability ratings when comparing the True and False Suspicion conditions. Meanwhile, if culpability depends on a broader recognition of one's unlawful behavior, then even the misguided suspicion that one is engaged in a different illicit activity (e.g., smuggling gold instead of drugs) should incriminate the defendant relative to the lack of any suspicion whatsoever.

Condition assignment impacted culpability ratings in a one-way ANOVA, $F(3, 606) = 69.29, p < 0.001$. We turned our attention to the specific pairwise comparisons highlighted previously: first, culpability did not differ in the comparison between False Suspicion and True Suspicion, $B = -0.35, t = -1.91, p = 0.23$. From the Bayesian perspective, this result provides merely anecdotal evidence in favor of the null (i.e., that specific knowledge does not elevate culpability), $BF_{01} = 1.77$. Second, culpability ratings were significantly higher in the False Suspicion condition than the No Suspicion condition, $B = -0.59, t = -3.16, p = 0.009$. This result constitutes moderate evidence in support of the alternative hypothesis: that is, that general knowledge does yield culpability, $BF_{10} = 3.74$. The remaining pairwise contrasts were all highly significant, $ps < 0.001$ (see also Table 4.2). Thus, our preliminary analyses indicated that culpability in cases of willful ignorance is motivated by the perpetrator's broader recognition of their unlawful behavior—and not by a detailed understanding of the circumstances of their complicity.

4.6.5.3 Social Preference

Condition assignment also influenced perceived social preference, $F(3, 606) = 17.00, p < 0.001$. Social preferences did not differ in the comparison between agents with False and True Suspicion, $B = 15.1, t = 0.61, p = 0.93$—which constituted substantial evidence in favor of the null, $BF_{01} = 6.73$. However, agents in the False Suspicion condition were seen as more antisocial than those in the No Suspicion condition, $B = 69.7, t = 2.77, p = 0.029, BF_{10} = 9.23$. The remaining pairwise contrasts were all statistically significant, $ps < 0.006$. In other words, the pattern of differences in culpability across conditions mirrored the pattern of broader inferences regarding the defendant's social preference.

4.6.5.4 Multiple Regression Analyses

To understand whether and which knowledge state accounted for the effect of condition, we entered specific knowledge, general knowledge, and both knowledge ascriptions in three consecutive regression models (see Figure 4.3, top panel). Entering specific knowledge in the model (Model 1) weakened the effect of condition, $F(3, 411) = 2.35, p = 0.072, \eta^2_p = 0.017$, and revealed a partial correlation between specific knowledge and culpability, $r_p = 0.21, 95\% CI[0.11, 0.30], p < 0.001$. Entering general knowledge in the model (Model 2) also weakened the effect of condition, $F(3, 408) = 3.54, p = 0.015, \eta^2_p = 0.026$, and revealed a partial correlation between general knowledge and culpability, $r_p = 0.33, 95\% CI[0.24, 0.41], p < 0.001$.

With both knowledge ascriptions together in the model (Model 3; restricted to the within-subjects data, $n = 219$), the effect of condition was rendered nonsignificant, $F(3, 213) = 0.74, p = 0.53$. Furthermore, there were no pairwise differences in culpability across conditions when conditioning on both knowledge ascriptions, all $ps > 0.48$. In this

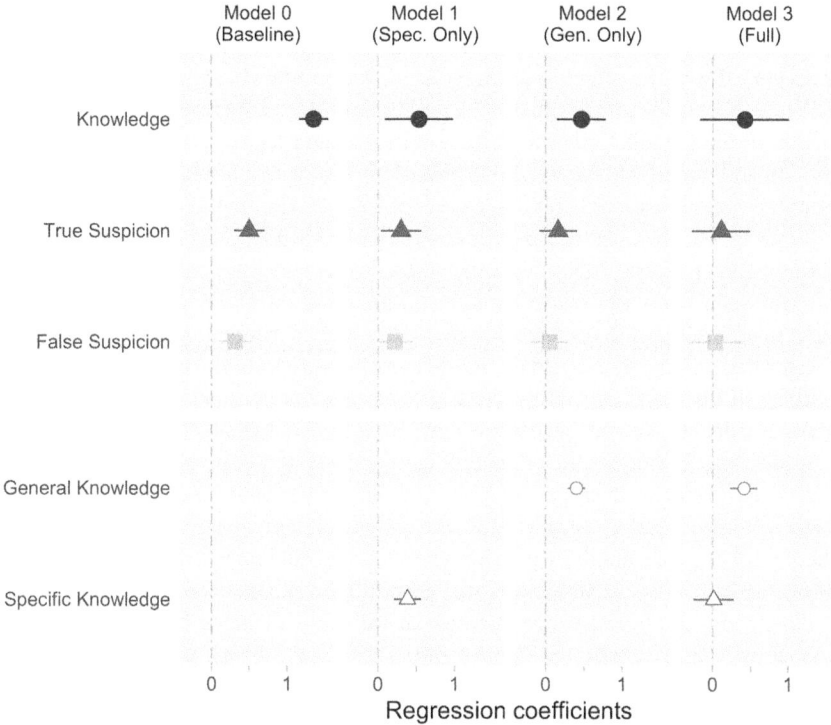

Figure 4.3 Results of Study 2. The figure displays the regression coefficients and 95 percent confidence intervals for each predictor in four separate regression models (Model 0, Model 1, Model 2, and Model 3) of culpability. *Model 0* functions as a comparison null model, without either knowledge rating as a predictor. *Model 1* includes *specific knowledge* ratings as a predictor, while *Model 2* includes *general knowledge* ratings as a predictor. *Model 3* includes both *specific and general knowledge* ratings as predictors. The top panel displays the effect of the knowledge and suspicion manipulations (dummy-coded), against the reference level (i.e., No Suspicion). The bottom panel displays the regression coefficients of participants' general and specific knowledge ratings. Culpability and knowledge ratings were scaled to one standard deviation, resulting in standardized coefficients in the bottom panel and semi-standardized coefficients in the top panel. © Lara Kirfel and Ivar R. Hannikainen.

same model, the effect of general knowledge ascriptions was statistically significant, $F(1, 213) = 51.53$, $p < 0.001$, $r_p = 0.29$, 95% $CI[0.17, 0.41]$, whereas the effect of specific knowledge ascriptions was not, $F(1, 213) = 0.04$, $p = 0.90$, $r_p = 01$, 95% $CI[0.13, 0.14]$ (see Figure 4.3 bottom panel). Taken together, these analyses suggest that general knowledge better accounts for the effect of condition on culpability than does specific knowledge.

4.7 General Discussion

In some prominent legal cases, a person was aware of a substantial risk that they were involved in criminal activity, and then deliberately avoided confirming any of the incriminating facts. Through the doctrine of willful ignorance, most Anglo-American legal systems prevent individuals from eschewing responsibility in these circumstances by allegorically burying their heads in the sand. Specifically, according to the doctrine, deliberate ignorance satisfies the mens rea requirement of knowledge in a criminal offense; and, as a result, the law ought to impute the same degree of liability for willfully ignorant and intentional crimes. These provisions raise a host of empirical predictions about how people ordinarily reason in cases of willfully ignorant wrongdoing.

Drawing on the methods of experimental jurisprudence (Prochownik, 2021; Sommers, 2021; Tobia, 2020), we interrogated laypeople's assessments of culpability and knowledge in a scenario resembling *United States v. Jewell*. By experimentally manipulating whether the defendant suspected certain incriminating facts, our studies revealed that willful ignorance does indeed constitute grounds for culpability. Though, contrary to the equal culpability thesis, people did *not* consider willfully ignorant agents as culpable as agents who knowingly committed the same crime.

A defining characteristic of willful ignorance is the fact that the defendant deliberately preserves their state of ignorance, often by avoiding any inquiry into the object of their suspicion. In our study, the defendant's culpability was unaffected by whether the requisite inquiry would have been easy or difficult to carry out or whether the circumstances would have raised suspicion in the average (or reasonable) person.

Finally, our studies also documented an influence of mens rea ascriptions on broader inferences about the agent's moral character. People expected willfully ignorant defendants to steal, but unsuspecting defendants to share equitably, if presented with a future opportunity to divide monetary rewards in a dictator game style task. This result provides some support for theories of willful ignorance that emphasize the perpetrator's "ill will" as grounds for their culpability (Yaffe, 2018). The "ill will" theory also dovetails with evidence in Study 2 that the accuracy of one's suspicion—for example, on the question of whether one was specifically aiding a drug-trafficking operation—did not impact verdicts of culpability. What appears to matter for conviction, and for inferences about the agents' antisocial character alike, is the broader suspicion that they were engaged in criminal wrongdoing.

4.7.1 Unequal Culpability

Whether and under what circumstances defendants in a state of willful ignorance should be held liable as if they had acted knowingly constitutes "the problem of willful ignorance." In our data, people radically distinguished between willfully ignorant and knowledgeable agents, hence violating the equal culpability assumption (Husak & Callender, 2019). Participants in our study were less inclined to say that the willfully ignorant defendant knew an incriminating fact p when compared to a defendant who unambiguously knew that p. Correspondingly, they were also less likely to convict the willfully ignorant agent.

To remain faithful to the "substitution principle" for knowledge, it is argued that the willful ignorance doctrine should not be applied *indiscriminately*, but only when the defendant acted with a form of willful ignorance rendering their behavior as culpable as the corresponding intentional offense (cf. Husak & Callender, 2019). Willful ignorance of an incriminating fact should be taken to satisfy the knowledge element of crime *only* in those cases in which the willfully ignorant defendant really is considered as culpable as an agent with knowledge (Husak & Callender, 2019; Sarch, 2016). While our study can only be seen as a first step toward further investigating ordinary and expert judgments about WI, the data suggest that the scope of WI may need to be further restricted. On the basis of our data involving lay participants, willful ignorance and actual knowledge do not appear to be treated as equally culpable.

Uncovering the circumstances in which ordinary people and legal experts assign equal culpability may help legal theorists and authorities ascertain when WI instructions to juries are warranted. Empirical studies can, at a minimum, serve as evidence concerning the extent to which the existing WI doctrine accords with folk intuition. Of course, whether technical legal concepts should be modeled after "folk" or ordinary notions has been hotly contested in recent scholarship (Jiménez, 2021; Tobia, 2022). Proponents, such as Simons (2021), argue that "[empirical studies] have important implications for whether WB [Willfull Blindness; WI] is a useful and viable criterion of criminal culpability, either in general or in specific legal contexts." For example, an empirically defensible definition of willful ignorance could involve the adoption of a third criterion, or the refinement of the existing criteria. In this regard, further research is needed to identify the factors that shape people's reasoning in cases of willful ignorance and the conditions under which the equal culpability assumption holds.

4.7.2 Mens Rea: Recklessness Plus?

Under traditional common law, the guilt or innocence of a defendant depends on whether they committed the crime (actus reus) and also intended to commit the crime (mens rea) (but see Kneer & Skoczeń, 2023). Many contemporary penal codes include various gradations within mens rea, depending on the surrounding elements of the crime. Recklessness and knowledge differ mainly along a cognitive dimension, that is, in the degree of conscious risk in which the defendant engages. In the taxonomy of mens rea states, WI could fall somewhere between knowledge and recklessness. In addition to recklessness, WI includes a non-cognitive, action-focused criterion: namely, the defendant's decision not to carry out an inquiry that would settle their suspicion. This way, the law gives weight to a non-epistemic aspect accompanying the mental state of willful ignorance.

Accordingly, all deliberately ignorant agents are reckless, but not all reckless agents are deliberately ignorant (Sarch, 2018; Simons, 2021). The difference between both types of mens rea lies in the opportunity for inquiry, and more specifically, its reasonableness. Suppose that an agent has a suspicion regarding the incriminating proposition *p*, but they actually have a valid reason not to acquire more information about *p*. For example, it could be impossible or unreasonable for the agent to acquire such knowledge, perhaps because the attempt would put them in danger. Then, although qualifying as reckless for engaging in illicit activity, the defendant would not be willfully ignorant and could not be punished under the WI doctrine. What then counts as sufficient reason for the omission of inquiry? The law concedes that, in a number of situations, an agent's decision not to act on their suspicion might not be justifiable, but "nearly justified." Sarch (2018) describes a scenario in which a drug manufacturer decides to overlook the potential (albeit, rare) side effects of a new drug because doing so would postpone its distribution and needlessly extend the suffering of a large number of patients. Sarch (2018) argues that, in such a case, the manufacturer's liability for any side effects of the drug would not be comparable to the liability derived from knowingly distributing a drug with those same side effects. If the omission of inquiry is almost justifiable, the agent might be considered reckless, but not deemed as culpable as a fully knowledgeable criminal.

In our study, we found evidence that the ease of inquiry, that is, whether it was easy or virtually impossible for the defendant to inspect the suspicious suitcase, did not influence evaluations of their culpability. This result raises the question of what qualifies as "reasonable inquiry" in the WI's second element, that is, the failure to "take reasonably available steps" to acquire knowledge. In the legal case *United States v. Heredia*, the court provides a first clarification of this element. They argue that an omission of inquiry due to "coercion, exigent circumstances or lack of meaningful choice" may not fall under the second criterion of WI, and in consequence, WI may not apply in such a case ("United States v. Heredia, 483 F. 3d 913 (9 th Cir.)(en banc), cert. denied, 76 USLW 3303 (US December 11, 2007) (No. 07-5762)," 2008). In *United States v. Heredia*, the defendant claimed that she could not allay her suspicion that the car might contain illegally smuggled drugs because it would have been unsafe for her to stop along the highway. While the manipulation in our study focused on practical obstacles, rather than on personal or moral reasons, precluding inquiry, the reasons for not wanting to know might be more complex than the mere unavailability or impracticality of information retrieval. In order to clearly distinguish recklessness from WI, our data point to the need to elaborate on the second defining criterion of WI.

4.7.3 Inferences from General Knowledge

In addition to potential legal-theoretical implications, our studies contribute empirical evidence toward the philosophical debate around the required *content* of knowledge for moral responsibility and legal culpability (Flanagan, de Almeida, Struchiner, & Hannikainen, 2022; Kirfel & Phillips, 2023; Levy, 2014; Sliwa, 2017; Talbert, 2017). What does an agent need to be aware of in order to qualify as responsible for the consequences of their actions? Philosophers have disputed the exact epistemic requirements of moral responsibility. Some argue that an agent must be aware of the exact consequences resulting from their actions in order to qualify as fully responsible (e.g., that littering will lead to an increase in mosquito populations in the area), while others argue that mere knowledge of its wrongness suffices (e.g., that littering causes harm) (Nelkin & Rickless, 2017; Sliwa, 2017; Vargas, 2005). Relatedly, whether *de re* or *de dicto* moral knowledge forms the basis for responsibility is likewise debated (Harman, 2011; Sliwa, 2017). The distinction between de dicto and de re awareness of moral significance (Harman, 2014; Sliwa, 2017) is often illustrated by circumstances in which an agent is aware (de dicto) of the general moral wrongness of their action, without being cognizant (de re) of its exact "wrong-making" features.

Our results support the view that attributions of culpability in the legal domain are motivated by perceptions of de dicto knowledge, that is, that the defendant possessed broadly (and not specifically) incriminating knowledge. This was reflected in people's judgments in the "False Suspicion" condition: An agent who suspected of the illegality of their behavior, but was mistaken about the details of their involvement (e.g., whether they were aiding a drug-trafficking or a gold-smuggling operation), was deemed as culpable as someone whose suspicion was correct about the details. Hence, specific knowledge about the precise manner of one's involvement in crime is seemingly irrelevant for culpability. This perspective dovetails with courtroom evidence: There is a growing skepticism that defendants must know all the details of extant regulations and statutes (Ambos, 2003) as long as they are aware of their existence and, under certain circumstances, a growing admission that a defendant can be convicted without a detailed grasp of the incriminating elements of their conduct (Schabas, 2002; Singer & Husak, 1999). In certain contexts, such a requirement would render convictions "virtually impossible" (see Ambos, 2003).

Strikingly, the patterns in people's judicial reasoning mirrored their broader inferences about the defendant's social preferences: In other words, agents with general knowledge of their criminal wrongdoing are perceived as having broader antisocial tendencies, extending into the future, regardless of whether their suspicion is correct. This result opens up promising avenues for future research to explore the connections between social and character inference on the one hand (in particular, how we infer the dispositions of potential social partners), and legal and moral appraisal on the other hand (see Hannikainen, 2019).

4.8 Conclusion

The court's decision in *United States v. Jewell* has been widely adopted throughout the United States and beyond as a framework for analyzing and deciding cases of willful ignorance. Debate among legal theorists suggests that the WI doctrine, although appealing as a tool to expedite prosecution (e.g., of white-collar crime, see ["U.K. 'Actively Avoided' Investigating Russian Interference, Lawmakers Find," 2020, July 20]), violates the key tenets of criminal law. Our results substantiated this concern in two ways: first, by showing that—in the eyes of lay judges—WI only partially satisfies the mens rea requirement, far below the level of genuine knowledge; and, second, by uncovering an intimate link between the cognitive processes that subserve judicial reasoning in criminal cases and those that support our extralegal everyday inferences about others' moral character. We therefore envision these studies not only as a contribution toward our understanding of this unique kind of "mens rea" but also as a vantage point from which to investigate the psychological basis of criminal conviction more generally.

Appendix A

Comprehension Check Questions

(1) "The fact that the route John is about to travel is a major drug trafficking route. . ."

    (i) is commonly known among most people,

    (ii) is completely unbeknownst to most people.

(2) "John . . ."

    (i) is aware of the drug trade on his travel route,

    (ii) is completely unbeknownst to most people.

(3) "When asked to transport the suitcase for the group of travellers,"

    (i) John is informed about the content of the suitcase.

    (ii) John is *not* informed about the content of the suitcase.

(4) Please fill in the statement such that it best described the scenario you just read: "John _ (1) what's inside the suitcase; opening the suitcase is actually (2). . ."

    (i) (1) checks ; (2) extremely easy

    (ii) (1) does not check ; (2) extremely easy

    (iii) (1) does not check ; (2) extremely difficult

References

Alexander, L., & Ferzan, K. K. (2009). *Crime and culpability: A theory of criminal law.* Cambridge: Cambridge University Press.

Alicke, M. D., & Weigel, S. H. (2021). The reasonable person standard: Psychological and legal perspectives. *Annual Review of Law and Social Science, 17,* 123–38.

Ambos, K. (2003). Some preliminary reflections on the mens rea requirements of the crimes of the icc statute and of the elements of crimes. In Vohrah, Lal Chand, et al. (Eds.), *Man's inhumanity to man.* Essays on International Law in Honour of Antonio Cassese (pp. 11–40). The Hague: Brill Nijhoff.

Ashworth, A., & Horder, J. (2013). *Principles of criminal law.* Oxford: Oxford University Press.

Charlow, R. (1991). Wilful ignorance and criminal culpability. *Texas Law Review, 70,* 1351.

Child, J. J. (2021). Knowledge by any other name: Alexander sarch on wilful ignorance. *Jurisprudence, 12* (2), 236–46.

Edwards, J. L. J. (1954). The criminal degrees of knowledge. *The Modern Law Review, 17*(4), 294–314.

Flanagan, B., de Almeida, G. F., Struchiner, N., & Hannikainen, I. R. (2022). Moral appraisals guide intuitive legal determinations. *Pre-print.*

Gettier, E. (1963). Is knowledge justified true belief? *Analysis, 23*(6), 121–3.

Ginther, M. R., Shen, F. X., Bonnie, R. J., Hoffman, M. B., Jones, O. D., Marois, R., & Simons, K. W. (2014). The language of mens rea. *Vanderbilt Law Review, 67,* 1327.

Guala, F., & Mittone, L. (2010). Paradigmatic experiments: The dictator game. *The Journal of Socio-Economics, 39*(5), 578–84.

Hannikainen, I. R. (2019). Ideology between the lines: Lay inferences about scientists' values and motives. *Social Psychological and Personality Science, 10*(6), 832–41.

Harman, E. (2011). Does moral ignorance exculpate? *Ratio, 24*(4), 443–68.

Harman, E. (2022). Ethics is hard! What follows? On moral ignorance and blame. Dana Kay Nelkin & Derk Pereboom (Eds.),*The Oxford handbook of moral responsibility.* Oxford: Oxford University Press.

Hellman, D. (2009). Willfully blind for good reason. *Criminal Law and Philosophy, 3*(3), 301–16.

Husak, D. N., & Callender, C. A. (2019). Wilful ignorance, knowledge, and the "equal culpability" thesis: A study of the deeper significance of the principle of legality. In *Criminal law* (pp. 203–44). London: Routledge.

Jaeger, C. B. (2020). The empirical reasonable person. *Alabama Law Review, 72,* 887.

Jiménez, F. (2021). Some doubts about folk jurisprudence: The case of proximate cause. *University of Chicago Law Review Online, 1.*

Jones, O. D., Ginther, M. R., Shen, F. X., Bonnie, R. J., Hoffman, M. B., & Simons, K. W. (2018). Decoding guilty minds: How jurors attribute knowledge and guilt. *Vanderbilt Law Review, 71,* 241.

Jones, O. D., Montague, R., & Yaffe, G. (2020). Detecting mens rea in the brain. *University of Pennsylvania Law Review, 169,* 1.

Kaplan, J., Weisberg, R., & Binder, G. (2014). *Criminal law: Cases and materials.* New York: Wolters Kluwer Law & Business.

Kirfel, L., & Lagnado, D. (2021). Changing minds—epistemic interventions in causal reasoning. *Pre-print.*

Kirfel, L., & Phillips, J. (2023). The pervasive impact of ignorance. *Cognition, 231,* 105316.

Kneer, M., & Skoczeń, I. (2023). Outcome effects, moral luck and the hindsight bias. *Cognition, 232,* 105258.

Levy, N. (2014). *Consciousness and moral responsibility.* Oxford University Press.

Luban, D. (1998). Contrived ignorance. *The Georgetown Law Journal, 87,* 957.

Marcus, J. L. (1993). Model penal code section 2.02 (7) and willful blindness. *The Yale Law Journal, 102*(8), 2231–57.

Mikhail, J. (2009). Moral grammar and intuitive jurisprudence: A formal model of un-conscious moral and legal knowledge. *Psychology of learning and motivation, 50,* 27–100.

Nelkin, D. K., & Rickless, S. C. (2017). Moral responsibility for unwitting omissions: A new tracing view. In D. K. Nelkin & S. C. Rickless (Eds.), *The Ethics and Law of Omissions* (pp. 106–29). Oxford: Oxford University Press.

Prochownik, K. M. (2021). The experimental philosophy of law: New ways, old questions, and how not to get lost. *Philosophy Compass, 16*(12), e12791.

Sarch, A. (2016). Equal culpability and the scope of the willful ignorance doctrine. *Legal Theory, 22*(3–4), 276–311.

Sarch, A. (2018). Willful ignorance in law and morality. *Philosophy Compass, 13*(5), e12490.

Sarch, A. (2019). *Criminally ignorant: Why the law pretends we know what we don't.* Oxford: Oxford University Press.

Sarch, A. F. (2014). Willful ignorance, culpability, and the criminal law. *St. John's Law Review, 88,* 1023.

Sarch, A. F. (2017). Beyond willful ignorance. *University of Colorado Law Review, 88*, 97.

Schabas, W. A. (2002). Mens rea and the international criminal tribunal for the former Yugoslavia. *New England Law Review, 37*, 1015.

Shen, F. X., Hoffman, M. B., Jones, O. D., & Greene, J. D. (2011). Sorting guilty minds. *New York University Law Review, 86*, 1306.

Sherrin, C. (2014). Wilful blindness: A confused and unnecessary basis for criminal liability. *UBC Law Review, 47*, 709.

Simons, K. W. (2021). The willful blindness doctrine: Justifiable in principle, problematic in practice. *Arizona State Law Journal, 53*, 655–79.

Singer, R., & Husak, D. (1999). Of innocence and innocents: The supreme court and mens rea since herbert packer. *Buffalo Criminal Law Review, 2*(2), 861–945.

Sliwa, P., Robichaud, P., & Wieland, J. (2017). On knowing what's right and being responsible for it. In *Responsibility: The epistemic condition* (pp. 127–45). Oxford: Oxford University Press.

Sommers, R. (2021). Experimental jurisprudence. *Science, 373*(6553), 394–5.

Stark, F. (2016). *Culpable carelessness: Recklessness and negligence in the criminal law.* Cambridge: Cambridge University Press.

Stark, F. (2020). The reasonableness in recklessness. *Criminal Law and Philosophy, 14*(1), 9–29.

Strawson, P. (2018). *Freedom and resentment.* Ithaca: Cornell University Press.

Talbert, M. (2017). Akrasia, awareness, and blameworthiness. In J. W. Wieland & P. Robichaud, *Responsibility: The epistemic condition* (pp. 127–45). Oxford: Oxford University Press.

Tobia, K. P. (2020). Legal concepts and legal expertise. Available at SSRN 3536564.

Tobia, K. P. (2018). How people judge what is reasonable. *Alabama Law Review, 70*, 293.

Tobia, K. P. (2022). Experimental jurisprudence. *The University of Chicago Law Review, 89*(3), 735–802.

U.K. 'Actively Avoided' Investigating Russian Interference, Lawmakers Find. (2020, July 20). *NPR Europe.* Retrieved from https://www.npr.org/2020/07/21/893443735/u-k -actively-avoided-investigating-russian-interference-lawmakers-find.

United states v. heredia, 483 f. 3d 913 (9 th cir.)(en banc), cert. denied, 76 uslw 3303 (us December 11, 2007)(no. 07-5762). (2008). *Harvard Law Review, 121*(125).

Valverde, M. (2009). *Law's dream of a common knowledge.* Princeton University Press.

Vargas, M. (2005). The trouble with tracing. *Midwest studies in philosophy, 29*, 269–91.

Wieland, J. W. (2019). Willful ignorance and bad motives. *Erkenntnis, 84*(6), 1409–28.

Wieland, J. W., & Robichaud, P. (2017). *Responsibility: The epistemic condition.* Oxford: Oxford University Press.

Williams, G. (1961). *Criminal law: The general part.* London: Stevens, 1983.

Williams, G. (1981). Recklessness redefined. *The Cambridge Law Journal, 40*(2), 252–83.

Williams, G. L. (1978). *Textbook of criminal law.* London: Stevens.

Yaffe, G. (2018). The point of mens rea: The case of willful ignorance. *Criminal Law and Philosophy, 12*(1), 19–44.

5

Culpability and Liability in the Law of Homicide:

Do Lay Moral Intuitions Accord with Legal Distinctions?

Paulo Sousa and Gary Lavery

The law of homicide has been created over the centuries by the courts and, more recently, by legislative bodies. It involves the most complex classification of offenses in criminal law, incorporating subtle differences in culpability and liability. Indeed, the law of homicide is "the melting-pot within which the features of the criminal law at large are fashioned" (Wilson, 2017, p. 355). This chapter provides new evidence on whether lay moral intuitions accord with differences of culpability and liability encoded in the law of homicide, focusing on the Anglo-American legal traditions (see LaFave & Scott, 1986; Wilson, 2017) and on UK and US subjects.[1] Thus, it contributes to debates regarding the structure of the lay concepts of culpability, liability, and intentional action and their congruence with legal concepts, which have been pivotal to the development of experimental philosophy in general and Xjur in particular (for recent reviews, see Prochownik, 2021; Sommers, 2021; Tobia, in press).

Joshua Knobe (2016) distinguishes three research focuses within experimental philosophy as far as conceptual analysis is concerned, using "conceptual analysis" in a sense that includes accounts of conceptual structure other than the classical view (e.g., accounts in terms of prototype structure rather than conditions that are individually necessary and jointly sufficient). A positive focus seeks to contribute to the philosophical tradition of conceptual analysis; a negative focus seeks to undermine the philosophical tradition of conceptual analysis; an indifferent focus seeks to do regular cognitive science but without any interest in conceptual analysis, philosophical or otherwise. We pursue a hybrid approach, focusing on doing regular cognitive science with an interest in conceptual analysis from a psychological point of view—after all, the study of concepts has been fundamental to the development of the cognitive sciences (Laurence & Margolis, 1999; Margolis & Laurence, 2015; Vicente & Manrique, 2016). Notably, our perspective pays special attention to the complex mapping between language and concepts, for we contend that only by taking this complexity into account can one make (theoretical and methodological) progress in the areas of moral psychology and Xjur (Sousa, 2005, 2009; Sousa & Holbrook, 2010; Sousa, Holbrook, & Swiney, 2015; Sousa & Swiney, 2016).

In the first section, we briefly delineate part of the rich polysemy in the language directly related to our topic. This section is crucial to distinguish some pertinent concepts, explicate our terminological decisions (and thus avoid confusion), and establish the background for delineating general hypotheses about the studies to be reported later and interpreting their results. In the second section, we provide a rational reconstruction of the concepts of culpability and liability in the law. Next, and in a similar vein, we characterize the different types of criminal homicides relevant to our research. Following this, we provide an overview of our research design. In the upcoming sections, we report three sets of results concerning people's moral intuitions about distinctions relevant to legal culpability and liability and the classification of different types of homicides. In the final section, we summarize our research findings, acknowledge limitations, evoke some broader issues, and emphasize the relevance of our approach to the development of moral psychology and Xjur.

5.1 A Word on Words and Concepts

Words such as "culpability," "responsibility," "blameworthiness," "fault," "guilt(y)," "liability," and "accountability," modified or not by the words "moral" or "legal," are polysemous. And their polysemy intersects inasmuch as these words may express the same concept (Sousa, 2009). We set apart four concepts that some of these words may express. For each concept, we indicate the word we employ to express it.

Some of these words may express CAUSE (e.g., "The flood was responsible for the damage" and "the flood is to blame for the damage"). We use the word "cause" thereof.

Some of these words may express AGENCY and/or CULPABILITY. We use the words "agency" and "culpability" thereof. To illustrate the difference between these concepts, consider the following scenarios:

> It occurs to Thomas that he will inherit a fortune when his aunt Laura dies. Thomas decides to kill his aunt and devises a plan to do so. Thomas is lying in wait when he sees Laura walking out to the car. He raises his rifle, gets her in the sights, and pulls the trigger. The bullet strikes and instantly kills Laura.

> It occurs to James that his aunt Andie keeps in her house some jewelry worth a fortune. James decides to steal his aunt's jewelry and devises a plan to do so. James is lying in wait when he sees Andie walking out to the car. After Andie takes her car and leaves, James breaks into the house, cracks the safe and steals the jewelry.

Thomas and James are similar in the degree of agency—they had plans guiding their actions and the same level of control over those plans and actions. However, Thomas is more culpable than James because his wrongdoing is more serious in terms of the level of harm involved. While the variable *level of harm* is relevant to the degree of culpability, it is not relevant to the degree of agency involved in the wrongdoing.

Some of the words given earlier may express a lay concept LIABILITY that represents the degree of punishment a person deserves for their actions. We use the word "liability" thereof. Ordinary people seem to see a fundamental connection between LIABILITY and CULPABILITY: the degree of punishment that a person deserves is based on their degree of culpability. In other words, a person deserves a degree of punishment that is proportional to their culpability: if a person is not culpable for their conduct, the person *deserves not to be punished* ("strong immunitivism"), and if a person is culpable for their conduct, the person *deserves to be punished in proportion to their degree of culpability* ("strong retributivism") (Zimmerman, 1988, 2011; see also Goodwin & Gromet, 2014). Although the legal concept of liability is not necessarily linked to the concept of culpability (i.e., legal systems allow "strict liability"), there is also an important connection between these concepts in criminal law.

5.2 Culpability and Liability in Criminal Law

In criminal law, one finds the criteria associated with culpability and liability in the structure of offenses and defenses.

5.2.1 Offenses

A criminal offense has two sides. Legal norms delineate what is legally forbidden; hence, a criminal offense exists when a person does what is legally forbidden by criminal law. The first side of a criminal offense corresponds to the definition of the conduct that is forbidden. Legal norms also delineate the punitive consequences of pursuing legally forbidden conduct. The second side of a criminal offense corresponds to its potential punishment delimited by criminal law.

The definition of conduct that is a criminal offense has two parts: one concerns the objective elements of the person's conduct, while the other concerns elements related to the mental states of the person.[2] The objective elements consist of three subparts: an act *qua* the bodily movements of the person, the results of the act (i.e., its causal consequences), and the objective circumstances involved—for example, a person may commit a criminal homicide by pulling the trigger of a gun (act) while the gun is loaded (circumstance), thus causing the death of another human being (result).

Different types of criminal offenses are ranked in terms of the resulting level of harm: all else being equal, causing the death of a human being is deemed worse than stealing their belongings. Since the result element of crimes ranks them by the level of the harm involved, and because *level of harm* is a variable that influences the degree of culpability and liability, this is one criterion that determines culpability and liability in the law: all else being equal, a person committing a criminal homicide is judged as more culpable and is liable to more punishment than a person committing a theft.

Because our focus is on one type of result/harm (i.e., the death of a human being), we leave aside the first part of the definition of offenses and deal only with the second part, namely, the elements related to mental states—often dubbed "fault elements" or "kinds/levels of culpability." Our characterization follows the Model Penal Code (MPC) schema, though without including its complete element analysis (see Dubber, 2015; Robinson & Grall, 1983), as it suffices here to concentrate on the result element. In the MPC schema, there are four distinct elements concerning mental states that may be attached to a result/harm element. In decreasing implied culpability, they are purpose, knowledge, recklessness, and negligence.

X acts *purposefully* concerning harm $H1$ if X has the aim of causing $H1$ via the act. The situation of X pulling the trigger of a gun with the aim of causing the death of Y evinces the purpose element. X acts *knowingly* concerning harm $H2$ if (i) X does not act purposefully concerning $H2$, but (ii) is aware that it is practically certain that $H2$ will be a side effect of the act. Situations that evince the knowledge element occur when X is acting purposefully concerning a distinct result (consisting of harm or not), and X knows that the act will cause harm as a side effect—for example, X sets a bomb off in the private jet of a politician with the sole aim of causing the politician's death but knowing that the bomb will also kill the pilot ($H2$).

It is important to note that, in contrast to the MPC schema, common-law schemas typically do not differentiate the purpose and knowledge elements in terms of culpability—these elements become disjunctive parts (with the same degree of implied culpability) of an offense element called "intention" or "intent" (see Dubber, 2015, pp. 58–9; LaFave & Scott, 1986, Vol. 1, pp. 303–4; Wilson, 2017, pp. 127–40). This view is prevalent in the UK: "a person acts (. . .) 'intentionally' concerning a result when (i) it is his purpose to cause it; or (ii) although it is not his purpose to cause that result, he knows that it would occur in the ordinary course of events (. . .)" (LAW COM, 1993, p. 8). And this view is still standard in the United States, even in codes somewhat influenced by the MPC: "'Intentionally' means that the actor either has a purpose to (. . .) cause the result specified, or is aware that his or her conduct is practically certain to cause that result" [Wisconsin's Criminal Code, 939.23(3)].

The other elements related to mental states, recklessness and negligence, occur in situations similar to that of the knowledge element but involve a component of risk rather than certainty: X acts *recklessly* or *negligently* concerning harm $H3$ if (i) X does not act purposefully concerning $H3$, and (ii) it is likely that $H3$ will be a side effect of the act. The difference between recklessness and negligence hinges on whether X envisages the risk of causing $H3$: with recklessness, X envisages the risk, whereas, with negligence, X does not. These elements also include a component that is not present in the characterization of the purpose and knowledge elements: the risky act constitutes a *gross* deviation from the standard of behavior that a reasonable person would observe in the situation (for a general discussion of the concept of a reasonable person, see Tobia, 2018).

It is important to note three points here. First, the notion of gross deviation from the standard of the reasonable person is a (vague) criterion to circumscribe the limits of criminal law—if the deviation from this standard is not gross, then it becomes a matter of civil law. The second point concerns the variables that determine the extent to which a risky act is unreasonable—that is, variables that determine the level of deviation from the reasonable person standard. All else being equal, the higher the risk of causing harm and the higher the level of the harm, the more unreasonable the risky act is. However, the reasonableness of a risky act is not simply a function of these two variables since it depends fundamentally on two other aspects of the reasonable person standard. One aspect, related to deviation in terms of negligence, concerns the level of knowledge and attention that a person should deploy in any specific situation to ascertain whether their act puts the welfare of others at risk. Humans have limited epistemic capacities, and the reasonable person standard takes such limitations into account. For instance, if a person hugs another person when the risk of transmitting a lethal disease is high, but where the person is asymptomatic, and the disease has yet to be identified, the hug does not constitute a departure from the reasonable person standard. The other aspect, related to deviation in terms of recklessness, concerns the justifiability of a risky act. Having envisaged that an act has risky side effects, humans must balance these side effects against the potential benefits related to the purpose of their act, and the reasonable person standard takes this balance into account. For instance, the performance of a delicate surgery, where there is a high risk that the patient will die, is justified if the surgery is a final attempt to save the patient's life—that is, taking the risk does not constitute a departure from the reasonable standard. Our last point is that, in adding a standard of reasonableness to the structure of offenses, the MPC incorporates into their structure a feature that is fundamental to the structure of defenses.

5.2.2 Defenses

Defenses are reasons to support the conclusion that a person is not culpable for causing harm, using "reason" à la Mercier & Sperber (2017) rather than in the more circumscribed senses found in the literature (e.g., Malle, Guglielmo, & Monroe, 2014). There are two types of defenses: justifications and excuses (Robinson, 1984).

Justifications exculpate the person because they indicate that the causation of harm is not wrong. In a way, justifications eliminate culpability by broadening the scope of what is permitted in specific situations. We have already indicated that justifications can relate to a situation of risk: if the aforementioned surgery causes the patient's death, the doctor is not culpable. Justifications may also relate to situations involving a knowledge element: in classic trolley dilemmas where a person causes the death of one human being as a known side effect of an act aimed at saving the lives of many others, people tend to think that the person's act is justified (hence the person is not culpable). However, justifications have been discussed primarily in relation to situations where the person's purpose is to cause harm and where the justification corresponds to the *motive* to cause harm: a person may cause the death of another person in order to avoid being mortally attacked (i.e., in self-defense) or in order to save other people's lives (i.e., in defense of others).

Excuses exculpate the person who causes harm because, although the causation of harm is deemed wrong, there is some abnormal disability or factor that leads to a condition that dissociates the person from the causation of harm, thus excusing the person.[3] In a way, excuses eliminate culpability by separating the issue of culpability from that of wrongdoing. The type of ignorance at stake in the aforementioned hugging case is an example—the person being asymptomatic and the disease being unknown to humanity excuse the person. Here, we focus on conditions that compromise a person's conscious control over their mental states and/or acts. One excusing condition occurs when a person acts and causes harm while being completely unaware of what they are doing and causing (e.g., a person who causes the death of another person while sleepwalking).[4] Another excusing condition occurs when a person has a strong misperception of reality—there is a voluntary act, and the person is aware of its consequences in the counterfactual reality implied by the misperception, but the person is unaware of the real nature of the act and its consequences (e.g., a person who causes the death of another person while hallucinating being attacked by a lion). A third excusing condition occurs when a person perceives the real nature of their act and its results but cannot resist the motivation to act (e.g., a person who causes the death of another person because they have an irresistible impulse or desire to kill the person). To reiterate, excusing conditions may be the consequence of an abnormal mental disability (in this case, they typically relate to an insanity defense) or of a more contingent abnormal factor. For example, a person may experience a hallucination as a schizophrenic episode or as an unexpected side effect of a medication.

All of the foregoing defenses may provide a partial exculpation instead of a complete one. For instance, if a person is perceived to have simply *diminished control* over their motivation to act, they may be deemed less culpable for the causation of harm rather than not culpable. These defenses may also interact or combine. For instance, the complete exculpation of the aforementioned hallucinating person also depends on the justifiability of the person's conduct in the context of the counterfactual reality implied by the hallucination—the killing of the lion was in self-defense. Finally, since defenses are reasons, and because what is deemed a good reason depends partially on a social agreement, their exculpatory force is not independent of what is perceived to be a reasonable person in a given social environment (i.e., their force may be related to an explicit or implicit comparison with what the reasonable person would do in the situation). For instance, in a social context where there is the normative expectation that a person should kill someone to preserve their honor (i.e., their right to respect—see Appiah, 2011; Stewart, 1994), such a killing would be (at least partially) justified, whereas, in a social context without this type of normative expectation, the killing would be unjustifiable.

5.3 The Law of Homicide

Homicides are conducts where a human being causes the death of another human being. Criminal homicides are homicides that meet the definition of a criminal offense (see LaFave and Scott, 1986; Wilson; 2017; for broader discussions, see Holder, 2007;

Mikhail, 2009). In this section, we characterize the criminal homicides most relevant to our research, including their definition and liability sides.

5.3.1 Murder

Murder is typically defined in terms of the presence of an element of "malice aforethought," forenamed as expressed or implied. We characterize two types of murder: one with expressed and the other with implied malice aforethought.

Historically, a homicide with an element of expressed malice aforethought meant that the homicide had a premeditated intention: the intention to cause death was formed in advance by cold-blooded deliberation, and the act that caused the death was an instance of planned activity (e.g., lying in wait to shoot). Such an element of premeditation still defines a subcategory of murder in many American codes, although sometimes the definition of "premeditation" makes this element innocuous: "the premeditation required in order to support a conviction of the crime of murder in the first degree must involve *more than a moment in point of time*" (Washington Criminal Code; our emphasis). However, this element has been dropped entirely from the definition of intentional murder in many US states (particularly those following the MPC schema—as we saw, the MPC does not list premeditation as a distinct element of culpability) and is absent in the UK definition of intentional murder. The type of murder we want to characterize here involves the intentional causation of death without requiring premeditation. Intentional causation relates to the common-law intention element that subsumes the MPC purpose and knowledge elements. This is the case in both the United Kingdom and United States since even those American states that follow the MPC schema do not acknowledge the distinction between purpose and knowledge as relevant in the context of the definition of murder. Thus, we define *intentional murder* as follows: X acts *purposefully* or *knowingly* concerning the death of Y and causes Y's death.

The type of murder with implied malice aforethought we characterize here typically expresses a "depraved heart" in terms of a "supreme indifference to human life." It occurs when a person does not act purposefully or knowingly concerning the death of a human being but acts in a way that puts other people at extreme risk of death, thereby causing a person's death. Examples would be piloting a speedboat through a packed crowd of swimmers just for fun (and causing the death of one of the swimmers) or shooting into a moving train full of passengers just to test one's gun (and causing the death of a passenger) (LaFave & Scott, 1986, Vol. 2, p. 230). This type of murder is listed in many US state codes, but, in the UK, it exists only in Scotland. There is some dispute on whether this type of murder should be defined in terms of the person envisaging and disregarding the extreme risk or simply in terms of the objective presence of the extreme risk (see, e.g., People v. Sanches, 2002). In other words, some think that a reckless element is necessary, whereas others think that it is not. To make this point explicit, we define two interpretations of *depraved-heart murder*: (i) X acts *recklessly* concerning the death of Y and causes Y's death, where the risk of causing Y's death was extreme (recklessness interpretation), and (ii) X acts *recklessly* or *negligently* concerning the death of Y and causes Y's death, where the risk of causing Y's death was extreme (objectivist interpretation).

In what respect do the said negligence and recklessness elements involve a reference to the reasonable person standard? It is important to note that these are homicide cases where it is utterly evident to any reasonable person that the act engenders an extreme risk of death. One argument supporting the objectivist interpretation is that these are cases where the presence of extreme risk is so obvious that whether there is an element of negligence or recklessness is irrelevant. In other words, these are cases where the lack of due attention to the situation is such a gross departure from the epistemic aspect of the reasonable person standard that the negligence element should not be factored in—that is, there can be no good excuse here. Furthermore, even if the person envisages the extreme risk, there can be no good justification for the risky act either.

Turning to murder's liability side, we equate intentional murder with first-degree murder and depraved-heart murder with second-degree murder. Regarding first-degree murder, we propose that its sentence ranges from thirty-two years to life in prison, whereas for second-degree murder, we propose that its sentence ranges from sixteen to thirty-two years in prison.[5]

5.3.2 Voluntary Manslaughter

Voluntary manslaughter is defined in tandem with intentional murder: cases of intentional murder may be mitigated by the presence of a partial defense, reducing them to the lesser offense of voluntary manslaughter.[6] Thus, what characterizes different versions of voluntary manslaughter is the different partial defenses in play. We delineate two partial defenses, restricting their characterization to situations of provocation.

One partial defense has the following components: (i) Y provokes X; (ii) due to the provocation, X attains a state of extreme anger ("heat of passion" and "sudden heat") that impairs X's self-control; (iii) under such a state, X kills Y; (iv) the provocation was grave enough to lead a reasonable person to a similar emotional reaction; (v) the time between the provocation and the killing was not sufficient for a reasonable person to cool off. In the United States, this type of partial defense is more frequent in states not aligned with the MPC. In the UK, the most recent formulation of this type of defense includes a clause that the provocation should also lead the person to have "a justifiable sense of being seriously wronged" (Wilson, 2017, pp. 371–84). This recent formulation makes the defense more akin to a partial justification than to a partial excuse related to impaired self-control (as is the case in the aforementioned formulation), though a partial justification concerning some sense of being subjected to injustice rather than to dishonor (as was the case in its much earlier formulation—see Horder, 1992).

The other partial defense has the following components: (i) Y provokes X; (ii) X is in a state of extreme emotional disturbance (hence X's self-control is impaired); (iii) due to the provocation and X's emotional state, X kills Y; (iv) there is a reasonable explanation or excuse for X's disturbed emotional state, though the criteria for what is reasonable should be determined from the point of view of X's situation. This defense is present in US states whose codes are aligned with the MPC (see, e.g., Kirchner & Galperin, 2002). It may exculpate a broader spectrum of homicides, even those that result from cold-blooded deliberation and planning. Because the criterion "from the point of view of X's situation" is vague and less tied to the reasonable person standard, there are strong similarities between this defense and that of diminished capacity, a resemblance contemplated by the MPC's drafters: "The term 'situation' is designedly ambiguous and is plainly flexible enough to allow the law to grow in the direction of taking account of mental abnormalities that have been recognized in the developing law of diminished capacity" [MPC 210.3(1)(b), comment 72 (1980)]. This type of extreme emotional-disturbance defense does not exist in the UK, although the UK has a defense of diminished capacity tied to voluntary manslaughter that can play a similar role (for a related discussion, see Mackay & Mitchel, 2003).

Turning to voluntary manslaughter's liability side, we propose that its sentence ranges from eight to sixteen years in prison.[7]

5.3.3 Involuntary Manslaughter

Involuntary manslaughter is defined in continuity with depraved-heart murder—indeed, in the United States, depraved-heart murder is sometimes classified as aggravated manslaughter (see New Jersey's code). In other words, involuntary manslaughter concerns situations where the risk of causing death is not extreme but nonetheless significant. There are analogous disputes concerning the interpretation of involuntary manslaughter. Here, however, this issue has specific implications in terms of types of homicide. Accordingly, we define three different types of involuntary manslaughter. We also contrast these types to the notion of negligence in tort law.

We define *objectivist manslaughter* as follows: X acts *recklessly* or *negligently* concerning the death of Y and causes Y's death, where the risk of causing Y's death was not extreme but nonetheless significant. In the United States, this type of definition is present in states that are not aligned with the MPC. One also finds this type of definition in the UK. The other two types of involuntary manslaughter are framed by the opposition between the recklessness and negligence elements. We define *reckless manslaughter* as follows: X acts *recklessly* concerning the death of Y and causes Y's death, where the risk of causing Y's death was not extreme but nonetheless significant. We define *negligent manslaughter* as follows: X acts *negligently* concerning the death of Y and causes Y's death, where the risk of causing Y's death was not extreme but nonetheless significant. These two types of manslaughter exist in US states more aligned with the MPC (e.g., New York) and may be described alternatively as "reckless homicide" and "negligent homicide." It is important to note that the notion of negligence in tort law does not correspond to any of the earlier given definitions. There are two reasons for this: (i) the foregoing definitions involve offense elements defined in the context of criminal law and (ii) tort negligence concerns a manner of behavior (e.g., medical malpractice) where a person "fails to satisfy an objective standard of carefulness or competence in breach of duty and in so doing causes the victim harm" (Wilson, 2017, p. 150). However, the definition of tort negligence aligns with the previous objectivist definition of manslaughter insofar as the contrast between the recklessness and negligence offense elements is not fundamental to either definition, while it is fundamental to the definitions of reckless and negligent manslaughter. Tort negligence differs from the three types of manslaughter insofar as it involves less than a gross deviation from the reasonable person standard.

For a homicide to be considered a crime rather than a tort, how significant should the level of risk involved be? In other words, what degree of risk would render a risky act a gross deviation from the reasonable person standard? Since the seriousness of the harm at stake is quite extreme (i.e., the death of a human being), we presume that even an act with a low risk of causing death may be understood as a gross deviation from the reasonable person standard. Now, given a significantly risky act, which level of inattentiveness pertaining to its harmful consequences constitutes such a gross deviation? Furthermore, if a person takes the risk while envisaging its harmful consequences, which lack of justification constitutes such a gross deviation? Concerning these questions, we let the reader reach their own conclusion by using their own intuitions about the reasonable person standard, akin to the legal system leaving a jury in a trial to answer such questions.

Turning to involuntary manslaughter's liability side, we propose the following liability ranges: six months to eight years in prison (objectivist manslaughter), six months to two years (negligent manslaughter), and four years to eight years in prison (reckless manslaughter).

5.4 Overview of Research Design

Our research presented subjects with pairs of contrasting scenarios akin to those introduced in Section 5.1. In that section, the two scenarios differ mainly on what each character did (kill or steal). In the pairs here, a character kills a human being in both scenarios (i.e., both scenarios describe a homicide), though the two scenarios differ in some aspects of the killing.

Before reading the paired scenarios, we instructed subjects to assume everything described by the scenarios to be literally true and focus exclusively on the facts described by the scenarios. We also indicated to subjects that we were interested in their own evaluation of the scenarios, not in what they think would be the legal view on the matter.

After reading the paired scenarios, subjects were asked, in a fixed order, the following two closed-ended questions about the main characters of the paired scenarios (e.g., about Ben and Sam):

In your opinion, would you place the blame on them equally for the death of Y?

Ben	☐	☐	☐	☐	☐	☐	☐	☐	☐
Sam	☐	☐	☐	☐	☐	☐	☐	☐	☐
	No Blame		A Little		Medium		A Lot of		Full Blame

In your opinion, do they deserve the same amount of punishment (in prison time)?

Ben	☐	☐	☐	☐	☐	☐	☐	☐	☐
Sam	☐	☐	☐	☐	☐	☐	☐	☐	☐
	None	6 Months	1 Year	2 Years	4 Years	8 Years	16 Years	32 Years	Life

The first probe operationalizes a culpability judgment, while the second probe operationalizes a liability judgment (cf. Robinson & Darley, 1995). Each probe was followed by an open-ended question asking participants to explain their options thoroughly. To help the reader keep track of our framework, Table 5.1 summarizes how the options of our liability measure map onto the liability range of each category of homicide discussed previously (however, see endnote 7).

The paired scenarios were part of a large paper-pencil survey where each subject received £20 for participation. Subjects were UK undergraduate students from Queen's University Belfast ($N = 152$; 48% male; 51% female; $M_{age} = 25$; no law student was included in the sample). The following three sections report the results of a subset of the paired scenarios from the survey. In each section, subjects responded to only one of its paired scenarios, although they responded to two paired scenarios across the three sections.[8]

Section 5.5, involving three pairs, reports results on whether subjects' judgments of culpability and liability are sensitive to the offense elements of purpose, knowledge, and risk (in terms of recklessness). In addition, in the context of the three paired scenarios, this section reports evidence on whether there are distinct lay concepts of intentional action that may correspond to distinct legal concepts (see Section 5.5.4 for details of the design). Section 5.6, involving two pairs, reports results on whether subjects' judgments of culpability and liability are sensitive to the contrast between objectivist and recklessness/negligence definitions of homicides. Section 5.7, involving three pairs, reports results on whether subjects' judgments of culpability and liability are sensitive to the partial or complete defenses discussed earlier. In each of the sections, we delineate the specific hypothesis for each paired scenarios. Our general hypothesis across all paired scenarios is that subjects' judgments will follow a strong immunitivist and retributivist pattern (i.e., subjects will accept both that if a person is not culpable, the person deserves not to be punished, and that if a person is culpable, the person deserves to be punished in proportion to their degree of culpability).

Table 5.1 Liability Range of Different Types of Criminal Homicide

Homicide Type	Liability Range								
	None	6 mths	1 yr	2 yrs	4 yrs	8 yrs	16 yrs	32 yrs	Life
Intentional Murder								X	X
Depraved-♥ Murder							X	X	
Voluntary Manslaughter						X	X		
Reckless Manslaughter					X	X			
Negligent Manslaughter		X	X	X					
Objectivist Manslaughter		X	X	X	X	X			

© Paulo Sousa and Gary Lavery.

5.5 Purpose, Knowledge, and Recklessness

5.5.1 Purpose versus Knowledge (Pair I)

The homicides in the first paired scenarios of this section differ on whether they include a purpose or a knowledge offense element. Both scenarios begin as follows:[9]

> The Summer Duck is very common in the summer but is rarely seen in the winter. As a prize, a hunting club has offered £90,000 to anyone who kills a Summer Duck in the wintertime. *X* is hunting, hoping to kill a Summer Duck and win the prize. After some hours, *X* has completely lost hope. *X* sees a huge build-up of snow on one of the nearby mountain peaks. Being an experienced hunter, *X* knows that the noise of a gunshot would surely cause an avalanche in such a situation. *X* notices someone walking underneath the huge build-up of snow.

The story continues in the purpose and knowledge scenarios, respectively, as follows:

> *X1* sees that it is his rich uncle who had come with him to do some hiking and from whom he will inherit £90,000. *X1* thinks: "If I shoot the gun, the avalanche will definitely kill my uncle." *X1* is in conflict, but his desire to get the inheritance money soon is stronger. *X1* shoots the gun into the air in order to kill his uncle. The avalanche occurs, and the uncle dies.

> *X2* sees that it is his poor uncle who had come with him to do some hiking. Suddenly, *X2* sees a Summer Duck flying overhead. *X2* thinks: "If I shoot the gun, the avalanche will definitely kill my uncle." *X2* is in conflict, but his desire to get the money prize is stronger. *X2* aims the gun at the Summer Duck and shoots in order to kill it. The bullet hits the target, and the Summer Duck dies. The avalanche occurs, and the uncle dies.

According to the aforementioned legal standards, these are two cases of intentional murder, with the same high degree of culpability and liability. Our research in the United States suggests that people do not distinguish between these cases either (Sousa, 2005). We propose a similar hypothesis here.

The two remaining paired scenarios in this section employ the same summer duck story to construct homicide scenarios that differ on the envisaged probability of causing death: from certainty to high risk to low risk. Our hypothesis regarding these pairs is that people are sensitive to this dimension: less envisaged probability leads to less culpability and liability.

5.5.2 Knowledge versus High Risk (Pair II)

The second pair contrasts a homicide with a knowledge offense element to a homicide with an envisaged high-risk offense element. Both scenarios begin as follows:

> The Summer Duck is very common in the summer but is rarely seen in the winter. As a prize, a hunting club has offered £90,000 to anyone who kills a Summer Duck

in the wintertime. *X* is hunting, hoping to kill a Summer Duck and win the prize. After some hours, *X* has completely lost hope.

The story continues in the knowledge and high-risk scenarios, respectively, as follows:

> *X1* sees a huge build-up of snow on one of the mountain peaks close to him. Being an experienced hunter, *X1* knows that the noise of a gunshot would surely cause an avalanche in such a situation. *X1* notices someone walking underneath the huge build-up of snow. *X1* sees that it is his uncle who had come with him to do some hiking. Suddenly, *X1* sees a Summer Duck flying overhead. *X1* thinks: "If I shoot the gun, the avalanche will definitely kill my uncle." *X1* is in conflict, but his desire to get the money prize is stronger. *X1* aims the gun at the Summer Duck and shoots in order to kill it. The bullet hits the target, and the Summer Duck dies. The avalanche occurs, and the uncle dies.

> *X2* sees a huge build-up of snow on one of the mountain peaks further away from him. Being an experienced hunter, *X2* knows that there is a substantial risk that the noise of a gunshot would cause an avalanche in such a situation. *X2* notices someone walking underneath the huge build-up of snow. *X2* sees that it is his uncle who had come with him to do some hiking. Suddenly, *X2* sees a Summer Duck flying overhead. *X2* thinks: "If I shoot the gun, there is a substantial risk of an avalanche, which would definitely kill my uncle." *X2* is in conflict, but his desire to get the money prize is stronger. *X2* aims the gun at the Summer Duck and shoots in order to kill it. The bullet hits the target, and the Summer Duck dies. The avalanche occurs, and the uncle dies.

These two cases of homicide may be interpreted in terms of the contrast between intentional murder and depraved-heart murder (in its recklessness interpretation). Our research in the United States also suggests that people see cases of extreme recklessness as involving a high degree of culpability and liability, though still distinct from intentional murder with a knowledge element (Sousa, 2005). We propose a similar hypothesis here.

5.5.3 High Risk versus Low Risk (Pair III)

The third pair contrasts a homicide with an envisaged high-risk offense element to a homicide with an envisaged low-risk offense element. For this pair, we slightly rephrased the second pair. The opposition of the previous pair "sees a huge build-up of snow on one of the mountain peaks *close to him* (versus *further away from him*)" was repeated here to manipulate perceptions of probability. Since these expressions denote vague predicates, it is plausible to assume that their interpretation would be pragmatically adjusted for the contrast between high risk ("close to him") and low risk ("further away from him"). Except for replacing "further away from him" with "close to him," the high-risk scenario here was the same as that of the second pair. Besides the "further away from him" detail, the low-risk scenario differed from the high-risk scenario of this pair in one other detail: "substantial risk" was replaced with "minimal risk."

Although we are dealing with a continuum, we hypothesized that this contrast would be the clearest to subjects. Moreover, we hypothesized that subjects in the high-risk scenario would assign punishment in the range of depraved-heart murder, while subjects in the low-risk scenario would assign punishment in the range of reckless manslaughter.

5.5.4 Lay Concepts of Intentional Action and Their Legal Counterparts

In the context of the previous three paired scenarios (after the culpability and liability probes), we investigated whether there are two distinct lay concepts of intentional action that may have legal counterparts.[10] Simplifying things, we characterize an aim-based lay concept as follows: X killed Y intentionally only if X aimed to cause Y's death (for a more detailed discussion, see Sousa & Holbrook, 2010; Sousa, Holbrook, & Swiney, 2015). Moreover, we characterize a choice-based lay concept as follows: X killed Y intentionally only if X chose to cause Y's death (see Sousa, 2005). Here we indicate how we probed whether ordinary people possess these two concepts of intentional action. In the following subsection, where we describe and discuss the results of the current section, we pursue the comparison with legal concepts.

In the context of the first pair, we predicted that both lay concepts of intentional action would be salient in relation to the uncle's death. The aim-based concept applies to the purpose scenario, though not to the knowledge scenario: while the former character aimed to cause the uncle's death with the gunshot, the latter character did not aim to cause the uncle's death with the gunshot (he aimed to cause the summer duck's death). The choice-based concept applies to both scenarios: knowing that a gunshot would cause an avalanche that would kill their uncle, both characters had a choice between shooting and preserving their uncle's life; hence, in deciding to shoot, they chose to cause their uncle's death. To test our prediction, we probed subjects' semantic intuitions directly. They were initially asked to read the following (emphasis as in the original):

> In the stories, *X1's aim was to kill his uncle* while *X2's aim was to kill the Summer Duck*. Thus, you may say:
>
> (A) X1 killed his uncle *intentionally*, but X2 did *not* kill his uncle *intentionally*.
>
> In the stories, both X1 and X2 *knew that a gunshot would cause an avalanche that would kill their uncles* and *decided to shoot the gun*. Thus, you may say:
>
> (B) *X1* and *X2* killed their uncles *intentionally*.

Next, subjects were asked which of the following options best describes their perceptions of the meaning (or meanings) of the word "intentionally":

☐ I could use the word "intentionally" only as in (A). For me, the meaning expressed in (B) does not sound familiar—strictly speaking, this is not a meaning of the word "intentionally."

☐ I could use the word "intentionally" only as in (B). For me, the meaning expressed in (A) does not sound familiar—strictly speaking, this is not a meaning of the word "intentionally."

☐ I could use the word "intentionally" as in (A) or as in (B). For me, both meanings sound familiar. These are simply two slightly different meanings of the word "intentionally."

☐ I could not use the word "intentionally" either as in (A) or as in (B). For me, both meanings sound unfamiliar. These are not meanings of the word "intentionally."

We hypothesized that a substantial number of subjects would either choose the third option or be divided between the first two options.

In the context of the remaining pairs, we predicted that only the choice-based concept would be salient and that this saliency would be apparent only in the knowledge scenario (i.e., the first scenario of the second pair). To test this prediction, we asked subjects whether one, both, or none of the characters of the paired scenarios killed their uncle intentionally. We hypothesized that most subjects would indicate that the character in the knowledge scenario killed intentionally, though much less so in the high- and low-risk scenarios.

5.5.5 Results and Discussion

Table 5.2 represents the percentage of subjects' ranks (of $X1$ and $X2$) in terms of both culpability and liability. Consistent with our general hypothesis, in all pairs, the vast majority of responses followed an immunitivist/retributivist pattern: punishment ranks did not contradict blame ranks.[11]

Table 5.2 Percentage of Subjects' Ranks (Combined)

Paired Scenarios	Rank Blame|Punish	Percentage (%)
I	$X1 = X2 \mid X1 = X2$	**70.5**
($N = 37$)	$X1 > X2 \mid X1 > X2$	**21.5**
	$X1 = X2 \mid X1 > X2$	5.5
	$X1 > X2 \mid X1 = X2$	2.5
II	$X1 = X2 \mid X1 = X2$	**74**
($N = 35$)	$X1 > X2 \mid X1 > X2$	**11.5**
	$X1 = X2 \mid X1 > X2$	3
	$X1 > X2 \mid X1 = X2$	11.5
III	$X1 = X2 \mid X1 = X2$	**28**
($N = 39$)	$X1 > X2 \mid X1 > X2$	**51.5**
	$X1 = X2 \mid X1 > X2$	15.5
	$X1 > X2 \mid X1 = X2$	5

Immunitivism/retributivism in bold. © Paulo Sousa and Gary Lavery.

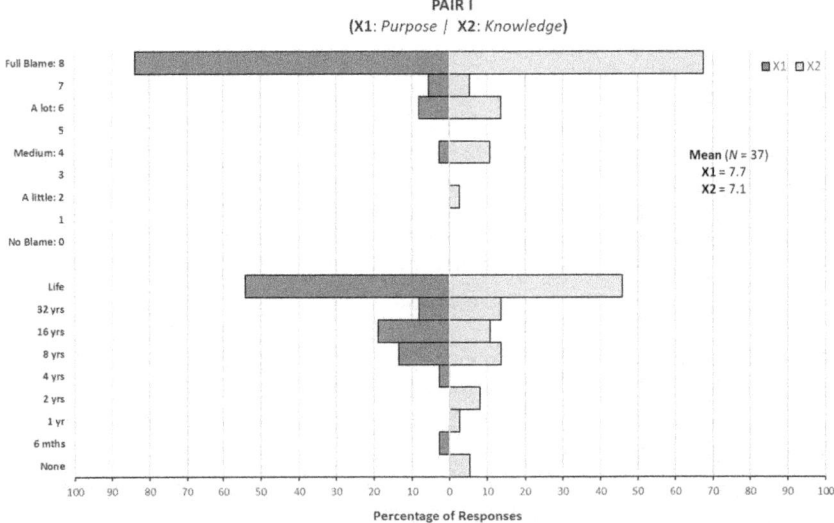

Figure 5.1 Results of pair I (purpose versus knowledge). © Paulo Sousa and Gary Lavery.

Figure 5.1 shows the results of pair I. Wilcoxon signed-rank tests indicated that there was a significant difference in culpability and liability judgments ($z = -2.72$, $p < 0.01$, $r = 0.32$ and $z = -2.84$, $p < 0.01$, $r = 0.33$). However, as Table 5.2 shows, 70.5 percent of subjects ranked the two characters as equal in blame and punishment. More specifically, the majority of subjects attributed full or almost full blame to both characters (*X1*: 89%; *X2*: 73%) and assigned either "thirty-two years" or "life" to them (*X1*: 62%; *X2*: 59.5%), which corresponds to the liability range of intentional murder. Hence, the overall pattern of results suggests that most subjects did not differentiate between the two homicides, seeing them instead as akin to intentional murder (as we initially hypothesized).

Figures 5.2 and 5.3 show the results of pairs II and III. Wilcoxon signed-rank tests indicated that there was a significant difference (in the predicted direction) in culpability and liability judgments in pair II ($z = -2.60$, $p < 0.01$, $r = 0.31$ and $z = -2.12$, $p < 0.05$, $r = 0.24$) and pair III ($z = -4.16$, $p < 0.001$, $r = 0.47$ and $z = -4.44$, $p < 0.001$, $r = 0.50$). These results support our hypothesis that a decrease in envisaged probability leads to a decrease in culpability and liability.

The contrast between the knowledge and high-risk scenarios in pair II was less accentuated than we hypothesized—the size of the difference in liability judgments, in particular, was small. Also, as Table 5.2 shows, 74 percent of subjects ranked the two characters as equal in blame and punishment. This seems partially due to an equalizing, anchoring effect, as some of the explanations given by subjects suggest that they either misinterpreted the knowledge scenario in terms of high risk ("They *both risked* and ultimately took the life of someone") or misinterpreted the high-risk scenario in terms of knowledge ("They *both knew* if they shot the duck their uncles would die"). Nevertheless, most subjects acknowledged this contrast but considered

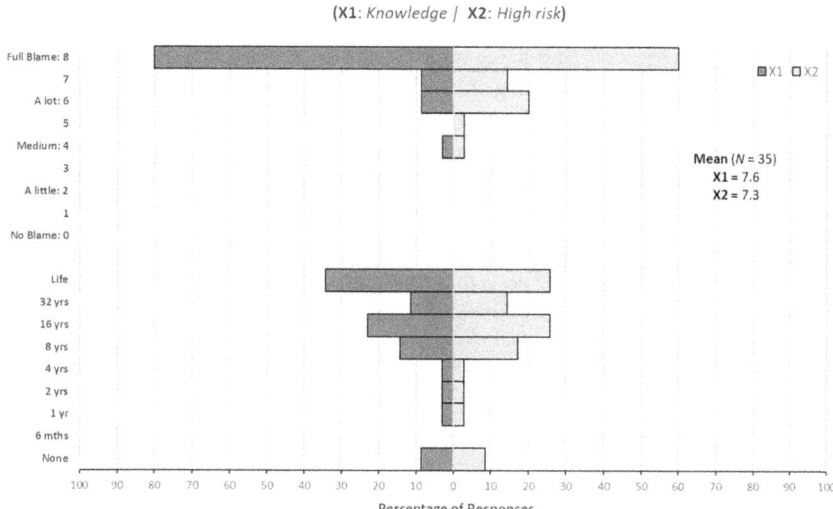

Figure 5.2 Results of pair II (knowledge versus high risk). © Paulo Sousa and Gary Lavery.

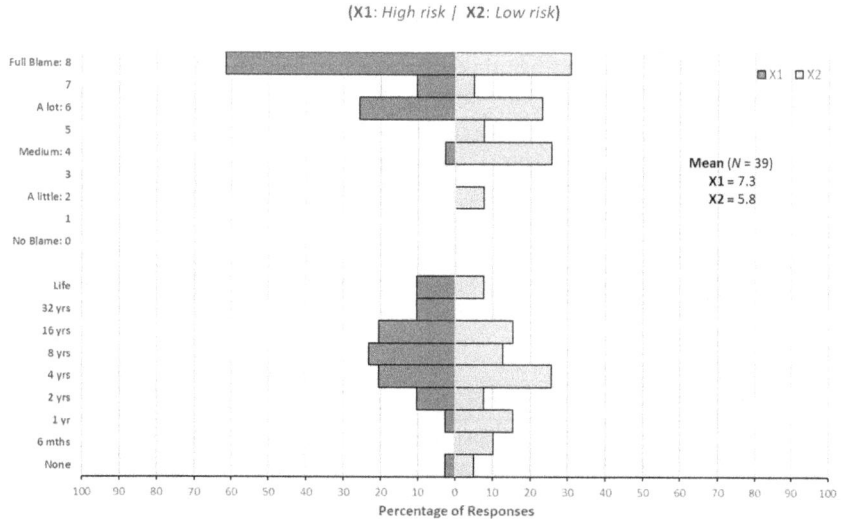

Figure 5.3 Results of pair III (high risk versus low risk). © Paulo Sousa and Gary Lavery.

it irrelevant to their judgments ("Even though *X1* was certain and *X2* was aware of a substantial risk, a substantial risk is enough to full blame . . . and to life in prison"). Indeed, while we expected the majority of subjects to assign punishment to *X2* within the range of depraved-heart murder, only by taking into account the entire murder range did we find a clear majority of subjects (65.5%). This was also the case in the assignment of punishment to *X1* (68.5%).

As we hypothesized, the contrast between the high-risk and low-risk scenarios in pair III was the clearest to subjects: only 28 percent ranked the two characters as equal in blame and punishment. And while there was a significant difference in culpability and liability judgments concerning *X1* and *X2* in all the pairs of this section, the effect size was much larger for pair III. We also hypothesized that subjects' liability judgments would be akin to the contrast between depraved-heart murder and reckless manslaughter. The results do not support our hypothesis. In the high-risk scenario, only 30 percent fell within the range of depraved-heart murder (i.e., from "16 years" to "32 years"). Although subjects' blame attributions were the same as in the previous comparison (i.e., $M = 7.3$), their perceptions of risk seem to have been adjusted down, thereby substantially diminishing the level of punishment assigned: in the previous comparison, the majority of punishment assignments fell within the murder range (65.5%), whereas here, the majority of assignments fell within the range of four to sixteen years (64%). On the other hand, in the low-risk scenario, only 38.5 percent assigned punishment within the range of reckless manslaughter (i.e., from four to eight years), with the remaining assignments being spread throughout the rest of the scale.

Regarding the issue of whether there are two distinct lay concepts of intentional action that may have legal counterparts, Table 5.3 represents subjects' responses on the meaning of "intentionally" and on whether each character killed their uncle intentionally.

In pair II, 60 percent of subjects judged that the character in the knowledge scenario killed his uncle intentionally, suggesting a lay concept of intentional action that is not aim based. As we proposed earlier, this concept is based on the perception of choice. This interpretation is also compatible with the decrease in judgments of intentionality evident in the high-risk and low-risk scenarios (for high risk: 37% in pair II and 30% in pair III; for low risk: 13% in pair III), as a decrease in the perception of probability decreases the perception of choice. Regarding pair I, 62 percent of subjects accepted

Table 5.3 Percentage of Responses on the Meaning of "Intentionally" (Pair I) and on Whether the Characters Killed Intentionally (Pairs II and III)

Paired Scenarios	Response Options	Percentage (%)
I	Only aim meaning	19
(N = 37)	Only choice meaning	19
	Both meanings	62
	None	0
II	Both killed intentionally	37
(N = 35)	Neither killed intentionally	40
	Only X1 killed intentionally	23
	Only X2 killed intentionally	0
III	Both killed intentionally	13
(N = 39)	Neither killed intentionally	69
	Only X1 killed intentionally	17
	Only X2 killed intentionally	0

© Paulo Sousa and Gary Lavery.

that there are two distinct meanings of "intentionally," meanings that, arguably, are related to the aim-based and choice-based concepts of intentional action. Moreover, the remaining subjects were divided on which meaning/concept "intentionally" expresses. This indicates that "intentionally" is polysemous both intra-individually and across individuals, a pattern of variation consistent with our hypothesis about the two lay concepts.

Concerning the issue of whether the aim-based and the choice-based concepts have legal counterparts, notice first that there can be no complete congruence between these lay concepts and legal concepts. Potential legal counterparts come from the types of actions arising from legal offense elements (e.g., from the MPC purpose element). However, legal offense elements and their related actions are technical definitions completely tied to a culpability schema, whereas analogous lay concepts of mental states and actions are not technical definitions, and they also have a role in our naïve theory of mind that is independent of judgments of culpability (e.g., in *explanations* of actions).

That being said, these results and our overall discussion indicate a robust congruence between lay and legal concepts (cf. Kneer & Bourgeois-Gironde, 2017). The aim-based concept of intentional action maps directly onto the type of action arising from the MPC purpose element. The choice-based concept of intentional action does not map directly onto any action arising from legal offense elements. It does not map onto the actions that arise from either the MPC purpose or knowledge elements because it subsumes both types of actions. It does not map onto the actions that arise from the common-law intention element because it has a basic structure (i.e., CHOICE), whereas the common-law intention element is structured simply as an exclusive disjunction (purpose or knowledge). Nevertheless, the rationale behind the common-law intention element (and its related actions) is akin to the choice-based concept. As legal scholars have emphasized, there is an implicit element of choice ("willfulness") that unifies the purpose and knowledge elements in opposition to the recklessness and negligence elements:

> Purposeful and knowing conduct is viewed as "wilful," while reckless conduct or less is at most "careless." Offenders whose conduct falls within the first category are condemned for "intentional" conduct; those in the latter are scolded for "taking risks." (Robinson, 1980, p. 819)

5.6 Recklessness, Negligence, and Objectivism

5.6.1 Envisaged High Risk versus Negligence (Pair IV)

One of the paired scenarios in this section contrasts the high-risk scenario of the previous section (pair III version) with an analogous negligence version of it. The difference in the negligence scenario is that, when the character sees a huge build-up of snow (initially or when he notices his uncle walking underneath it), he does not recall the risk involved: "Although *X2* is an experienced hunter, he does not remember that there is a substantial risk that the noise of a gunshot would cause an avalanche in such a situation." Thus, the character shoots the gun without envisaging the risk of causing his uncle's death: "Without any thought about the risk of an avalanche crossing his mind, X2 aims the gun and shoots in order to kill the Summer Duck."

We contrasted these two cases of homicide to test the opposition between objectivist interpretations/definitions, which do not deem the distinction between the recklessness and negligence elements relevant (such as in objectivist depraved-heart murder and objectivist manslaughter), and those interpretations/definitions that take the distinction to be relevant (such as in reckless depraved-heart murder, reckless manslaughter, and negligent manslaughter). Because of how both stories are narrated, we hypothesized that subjects would realize that the causal link between a gunshot and an avalanche should be evident to an experienced hunter. Furthermore, because X2 has no recollection of this link (neither when he initially sees the build-up of snow nor when he saw his uncle walking beneath it), we presumed that this would be indicative of a gross deviation from the level of knowledge and attention that a reasonable person (in this case, *qua* the reasonable hunter) should deploy in the situation. The objectivist position predicts that most subjects will judge X1 and X2 equally in culpability and liability. However, we hypothesize that most subjects will judge X1 more severely in this respect, interpreting the contrast as akin to the difference between reckless depraved-heart murder/manslaughter and negligent manslaughter.

5.6.2 Envisaged Very Low Risk versus Negligence (Pair V)

The other pair in this section involves scenarios that may be interpreted as crossing the boundary between criminal and civil law, as the probability of causing death is very low. We aimed to test objectivist and non-objectivist positions more broadly, considering tort negligence as a kind of objectivist position similar to objectivist manslaughter (see related discussion in Section 5.3.3). Both scenarios begin by stating that, during the last few months, the characters have been completely involved with getting their job affairs in order. However, while one character keeps postponing getting new car tires despite noticing that they are virtually bald, the other character has not noticed his car's bald tires. Next, on a very rainy day, both characters go to their respective garages to get their cars to go to work. However, the characters differ on whether they perceive the risk:

> It occurs to X1 that it is risky to use his car in this weather. However, X1 thinks that if he waits for a bus or if he calls a taxi, he will arrive late for the important meeting that he has with the president of the company.

> X2 is so focused on the important meeting he has with the president of his company that it does not occur to him to look at the tires.

Both scenarios end as follows:

> X is driving his car down a city street. X is driving under the speed limit, and he is very attentive to his driving. The light ahead turns red, and the street is immediately

filled with pedestrians. *X* steps on the break in time, but the car does not stop, due to its bald tires. The car strikes a pedestrian. The pedestrian instantly dies.

These two scenarios may be interpreted simply as a case of tort negligence inasmuch as both drivers are behaving in a manner that violates the (legal) duty of care of a reasonable driver. From this perspective, the tort-objectivist prediction is that *X1* and *X2* should not receive any punishment in prison time. However, this depends on how one interprets the following: (i) the level of risk of causing death at stake; (ii) the extent to which being distracted by one's job affairs and having an important meeting serve as an excuse not to pay attention; (iii) the extent to which envisaging the risk of an accident involves foreseeing the risk of causing death, and (iv) the extent to which taking the risk to be on time for an important meeting serves as a reasonable justification. Consequently, such homicides may also be construed as criminal homicides. In such cases, the objectivist position holds that both scenarios are equivalent *qua* cases of objectivist manslaughter, the prediction being that *X1* and *X2* should receive the same punishment in terms of prison time. Our general alternative hypothesis concerning these scenarios is that most subjects will judge *X1* more severely because, presumably, they reject objectivism.

5.6.3 Results and Discussion

Table 5.4 represents the percentage of subjects' ranks (of *X1* and *X2*) in terms of both culpability and liability. Consistent with our general hypothesis, the vast majority of responses followed an immunitivist/retributivist pattern.

Figures 5.4 and 5.5 show the results of pairs IV and V. Wilcoxon signed-rank tests indicated that there was a significant difference (in the predicted direction) in culpability and liability judgments in pair IV ($z = -5.26, p < 0.001, r = 0.59$ and $z = -5.25, p < 0.001, r = 0.59$) and in pair V ($z = -4.75, p < 0.001, r = 0.55$ and $z = -3.90, p < 0.001, r = 0.45$).

In pair IV, the effect sizes of both differences were quite large, and as Table 5.4 shows, 85 percent of subjects ranked *X1* as more deserving of blame and punishment. More specifically, while 77.5 percent of subjects attributed full or almost full blame to *X1*, only 7.5 percent made such attribution to *X2*. And while 62.5 percent of subjects assigned punishment to *X1* within the range of reckless manslaughter and depraved-

Table 5.4 Percentage of Subjects' Ranks (Combined)

Paired Scenarios	Rank Blame|Punish	Percentage (%)
IV	$X1 = X2 \mid X1 = X2$	5
(N = 40)	$X1 > X2 \mid X1 > X2$	**85**
	$X1 > X2 \mid X1 = X2$	5
	$X1 = X2 \mid X1 > X2$	5
V	$X1 = X2 \mid X1 = X2$	21.5
(N = 37)	$X1 > X2 \mid X1 > X2$	**48.5**
	$X1 > X2 \mid X1 = X2$	30

Immunitivism/retributivism in bold. © Paulo Sousa and Gary Lavery.

PAIR IV
(**X1**: *High risk* | **X2**: *Negligence*)

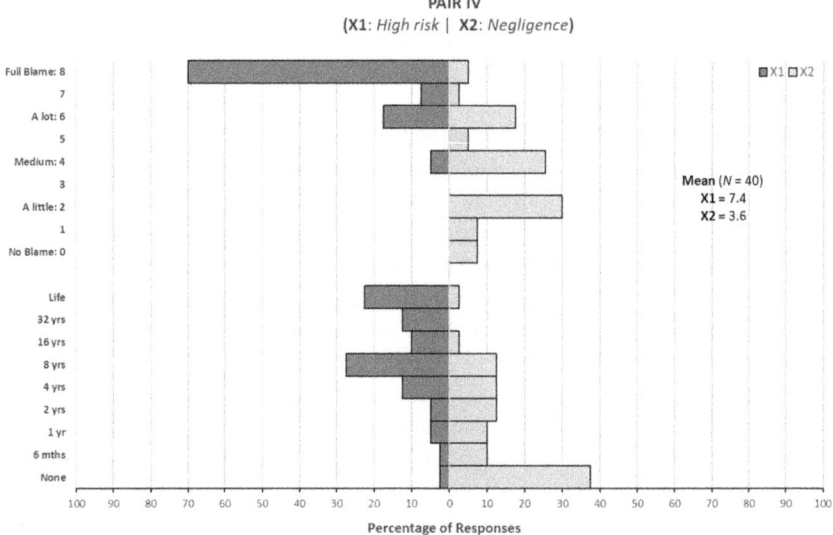

Figure 5.4 Results of pair IV (envisaged high risk versus negligence). © Paulo Sousa and Gary Lavery.

heart murder (i.e., from "four years" to "thirty-two years"), only 27.5 percent made such an assignment to *X2*. These results are more consistent with our hypothesis than the objectivist position.

The liability results of the negligence scenario were somewhat surprising. We expected most subjects to assign punishment within the range of negligent manslaughter (i.e., "six months" to "two years"), yet only 32.5 percent of them did so. Intriguingly, 37.5 percent of subjects assigned no punishment at all. Since the absence of criminal punishment indicates the lack of a crime, it is possible that some subjects deemed information about negligence as insufficient to constitute a solid foundation for a judgment of criminal liability. In line with this hypothesis, some subjects sometimes invoked "the unknown of negligence" rationale (i.e., what would *X2* have done if, as with *X1*, the thought of the avalanche had crossed his mind?), either by presuming that *X2* would have done otherwise ("*X2*, one presumes, would not have shot if he had remembered about the substantial risk of an avalanche"), or by claiming that one cannot judge in the absence of such evidence ("*X2* may have made a completely different decision if he had remembered. We can't judge him on anything else than what we do know"). Alternatively, it is possible that the narrative of the scenario was not realistic enough to suggest a gross deviation from the level of knowledge and attention that a reasonable hunter should deploy in the situation. Indeed, most subjects emphasized that what happened was simply an accident ("*X2* killed his uncle through an unanticipated accident").

Concerning pair V, although the effect sizes related to both differences were large, the overall pattern of results was more equivocal. As Table 5.4 shows, 48.5 percent of subjects ranked *X1* more deserving of blame and punishment. This result is more consistent with our hypothesis than with the objectivist position. However, as Table 5.4 also

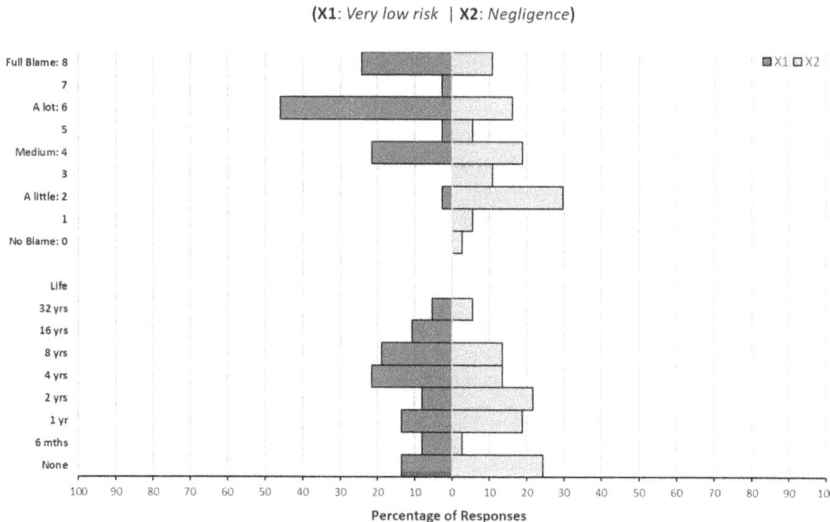

Figure 5.5 Results of pair V (envisaged very low risk versus negligence). © Paulo Sousa and Gary Lavery.

shows, subjects were divided in their liability judgments (i.e., 48.5% for *X1* > *X2* versus 51.5% for *X1* = *X2*). In other words, more than half of the subjects (nineteen) made objectivist liability judgments—in terms of no punishment (five) or some punishment (fourteen). The five tort-objectivist subjects did not seem to perceive gross deviation from the reasonable person standard ("It is easy to overlook your tires when you have a busy schedule . . ."). The fourteen objectivist-manslaughter subjects, who typically assigned "one year" to "eight years" of punishment, seem to think that there is such gross deviation. ("Both showed immense signs of carelessness.") On the other hand, the non-objectivist subjects (eighteen) invariably emphasized that *X1* was aware of the risk.

The vast majority of subjects (78.5%) attributed more blame to *X1*, invariably emphasizing that *X1* was aware of the risk. Interestingly, many of these subjects assigned the same punishment to *X1* and *X2*, which seems to evince a non-retributivist pattern (see Table 5.4, 30%). Additionally, some of these subjects assigned no punishment (four out of eleven). Would these subjects have differentiated between *X1* and *X2* if they had been given alternative ways of assigning punishment (other than prison time)? This remains an open question. More generally, it is possible that our punishment measure was not sensitive enough to probe for differences in liability judgments.

5.7 Partial and Complete Defenses

5.7.1 Extreme Disturbance versus Heat of Passion (Pair VI)

One of the paired scenarios in this section contrasts two homicides that may be interpreted in terms of the distinction between the emotional-disturbance and heat-of-passion versions of voluntary manslaughter. Both scenarios begin by describing a character who has been married to his wife for ten years. The story continues in the emotional-disturbance and heat-of-passion scenarios, respectively, as follows:

> *X1* has been under extreme emotional distress. Not long ago, he lost his job, and his parents and only brother died in a tragic car accident. Now, his beloved wife leaves him to live with a rich man. In addition, his wife does not miss an opportunity to make him jealous by showing off her new lifestyle. *X1* says that he does not want to see her anymore, but she insists on passing by or calling to relate the details of her happiness. Also, she keeps going with her new partner to the places that *X1* frequents. *X1* starts to have strong desires to kill his wife. He tries to avoid the idea of killing his wife, but he is feeling too weak to control himself. *X1* ends up succumbing to the idea of killing his wife and devises a plan to do so. *X1* is lying in wait when he sees his wife walking out to the car with her new partner. He raises his rifle and aims at his wife's heart. *X1* pulls the trigger and the bullet goes directly into her heart. His wife instantly dies.

> *X2* loves his wife and thinks that she is the most trustworthy person he has ever met. One day, *X2* decides to leave work early, buy some flowers and surprise his wife. When he arrives home and opens the door of their bedroom, he sees his wife having sex with another man. The scene causes feelings of anger to rush over *X2*. Completely enraged, he goes to the closet, grabs his handgun, and shoots his wife. His wife instantly dies.

Not long ago, women's sexual infidelity or betrayal would constitute a partial defense reducing a charge of intentional murder (with a purpose element) to that of voluntary manslaughter. More recently, and for very good reasons, the criminal law has attempted to eliminate this bias against women by putting in place quite strong restrictions on the usage of partial defenses related to women's sexual infidelity and breakups, thus permitting such defenses only in exceptional circumstances. For example, in the UK, this partial defense only has force when the killing was driven by a justifiable sense of being subjected to injustice rather than by jealousy and/or a sense of being subjected to dishonor (see Wilson, 2017, pp. 380–1). The provocations in our scenarios may be interpreted as constituting such a circumstance. Both stories suggest some unfairness on the part of the wives. Furthermore, the husbands killed only their wives, indicating that the primary motive was not jealousy and/or a sense of being subjected to dishonor. Our research in the United States suggests that many people do not differentiate between these two cases in terms of culpability and that they judge them less severely than cases of intentional murder with a purpose element (see Sousa, 2005). Accordingly, we hypothesized that a significant number of subjects would not differentiate between these two cases and would interpret them as involving a partial defense that reduces their liability judgments from the range of intentional murder to that of a lesser offense (e.g., voluntary manslaughter or second-degree murder—see endnote 7).

5.7.2 Real Self-Defense versus Hallucinatory Self-Defense (Pair VII)

Another pair in this section contrasts a real case of self-defense homicide to a hallucinatory self-defense one. Both scenarios begin as follows:

> *X* lives with his wife. In the middle of the night, *X* wakes up and goes to the bathroom at the end of the corridor. When returning to their bedroom, he sees a large man with a huge axe coming ferociously to attack him. *X* thinks that the large man is a robber trying to kill him and his wife. Completely terrified, *X* runs to his workroom, grabs his handgun and shoots the man. The man instantly dies.

The story ends in the real self-defense and hallucinatory self-defense scenarios, respectively, as follows:

> The large man was indeed a robber trying to kill *X1* and his wife. *X1* feels totally justified in defending himself and his wife.

> Suddenly, *X2* sees that the large man was in fact his wife, who got up to see what he was doing. *X2* feels totally confused—he cannot explain such a hallucination. It turns out that his hallucination was the effect of an interaction between two new medicines he had just started to take. This interaction, which was completely unknown by the medical community before this occurrence, causes momentary brain dysfunctions with extremely vivid hallucinations.

We hypothesized that *X1* and *X2* would be completely exculpated—in terms of either a complete justification or a complete excuse (coupled with a justification in the counterfactual world implied by the hallucination).

5.7.3 Sleepwalking without Love versus Sleepwalking with Love (Pair VIII)

The last pair in this section contrasts two sleepwalking homicides—one in a scenario suggesting that there may have been some unconscious motivation to kill, and another in a scenario with no such suggestion. Both scenarios begin by stating that the characters and their wives have been married for ten years. Next, each scenario describes a different relationship state, namely one where love is absent and another where it is present:

> *X1* does not love his wife anymore and is completely bored by their marriage. *X1* would like to see his wife dead, but for moral reasons he would never do anything to hurt her. *X1* has been thinking about asking for a divorce but keeps postponing it.

> They [*X2* and his wife] love each other and their life together has always been warm and joyful.

Both scenarios end with an episode of sleepwalking as follows:

> One night, some hours after they are asleep, X starts to dream that he is hunting deer. X gets up, goes to his workroom, grabs his rifle, returns to their bedroom and shoots his wife. His wife instantly dies. X then goes to the living room and lies on the couch with the rifle by his side. It turns out that X killed his wife while sleepwalking. When he wakes up, X can't remember anything that happened. X had never sleepwalked before.

Because a person has no conscious control over their thoughts and actions while sleepwalking, we hypothesized that both $X1$ and $X2$ would be completely exculpated.

5.7.4 Results and Discussion

Table 5.5 represents the percentage of subjects' ranks (of $X1$ and $X2$) in terms of culpability and liability. Consistent with our general hypothesis, the majority of responses followed an immunitivist/retributivist pattern.

Figure 5.6 shows the results of pair VI. Wilcoxon signed-rank tests indicated that there was a significant difference in culpability judgments ($z = -2.23$, $p < 0.05$, $r = 0.26$), but not in liability judgments ($z = -0.78$, $p > 4.0$ $r = 0.09$).[12] Our hypothesis that a significant number of subjects would not differentiate between these two cases was broadly confirmed. There was no significant difference in liability judgments, and while there was a significant difference in culpability judgments, the

Table 5.5 Percentage of Subjects' Ranks (Combined)

Paired Scenarios	Rank Blame|Punish	Percentage (%)
VI	$X1 = X2 \mid X1 = X2$	**28.5**
($N = 35$)	$X1 > X2 \mid X1 > X2$	**23**
	$X1 < X2 \mid X1 < X2$	**8.5**
	$X1 > X2 \mid X1 = X2$	14
	$X1 = X2 \mid X1 < X2$	14
	$X1 = X2 \mid X1 > X2$	6
	$X1 < X2 \mid X1 = X2$	3
	$X1 < X2 \mid X1 > X2$	3
VII	$X1 = X2 \mid X1 = X2$	**34.5**
($N = 38$)	$X1 > X2 \mid X1 > X2$	**26.5**
	$X1 < X2 \mid X1 < X2$	**2.5**
	$X1 > X2 \mid X1 = X2$	31.5
	$X1 = X2 \mid X1 < X2$	2.5
	$X1 = X2 \mid X1 > X2$	2.5
VIII	$X1 = X2 \mid X1 = X2$	**64**
($N = 39$)	$X1 > X2 \mid X1 > X2$	**15.5**
	$X1 > X2 \mid X1 = X2$	18
	$X1 = X2 \mid X1 > X2$	2.5

Immunitivism/retributivism in bold. © Paulo Sousa and Gary Lavery.

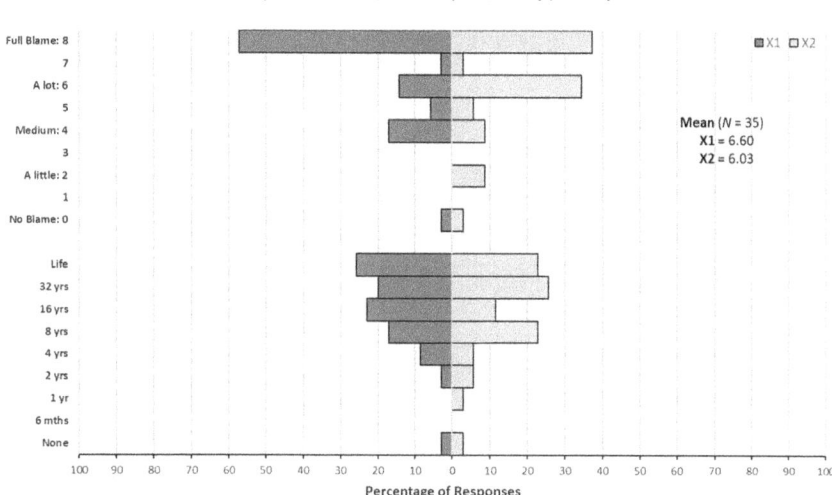

Figure 5.6 Results of pair VI (extreme disturbance versus heat of passion). © Paulo Sousa and Gary Lavery.

effect size was not large. And although Table 5.5 shows that only 28.5 percent of subjects judged *X1* and *X2* as equal in both culpability and liability, it also shows that, in total, about half of the subjects judged them as being equal in culpability (48.5%) or liability (45.5%). Our hypothesis that a significant number of subjects would perceive the two cases as involving a partial defense was also broadly confirmed. Blame means were lower compared to those pertaining to the case of intentional murder with a purpose element of pair I (*X1*: 6.6; *X2*: 6.0 versus *X1*: 7.7). Moreover, there was an apparent reduction in punishment assignment within the intentional murder range (i.e., "32 years" or "life") in comparison to the same case of pair I (*X1*: 46%; *X2*: 48.5% versus *X1*: 62%), indicating that a significant number of subjects judged the homicides as akin to a lesser offense, though not necessarily in the range of voluntary manslaughter (see endnote 7).

Figure 5.7 shows the results of pair VII. Wilcoxon signed-rank tests indicated that there was a significant difference in culpability judgments ($z = -3.88, p < 0.05, r = 0.45$) but not in liability judgments ($z = -1.87, p > 0.05, r = 0.21$). Furthermore, Table 5.5 shows that, in total, 58 percent of the subjects attributed more blame to *X1* than *X2*, while only 29 percent assigned more punishment to *X1* than *X2*. These results indicate a discrepancy between judgments of culpability and liability.

Overall, the liability results support our hypothesis. The majority of subjects assigned "no punishment" to *X2* (71%). Subjects assigned "no punishment" to *X1* to a lesser degree (58%), one possible reason being that situations of self-defense can be interpreted as not wholly justified. For example, some subjects assumed that *X1* had a better alternative: "If *X1* had time to grab a handgun, he had time to call the police." This also explains why 29 percent of subjects assigned more punishment to *X1* than *X2*.

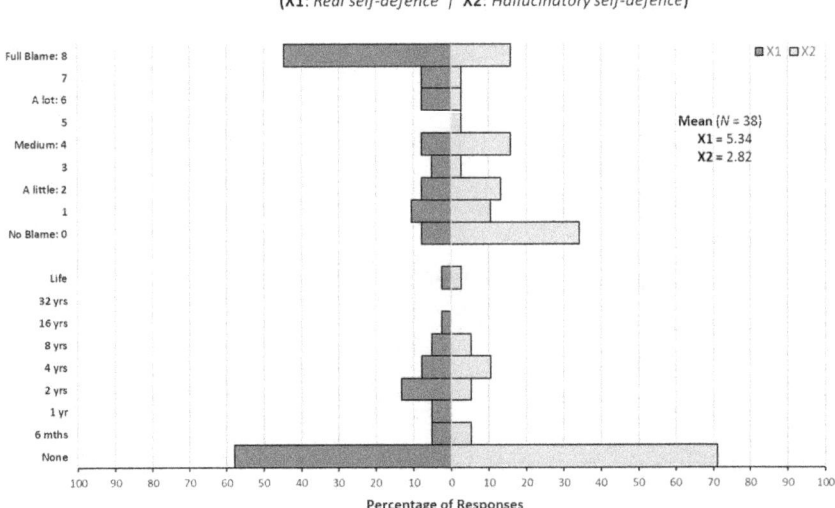

Figure 5.7 Results of pair VII (real self-defense versus hallucinatory self-defense). © Paulo Sousa and Gary Lavery.

Overall, the culpability results seem anomalous: why did so many subjects attribute much more blame to *X1* than *X2*? Because 37 percent of subjects (13) attributed "full blame" to *X1* yet assigned "no punishment" to both *X1* and *X2*, we propose that these subjects interpreted "blame" in terms of either CAUSE or AGENCY rather than CULPABILITY—reasons *qua* justifications are relevant to CULPABILITY, but not to CAUSE or AGENCY, which are purely descriptive concepts. Five of the thirteen subjects seemed to interpret the questions in terms of CAUSE since they attributed "full blame" to both *X1* and *X2*. Thus, these subjects chose "full blame" to indicate that *X1* and *X2* caused the deaths—accordingly, they said: "They both killed them. No one else did it." And eight of the thirteen subjects seemed to interpret the questions in terms of AGENCY since they attributed "full blame" to *X1* but "no blame" to *X2*. As a contrast to *X2*, who was neither aware nor in control of his actions, these subjects chose "full blame" to indicate that *X1* evinced a high degree of agency—accordingly, they said: "*X1* was fully aware of his actions and consequences." This second point also partially explains why many responses followed a non-retributivist pattern (Table 5.5, "*X1* > *X2* | *X1* = *X2*," 31.5%) since the previous eight subjects were among the twelve subjects whose responses evinced this pattern.

Figure 5.8 shows the results of pair VIII. Wilcoxon signed-rank tests indicated that there was a significant difference in culpability and liability judgments ($z = -3.25$, $p < 0.001$, $r = 0.36$ and $z = -2.53$, $p < 0.05$, $r = 0.28$, respectively). While 64 percent of subjects ranked the two characters as equal in blame and punishment, these results do not fully support our hypothesis. More than half of the subjects assigned no punishment to *X1* (54%) and *X2* (56.5%). And if one considers the

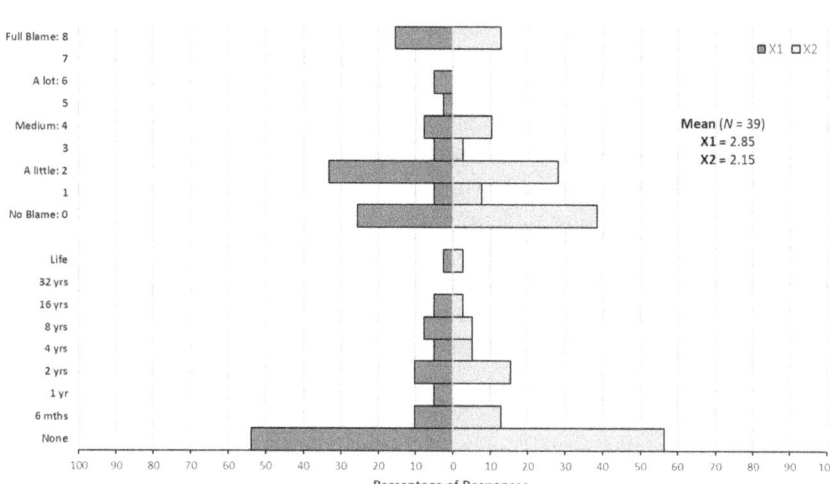

Figure 5.8 Results of pair VIII (sleepwalking without love versus sleepwalking with love). © Paulo Sousa and Gary Lavery.

remaining assignments, there was little difference between *X1* and *X2*. Still, somewhat unexpectedly, many subjects assigned a high level of punishment to both characters—many subjects assigned punishment from "two years" to "sixteen years" (*X1*: 28%; *X2*: 28%). One possibility is that many subjects did not find the sleepwalking scenarios completely believable.

Fewer subjects attributed "no blame" to *X1* (25.5%) and *X2* (38.5%) than we expected, and blame means were also higher than we expected. However, one partial explanation for this relates to the same type of problem identified in the previous pair. Five subjects (13%) attributed full blame to *X1* and *X2*. These same subjects assigned very low or no punishment at all to the characters, suggesting that they interpreted the question in terms of CAUSE rather than CULPABILITY—accordingly, they said: "They caused the death, sleepwalking or not." We assumed that subjects would not differentiate between *X1* and *X2* in culpability, yet they did. In this respect, most subjects emphasized *X2*'s unconscious desires–accordingly, they said: "His state of mind may have influenced the killing subconsciously."

5.8 General Discussion and Conclusion

Overall, our results suggest that ordinary people in the UK are sensitive to distinctions relevant to legal culpability and liability and the classification of different types of homicides in the context of Anglo-American legal traditions. Our results also suggest that people's moral intuitions, as evinced by their judgments of culpability and liability, are commensurable with legal views.

The Anglo-American legal system is broadly constrained by a strong principle of immunitivism (i.e., do not punish the innocent) and retributivism (i.e., punish the guilty according to their degree of culpability). The judgments of the subjects in our research followed a strong immunitivist and retributivist pattern. One limitation here is that our usage of the word "desert" to frame the liability measure ("do they deserve the same amount of punishment?") allows for an alternative interpretation: rather than showing that our subjects endorse immunitivism/retributivism, their response pattern may reveal simply that they possess an immunitivist/retributivist concept of punishment (i.e., that they understand the concept of desert related to deserved punishment in terms of the concept of culpability). However, subjects' justifications of their judgments seem to indicate that they possess this concept of deserved punishment and that they endorse immunitivism/retributivism. Moreover, showing that people possess this immunitivist/retributivist concept of punishment is not a trite result: the type of desert related to punishment is not the same type of desert related to culpability, and it might have been understood in terms of the concept of wrongdoing simply rather than the concept of culpability (for a detailed discussion, see Zimmerman, 1988, Chapter 5).

The Anglo-American legal concepts of culpability and liability are embedded in a complex structure of offenses, framed by a schema of offense elements related to mental states (purpose, knowledge, recklessness, and negligence), and in a complex structure of defenses, framed by justifications and excuses (complete or partial). The judgments of the subjects in our research were compatible with the different degrees of culpability implied by the legal schema, even deemphasizing what the legal system frequently deemphasizes, such as the difference in culpability implied by the MPC distinction between the purpose and knowledge offense elements. Their judgments also took defenses into account, even in a qualified, partial way, as when, in the emotional-disturbance and heat-of-passion scenarios, the assigned punishment was reduced to a range below that of intentional murder. Granted, there is no unified legal view on many of the issues we discussed in this chapter. Nonetheless, our results also suggest that the variability in legal views is often accompanied by a related variability in subjects' judgments—for example, the different legal views on the relevance of the distinction between recklessness and negligence were somewhat mirrored in their judgments.

Of course, our claims must be taken with caution. Our samples were small and included only university students. Additional research with a larger and more representative sample is needed to ascertain whether our results generalize to other societal sectors. Moreover, we probed each type of issue by using one or two situations of homicide. Additional research with a broader range of stimuli is required to determine whether our results generalize to different homicide situations. Turning to the other side of the comparison, our claims are also limited by those aspects of the legal system that we selected to contrast with lay moral intuitions. For example, we included only cases of "expressed and implied malice murder," thus leaving aside cases of "constructive malice murder" (e.g., felony murder), where consequentialist aspects of the legal system play a more fundamental role. Hence, it is probable that people's moral intuitions and legal views diverge much more about such types of homicides (e.g., see Robinson & Darley, 1995, pp. 169–80) or other liability aspects of the legal system that are more constrained by consequentialist concerns. More broadly, we are not claiming that a notion of just deserts always constrains legal systems or that lay moral intuitions will always accord, to some extent, with legal views—in brutish dictatorships, for instance, the compatibility between lay moral intuitions and legal views may collapse completely.

We conclude by retaking a recurrent theme in this chapter and a related claim we made in the introduction. Throughout the chapter, we discussed aspects of the complex mapping between language and concepts in the context of our topic (e.g., when discussing the polysemy of "blame" and "responsibility" or of "acting intentionally"). And we claimed that one should adopt a fine-grained approach to this mapping to make progress in the areas of moral psychology and Xjur, both theoretically and methodologically. We have argued elsewhere that much of the empirical literature on judgments of responsibility or blame is unintelligible because the rich polysemy of "responsibility" and "blame" is either underestimated or handled inappropriately (Sousa, 2005, 2009). We have also argued that, to thoroughly explain Knobe Effects in judgments of intentional action (Knobe, 2003a, 2003b) and clearly envisage their legal implications, one needs to bring the polysemy of "acting intentionally" into the picture (Sousa & Holbrook, 2010). Here, we indicate two simple aspects of our results that highlight the importance of pursuing a fine-grained approach.

In the absence of such an approach, how should one interpret those subjects, in the real self-defense scenario (see Figure 5.7), who attributed "full blame" and assigned "no punishment"? Did these subjects attribute a high degree of culpability for the death of a human being yet think that the culprit did not deserve punishment? Is there a significant minority that departs entirely from the legal view? Although some people are quite willing to forgive or are so pacifist that they abhor any type of punishment, subjects' "no punishment" explanations were not consistent with these possibilities. Hence, the foregoing response pattern is, theoretically speaking, puzzling. Nevertheless, if one considers that "blame" can also express CAUSE or AGENCY, a solution to the puzzle ensues.

In the study of moral judgments, subjects are asked to make specific judgments (at the researcher's discretion). To operationalize the culpability question, we employed the expression "place the blame" with the aim that this would activate the concept CULPABILITY. However, as our solution to the earlier puzzle indicates, this was not always the case. Can one improve the formulation of the question so that it more reliably activates the moral concepts and related judgments one wants to study? We propose that this can be achieved only by developing a fine-grained approach to the mapping between language and concepts.

Acknowledgement

Corresponding author: paulo.sousa@qub.ac.uk. We want to thank Karolina Prochownik, Stefan Magen, and an anonymous reviewer for their comments and suggestions. The research reported here was supported by *The British Academy* (grant number: SG-51501).

Notes

1 Most subjects in the studies reported herein were from the UK, though we shall introduce similar research with US subjects.

2 These parts are traditionally described by the distinction between actus reus and mens rea. We avoid this distinction because it is confusing: leaving aside the fact that mens rea is often used in a broader sense that also includes mental states related only to defenses, the distinction dissolves at too many points (see Robinson, 2002). For example, a general principle of the actus reus is that it involves voluntary bodily movements; hence, a property related to mental states (i.e., voluntariness) is deemed fundamental to the actus reus. However, we do not presume that our reframing of this distinction solves all its problems.

3 Note, however, that excuses have force only when the person is deemed not culpable for the abnormal disability or factor leading to the excusing condition.

4 This and more extreme cases of automatism, such as acts occurring during an epileptic seizure, are often interpreted as violations of the general principle of the actus reus mentioned earlier (see footnote 2).

5 The reader should keep in mind that our liability schema is a simplification and somewhat arbitrary since our main purpose is to establish an anchor to discuss the results of our research. The United States attaches minimum sentences for first-degree murder and second-degree murder (with much variability across states), and the trial judge determines the exact sentence according to certain mitigating or aggravating factors (in certain US states, the sentence may be the death penalty). In the UK, which has neither degrees of murder nor the death penalty, a life sentence is mandatory for murder. However, the culprit may be released "on license" after a certain period, no less than the minimum term set by the trial judge, which again depends on certain mitigating or aggravating factors (see Criminal Justice Act 2003). We characterize our liability ranges as intersecting between crime categories because these mitigating and aggravating factors can make a critical difference.

6 This partial defense may be formulated as a failure of proof defense or as an offense modification defense, a distinction that we leave aside (see Robinson, 1982). For those not acquainted with the legal system, the general issue here is whether a successful defense denies an element of the offense definition, in which case the person is deemed not to have committed the crime at all (and hence is not culpable/liable for it), or whether it brings into the picture an exculpating factor independent of the offense definition, in which case the person is deemed to have committed the crime, but is not culpable/liable for it (i.e., there is "facial" but no "actual" liability).

7 It is important to point out an intricacy we left aside in our characterization of *intentional murder*, which springs from its connection to voluntary manslaughter and partial defenses: the liability of cases of intentional murder not reduced to voluntary manslaughter because the partial defense was not completely satisfied may still be reduced to second-degree murder (i.e., to a range from sixteen years to thirty-two years in prison). This corresponds to a category of second-degree murder distinct from depraved-mind murder: *second-degree intentional murder.*

8 A more detailed description of the design and materials of the survey, including its overall data and the data reported in this chapter, can be found on the OSF page of this project: https://osf.io/cvmwk/.

9 In the description of the paired scenarios here and in the following, we replaced the original proper names of the main characters of each scenario with "*X*" (to refer to the

main character of either scenario) or with "*X1*" (to refer to the main character of the first scenario) or with "*X2*" (to refer to the main character of the second scenario).

10 To keep with the legal concept of result (as distinct from act), our discussion thus far has been phrased mainly in terms of the language of causal descriptions (e.g., "to *cause the death* of a human being") rather than the language of action descriptions (e.g., "to *kill* a human being"). We now use both phrasings in our discussion, treating them, for our purposes here, as roughly equivalent (cf. Fodor, 1970).

11 Rather than reporting the correlations between culpability and liability judgments for *X1* and *X2*, we report the data in this way because it provides more information relating to our current discussion and because, arguably, it can disentangle different immunitivist/retributivist response patterns. Of course, our reporting method is not infallible since the "*X1* = *X2*|*X1* = *X2*" pattern may involve responses that are non-retributivist. For example, if a subject attributes full blame to *X1* and *X2* and assigns no punishment to them, this may not correspond to a retributivist pattern (we use "may" here because it remains a possibility that this subject would assign some type of punishment, other than prison time). However, only a minority of the subjects evinced this type of response in our data. Later, we argue that this type of response indicates that the subject interpreted the blame question in terms of CAUSE or AGENCY, rather than CULPABILITY. Overall, there was a strong correlation between judgments of culpability and liability in our data (rho = 0.609, $p < 0.001$, $N = 600$). And of the forty-seven "no blame" attributions (to *X1* or *X2*), thirty-seven (79%) indicated immunitivism (i.e., assigned no punishment).

12 The variable *gender* did not contribute to any differences in the results here.

References

Appiah, K. A. (2011). *The honor code: How moral revolutions happen.* New York: WW Norton & Company.

Dubber, M. D. (2015). *An introduction to the model penal code.* New York: Oxford University Press.

Fodor, J. A. (1970). Three reasons for not deriving "kill" from "cause to die." *Linguistic Inquiry, 1*(4), 429–38.

Goodwin, G. P., & Gromet, D. M. (2014). Punishment. *WIREs Cognitive Science, 5,* 561–72.

Horder, J. (1992). *Provocation and responsibility.* Oxford: Clarendon Press.

Horder, J. (2007). *Homicide law in comparative perspective.* Oxford: Hart.

Kirschner, S., & Galperin, G. (2002). The defense of extreme emotional disturbance in New York County: Pleas and outcomes. *Behavioral Sciences and the Law, 20,* 47–50.

Kneer, M., & Bourgeois-Gironde, S. (2017). Mens rea ascription, expertise and outcome effects: Professional judges surveyed. *Cognition, 169,* 139–46.

Knobe, J. (2003a). Intentional action in folk psychology: An experimental investigation. *Philosophical Psychology, 16,* 309–24.

Knobe, J. (2003b). Intentional action and side-effects in ordinary language. *Analysis, 63,* 190–3.

Knobe, J. (2016). Experimental philosophy is cognitive science. In J. Sytsma & W. Buckwalter (Eds.), *A companion to experimental philosophy* (pp. 37–52). Malden: Wiley Blackwell.

LaFave, W. R. & Scott, A. W. (1986). *Substantive criminal law* (Vols. 1 and 2). St. Paul: West Publishing Co.

Laurence, S., & Margolis, E. (1999). *Concepts and cognitive science*. Cambridge, MA: The MIT Press.

Mackay, R. D. & Mitchell, B. J. (2003). Provoking diminished responsibility: Two pleas merging into one? *Criminal Law Review,* (November), 745–59.

Malle, B. F., Guglielmo, S., & Monroe, A. E. (2014). A theory of blame. *Psychological Inquiry, 25*(2), 147–86.

Margolis, E., & Laurence, S. (2015). *The conceptual mind—New directions in the study of concepts*. Cambridge, MA: The MIT Press.

Mercier, H., & Sperber, D. (2017). *The enigma of reason*. Harvard University Press.

Mikhail, J. (2009). Is the prohibition of homicide universal-evidence from comparative criminal law. *Brooklyn Law Review, 75*, 497–515.

Prochownik, K. M. (2021). The experimental philosophy of law: New ways, old questions, and how not to get lost. *Philosophy Compass, 16*(12), e12791.

Robinson, P. H. (1980). A brief history of distinctions in criminal culpability. *Hastings Law Journal, 31*, 815.

Robinson, P. H. (1982). Criminal law defenses: A systematic analysis. *Columbia Law Review, 82*(2), 199–291.

Robinson, P. H. (1984). *Criminal Law Defenses (Volumes 1 and 2)*. St. Paul: West Publishing CO.

Robinson, P. H. (2001). Mens rea. In J. Dressler (Ed.), *Encyclopaedia of crime & justice* (pp. 995–1006). Macmillan Library Reference.

Robinson, P. H., & Darley, J. M. (1995). *Justice, liability, and blame: Community views and the criminal law*. Boulder: Westview Press.

Robinson, P. H., & Grall, J. A. (1983). Element analysis in defining criminal liability: The model penal code and beyond. *Stanford Law Review, 35*, 681–762.

Sommers, R. (2021). Experimental jurisprudence. *Science, 373*(6553), 394–5.

Sousa, P. (2005). *The American folk concept of moral fault-responsibility—an exploration* (Unpublished doctoral dissertation). The University of Michigan.

Sousa, P. (2009). A cognitive approach to moral responsibility: The case of a failed attempt to kill. *Journal of Cognition and Culture, 9*(3–4), 171–94.

Sousa, P., & Holbrook, C. (2010). Folk concepts of intentional action in the contexts of amoral and immoral luck. *Review of Philosophy and Psychology, 1*(3), 351–70.

Sousa, P., Holbrook, C., & Swiney, L. (2015). Moral asymmetries in judgments of agency withstand ludicrous causal deviance. *Frontiers in Psychology, 6*: 1380.

Sousa, P., & Swiney, L. (2016). Intentionality, morality, and the incest taboo in Madagascar. *Frontiers in psychology, 7*, 494.

Stewart, F. H. (1994). *Honor*. Chicago: University of Chicago Press.

Tobia, K. (2018). How people judge what is reasonable. *Alabama Law Review, 70*, 293–359.

Tobia, K. P. (in press). Experimental jurisprudence. *University of Chicago Law Review, 89*(3), 735–802.

Vicente, A., & Manrique, F. M. (2016). The big concepts paper: A defence of hybridism. *The British Journal for the Philosophy of Science, 67*(1), 59–88.

Wilson, W. (2017). *Criminal law*. London: Pearson.

Zimmerman, M. J. (1988). *An essay on moral responsibility*. Totowa: Rowman & Littlefield.

Zimmerman, M. J. (2011). *The immorality of punishment*. Peterborough: Broadview Press.

Causation and the Silly Norm Effect

Levin Güver and Markus Kneer

6.1 Introduction

6.1.1 The Correspondence Assumption

Whereas in certain domains, the law relies on terms of art (e.g., "injunction," "double jeopardy," "punitive damages," and "bankruptcy"), in others—in particular in criminal law—it invokes, or takes itself to invoke, the plain everyday meaning of the expressions used. This is unsurprising: citizens, standardly not equipped with a law degree, must understand what the law says in order to adhere to it. Furthermore, in common-law jurisdictions, non-experts help decide court cases in jury trials. And when it comes to disputes in statutory interpretation among judges, turning to ordinary meaning is one, if not—as some scholars and practitioners argue[1]—*the* evident strategy to resolve them.[2]

According to what we term the correspondence assumption, certain central legal expressions are taken to refer to the same concepts as their corresponding ordinary language analogues (at least within designated spheres of the law). Candidate concepts for the correspondence assumption are plentiful. *Consent* is one. At a recent sexual misconduct trial in the United States, the judge refused to provide conceptual classification and stated that "the jury will decide what consent means to them" (Puente, Sloan, & Deerwester, 2018; for empirical work on the notion of consent, see Sommers, 2020). The expression "reasonable" and the concept it denotes constitute another example. As Gardner (2015) writes, the reasonable person standard "exists to allow the law *to pass the buck*, to help itself *pro tempore* to standards of justification that are not themselves set by the law" (p. 36). Naturally, for a maneuver of this sort to even begin to make sense, it must be assumed that the lay person's concept of reasonableness fits the law's demands.[3]

In many jurisdictions, the central mens rea concepts, such as intention, are subject to the correspondence assumption—which is perhaps one of the key reasons why, very frequently, they are left partially or entirely uncodified.[4] The English courts have made this explicit stating that "the legal meaning of the word 'intention' is the ordinary meaning of the word" (Herring, 2012, p. 135). In *R v. Moloney* [1985], Lord Bridge put it as follows:

The golden rule should be that, when directing a jury on the mental element necessary in a crime of specific intent, the *judge should avoid any elaboration or paraphrase of what is meant by intent, and leave it to the jury's good sense to decide whether the accused acted with the necessary intent,* unless the judge is convinced that, on the facts and having regard to the way the case has been presented to the jury in evidence and argument, some further explanation or elaboration is strictly necessary to avoid misunderstanding.[5]

Indeed, the courts have been very reluctant to provide the jury with further directions on intention, doing so only in "very rare"[6] or "very exceptional"[7] cases.[8]

6.1.2 Correspondence Trouble

Where correspondence is assumed, a complication can arise: although the law takes a certain legal expression *E* to mirror ordinary language, its application in daily life differs from what the law presumes. The divergence can be due to one of two reasons: misalignment in *application only* or misalignment in *semantics*. In the former case, the assumption of correspondence holds good in so far as the legal expression *E* and its ordinary language equivalent are semantically on a par—they mean the same. However, the application of the ordinary language expression sometimes differs radically from what the law assumes due to either pragmatics or bias.[9] Consider the expression "intention" and its cognates, for which English law assumes correspondence. Problematically, lay attribution of intentionality is sensitive to outcome valence (good v. bad, the Knobe Effect)[10] and outcome severity (the Severity Effect).[11] The Knobe Effect threatens to undermine a meaningful distinction between the mentes reae knowledge and intention for bad outcomes.[12] Both the Knobe Effect and the Severity Effect put pressure on the conceptual and procedural independence of actus reus and mens rea, since features of the former (outcome valence or severity) influence the attribution of the latter. Importantly, the problem is not limited to the judgments of lay juries. Legal professionals, including judges, also manifest the Knobe Effect[13] and the Severity Effect[14] for intentionality attributions. Differently put, even if the folk (as well as experts) would reflectively endorse certain implicit and explicit constraints the law imposes on the concept of intention (such as the possibility of a hard distinction between knowingly and intentionally committing a crime), its standard *application* can still be inconsistent with these assumptions.

The *second* complication that can arise with respect to the correspondence assumption runs deeper than the first. It goes beyond application, pragmatics, and potential bias and instead regards the very semantics of the expression at stake. In such a case the folk expression *E* does not actually mean what the law takes it to mean, and this explains why folk applications of the concept designated by *E* defy legal expectations. Differently put, the folk use or application might be perfectly adequate—what are off are the legal hypotheses as to what the folk concept *E* and its apparently corresponding legal equivalent actually mean. The aforementioned concept of reasonableness is a good example, since it might defy legal expectations in two orthogonal ways: *normativity* and *outcome dependence*.[15]

There is an extensive debate among legal scholars as to whether "reasonable" is best understood as a *descriptive* expression (such that what is reasonable is what the *ordinary* person would do), a prescriptive or normative expression (such that what is reasonable is what the *responsible, prudent,* or perhaps somewhat *ideal* citizen would do), or possibly a *hybrid* expression (or what philosophers refer to as a "thick" expression, having both descriptive and normative components).[16] Despite outsourcing the meaning of the expression to the folk, the law *does* speculate about, and thus constrain, what it can mean. Consider, for instance, the staggering variety of explanations of the reasonable person standard for negligence across jury instructions in US sates. Some of those are more in tune with a descriptive standard (focusing on "ordinary" conduct, such as Texas), and others—explicated in terms of the "reasonably careful" person (e.g., Illinois or Florida)—suggest a normative standard.[17] As Tobia's (2018) empirical work shows, however, the folk concept of *reasonable* seems to be hybrid. If so, its semantics is inconsistent with legal constraints that explicate it in purely descriptive or purely normative terms.

Perhaps an even more glaring divergence arises as regards the law's insistence on the outcome independence of what is reasonable. In evaluating criminal negligence, we must consider the defendant's conduct in light of "the circumstances known to him [or her]" so as to assess whether his or her conduct "involves a gross deviation from the standard of care that a reasonable person would observe *in the actor's situation.*"[18] What matters are the agent's epistemic circumstances ex ante, not what one might come to learn about the action's consequences ex post.[19] The folk concept of reasonableness, however, seems to be strongly sensitive to outcome information: decisions and actions undertaken from the same epistemic point of view are judged more or less reasonable depending on whether the outcome is good or bad. This is not just a matter of a possibly biased, outcome-sensitive *application* of the expression "reasonable." Even when the effect of the hindsight bias is corrected for, the folk seem to insist that outcome information matters to judgments of reasonableness (see the findings in Kneer, 2021).

6.1.3 The Correspondence Assumption with Respect to Causation

So far, we have explained what we call the correspondence assumption, provided a few examples, and examined two distinct types of problems that can arise in the wake of assumptions of this sort. With the basic conceptual framework in place, we will now turn to the concept of causation, which constitutes the topic proper of this chapter. Here too, we take it that there are at least decent grounds to hold that the correspondence assumption is in place for certain jurisdictions.

Causation lies at the heart of both tort law and criminal law. The actus reus (the "guilty act") is one of the two central requirements for criminal culpability besides mens rea (the "guilty mind"). In the rather rare cases of strict liability, the actus reus by itself can suffice. There's considerable evidence that common-law jurisdictions, which overwhelmingly task lay juries with the process of determining causation, endorse the correspondence assumption (see Summers, 2018). Hart and Honoré's (1959) contention that the legal notion of causation should be that of the "plain man" (p. 1) has been echoed many times by British and American courts. In a landmark English case, Lord Wright argued that "[c]ausation is to be understood as the man in the street, and not as the scientist or the metaphysician, would understand it."[20] A Scottish court under Lord Thomson highlighted that they would rather follow "the practical experience of the reasonable man" than "the theoretical speculations of the philosopher."[21] The US Supreme Court, in the much-cited *Burrage v. United States*, stated that courts should rely on "the common understanding of causation" and explicate causal relations with reference to what it "is natural to say."[22] It thus comes as no surprise that Knobe and Shapiro's (2021) analysis of a multitude of US cases concludes that "judges who invoke the doctrine of proximate causation [. . .] are doing what the rules tell them to do, namely, to engage in *ordinary causal reasoning*" (p. 235, emphasis added).[23]

Assumed correspondence between a certain legal concept and its folk analogue does not mean that the law defers to the folk, whatever their concept might be. Even when explicit definitions are lacking, partial clarifications (e.g., in the case of "reasonable" discussed earlier) or legal procedure constrain the concept of interest and its application. A question of fundamental importance is thus whether a particular folk concept *C*, to which the law wants to avail itself, is broadly consistent with the constraints it takes to govern said concept. To make some progress in this regard as concerns the concept of causation, we will proceed as follows: in Section 6.2, we examine the legal notion of causation in the United States. Section 6.3 surveys several accounts of the folk notion of causation and discusses ways in which they could correspond with the American legal analogue (or at least certain scholarly interpretations thereof). In the remainder of the chapter, we report a series of studies that casts doubt on the suggestion that the law should invoke the "ordinary man's" concept of causation.

6.2 Causation in the Law

Common-law jurisdictions have converged on a two-layer model of causation for both criminal law and the law of torts, distinguishing between factual cause and legal cause. In a first step, the courts determine whether the action in question was the factual cause of the outcome. A factual cause is determined by employing the *but-for* test: an action is deemed the cause of an event *X* if, *but-for* the action, *X* would not have come about. Simply put, if *X* is a factual cause of consequence *Y*, *X* is a necessary condition for *Y*'s occurrence.[24] Factual causation is, however, unable to capture all constellations with which the courts are confronted in their day-to-day activities.[25] It is thus in a second step—that of *legal causation*—that the courts distinguish legally *relevant* causal factors from irrelevant ones, reducing the extensive class of factual causes to those that are of import for the determination of legal responsibility.

There is no "clear [and] crisp definition" (Moore, 2019, Section 6.2.3) of proximate causation in the United States, though we can sort the multitude of formulas employed by the courts into two overarching clusters. The first takes proximate causation to be a reflection of *actual* causal relations *in the world*, whereas the second cluster employs "policy-based" (Posner, 1986, p. 181) tests, that is, tests that take normative factors, such as considerations of justice and social interests, into account (see Moore, 2019, Section 6.5.3). A prominent example of the former cluster is the test of *directness* and an example of the latter is the test of *reasonable foreseeability*.[26]

According to the test of directness, proximate causation is established if the causal connection between an action and outcome is sufficiently direct and there is no intervening factual cause that supersedes the defendant's action (i.e., there is no further cause that stands between the defendant's action and the harmful outcome).[27] Consider the following example: in a moment of inattentiveness, *A* swings her golf club and hits *B* in the face, breaking his nose. *B* requires medical attention. On his way to the hospital, *B* is hit by a bolt of lightning and dies instantly. Is *A*'s action the proximate cause of *B*'s death? Undeniably, her action was a factual cause: had *A* not hit *B* in the face, *B* would not have been struck by lightning on his way to the hospital. Nevertheless, the lightning supersedes *A*'s doing, it severs the causal chain between the injury and the death. If, on the other hand, we were to modify the example so that *A*'s golf swing kills *B* on the spot, the causal relation would be sufficiently *direct* to consider *A* the proximate cause of *B*'s death.

In applying the test of foreseeability, courts probe whether the defendant could, at the time of her action, have reasonably foreseen the resulting harm.[28] The underlying rationale is that it is unfair to hold someone legally accountable for an unforeseeable outcome, as this would largely constitute an instance of bad luck. Since what is *reasonably* foreseeable may be subject to a wide range of value judgments (for reasonableness, see the references in Section 6.1.2), the test of foreseeability can plausibly be taken to carry normative import. To illustrate, consider the following situation: *A* is speeding past a busy town square, just ahead of which *B* is crossing the road. *A*, who is unable to react in time, collides with and fatally injures *B*. Given that *A* could, at the time of driving, have reasonably foreseen that speeding past a well-frequented area is a recipe for disaster, her doing is regarded the proximate cause of *B*'s death. However, if *A* is not speeding but instead driving attentively, and *B*—in an unpredictable manner—runs onto the road, the legal assessment would change: the accident is not judged reasonably foreseeable, and *A* is absolved of legal liability.[29]

There is a long-standing legal dispute concerning proximate causation in the law.[30] Two camps can be distinguished. Legal formalists treat proximate causation as a descriptive enterprise. On their view, causation is taken to be something in the world, and when the courts select a proximate cause, they simply single out a special class of factual causes that are sufficient in causal strength to be considered *the* legal cause of a certain outcome.[31] Legal realists disagree. They claim that when the courts speak of proximate causation, they do not take themselves to be pointing out a state of affairs in the world. Instead, courts employ the veiling language of proximate causation to make normative ascriptions of responsibility—judgments that are based to a considerable extent on moral and policy considerations.[32]

The dispute itself has a descriptive and a prescriptive dimension. On the one hand, it concerns the question as to *what the courts are really doing*, or the *practice* of the law. What are the psychological mechanisms by virtue of which judges come to reach a verdict? Formalists contend that it is *via* the deductive application of certain rules and tests (Schauer, 1988), examples of which we have already seen. According to legal

		Practice	
		Descriptive	**Normative**
Nature	**Descriptive**	Formalism	Weak realism
	Normative	–	Strong realism

Figure 6.1 Formalism and Realism.

realists, however, judges construe the causal query as "post hoc justification for the moral judgment [they have] already made" (Knobe & Shapiro, 2021, p. 171), deciding ultimately "with their sense of justice and social utility" (p. 176).[33] On the other hand, there is disagreement as to how courts *ought* to assess proximate causation or what the *nature* of the law demands. Should the law exclusively rely on judgments free of normative considerations to establish proximate causation? Or do such normative factors have their proper place in such decisions?

The positions discussed can be plotted in a matrix distinguishing what the courts should do according to the nature of the law, and what they actually do in practice. Formalists will contend that proximate causation is descriptive in both nature and practice; *weak* realists argue that there is a mismatch between descriptive doctrine and normative legal reality, while *strong* realists take proximate causation to be rightfully normative in both nature and practice (see Figure 6.1).[34]

Let's take stock. Causation is commonly assessed in two layers. The first layer, that of *factual* causation, refers to an entirely descriptive, counterfactual notion of causation. The second layer—that of proximate causation—is established through a multitude of tests, of which we have exemplarily assessed the test of directness and that of foreseeability in the context of both criminal and tortious liability. We then briefly reconstructed the long-standing debate between legal formalists and legal realists along two dimensions—those of proximate causation's nature and practice—and distinguished three distinct positions, that is, formalism, weak realism, and strong realism.

Interestingly, however, this dichotomy between descriptive and normative theories of causation is not limited to the legal sphere and extends to the psychological literature. Given that courts tend to postulate correspondence between the legal and the folk concepts of causation, we will turn to the psychological literature next.

6.3 Theories of the Folk Concepts of Causation

6.3.1 The Norm Effect

We have argued that there is evidence that in common-law jurisdictions like the United States and the United Kingdom, a correspondence assumption is in place for causation. For correspondence to hold, the folk concept must be consistent with the constraints the law imposes on the legal concept of causation. Having briefly sketched how causation is established in the law in the previous section, we will turn to recent empirical work on the folk concept of causation. More precisely, we will focus on one aspect of this large body of work, according to which perceived causation is sensitive to salient norm violations (the *norm effect*).[35]

Consider the following situation (henceforth *Rollerblading*), which is based on a Swiss Federal Court case:[36] Mark is rollerblading on a footpath, and Lauren is walking ahead of him. Suddenly, a cat jumps out of the brush. In an attempt to evade it, Lauren steps into the lane of Mark. Mark crashes into Lauren. Who or what caused the accident? It seems natural to deem the cat as the cause of the accident. This intuition is consistent with recent findings concerning *normality* in the ascription of causation, highlighting that people tend to elevate the causal contribution of *abnormal* events— here, the suddenly appearing cat—in jointly causal structures.[37]

Now consider a variation of the scenario, in which everything is held fixed, except that it is legally *prohibited* to skate on the footpath. This is an example of an injunctive norm, as it expresses not what typically happens (a statistical norm), but what *ought* or *ought not to* be done. Despite the prohibition, Mark is rollerblading on the same footpath that Lauren is walking on. Lauren sidesteps the cat, walks into Mark's lane and the two collide. Who caused the accident? In this case, our response might differ from the original case, or so a series of empirical studies on the folk concept of causation suggests.[38] When two agents—one of them in violation of an injunctive norm—jointly bring about an outcome, the norm-violating agent is deemed more causal. This effect, standardly known as the norm effect, extends to scenarios where an outcome is brought about by a single agent, once in a norm-conforming and once in a norm-violating manner (Livengood, Sytsma, & Rose, 2017; Sytsma, Livengood, & Rose, 2012).

6.3.2 The Folk Concept of Causation

6.3.2.1 *The Counterfactual and the Pragmatic View*

There are at least four families of accounts in the literature, which purport to explain the norm effect, the first of which is known as the Counterfactual View. According to its proponents, norm violations—be they of the prescriptive or descriptive kind— motivate people to reason about counterfactual scenarios in which the agent adhered to the norm in question.[39] For Hitchcock and Knobe (2009), this is mainly the case for *abnormal* causes, which give rise to this kind of counterfactual reasoning to a significantly higher degree than normal causes. Such counterfactual reasoning, they hold, renders the abnormal factor more salient, and thus increases perceived causal contribution.

Proponents of the Pragmatic View, by contrast, hold that the locution "*A* caused *B*" can be read in one of two ways (Samland & Waldmann, 2014, 2015, 2016). Under the narrow reading, it refers to the descriptive causal processes linking events *A* and *B*. Under the broad reading, it refers to an assessment of *accountability*, a notion which extends beyond the descriptive into the normative realm. Judgments of causation in this sense are sensitive to considerations like the agent's foresight of the outcome, their desire to bring it about, and of course also norms and whether the agent was aware of them (see Samland & Waldman, 2016, p. 165). Different contexts trigger different uses of "cause" which is, according to the Pragmatic View, what explains the norm effect.

6.3.2.2 *The Bias View and the Responsibility View*

In this chapter, we will not have much to say about the Counterfactual and Pragmatic Views. We'll predominantly focus on the Bias View and the Responsibility View, whose import for legal causation is (perhaps) clearer and more pronounced. On the Bias View (by and large Alicke's Culpable Control Model), ordinary people have a descriptive *concept* of causation, yet in *attributing* causation they fall victim to a pervasive bias (Alicke, 1992, 2000; see also Lagnado & Channon, 2008). When an agent breaks a norm, people blame her for doing so. In an implicit act of backward rationalization, their desire to blame the norm-violating agent triggers attributions of causality, even though people would agree in reflective judgment that causation does not depend on normative factors (see also Rose, 2017, p. 1327). This effect is not limited to the violation of norms. Rather, any factor that is able to elicit a desire to blame the agent— such as an agent's bad general character, wicked motives, race, gender, status, and ideology—can have downstream consequences and distort laypeople's attribution of causation.[40] Common to these factors is that people view the agent in a negative light and then project factors that justify their desire to blame them post hoc (Alicke, Rose, & Bloom, 2011, p. 670).

Take the following schematic illustration of the Bias View (Figure 6.2a): there are factors that affect blame independently of causation—whether appropriately so (e.g., mens rea—solid black arrow) or not (e.g., race, gender, and status—dashed black arrow). Furthermore, there are descriptive factors pertinent to causation (e.g., how directly the agent was involved in bringing about the outcome) that do and should affect causation, and therefore blame (solid gray arrows). There is, however, also a variety of factors that affect causation *via* blame (dashed black arrow). Although they should *not* matter for causation, an increase in perceived blame is inadequately justified post hoc by means of an increase of the ascribed causal contribution of the agent. Note that on this view, there are two ways the bias can arise: naturally, factors that inappropriately influence blame might distort perceived causation (dashed black paths). However, factors that appropriately influence blame (e.g., mens rea), yet that are conceptually independent from causation proper, might too (solid black and dashed black paths). Whereas in such a case "blame amateurs," as Alicke calls them, get it wrong only once, in the former case, they get it wrong twice (Alicke, 2008, p. 179).

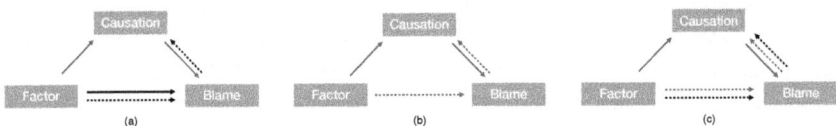

Figure 6.2 Schematic illustrations of the Bias View (6.2a), the Anything-Goes View (6.2b), and the Responsibility View (6.2c). © Levin Güver and Markus Kneer.

The Responsibility View, by contrast, holds that the influence of norms on causal judgment is not a *bug* but a *feature* (Livengood, Sytsma, & Rose, 2017, p. 284). The folk are not systematically biased in the application of a descriptive concept of causation—rather, the ordinary concept of causation is inherently normative.[41] The meaning of "X caused Y" is, in Sytsma's (2022) terminology, "quite similar" to "X is *responsible* for Y" (p. 6). Responsibility, in turn, is taken to encompass "broadly *moral* evaluations" (Sytsma, 2020, p. 21), though the notion is not further specified. Perceived responsibility can be increased not only through norm violations but also due to factors relevant to the mental state of the agent, such as her *foresight* or *desire* of the outcome (see Sytsma, 2019 and for interested related findings, Kirfel & Lagnado, 2021).

When we attempt to schematize the Responsibility View, it is not entirely clear what, exactly, it entails. The most permissive extrapolation of causal and moral responsibility being "quite similar" is that *any* factor that affects the one, can (though need not necessarily) affect the other (Figure 6.2b). Uncontroversially, descriptive features that affect causation can have an impact on blame (solid gray arrows). On a maximally permissive account, the folk concept of causation would be such that *any* factor that has an impact on *perceived* blameworthiness can have an impact on causation (dashed gray arrows). This *Anything-Goes View*—primarily discussed for didactic reasons here—is surely not what Sytsma and Livengood have in mind. True, the view makes room, for instance, for norm infractions to influence blame and therefore perceived causation, a point Sytsma defends at length. But it overgenerates: if an agent's gender impacts perceived blame in misogynistic ways, then—on this view—it would be fine to wind up with a difference in causal attribution across gender. An account of this sort, needless to say, cannot helpfully be contrasted with the Bias View, since it rules out the possibility of bias from the get-go.

What, exactly, is Sytsma's view? Following Alicke, Sytsma acknowledges the distinction between features that are "peripheral" to moral responsibility—such as, for example, "the actor's or victim's race and character" (Alicke, Rose, & Bloom, 2011, p. 674)—and those that are not (Sytsma, 2019, p. 4, 2022, pp. 11–12). Differently put, Sytsma agrees with Alicke that there are factors that *appropriately* influence moral responsibility and blame and those that do so *inappropriately*. But once *actual moral responsibility* and *perceived moral responsibility* can come apart (in contrast to the Anything-Goes View), the possibility of bias is back, and the differences between the two accounts of causation can be stated clearly. On the Responsibility View, we take the following to hold good (Figure 6.2c): uncontroversially, factors that have a direct influence on causation can have downstream normative consequences on blame (solid gray arrows). However—and this is the distinguishing feature of the account—factors that *appropriately* influence blame can also have an appropriate impact on perceived causation (dashed gray arrows). Differently put, certain factors, such as salient norms, that prima facie have no clear connection to causation can impact it nonetheless in virtue of their justified impact on perceived moral responsibility or blame. However—and this prevents the account from collapsing into an unpalatable Anything-Goes View—not just any factor that has an influence on perceived blame has a *valid* impact on causation: factors—like, for example, race, gender, or general character—that *bias* blame are not considered appropriate influences on perceived causation (dashed black arrows).

6.3.2.3 Recent Support for the Responsibility View

The Responsibility and Bias Views make similar predictions for the *Rollerblading* case stated earlier. They both hypothesize that the violation of a reasonable and pertinent norm will affect blame (or moral responsibility) and thus—on one account adequately and on the other inadequately—attributed causality. Differently put, the predictions of the two views are identical with regard to all and only those factors that justly bear on moral responsibility. The two views do, however, come apart as concerns factors that should *not* bear on—or are "peripheral to"—moral responsibility or blame. According to the Bias View, such peripheral factors, which *inappropriately* influence perceived blame, will increase perceived causality just like nonperipheral ones. The Responsibility View, however, predicts that they will not—which is what prevents it to collapse into the Anything-Goes View.

One peripheral feature already briefly mentioned earlier may be the agent's *general character*. Assume that two agents *A* (a good person) and *B* (a bad person) do the exact same thing with the same state of mind, and their actions lead to a harmful outcome. Whether or not the agent is a good person should not matter for the assessment of their moral responsibility for the harmful outcome. The Responsibility View thus predicts the perceived causal contribution of the two agents to be the same. The Bias View, however, hypothesizes that factors normatively irrelevant or "peripheral" to moral responsibility, like general character, might well have an impact on blame, and—in an attempt of post hoc justification thereof—on perceived causality.

In a famous experiment, Alicke (1992)—the main proponent of the Bias View—tested the prediction. He designed a vignette where a speeding driver collides with another car. In one version, he was speeding to hide an anniversary present for his parents (good character); in the other, the driver was speeding to hide a vial of cocaine from his parents (bad character). Participants deemed the driver significantly more causal in the latter version. On Alicke's view, this is because our desire to blame the bad driver more than the good driver makes us exaggerate his causal contribution. Sytsma (2019) disagrees, hypothesizing that the two vignettes trigger not only different inferences as to the agents' general character, but also as concerns their driving ability, a feature which is relevant to causal assessment. And indeed, Sytsma shows, if driving ability is held fixed across scenarios, the effect of character on causation disappears.

In further studies with a different scenario (*Lauren Alone*, first used in Livengood, Sytsma, & Rose, 2017), Sytsma shows that manipulating character only affects causality if it also affects the attribution of inculpating states of mind (in particular, knowledge). In the scenario, Lauren works for a company that has an unstable mainframe. The company does not know that the mainframe will crash if anyone logs into it. One day, Lauren logs into the mainframe, and the system crashes. Following the crash, the company institutes a policy that forbids its employees from logging into the mainframe. In one study, Sytsma manipulates the agent's character (*not specified* v. *bad*) and her mental states concerning the system crash (*not specified* v. *specified as absent*). He finds that character has an effect on causal judgment when knowledge and desire are left unspecified. When it is explicitly stated that the agent lacks knowledge or desire of the bad outcome, the effect disappears. What this suggests is that the participants draw an inference from bad character to an inculpating attitude toward the outcome, which then influences causal judgment because it does—and should—influence moral responsibility. In further studies, Sytsma finds that participants' causal judgments are most sensitive to the agent's knowledge of the outcome (i.e., the system crash) and, to a lesser extent, to her desire to bring it about (see also Kirfel & Lagnado, 2021).

In a nutshell, then, Sytsma shows that what really drives Alicke's astonishing results is not general character (a feature peripheral to both moral responsibility and causation), but other features (ability, mens rea) which can covary with the former, but which are not peripheral to moral responsibility (and thus, on Sytsma's view, causation).

6.4 Matching Legal and Psychological Accounts

The legal and psychological accounts discussed have prescriptive and descriptive features: they take position as to the *nature* of causation and its *actual attribution*, be it in court or our day-to-day lives. Formalists argue that the legal concept of causation is descriptive and that's how it is applied (i.e., solid gray arrows only in any of our graphs). Weak realists also hold that the legal concept of causation is descriptive, though its application has certain normative facets. Those who are vocal in their critique of the normative application of what is ultimately a descriptive concept presumably agree—by and large—with Alicke's account (Figure 6.2a). Strong realists, by contrast, argue that there is no genuine mismatch between the application of the legal concept of causation and its nature: the concept is sensitive to normative factors, so its application can be, too. This seems—at least prima facie—a good fit for Sytsma's Responsibility View. Naturally, if Sytsma's account as to what the folk concept is were correct, then some strong realist account of legal causation fits the Folk View of Causation (at least broadly). We would have actual correspondence between the legal expression (and concept) on the one hand and the folk accounts thereof.

Despite the prima facie room for convergence just discussed, a lot depends on the details. Take the factor of mens rea as an example. The law draws a strict conceptual and procedural distinction between mens rea on the one hand and the actus reus (the "guilty act") on the other. Culpable are only those who fulfill both requirements (except in cases of strict liability). Whereas Sytsma's Responsibility View might make room for a legitimate impact of mens rea on causation via responsibility (solid gray arrows, Figure 6.3), an account of this sort breaks with the hard distinction between mens rea and actus reus. According to Western criminal law and torts, the fact that a certain factor, like mens rea, appropriately increases perceived moral responsibility does not warrant an inference as to heightened causal contribution (solid gray and dashed black arrows, dashed black indicating an error/bias).

Let's take an example: suppose that we face a *many hands problem*, meaning we cannot clearly attribute causal responsibility for a harmful consequence to any of the many agents involved. Now it turns out that one agent, François, acted

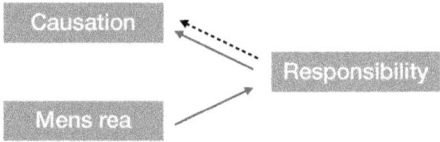

Figure 6.3 The implications of the Responsibility View for the law. © Levin Güver and Markus Kneer.

with knowledge (i.e., was practically certain the harm would occur), whereas all others were merely aware of a substantial risk (i.e., acted recklessly). On the moral scoreboard, François' standing is naturally somewhat worse in this case, but does this mean that he is more *causally* responsible? According to most legal accounts of causation (and interpretations thereof), the answer is negative. Sytsma's view, however, can—and *does* (see Sytsma, 2019, pp. 5–6)—make room for such an inference. What this shows, in short, is that from the legal point of view not just any normatively relevant factor warrants an inference to causation. On the Responsibility View of Causation, however—or at least this is what can be gleaned from Sytsma's papers—any factor that *appropriately* influences perceived moral responsibility (and what can be more paradigmatic than mens rea?) can justly exert some influence on perceived causation.

Taking stock: certain versions of strong realism map onto Sytsma's Responsibility View. Causation can legitimately be influenced by normative features, be it the infraction of a pertinent rule or other factors that appropriately influence moral responsibility. Whether the latter can include mens rea depends on the particular type of strong realism at stake. Naturally, to maintain a firm distinction between mens rea and actus reus, it is not appropriate to count all factors which, like mens rea, legitimately impact responsibility as adequate desiderata for attributed causal responsibility. In contrast to strong realists, weak realists might sympathize with Alicke's Bias View: causation, on this account, is a robustly descriptive phenomenon, but in "blame validation mode" its attribution is frequently marred by normative factors.

The details of this admittedly rough matching of legal and psychological accounts of causation might seem to matter a lot—except if it could be *shown* that the folk attribution of causation fits the predictions of the Bias View. This is what we will attempt to do in the following. If our findings are on the right track, the correspondence assumption as regards causation (no matter potential restrictions of scope) is problematic: the law might be well advised to distance itself from the folk concept of causation and should have a close look over the latter's shoulders in juror trials.

6.5 Setting the Stage for the Experiments

According to the Responsibility View, certain situational features, such as the character of the agent should not have a *direct* impact on perceived causation. As Sytsma has shown, in fact it doesn't: the influence of character on perceived causation is mediated by perceived mens rea, that is, the knowledge and desire to bring about a harmful outcome. Since mental states do play a legitimate role in the assessment of moral responsibility, it is only reasonable, on his view, that they also influence causality attributions. Just like mens rea, the violation of pertinent, contextually salient norms also does—and should—influence perceived causation.

The Responsibility View and the Bias View, we said, make identical predictions concerning perceived causation when an agent violates a norm pertinent to a harmful consequence of the agent's action. The predictions of the two views come apart as regards features "peripheral" to moral responsibility (such as character, race, status, gender, etc.). Alicke expects them to influence causation just the same; Sytsma does not (at least as long as they do not have an impact on a factor that legitimately influences moral responsibility). One such peripheral factor might be norms whose infraction is *nonpertinent* to the harmful outcome. Contrast two versions of the *Rollerblading* scenario: in one, skaters are not allowed on the footpath. In the other, they must wear a helmet—a rule that is aimed at their own protection. In the first case, where Mark is not supposed to skate on the path, he might legitimately be considered morally responsible for the accident with Lauren. However, in the second case, his moral responsibility should not be sensitive to the fact that he violates a norm. The rule to wear a helmet is supposed to protect *him*, and it simply isn't pertinent to the moral assessment or causal structure of the accident. This thought can be dramatized by invoking a patently silly norm: assume that people are only allowed to skate on the path if they like pizza, own a pet, or wear a gray T-shirt. On any account of moral responsibility worth its salt, moral responsibility should not be sensitive to the infraction of norms of this sort. On Sytsma's view, causation should thus not be sensitive to them either. Here we will present two experiments that explore whether they are.

6.6 Experiment 1

In our first experiment, we set out to test whether the effect of increased causality attribution is limited to pertinent norms or whether it extends to norms not pertinent to the consequences and even to outright silly norms. For the scenario, we used the *Rollerblading* vignette introduced in Section 6.3.1.[42]

6.6.1 Participants

Responses were collected from 278 participants on Amazon Mechanical Turk. The IP address was restricted to the United States. As preregistered,[43] participants were excluded if they failed an attention check, spent less than ten seconds reading the vignette, failed the comprehension question, or were not native English speakers. In total, 220 participants remained (female: 44%; mean age: 43 years, $SD = 13$ years, range: 22–74 years).

6.6.2 Methods and Materials

Participants were shown a vignette (*Rollerblading*) in which Mark was rollerblading on the same footpath that Lauren was walking on. It read as follows (conditions in square brackets):

One recent summer afternoon, Mark is rollerblading outside. The path Mark is on is commonly used by cyclists, rollerbladers and pedestrians. [However, there is a sign stating that it is forbidden to be on the path as a cyclist or rollerblader. Cyclists and rollerbladers are fined $100 if they use the path.] / [However, it is forbidden to be on the path as a cyclist or rollerblader unless one wears a helmet. Mark is not wearing a helmet. He is thus not allowed to be on the path.] / [However, it is forbidden to be on the path as a cyclist or rollerblader unless one wears a gray t-shirt. Mark is not wearing a gray t-shirt. He is wearing a blue t-shirt. He is thus not allowed to be on the path.]

One of these pedestrians is Lauren, who is walking ahead of Mark.

Suddenly a cat jumps onto the path right in front of Lauren. Lauren is startled and steps to the left to evade it.

Mark, who is approaching speedily on rollerblades from behind, collides with Lauren. The collision sweeps her off her feet and knocks her to the ground. Lauren sustains bruises all over.

Participants were randomly assigned to one of four conditions. In the *no norm* condition (displayed above without the addition of brackets), no norms as to the usage of the path were specified. In the *norm* condition, rollerbladers and cyclists were not allowed to use the path (first bracketed phrase). In the *nonpertinent norm* condition, rollerbladers and cyclists were only allowed to use the path if they wore a helmet, which Mark didn't do (second bracketed phrase). In the *silly norm* condition, everybody on the path was required to wear a gray T-shirt, and Mark's shirt was blue (third bracketed phrase).

Having read the scenario, participants had to answer a binary True/False comprehension question to confirm that they had read the vignette attentively and were aware both of Mark's action and its norm status. Participants were then asked questions about the causal contribution of Mark and the cat toward the accident. On a 7-point Likert scale, they had to report their agreement or disagreement with the following claims (labels in bold omitted):

Causation Mark: "Mark caused the accident." (1 = completely disagree; 7 = completely agree)

Causation Cat: "The cat caused the accident." (1 = completely disagree; 7 = completely agree)

Next, we tested two types of mental state ascriptions to Mark: knowledge and desire. As discussed earlier, Sytsma (2019) has shown that even when causality attributions *seem* to be influenced by peripheral features (character in Alicke's cases, nonpertinent or silly norms in our case), the latter might actually impact features that *are* pertinent to moral responsibility—and on Sytsma's view, therefore causal responsibility. In Sytsma's replications of Alicke's famous cases, the impact of character on perceived causation was mediated by knowledge and desire attributions which are (at least on Sytsma's view) nonperipheral to the causation question.[44] The questions asked to what extent people agreed or disagreed with the following claims (labels in bold omitted):

Knowledge: "Mark knew that the accident would occur." (1 = completely disagree; 7 = completely agree)

Desire: "Mark desired the accident." (1 = completely disagree; 7 = completely agree)

Finally, we tested three types of moral judgment: blame, moral responsibility, and deserved punishment,[45] to see how they behave with respect to different types of norm violations (labels in bold omitted):

Blame: To what extent do you think that Mark is blameworthy, if at all, for the accident? (1 = not at all blameworthy; 7 = totally blameworthy)

Responsibility: To what extent do you think that Mark is *morally* responsible, if at all, for the accident? (1 = not at all morally responsible; 7 = totally morally responsible)

Punishment: How much punishment, if any, does Mark deserve for the accident? (1 = no punishment at all; 7 = severe punishment)

6.6.3 Results

We ran one-way ANOVAs to test the impact of norms (no norm, pertinent norm, nonpertinent norm, and silly norm) on all dependent variables (Table 6.1). Figure 6.4 provides an overview of the most important findings. We found that norm type had a significant effect on causation and moral judgment (all $ps < 0.001$). The effect size for Mark being the cause was large ($\eta^2 = 0.218$) and the same held for all three moral variables (all

Table 6.1 One-Way ANOVAs Exploring the Influence of Norms on Causality Ascriptions, Mental States, and Moral Judgments

	df	*F*	*p*	η^2
Causation Mark	3	20.03	<.001	.218
Causation Cat	3	8.26	<.001	.103
Knowledge	3	3.92	.009	.052
Desire	3	1.23	.298	.017
Blame	3	40.39	<.001	.359
Responsibility	3	36.45	<.001	.336
Punishment	3	35.68	<.001	.331

© Levin Güver and Markus Kneer.

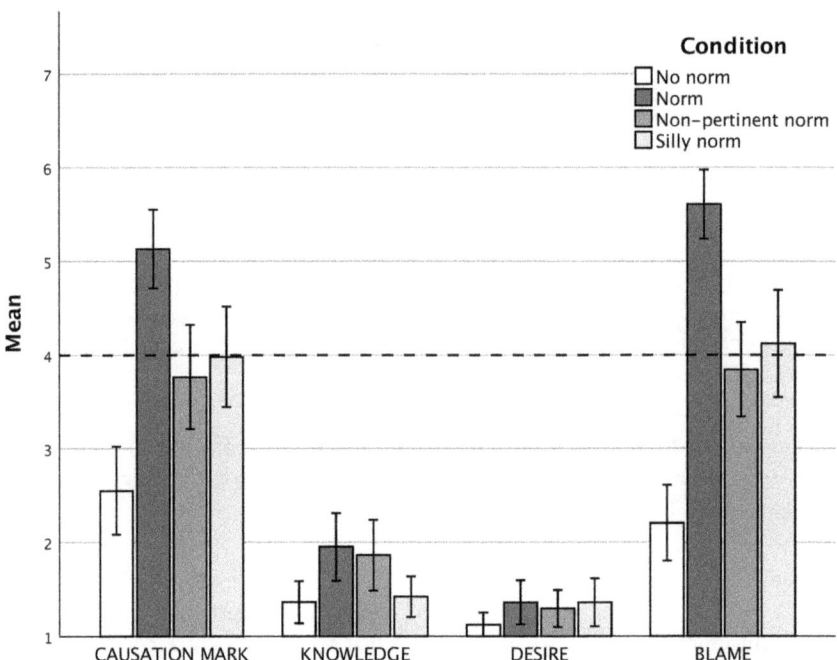

Figure 6.4 Comparison of means across all four conditions. Error bars denote 95 percent confidence intervals. © Levin Güver and Markus Kneer.

η^2s > 0.330). The effect of norm type on desire was nonsignificant ($p = 0.298$) and, although it reached significance for knowledge ($p = 0.009$), here the effect size was small ($\eta^2 = 0.052$).

According to Sytsma's view, perceived causality should covary with perceived moral responsibility (or moral blame). Across all four norm-type conditions, Mark's causal contribution correlated strongly with moral responsibility ($r = 0.77$) and blame ($r = 0.84$), in line with Sytsma's hypothesis. We also ran a mixed ANOVA (within-subject factor: judgment type—causation v. responsibility; between-subject factor: norm type—no norm v. norm v. nonpertinent norm v. silly norm). Again confirming Sytsma's view, we found that, aggregating across the four norm-type conditions, participants' causality judgments did not differ significantly from their judgments of responsibility ($F(1,216) = 0.001, p = 0.972, \eta_p^2 = 0.000$). In a similar mixed ANOVA with causation v. blame as the within-subject factor, we also found no significant difference in the attribution of these two DVs ($F(1,216) = 1.25, p = 0.265, \eta_p^2 = 0.01$).

To explore the impact of norms in more detail, we ran independent samples t-tests for the contrasts between the norm, nonpertinent and silly norm conditions with the no norm condition respectively.

6.6.3.1 No Norm v. Norm

The findings of the *no norm* and *norm* conditions are visualized in Figure 6.5. Contrasting *no norm v. norm* results, we found that participants deemed Mark

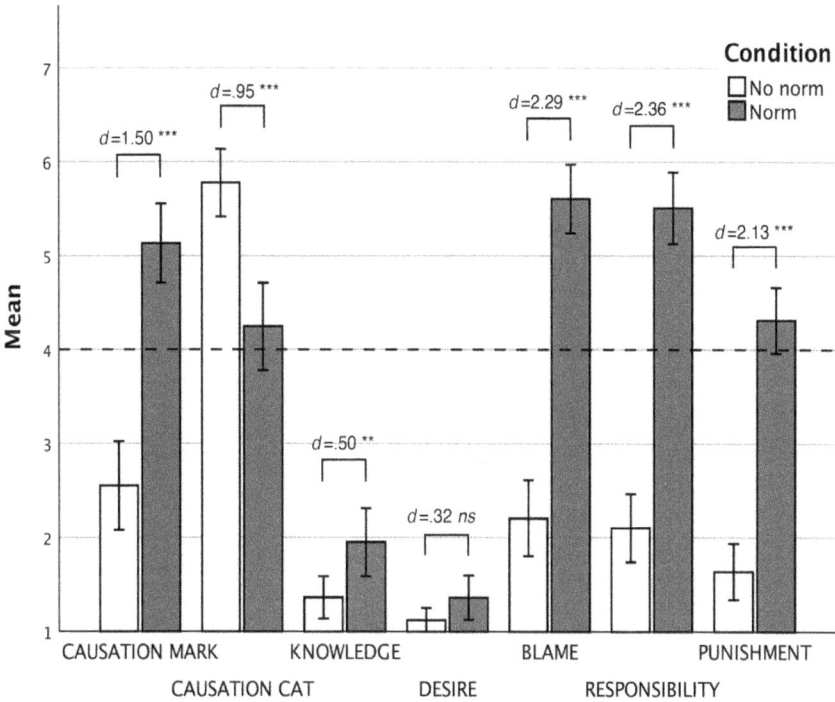

Figure 6.5 Comparison of means between the *no norm* and *norm* conditions. Effect sizes are given in terms of Cohen's *d*; * indicates $p < 0.05$, ** indicates $p < 0.01$, and *** indicates $p < 0.001$. Error bars denote 95 percent confidence intervals. © Levin Güver and Markus Kneer.

significantly more causal in the *norm* condition than the *no norm* condition ($p < 0.001$, $d = 1.50$, a large effect). This is consistent with previous findings (see note 35). There was also a significant and pronounced effect on the moral variables of blame, responsibility, and punishment (all $ps < 0.001$, all $ds > 2.12$, which are large effects). Additionally, participants considered Mark to have had significantly more foreknowledge of the accident ($p = 0.007$, $d = 0.50$, a medium-sized effect). There was no significant effect of norm status on perceived desire to cause an accident ($p = 0.080$).

6.6.3.2 No Norm v. Nonpertinent Norm

A comparison of the *no norm* and *nonpertinent norm* conditions revealed a similar effect as the one just discussed: in the nonpertinent norm conditions, participants gave significantly higher ratings for all DVs (all $ps < 0.031$) except the desire to cause an accident ($p = 0.136$), see Figure 6.6. Participants thus judged Mark significantly more causal in the *nonpertinent* norm condition than the *no norm* condition and the effect size was considerable ($d = 0.65$), despite the fact that Mark violated a norm that was peripheral to the outcome and (we take it) to his moral responsibility. As the data shows, however, the folk disagree with this assessment (for the moral variables all $ds > 0.97$).

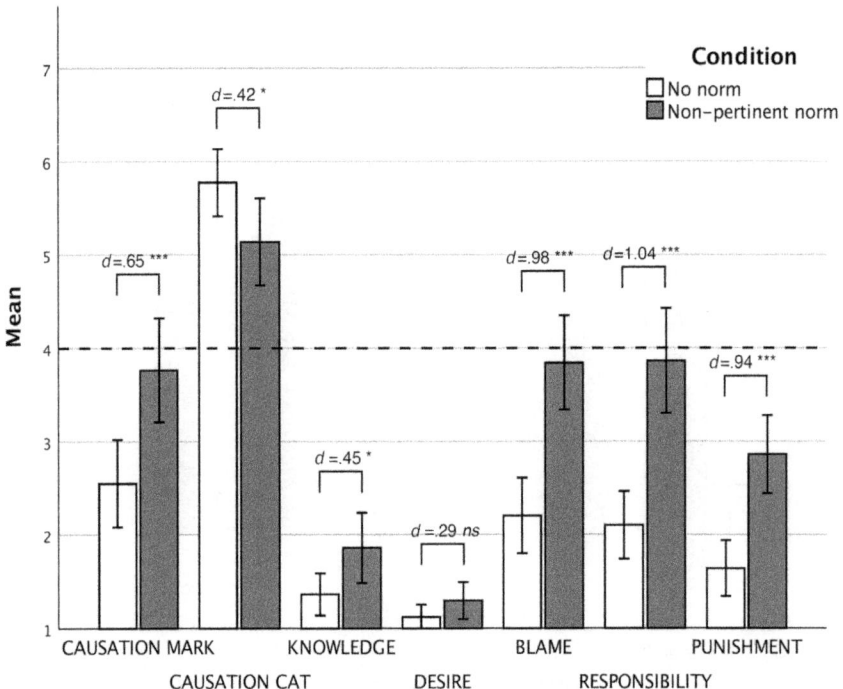

Figure 6.6 Comparison of means between the *no norm* and *nonpertinent norm* conditions. Effect sizes are given in terms of Cohen's *d*; * indicates *p* < 0.05, ** indicates *p* < 0.01, and *** indicates *p* < 0.001. Error bars denote 95 percent confidence intervals. © Levin Güver and Markus Kneer.

6.6.3.3 *No Norm v. Silly Norm*

Comparing the no norm and silly norm conditions, we found a significant difference for causality attributions and the moral variables (all *ps* < 0.001; see Figure 6.7), though we did not find a significant difference in knowledge or desire attributions (*ps* > 0.098). Again, the impact of a norm—albeit a silly one in this case—on causation was close to large in size (*d* = 0.78).

6.6.4 Discussion

Our experiment replicated previous findings according to which the violation of a norm pertinent to the moral assessment of an action influences perceived moral responsibility and—in line with the Responsibility View of Causation—the perceived causal contribution of the agent. Two conditions, in which the norm was either not pertinent to the consequences that ensued, or else patently silly, however, cast doubt on the plausibility of Sytsma's view. Since they are peripheral to moral responsibility, neither the nonpertinent or silly norm violations *should* influence responsibility or blame and hence causation. However, they do. This is in line with

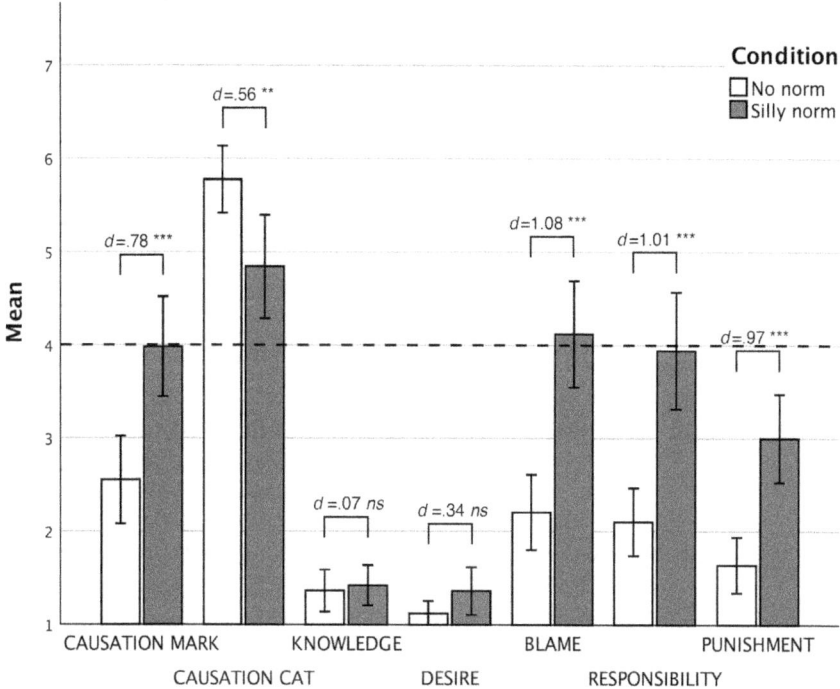

Figure 6.7 Comparison of means between the *no norm* and *silly norm* conditions. Effect sizes are given in terms of Cohen's *d*; * indicates $p < 0.05$, ** indicates $p < 0.01$, and *** indicates $p < 0.001$. Error bars denote 95 percent confidence intervals. © Levin Güver and Markus Kneer.

Alicke's Culpable Causation Model: justified or not, bad outcomes frequently trigger blame, and when they do, people tend to rationalize their inclination to "stick it" to the agent either by exaggerated attributions of mens rea or causal contribution. Where attempts of post hoc blame justification via mens rea seem implausible (as in our scenario: all means for knowledge < 2.00, all means for desire < 1.50, no significant differences for either in the silly norm case), people seem to resort to causation.

The results are robust: we have replicated them in two further preregistered studies, each of which used a different scenario. Consistent with the findings here reported, we found a significant and pronounced effect of nonpertinent and silly norms on blame, moral responsibility, and causation. Their effect on attributed desire and knowledge was nonsignificant.

A proponent of the Responsibility View, we take it, could respond in one of two ways: *first*, they might argue that what actually matters is not *warranted* moral responsibility or blame but *ascribed* moral responsibility or blame. And indeed, the correlations between causation on the one hand and ascribed responsibility and blame on the other hand are strong in our study (across conditions, *rs* > 0.76, in all individual conditions *rs* > 0.60, see Supplemental Materials for details in note 43). But on such an interpretation, the Responsibility View collapses into the aforementioned Anything-Goes View (Section 6.3.2.2). Many factors peripheral to moral responsibility proper—such as race, gender, character, status, and, as it turns out, the breaching of silly norms—can influence perceived blame. Since such biased moral assessments are inadequate, it is not clear why their post hoc justifications of exaggerated causation attributions should be any better.

Sytsma would agree with this assessment, we take it: after all he goes through considerable efforts to show that the impact of the "morally peripheral" feature of general character in Alicke's (1992) experiments is driven by a confound (driving ability). He further shows that, when no such confound is present, the effect of general character on causation unfolds via mens rea attribution, and mens rea is certainly relevant for moral responsibility. As discussed, we do not find an effect of the silly norm on mens rea (neither do we find one in the replications). Hence, the silly norm effect on causation is not easily explained by reference to attributed knowledge or desire. But this is where the *second* possible and certainly more plausible objection to our experiment might arise: the mens rea questions we ran following Sytsma's studies might be inadequate for the specific case at hand. In our scenario, one might argue, it simply makes little sense to attribute *foresight* (or knowledge) of an accident, so it is unsurprising that we could not detect a significant difference across conditions. However, other types of mens rea could well be relevant. The most plausible candidate is reasonable foreseeability of an accident and thus carelessness (i.e., the legal category of negligence). This is indeed a promising consideration: norm violators of any sort might be deemed careless rascals, and an increase in perceived moral responsibility, blame, and causal contribution might thus be traced back to an increase in negligence.

In short, Sytsma might hypothesize that the violation of a nonpertinent or silly norm triggers justified inferences regarding mens rea (negligence), and since these are relevant for moral responsibility these can have justified effects on perceived causation. Interestingly, the law makes room for similar considerations pertaining to the actus reus: as we have seen in Section 6.2, both criminal law and the law of torts employ tests of foreseeability in their assessment of legal causation. By testing not Mark's foresight of the accident, but its foreseeability, we can thus make headway on multiple fronts. We set out to test these hypotheses in the following experiment.

6.7 Experiment 2

6.7.1 Participants

We collected responses from 315 participants on Amazon Mechanical Turk. Their IP address was restricted to the United States. As preregistered,[46] we excluded participants who failed an attention check, spent less than ten seconds reading the vignette, or were not native English speakers. In total, 284 participants remained (female: 52%; mean age: 41 years, $SD = 12$ years, range: 20–78 years).

6.7.2 Methods and Materials

Participants were presented with the *Rollerblading* vignette from Experiment 1, though it was split into two parts. In the first step, participants were told that Mark was rollerblading on the path, that Lauren was walking ahead of him, and what type of norm applied (if any)—there being again four conditions: in the *no norm* condition, no further information was specified. In the *norm* condition, participants were told that Mark was not allowed to rollerblade on the path. In the *nonpertinent norm* condition, they were told that rollerbladers were required to wear a helmet, and Mark was not wearing one. In the *silly norm* condition, participants were told that everyone on the path was required to wear a gray T-shirt, whereas Mark was wearing a blue one.

Having read the first part of the vignette, participants were then asked to make an ex ante judgment as to the *foreseeability* of an accident.[47] The question read as follows (label in bold omitted):

> **Foreseeability:** To what extent do you agree or disagree with the following statement: "Mark could have reasonably foreseen the occurrence of an accident."
> (1 = completely disagree; 7 = completely agree)

Afterward, participants were shown the second part of the vignette, which detailed the appearance of the cat, Lauren's stepping into Mark's lane, and the ensuing collision. They were then asked to rate Mark's causal contribution toward the accident, the cat's causal contribution, the extent to which Mark is to be blamed and morally responsible for the accident, and how much punishment he deserves. The questions were phrased exactly as in Experiment 1 (see Section 6.6.2).

6.7.3 Results

We ran one-way ANOVAs to explore the influence of the four norm-type conditions on the dependent variables (see Table 6.2). Figure 6.8 provides an overview of the most important findings. We found a nonsignificant difference in participants' assessments of foreseeability across the four conditions ($p = 0.059$, $\eta^2 = 0.026$). Nevertheless, the effect of norm type on Mark's causal contribution and all moral variables was significant ($ps < 0.001$) and large in size for all DVs ($\eta^2 s > 0.194$).

Table 6.2 One-Way ANOVAs Exploring the Influence of Norms on Foreseeability, Causality, and Moral Judgments

	df	*F*	*p*	η^2
Foreseeability	3	2.51	.059	.026
Causation Mark	3	22.57	<.001	.195
Causation Cat	3	7.22	<.001	.072
Blame	3	33.99	<.001	.267
Responsibility	3	42.10	<.001	.311
Punishment	3	31.89	<.001	.255

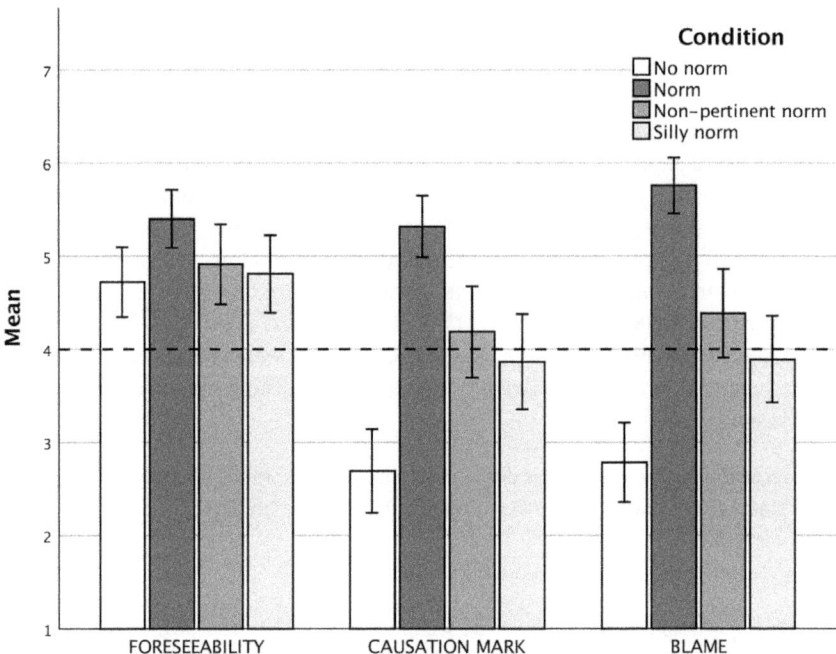

Figure 6.8 Comparison of means across all four conditions. Error bars denote 95 percent confidence intervals. © Levin Güver and Markus Kneer.

6.7.3.1 No Norm v. Norm

A comparison of the *no norm* and *norm* conditions revealed a significant difference for judgments of foreseeability ($p = 0.006$, $d = 0.47$, a medium-sized effect), see Figure 6.9. Participants also deemed Mark significantly more causal in the *norm* condition than the *no norm* condition ($p < 0.001$, $d = 1.62$, a very large effect), replicating the results of Section 6.6.3.1. There was also a significant and pronounced effect on the moral variables of blame, responsibility, and deserved punishment (all ps < 0.001, all ds $>$ 1.79, which are very large effects).

6.7.3.2 No Norm v. Nonpertinent Norm

In comparing the *no norm* and *nonpertinent norm* conditions, we found no significant difference in judgments of foreseeability ($p = 0.507$, $d = 0.12$). Nevertheless, norm type had a pronounced impact on Mark's causal contribution ($p < 0.001$, $d = 0.77$, close to a large effect) and the moral variables (ps < 0.001, ds > 0.85, large effects), see Figure 6.10.

6.7.3.3 No Norm v. Silly Norm

Comparing the *no norm* and *silly norm* conditions, we found no significant difference in judgments of foreseeability ($p = 0.757$, $d = 0.05$). There was, however, a

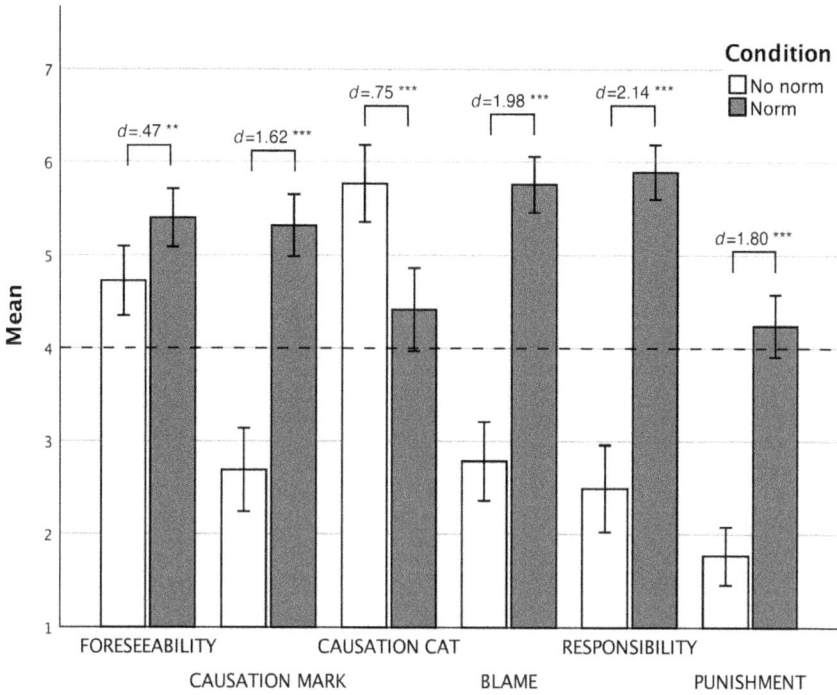

Figure 6.9 Comparison of means between the *no norm* and *norm* conditions. Effect sizes are given in terms of Cohen's *d*; * indicates $p < 0.05$, ** indicates $p < 0.01$, and *** indicates $p < 0.001$. Error bars denote 95 percent confidence intervals. © Levin Güver and Markus Kneer.

significant effect of norm type on Mark's causal contribution ($p = 0.001$, $d = 0.58$, a medium-sized effect) and on blame, responsibility, and punishment ($ps < 0.002$, $ds > 0.58$), see Figure 6.11.

6.7.4 Discussion

Our experiment produced several findings. *First*, we replicated the results from Experiment 1 and the literature more generally as regards the comparison between the no norm v. norm conditions: the presence of a pertinent norm has a significant and large effect on perceived causation ($d = 1.62$) and the moral variables (all $ds > 1.79$). Note, however, that it is unlikely that this effect can be fully accounted for by foreseeability. Here, too, we found a significant norm effect, though its size is comparatively small ($d = 0.47$). We do not want to suggest that this needs to be problematic for either Sytsma's Folk View of Causation or certain accounts of legal causation. For instance, the findings do not pose a problem for *strong* realist readings of proximate causation, as they might concede from the get-go that a plethora of broadly normative factors can play into one's causal judgment—a position consistent with Sytsma's Responsibility View.

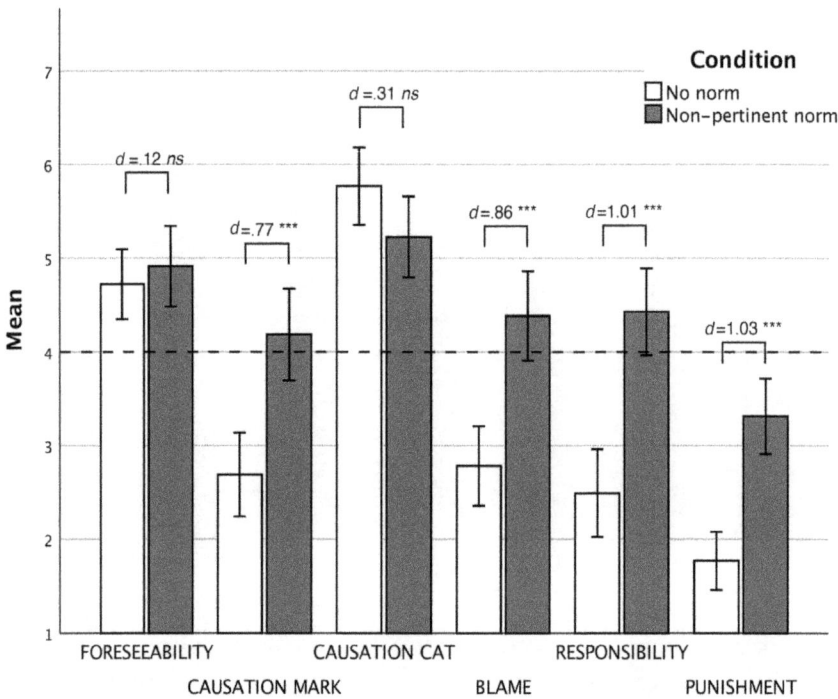

Figure 6.10 Comparison of means between the *no norm* and *nonpertinent norm* conditions. Effect sizes are given in terms of Cohen's *d*; * indicates $p < 0.05$, ** indicates $p < 0.01$, and *** indicates $p < 0.001$. Error bars denote 95 percent confidence intervals. © Levin Güver and Markus Kneer.

What *is* problematic for most accounts is our *second* set of findings. According to the Responsibility View and by and large any account of legal causation, nonpertinent or silly norms should not influence causation directly. They certainly also shouldn't influence causation via reasonable foreseeability, since what is *reasonably* foreseeable simply doesn't depend on what kinds of nonpertinent or silly norms happen to be in place. And in fact, the folk concurs here: contrasts of no norm v. nonpertinent norm as well as no norm v. silly norm revealed no significant effect of norm type on foreseeability ($ps > 0.506$). Problematically, however, both for the nonpertinent norm and the silly norm conditions Mark's causal contribution was judged as significantly more pronounced than in the no norm condition ($ps < 0.002$, $ds > 0.57$). Overall, then, our findings suggest that features peripheral to causation according to the law and any plausible version of the Responsibility View nonetheless do influence perceived causation, and that this *cannot* be explained with reference to foreseeability.

6.8 General Discussion

In certain domains, the law assumes that a legal expression *E* corresponds to its natural language analogue. Explicit clarification, established procedures, or case law provide

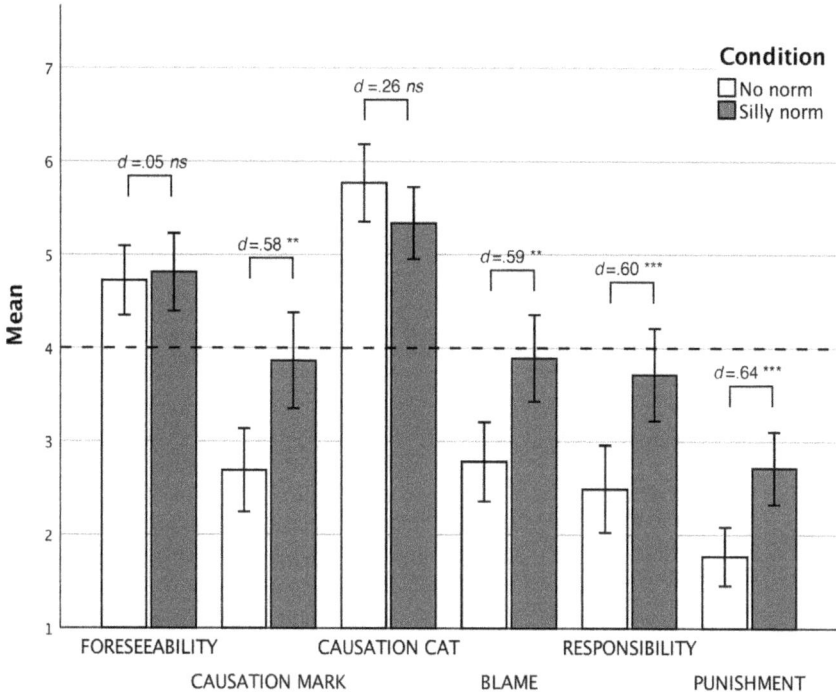

Figure 6.11 Comparison of means between the *no norm* and *silly norm* conditions. Effect sizes are given in terms of Cohen's *d*; * indicates *p* < 0.05, ** indicates *p* < 0.01, and *** indicates *p* < 0.001. Error bars denote 95 percent confidence intervals. © Levin Güver and Markus Kneer.

constraints on what such expressions can mean in the legal context—whether or not the law's take on the ordinary meaning of *E* is in fact correct. For some expressions the constraints are minimal (e.g., as concerns "reasonable" in the United States and the United Kingdom) or entirely absent (e.g., "intention," which is left uncodified in many jurisdictions, see note 4). For others, like causation, where at least in the United States and the United Kingdom, a correspondence assumption is arguably in place, the constraints are rather ample. Naturally, *presumed* and *actual* correspondence and the potential divergence that can arise are of particular importance in common-law jurisdictions, where jurors are tasked with evaluating causation.

One important facet of correspondence concerns the question whether an expression (and denoted concept) is descriptive, normative, or hybrid (i.e., "thick" in philosophical jargon). The expression "reasonable" raises this question and so does the expression "cause" and cognates. Formalists argue that the doctrine of proximate causation is stated descriptively and—by and large—applied in such a fashion (naturally, the occasional slip does not mean that there are *systematic* mistakes). The law's explicit correspondence assumption (see, e.g., *Burrage*) stands and falls with what the folk expression of "cause" actually means and what the concept it denotes actually is. If, like Alicke, we hold that its sensitivity to nondescriptive factors such as manifested by the norm effect is a bias, the possibility of correspondence in the *semantics* across folk and legal concept is possible. The fact that the folk *application* of the concept is systematically distorted by normative factors would mean that, in court, the law should be vigilant that lay jurors don't make mistakes. Suppose, on the other hand, that Sytsma were correct, such that the normatively inflected folk attributions of causation are in line with an unobjectionably normative folk concept of causation. From a formalist point of view, correspondence is thus no longer tenable: the *semantics* of the legal expression and that of the folk expression differ radically. In such a case, the law would be well advised to reign in its speculations as to correspondence and explicitly instruct jurors that in court, "cause" means something quite distinct from what it means on the street. So, in a nutshell, on formalist premises, the norm effect either poses a *threat* to the adequate *application* of the concept of cause in court by jurors (Bias View of the Folk Concept) or testifies to a difference in *semantics*, which means assumptions as to correspondence must be retired (Responsibility View of the Folk Concept).

Let's turn to *weak* realism, which holds that the letter of the law operates with a descriptive concept of causation, yet its application in court tends to be systematically inflected. If this is seen as problematic, and if we agreed with Alicke's account of folk causation, an eerie correspondence is in place. Semantically, the legal and the folk expression "cause" are on a par, yet *in and outside court* people are prone to systematic bias. If, by contrast, we agreed with Sytsma, then correspondence would once again be under pressure: the folk concept makes room for normative factors; the legal concept does not. And even if this were not to matter much given that the application of either concept is, in fact, frequently normative—that is, there's correspondence in application, though not in semantics—this would be quite a formidable mess.

What about *strong* realism? The classical norm effect can be accounted for by the strong realist position. However, on this view, too, the influence of nonpertinent and silly norms nevertheless spells trouble. Even a strong realist account of legal causation, we take it, does not amount to an Anything-Goes View, according to which any factor that might influence *perceived* moral responsibility can also legitimately influence causation. Consequently, even strong realists should, and presumably would, be alarmed by the silly norm effect on causal judgment—at least if they assume correspondence between the legal and the folk concept of causation.

So much for the possible *legal* implications of the norm effect and the silly norm effect. In our experiments, we have also tried to make progress regarding the question as to what, exactly, the folk concept of causation really is. Everyone, we take it, agrees that violations of silly norms should *not* influence perceived causation—at least if they do not impact the foreseeability of consequences or other morally *relevant* mediators. However, we found a substantial effect of silly and nonpertinent norms on causation, and we ruled out potential confounds due to foresight, desire, and foreseeability. This is problematic for Sytsma's view. As discussed at length, the fact that nonpertinent and silly norms affect perceived moral responsibility and that the latter correlates strongly with causation is of little help: the violation of silly norms, just as an agent's gender or race, should affect *neither* moral responsibility *nor* causation.

Our findings concerning the inadequate influence of silly norms on causation allow one of two interpretations: *first*, one might take them to support a *winner-takes-it-all* victory of Alicke's view. The silly norm effect suggests that people's desire to blame the agent led them to project the necessary causal prerequisites post hoc. But if this is so for morally peripheral factors, there's little reason to assume that the *process* of judgment for nonperipheral factors is much different—and it is this process that Alicke's account is about. On this interpretation, then, the legal implications we traced out under the premise of Alicke's account being correct would hold good.

Alternatively, one might opt, *second*, for a more limited conclusion. According to the latter, we still cannot adequately say whether Alicke or Sytsma are right as regards nonperipheral normative factors such as the (nonsilly) norm effect. Only as regards clearly peripheral factors—like the violation of silly norms—Alicke has a point. On a modified account of Sytsma's view, there are thus factors that appropriately and inappropriately influence folk attributions of causation. For this to be convincing, what's needed is of course some explanation why the processing of morally peripheral and nonperipheral factors should invoke different *psychological* mechanisms. We doubt that an explanation of this sort is easy to come by. What is obvious is that the earlier-expressed recommendations of caution and care as regards the possibly biased *application* of the concept of causation in court are very much in order. One might take these warnings to be restricted in scope to *juror* trials. But we have limited trust in legal expertise when deep-seated patterns of judgment distortion are at stake. Given that legal experts are just as sensitive to the Knobe Effect and the Severity Effect on mens rea attribution (Kneer & Bourgeois-Gironde, 2017; Kneer et al., ms), even when the mode of presentation is the exact same as in court (Kneer & Bublitz, ms), we doubt that all is gas and gaiters when it comes to causation. Given the powerful impact of morally peripheral normative factors on causation among laypeople, future research should address whether experts do any better in this regard.

6.9 Conclusion

Is the folk concept of causation suited for legal purposes? Does it make sense for the law to rely on "the practical experience of the reasonable man" rather than "the theoretical speculations of the philosopher" in this regard?[48] The response to these questions depends in part on what the folk concept is, and in part on the legal constraints it needs to live up to. In this chapter, we have provided an example of how an inquiry of this sort can proceed, focusing on just one facet of the empirical literature about causation, namely, the norm effect.

The norm effect demonstrates that folk *attributions* of causality are sensitive to normative factors. Whether this shows that the folk *concept* of causation is inherently normative, however, is a matter of debate. On Sytsma's Responsibility View the question is answered in the affirmative. According to Alicke's Culpable Control Model, the norm effect constitutes a bias. One can thus draw a very rough analogy between these folk psychological views on the one hand, and strong and weak realism about causation in the law on the other.

In our experiments, we have shown that the violation of morally nonpertinent and silly norms *also* has a powerful effect on causality ascriptions. Furthermore, we found that these effects cannot be explained by a potentially legitimate difference in the foreseeability of possible consequences. Effects of this sort thus constitute a bias, we take it, *both* on Sytsma's *and* Alicke's account. Do these findings suggest that the standard (pertinent) norm effect familiar from the literature—as well as other normative factors—must *also* be treated as a bias? This question requires further research. Whether or not the answer is "yes," it is evident, however, that the law should be cautious about reliance on the folk concept of causation and its application, as the latter might not be what the law *takes* them to be. If the folk concept of causation is normative, it might be unsuited for legal purposes, at least if we share formalist or weak realist premises. Even on strong realist assumptions, however, it is hard to make sense of a concept of causation that is susceptible to factors like character, gender, or silly norms. Courts must thus strive to limit inappropriate normative influences on causation judgments, in particular in juror trials, no matter how broad the class of legitimate normative influences is defined.

Notes

1 E.g., Brannon (2015); Kavanaugh (2016); Solan and Gales (2016).
2 For further reflections on the relation between ordinary and legal language, see, for example, Jiménez (2021); Knobe and Shapiro (2021); Prochownik (2022); Tobia (2020, 2022).
3 See, for example, Westen (2008); Moran (2010); Gardner (2015); Zipursky (2015); Mangini (2018).
4 Both intention and knowledge are left uncodified in, for example, England, Germany (see the glaring lack in § 15 German Penal Code), France, the Netherlands, and Spain.
5 *R v Moloney* [1985] AC 905, 926 (italics added).
6 See *R v McNamara (Richard)* [2009] EWCA Crim 2530.
7 See *R v Allen* [2005] Crim LR 698; *R v Phillips* [2007] EWCA Crim 1042.
8 Herring (2012) makes the plausible assumption that the courts have not elaborated further on what the ordinary meaning of intention *actually* is because they think "it is obvious" (p. 135).
9 Note that for many puzzling phenomena (e.g., the Knobe Effect concerning intention and the norm effect concerning causation) for which one type of account is available (say, a pragmatic explanation) and the other one is standardly available also (a bias account).
10 Knobe (2003, 2006), for reviews see Cova, Lantian, and Boudesseul (2016); Feltz (2007), for early discussion in the legal context see Nadelhoffer (2006) and Kobick and Knobe (2009).
11 According to this effect, more severe outcomes correlate positively with the willingness to attribute intentionality. See Kneer and Bourgeois-Gironde (2017); Olier and Kneer (ms), and for a large cross-cultural replication of the effect with samples from over a dozen countries from the Americas, Asia, and Europe, see

Kneer et al. (ms). For a review of outcome effects broadly conceived, see Robbennolt (2000).

12 Whereas the Knobe Effect blurs the boundary between knowledge and intention, the boundary between knowledge and *recklessness*, too, seems to be susceptible to influences not anticipated by lawgivers. In an experiment conducted by Severance, Goodman, and Loftus (1992), lay participants were presented with the MPC definitions of the four mentes reae and asked to apply the terms to different legally relevant scenarios. Surprisingly, participants were unable to distinguish knowledge from purpose, recklessness, or negligence—indeed, the only distinction they could reliably make was between intention and negligence (p. 115). Further studies have confirmed the boundary between knowledge and recklessness to be especially opaque, see Shen, Hoffman, Jones, Greene, and Marois (2011, pp. 1337, 1343); similarly, Levinson (2005), though *contra* Robinson and Darley (1995); Vilares et al. (2017).

13 For French legal experts, see Kneer and Bourgeois-Gironde (2017) and Bourgeois-Gironde and Kneer (2018). For US experts, see Tobia (2020).

14 For French legal experts, see Kneer and Bourgeois-Gironde (2017); for conflicting results, see Prochownik, Krebs, Wiegmann, and Horvath (2020); Tobia (2020). Although the evidence seems mixed, a large cross-cultural replication with experts from the UK, Brazil, Poland, and the Netherlands finds a robust effect for each sample, see Kneer et al. (ms).

15 Naturally, if one considers the outcome sensitivity of the expression "intentional" to be part of its ordinary language *semantics*, as some have argued, this expression, too, falls under the second category of correspondence trouble.

16 See, for example, Gardner (2001, 2015); Tobia (2018); Westen (2008); Zipursky (2015).

17 Note that "careful" has a normative ring to it, which the related noun "care" (in contrast to "carefulness") does not. The fact that the latter is frequently invoked—for example, in formulations of "ordinary care"—does not necessarily import normativity. One can effect an action with "ordinary care" and yet fail to satisfy standards of "reasonable carefulness."

18 Section 2.02(d) MPC (italics added); for another example, see Section 210.3 MPC regarding manslaughter.

19 The same point holds for Torts (Third Restatement) §3, according to which negligence turns on the "*foreseeable* likelihood" of harm and the "*foreseeability* severity of any harm," since foreseeability is tied clearly to the ex ante circumstances of the agent. More on this in footnote 47.

20 *Yorkshire Dale Steamship Co Ltd v Minister of War Transport* [1942] AC 691 (HL) 706. In a similar vein, Lord Salmon argued in *Alphacell Ltd v Woodward* [1972] A.C. 824, 847, that "[w]hat or who caused an event to occur is essentially a practical question of fact which can best be answered by ordinary common sense than abstract metaphysical theory."

21 *Blaikie v British Transport Commission* [1961] SC 44, 49, reaffirmed in *Kane v HM Advocate* [2009] HCJAC 8.

22 *Burrage v. United States*, 571 US 204 (2014). Representative in the realm of factual causation are, for example, Dressler (2012, p. 160) and Solan and Darley (2001, pp. 271–2). For a plethora of further references, see Macleod (2019, pp. 982–5), Tobia (2021, pp. 91–2), and Summers (2018, pp. 3–5).

23 See also Lagnado and Gerstenberg (2017), who argue that "legal concepts of causation are closely related to everyday causal reasoning" (p. 565).

24 See, for example, Fletcher (1998, 2000); Dressler (2015, § 14); Herring (2018, pp. 80–96); and Section 2.03(1)(a) Model Penal Code. Some authors have argued for modified forms of the test for factual causation, see, for example, Harpwood (2009) and Elliott and Quinn (2017).

25 The *but-for* test is both over- and under-inclusive in certain respects, as it faces well-known complications with situations of *overdetermination* and *preemption*, see Stuckenberg (2014) for a review, and see also the recent empirical findings by MacLeod (2019).

26 In recent years, the test of directness has fallen out of favor and was largely replaced by the criterion of foreseeability in the assessment of tortious conduct (see Owen, 2009; Goldberg & Zipursky, 2010; but cf. Keeton, 1963), whereas both criteria are used conjunctively in criminal law (Dressler, 2015, pp. 189–90). As to their general interrelation, cf. Grady (2002, pp. 9–10).

27 See, for example, Dressler (2015, p. 190); *State v. Dunn* 850 P.2d 1201, 1215. For the law of torts, cf. Epstein and Sharkey (2020); Harpwood (2000, pp. 158–9).

28 Cf. the slightly different formulations of the foreseeability test depending on whether causation or, for example, questions of tortious duty (Harpwood, 2000, pp. 31–2) or its breach (Simons, 2002, pp. 291–4) are at stake. Courts oftentimes fail to conceptually hold these two layers—those concerning breach and causation—apart, cf. Harpwood (2000, p. 27); see also Brown (2023).

29 The courts emphasis on the foreseeability of an outcome is backed by recent empirical work on causal cognition, see Kirfel and Lagnado (2021). A third test of proximate causation which Hart and Honoré (1959) were early to allude to—namely, one that probes the atypicality or abnormality of the causal chain—has also received strong support from the literature on causal cognition, see, for example, Halpern and Hitchcock (2015); Hitchcock and Knobe (2009); Icard, Kominsky, and Knobe (2017).

30 Thus, Grady (2002, p. 2) writes that "[n]o common law doctrine is more puzzling than the proximate cause limitation on negligence liability," and Swisher (2002, p. 351) reiterates: "In all of Anglo-American law, there is no concept that has been [. . .] so pervasive—and yet so elusive—as the causation requirement."

31 See, for example, Beale (1920); Kadish (1985); Schauer (1988); Hart and Honoré (2002); for an overview Moore (2009).

32 See, for example, Green (1929); Keeton (1963), Prosser and Keeton (1984); for a comprehensive overview Leiter (2005).

33 For instance, comprehensive analysis of case law in common-law jurisdictions gives reason to believe that key elements of proximate causation (e.g., "directness" for the United States and "operativeness" and "substantiveness" for the United Kingdom) are judged highly inconsistently—judgments that can only be made sense of after taking into account the court's "sense of justice" or "public policy considerations," Dressler (2015, p. 189). For a similar analysis concerning Swiss case law, see Frei (2010).

34 Increasing support for the strong realist position can be found throughout the Restatement of Torts, which, in the Second Restatement, rebranded proximate causation to "legal causation," and in the Third Restatement, had the duty analysis usurp the concept entirely, see American Law Institute (1985). Arguably, both Harper, James, and Gray (1986) and Prosser, Keeton, Dobbs, Keeton, and Owen (1984) can be considered *strong* realists as well.

35 For example, Knobe and Fraser (2008); Gerstenberg and Icard (2020); Hitchcock and Knobe (2009); Knobe (2009); Kirfel and Lagnado (2017); Kominsky, Phillips,

Gerstenberg, Lagnado, and Knobe (2015); Livengood, Sytsma, and Rose (2017); Samland and Waldmann (2015, 2016); Sytsma (2019); Schwenkler and Sytsma (ms); for a review see Willemsen and Kirfel (2019).

36 Swiss Federal Court verdict of April 18, 2011, 6B_974/2010.

37 For example, Halpern and Hitchcock (2015); Hitchcock and Knobe (2009); Icard, Kominsky, and Knobe (2017); Kominsky et al. (2015); Kahneman and Miller (1986). The origins of such normality-based accounts can be traced back to at least Hart and Honoré (1959, p. 10).

38 For example, Alicke, (1992, 2000); Alicke, Rose, and Bloom (2011); Hitchcock and Knobe (2009); Knobe (2006); Knobe and Fraser (2008); Samland and Waldmann (2016); Sytsma (2019); Sytsma, Livengood, and Rose (2012).

39 Halpern and Hitchcock (2015); Henne, Kulesza, Perez, and Houcek (2021a); Henne, O'Neill, Bello, Khemlani, and De Brigard (2021b); Hitchcock and Knobe (2009); Icard, Kominsky, and Knobe (2017); Kominsky et al. (2015); cf. also Gerstenberg, Goodman, Lagnado, and Tenenbaum (2015); Halpern and Pearl (2005); Lagnado, Gerstenberg, and Zultan (2013); Woodward (2008).

40 Alicke (1992, 2000); Alicke, Rose, and Bloom (2011); on blame more generally, see Malle, Guglielmo, and Monroe (2014).

41 Livengood, Sytsma, and Rose (2017); Sytsma (2020); Sytsma, Livengood, and Rose (2012). Differently put, "we are simply dealing with the judgments that result from the correct application of a normative concept akin to responsibility or accountability. [. . .] The explanation of the norm effect is simply that we ordinarily use the lemma 'cause' in a normative way" (Sytsma, 2022, p. 28).

42 *Rollerblading* is adapted from a judgment of the Swiss Federal Court, 6B_974/2010 from April 18, 2011.

43 Available under https://aspredicted.org/ve2p4.pdf. Supplemental Materials and data for this and all further experiments can be found on the project's OSF site at https://osf.io/8meca/.

44 For interesting similar findings, see Kirfel and Lagnado (2021). Kirfel and Lagnado defend an account according to which folk causation depends on *foreseeability* rather than moral responsibility.

45 We distinguished between blame and moral responsibility mainly because Alicke invokes the former and Sytsma the latter in their accounts, though neither gives a definition of either. We included deserved punishment as a further measure since it is of direct relevance to the law on the one hand, and since there is an ongoing debate as to whether blame and punishment judgments draw on the same process of judgment. Cushman (2008) argues that this is the case, and Kneer and Machery (2019) and Frisch, Kneer, Krueger, and Ullrich (2021) challenge the view.

46 Available under https://aspredicted.org/j3sx5.pdf.

47 Note that the law explicitly highlights that reasonable foreseeability is foreseeability ex ante, not ex post (for the law of torts: Goldberg & Zipursky, 2010; cf. also Owen, 2009, pp. 1281–2, 1294; for criminal law: Dressler, 2015, pp. 189–90). So as to avoid serious worries regarding a potential hindsight bias when it comes to the assessment of negligence (see, e.g., Kamin & Rachlinski, 1995; Kneer, 2021; Kneer & Skoczeń, 2023), the question concerning foreseeability was presented to participants before the outcome (i.e., the accident) was described.

48 As expressed by Lord Thomson in *Blaikie v British Transport Commission* [1961] SC 44, 49.

References

Alicke, M. D. (1992). Culpable causation. *Journal of Personality and Social Psychology*, *63*(3), 368–78.

Alicke, M. D. (2000). Culpable control and the psychology of blame. *Psychological Bulletin*, *126*(4), 556–74.

Alicke, M. D. (2008). Blaming badly. *Journal of Cognition and Culture, 8*(1–2), 179–86.

Alicke, M. D., Rose, D., & Bloom, D. (2011). Causation, norm violation, and culpable control. *The Journal of Philosophy, 108*(12), 670–96.

American Law Institute. (1985). *Model Penal Code and Commentaries (Official Draft and Revised Commentaries): With text of Model Penal Code as adopted at the 1962 annual meeting of the American Law Institute at Washington, D.C., May 24, 1962.* American Law Institute.

Beale, J. H. (1920). The proximate consequences of an act. *Harvard Law Review, 33*(5), 633–58.

Bourgeois-Gironde, S., & Kneer, M. (2018). Intention, cause, et responabilité: Mens rea et effet Knobe. In S. Ferey & F. G'Sell (Eds.), *Causalité, Responsabilité et Contribution à la Dette* (pp. 117–44). Bruylant.

Brannon, V. C. (2015). Statutory interpretation: Theories, tools, and trends, *Congressional Research Service Reports, R45153,* 1–64.

Brown, T. R. (2023). Minding accidents. *University of Colorado Law Review, 43*(1), 89–148.

Cova, F., Lantian, A., & Boudesseul, J. (2016). Can the Knobe effect be explained away? Methodological controversies in the study of the relationship between intentionality and morality. *Personality & Social Psychology Bulletin, 42*(10), 1295–308.

Cushman, F. (2008). Crime and punishment: Distinguishing the roles of causal and intentional analyses in moral judgment. *Cognition, 108*(2), 353–80.

Dressler, J. (2012). *Understanding criminal law* (6th ed.). LexisNexis.

Dressler, J. (2015). *Understanding criminal law* (7th ed.). LexisNexis.

Elliott, C., & Quinn, F. (2017). *Tort law* (11th ed.). Pearson.

Epstein, R. A., & Sharkey, C. M. (2020). *Cases and materials on torts* (12th ed.). Wolters Kluwer.

Feltz, A. (2007). The Knobe effect: A brief overview. *The Journal of Mind and Behavior, 28*(3/4), 265–77.

Fletcher, G. P. (1998). *Basic concepts of criminal law.* Oxford University Press.

Fletcher, G. P. (2000). *Rethinking criminal law.* Oxford University Press.

Frei, M. A. (2010). *Der rechtlich relevante Kausalzusammenhang im Strafrecht im Vergleich mit dem Zivilrecht: Adäquate Kausalität und Voraussehbarkeit, Gefahrschaffung, Risikoverringerung, erlaubtes Risiko, Vertrauensgrundsatz, rechtmässiges Alternativverhalten, Schutzzweck der Norm, eigenverantwortliche Selbstgefährdung, Handeln auf eigene Gefahr, allgemeines Lebensrisiko und Sozialadäquanz* (Vol. 56). Schulthess.

Frisch, L. K., Kneer, M., Krueger, J. I., & Ullrich, J. (2021). The effect of outcome severity on moral judgment and interpersonal goals of perpetrators, victims, and bystanders. *European Journal of Social Psychology.* Online first, available under https://doi.org/10.1002/ejsp.2805.

Gardner, J. (2001). The mysterious case of the reasonable person. *The University of Toronto Law Journal, 51*(3), 273–308.

Gardner, J. (2015). The many faces of the reasonable person. *Law Quarterly Review, 131*(1), 563–84.

Gerstenberg, T., Goodman, N. D., Lagnado, D. A., & Tenenbaum, J. (2015). How, whether, why: Causal judgments as counterfactual contrasts. In D. C. Noelle, R. Dale, A. S. Warlaumont, J. Yoshimi, T. Matlock, C. D. Jennings, & P. P. Maglio (Eds.), *Proceedings of the 37th annual conference of the cognitive science society* (pp. 782–7). Cognitive Science Society.

Gerstenberg, T., & Icard, T. (2020). Expectations affect physical causation judgments. *Journal of Experimental Psychology: General, 149*(3), 599–607.

Goldberg, J. C. P., & Zipursky, B. C. (2010). *Torts.* Oxford University Press.

Grady, M. F. (2002). *Proximate cause decoded.* UCLA *Law Review, 50*, 293–335.

Green, L. (1929). Are there dependable rules of causation? *University of Pennsylvania Law Review, 77*(5), 601–28.

Halpern, J. Y., & Hitchcock, C. (2015). Graded causation and defaults. *The British Journal for the Philosophy of Science, 66*(2), 413–57.

Halpern, J. Y., & Pearl, J. (2005). Causes and explanations: A structural-model approach. Part I: Causes. *The British Journal for the Philosophy of Science, 56*(4), 843–87.

Harper, F., James, F. Jr., & Gray, O. S. (1986). *The law of torts* (2nd ed., Vol. 4). Little, Brown and Company.

Harpwood, V. (2000). *Principles of tort law.* Cavendish.

Harpwood, V. (2009). *Modern tort law.* Routledge–Cavendish.

Hart, H. L. A., & Honoré, T. (1959). *Causation in the law.* Clarendon Press.

Hart, H. L. A., & Honoré, T. (2002). *Causation in the law* (2nd ed. 1985, repr.). Clarendon Press.

Henne, P., Kulesza, A., Perez, K., & Houcek, A. (2021a). Counterfactual thinking and recency effects in causal judgment. *Cognition, 212,* 104708.

Henne, P., O'Neill, K., Bello, P., Khemlani, S., & De Brigard, F. (2021b). Norms affect prospective causal judgments. *Cognitive Science, 45*(1), e12931.

Herring, J. (2012). *Criminal law: Text, cases, and materials* (5th ed.). Oxford University Press.

Herring, J. (2018). *Criminal law: Text, cases, and materials* (8th ed.). Oxford University Press.

Hitchcock, C., & Knobe, J. (2009). Cause and norm. *The Journal of Philosophy, 106*(11), 587–612.

Icard, T. F., Kominsky, J. F., & Knobe, J. (2017). Normality and actual causal strength. *Cognition, 161,* 80–93.

Jiménez, F. (2021). Some doubts about folk jurisprudence: The case of proximate cause. *The University of Chicago Law Review Online.* Available under https://doi.org/10.2139/ssrn.3815405.

Kadish, S. H. (1985). Complicity, cause and blame: A study in the interpretation of doctrine. *California Law Review, 73*(2), 323–410.

Kahneman, D., & Miller, D. T. (1986). Norm theory: Comparing reality to its alternatives. *Psychological Review, 93*(2), 136–53.

Kamin, K. A., & Rachlinski, J. J. (1995). Ex post ≠ ex ante: Determining liability in hindsight. *Law and Human Behavior, 19*(1), 89–104.

Kavanaugh, B. M. (2016). Fixing statutory interpretation: Review of "Judging Statutes" by Robert A. Katzmann. *Harvard Law Review, 129*(8), 2118–63.

Keeton, R. E. (1963). *Legal cause in the law of torts.* Ohio State University Press.

Kirfel, L., & Lagnado, D. (2017). "Oops, I did it again." The impact of frequent behaviour on causal judgement. In R. Granger, U. Hahn, & R. Sutton (Eds.), *Proceedings of the 39th annual meeting of the cognitive science society* (pp. 2420–5). Cognitive Science Society.

Kirfel, L., & Lagnado, D. (2021). Causal judgments about atypical actions are influenced by agents' epistemic states. *Cognition, 212,* 104721.

Kneer, M. (2022). Reasonableness on the Clapham Omnibus: Exploring the outcome-sensitive folk concept of reasonable. In P. Bystranowski, J. Bartosz, & P. Maciej (Eds.), *Judicial decision-making: Integrating empirical and theoretical perspectives* (pp. 25–48). Springer Nature.

Kneer, M., & Bourgeois-Gironde, S. (2017). Mens rea ascription, expertise and outcome effects: Professional judges surveyed. *Cognition, 169,* 139–46.

Kneer, M., & Bublitz, J. C. (ms). Outcome effects on mens rea attribution: A comparative study with German legal experts, law students and laypeople (in prep.).

Kneer, M., Hannikainen, I., Zehnder, M.-A., Almeida, G., Aguiar, F., Bystranowski, P., . . . Struchiner, N. (ms). Outcome effects on mental state ascriptions across cultures (in prep.).

Kneer, M., & Machery, E. (2019). No luck for moral luck. *Cognition, 182,* 331–48.

Kneer, M., & Skoczeń, I. (2023). Outcome effects, moral luck and the hindsight bias. *Cognition, 232,* 105258.

Knobe, J. (2003). Intentional action and side effects in ordinary language. *Analysis, 63*(279), 190–4.

Knobe, J. (2006). *Folk psychology, folk morality* (Dissertation). Princeton University.

Knobe, J. (2009). Folk judgments of causation. *Studies in History and Philosophy of Science Part A, 40*(2), 238–42.

Knobe, J., & Fraser, B. (2008). Causal judgment and moral judgment: Two experiments. In W. Sinnott-Armstrong (Ed.), *Moral Psychology* (Vol. 2, pp. 441–7). MIT Press.

Knobe, J., & Shapiro, S. J. (2021). Proximate cause explained: An essay in experimental jurisprudence. *University of Chicago Law Review, 88,* 165–236.

Kobick, J., & Knobe, J. (2009). Interpreting intent: How research on folk judgments of intentionality can inform statutory analysis. *Brooklyn Law Review, 75*(2), 409–31.

Kominsky, J. F., Phillips, J., Gerstenberg, T., Lagnado, D., & Knobe, J. (2015). Causal superseding. *Cognition, 137,* 196–209.

Lagnado, D. A., & Channon, S. (2008). Judgments of cause and blame: The effects of intentionality and foreseeability. *Cognition, 108*(3), 754–70.

Lagnado, D. A., & Gerstenberg, T. (2017). Causation in legal and moral reasoning. In M. R. Waldmann (Ed.), *The Oxford handbook of causal reasoning* (pp. 565–601). Oxford University Press.

Lagnado, D. A., Gerstenberg, T., & Zultan, R. (2013). Causal responsibility and counterfactuals. *Cognitive Science, 37*(6), 1036–73.

Leiter, B. (2005). American legal realism. In M. P. Golding & W. A. Edmundson (Eds.), *The blackwell guide to the philosophy of law and legal theory* (pp. 50–66). John Wiley & Sons, Ltd.

Levinson, J. D. (2005). Mentally misguided: How state of mind inquiries ignore psychological reality and overlook cultural differences. *Howard Law Journal, 49*(1), 1–29.

Livengood, J., Sytsma, J., & Rose, D. (2017). Following the FAD: Folk attributions and theories of actual causation. *Review of Philosophy and Psychology, 8*(2), 273–94.

Macleod, J. (2019). Ordinary causation: A study in experimental statutory interpretation. *Indiana Law Journal, 93*(3), 957–1030.

Malle, B. F., Guglielmo, S., & Monroe, A. E. (2014). A theory of blame. *Psychological Inquiry, 25*(2), 147–86.

Mangini, M. (2018). Toward a theory of reasonableness. *Ratio Juris, 31*(2), 208–30.

Moore, M. S. (2009). *Causation and responsibility: An essay in law, morals, and metaphysics*. Oxford University Press.

Moore, M. S. (2019). Causation in the law. In E. N. Zalta (Ed.), *The Stanford encyclopedia of philosophy*. Metaphysics Research Lab, Stanford University. Available under https://plato.stanford.edu/archives/win2019/entries/causation-law/.

Moran, M. (2010). The reasonable person: A conceptual biography in comparative perspective. *Lewis & Clark Law Review*, *14*(4), 1233–83.

Nadelhoffer, T. (2006). Bad acts, blameworthy agents, and intentional actions: Some problems for juror impartiality. *Philosophical Explorations*, *9*(2), 203–19.

Olier, J. G., & Kneer, M. (ms). The Knobe effect as an instance of a Severity effect (under review).

Owen, D. (2009). Figuring foreseeability. *Wake Forest Law Review*, *44*(5), 1277–308.

Posner, R. A. (1986). Legal formalism, legal realism, and the interpretation of statutes and the constitution. *Case Western Reserve Law Review*, *37*(2), 179–217.

Prochownik, K. (2022). Causation in the law, and experimental philosophy. In P. Willemsen & A. Wiegmann (Eds.), *Advances in Experimental Philosophy of Causation* (pp. 165–88). Bloomsbury Publishing.

Prochownik, K., Krebs, M., Wiegmann, A., & Horvath, J. (2020). Not as bad as painted? Legal expertise, intentionality ascription, and outcome effects revisited. In S. Denison, M. Mack, Y. Xu, & B. C. Armstrong (Eds.), *Proceedings of the 42nd annual conference of the cognitive science society* (pp. 1930–6). Cognitive Science Society.

Prosser, W. L., Keeton, W. P., Dobbs, D. B., Keeton, R. E., & Owen, D. G. (1984). *Prosser and Keeton on the law of torts* (5th ed.). West Publishing Co.

Puente, M., Sloan, G., & Deerwester, J. (2018, April 25). Bill Cosby retrial, day 13: Jury Adjourns for night after seeking definition of consent. *USA Today*. https://www.usatoday.com/story/life /2018/04/25/bill-cosby-retrial-day-13-jury-begins-deliberati ons/548593002 [https:// perma.cc/2ADC-BTZH].

Robbennolt, J. K. (2000). Outcome severity and judgments of 'Responsibility': A meta-analytic review. *Journal of Applied Social Psychology*, *30*(12), 2575–609.

Robinson, P., & Darley, J. (1995). *Justice, liability, and blame: Community views and the criminal law*. Westview Press.

Rose, D. (2017). Folk intuitions of actual causation: A two-pronged debunking explanation. *Philosophical Studies*, *174*(5), 1323–61.

Samland, J., & Waldmann, M. R. (2014). Do social norms influence causal inferences. In P. Bello, M. Guarini, M. McShane, & B. Scassellati (Eds.), *Proceedings of the 36th annual conference of the cognitive science society* (pp. 1359–64). Cognitive Science Society.

Samland, J., & Waldmann, M. R. (2015). Highlighting the causal meaning of causal test questions in contexts of norm violations. In D. C. Noelle, R. Dale, A. S. Warlaumont, J. Yoshimi, T. Matlock, C. D. Jennings, & P. P. Maglio (Eds.), *Proceedings of the 37th annual conference of the cognitive science society* (pp. 2092–7). Cognitive Science Society.

Samland, J., & Waldmann, M. R. (2016). How prescriptive norms influence causal inferences. *Cognition*, *156*, 164–76.

Schauer, F. (1988). Formalism. *Yale Law Journal*, *97*(4), 509–48.

Schwenkler, J., & Sytsma, J. (ms). Reversing the norm effect on causal attributions (preprint). Available under http://philsci-archive.pitt.edu/18220/.

Severance, L. J., Goodman, J., & Loftus, E. F. (1992). Inferring the criminal mind: Toward a bridge between legal doctrine and psychological understanding. *Journal of Criminal Justice*, *20*(2), 107–20.

Shen, F., Hoffman, M., Jones, O., Greene, J., & Marois, R. (2011). Sorting guilty minds. *New York University Law Review, 86*, 1306–60.

Simons, K. W. (2002). Dimensions of negligence in criminal and tort law. *Theoretical Inquiries in Law, 3*(2), 1–57.

Solan, L. M., & Darley, J. M. (2001). Causation, contribution, and legal liability: An empirical study. *Law and Contemporary Problems, 64*(4), 265–98.

Solan, L. M., & Gales, T. (2016). Finding ordinary meaning in law: The judge, the dictionary or the corpus? *International Journal of Legal Discourse, 1*(2), 253–76.

Sommers, R. (2020). Commonsense consent. *Yale Law Journal, 129*(8), 2232–324.

Stuckenberg, C.-F. (2014). Causation. In M. D. Dubber & T. Hörnle (Eds.), *The Oxford handbook of criminal law*. Oxford University Press.

Summers, A. (2018). Common-sense causation in the law. *Oxford Journal of Legal Studies, 38*(4), 793–821.

Swisher, P. N. (2002). Insurance causation issues: The Legacy of Bird v. St. Paul Fire & Marine Ins. Co. *Nevada Law Journal, 2*, 351–85.

Sytsma, J. (2019). The character of causation: Investigating the impact of character, knowledge, and desire on causal attributions (preprint). Available under http://philsci-archive.pitt.edu/16739/.

Sytsma, J. (2020). Causation, responsibility, and typicality. *Review of Philosophy and Psychology*. Online first, available under https://doi.org/10.1007/s13164-020-00498-2.

Sytsma, J. (2022). The responsibility account. In P. Willemsen & A. Wiegmann (Eds.), *Advances in experimental philosophy of causation* (pp. 145–64). Bloomsbury Publishing.

Sytsma, J., Livengood, J., & Rose, D. (2012). Two types of typicality: Rethinking the role of statistical typicality in ordinary causal attributions. *Studies in History and Philosophy of Science Part C: Studies in History and Philosophy of Biological and Biomedical Sciences, 43*(4), 814–20.

Tobia, K. (2018). How people judge what is reasonable. *Alabama Law Review, 70*(2), 293–359.

Tobia, K. (2020). Legal concepts and legal expertise (working paper). Available under https://doi.org/10.2139/ssrn.3536564.

Tobia, K. (2021). Law and the cognitive science of ordinary concepts. In B. Brozek, J. Hage, & N. Vincent, *Law and mind: A survey of law and the cognitive sciences* (pp. 86–96). Cambridge University Press.

Tobia, K. (2022). Experimental jurisprudence. *University of Chicago Law Review, 89*. Available under https://doi.org/10.2139/ssrn.3680107.

Vilares, I., Wesley, M. J., Ahn, W.-Y., Bonnie, R. J., Hoffman, M., Jones, O. D., . . . Montague, P. R. (2017). Predicting the knowledge–recklessness distinction in the human brain. *Proceedings of the National Academy of Sciences, 114*(12), 3222–7.

Westen, P. (2008). Individualizing the reasonable person in criminal law. *Criminal Law and Philosophy, 2*(2), 137–62.

Willemsen, P., & Kirfel, L. (2019). Recent empirical work on the relationship between causal judgements and norms. *Philosophy Compass, 14*(1), e12562.

Woodward, J. (2008). Psychological studies of causal and counterfactual reasoning. In C. Hoerl, T. McCormack, & S. R. Beck (Eds.), *Understanding counterfactuals, understanding causation* (pp. 16–53). Oxford University Press.

Zipursky, B. (2015). Reasonableness in and out of negligence law. *University of Pennsylvania Law Review, 163*, 2131–70.

Part III

(New) Methods and Topics in Experimental Jurisprudence

7

Ordinary Meaning and Consilience of Evidence

Justin Sytsma

Both philosophy and legal interpretation are often concerned with assessing the ordinary meaning of important terms or phrases (or with the concepts beings expressed by those terms when used with their ordinary meaning).[1] And researchers in both areas have begun to urge that ordinary meaning is an empirical question. Interestingly, some recent work in these areas suggests seemingly opposed views about the use of one source of empirical evidence in investigating ordinary meaning—the tools of corpus linguistics. Some work in experimental jurisprudence has pushed for moving beyond textual sources, including the use of linguistic corpora, and toward survey methods in legal interpretation (Tobia, 2020; Klapper, Schmidt, & Tarantola, ms). In fact, Klapper et al. seem to suggest that we should prefer survey methods *over* corpus methods, holding that "the best way to discern ordinary meaning is to simply ask ordinary people how they would read and apply a disputed term" and making the argument that "properly executed, survey methods offer marked theoretical advantages over current means of ascertaining ordinary meaning" (20). Such work leads two advocates of the use of corpus methods in legal interpretation to contend with "a range of scholars seeking to pump the brakes on or outright repudiate the utility of corpus tools in the law" (Lee & Mouritsen, 2021, pp. 278–9).

In contrast, questionnaire methods have been the dominant approach in experimental philosophy, although they are certainly not the only methods that have been employed (Sytsma & Livengood, 2016). Recently, however, some philosophers have urged that corpus methods "should be added to the philosopher's toolkit" (Caton, 2020, p. 51) and that they can productively supplement the more common questionnaire methods employed by experimental philosophers.[2] For instance, Bluhm (2016, p. 104) notes some potential issues with questionnaire methods and suggests that one way to alleviate them is to turn to corpus methods, "not to supplant, but to supplement." In similar fashion, Sytsma, Bluhm, Willemsen, and Reuter (2019, p. 233) conclude that corpus methods should be seen "as a fruitful addition to the methodological toolbox of experimental philosophy" and Ulatowski, Weijers, and Sytsma (2020) note that "one advantage of corpus methods for experimental philosophy is that they can offer a further way to test our hypotheses, one free of some encumbrances common in more standard experimental contexts, even as it inevitably introduces others." The suggestion is that corpus methods can often complement more traditional experimental methods, with the hope of providing a consilience of evidence with regard to hypotheses about ordinary meaning and ordinary concepts.

At first glance, there would seem to be a tension in these attitudes about corpus methods. This seeming tension recommends taking a closer look, and doing so, I believe, helps to draw out several important methodological points concerning the use of corpus and questionnaire methods. Most importantly, I argue that there is seldom a silver bullet when it comes to answering complex empirical questions and that different types of methods, including corpus and questionnaire methods, can often be used together to paint a fuller picture of a phenomenon of interest. To draw this out I will focus on a famous legal hypothetical—the meaning of "vehicle" in ordinances like "no vehicles in the park" (Hart, 1958)—that plays a prominent role in the recent methodological debates in legal interpretation.

Here is how I will proceed. In Section 7.1, I briefly discuss ordinary meaning and illustrate the corpus methods that I'll focus on. In Section 7.2, I present and then expand upon Lee and Mouritsen's corpus analysis of "vehicle." In Section 7.3, I consider a specific concern raised by Tobia, the supposed nonappearance fallacy, and some of the questionnaire results he presents. In Section 7.4, I then consider the questionnaire results that Klapper et al. report.

7.1 Ordinary Meaning and Linguistic Context

Lee and Mouritsen (2018) advocate for the use of corpus methods in addressing empirical questions about ordinary meaning in the law. One illustration they provide involves the iconic problem of the meaning of "vehicle" in the rule "no vehicles in the park" (Hart, 1958). The same hypothetical is subsequently taken up by Tobia (2020) and Klapper, Schmidt, and Tarantola (ms), who raise concerns about the use of the corpus methods employed by Lee and Mouritsen in assessing ordinary meaning. While these groups take opposing views with regard to how best to empirically assess the ordinary meaning of "vehicle," employing either corpus methods or one of two types of questionnaire methods, I'll argue that the results for these methods are in fact consistent and that together they provide a fuller picture of the ordinary meaning.

While Lee and Mouritsen, Tobia, and Klapper et al. all argue convincingly that ordinary meaning is of clear importance in legal interpretation, what is meant by "ordinary meaning" is not itself so clear. As Lee and Mouritsen (2018, p. 127) put it, "ironically, we have no ordinary meaning of 'ordinary meaning.'" Given vagueness with regard to what we are after when we look to assess ordinary meaning, I suggest that a single type of study is unlikely to be satisfactory.

There are numerous issues to be disentangled here, including that different theories of legal interpretation will suggest different perspectives on "ordinary meaning." One important issue concerns the role of linguistic context in shaping how a word or phrase is understood. It is clear that how a word or phrase is understood is often contingent on the context in which it is used. To give a simple illustration, asking someone to "set the table" suggests a quite different sense of "table" than if you were to ask them to "format the table." And, in fact, these correspond with the first two senses of the noun "table" defined in a common online dictionary:

[1] A piece of furniture with a flat top and one or more legs, providing a level surface for eating, writing, or working at.

[2] A set of facts or figures systematically displayed, especially in columns. (Lexico.com, April 26, 2021)

With this in mind, one question we might ask with regard to ordinary meaning is how a word is most commonly used across contexts. And for such questions, the tools of corpus linguistics can be of great help. To illustrate, we can check a common, balanced corpus such as the *Corpus of Contemporary American English* (COCA) to get a sense of how often the noun "table" is used in something roughly like each of the dictionary senses just noted.[3] For instance, continuing with our toy example we can look at the most common *collocates* of the noun "table"; that is, the terms that occur most frequently near this term in the corpus. The results for COCA suggest that the noun is most often used in the furniture sense, with the top four collocates each suggesting this sense ("sit," "kitchen," "coffee," and "chair") and seven of the top 10 ("dinner," "dining," and "round"). The remainder of the top 10 collocates, however, instead suggest the information display sense ("present," "figure," and "content").

Alternatively, we can use the *Key Word in Context* (KWIC) feature to provide a sample of the texts, or *concordance lines*, in which "table" is used as a noun in COCA. A survey of a random sample of 100 concordance lines suggests that a little more than half employ the furniture sense (or a use derived from it, such as phrases like "table manners" and "table cloth"), while roughly a third employ the information display sense (including references to database tables). Most of the remainder involve idiomatic or metaphorical expressions related to the furniture sense, such as "off the table" and "ran the table." Together, these results suggest, not surprisingly, that "table" is most frequently used in the furniture sense, although the information display sense is also reasonably common.

We might also ask questions about the specifics of a given broad sense of a term. For example, we might ask just which things are typically counted as tables in the furniture sense and whether the dictionary definition previously given adequately captures the extension of the term as ordinarily used. Again, the methods of corpus linguistics can help. For instance, looking through concordance lines for the noun "table" on COCA, we find uses such as "pool table" and "bedside table" that are not (typically or primarily) used for eating, writing, or working at. Noting such exceptions, we might ask about the relative frequency of talking about different types of tables (in the furniture sense). One reason to do so is that this will provide an initial indication of what people are most likely to assume is meant by a generic reference to a "table."[4] And here we might note, for instance, that the *frequency count* for occurrences of "dinner table" is roughly three times larger than for "pool table" and two and a half times larger than for "bedside table."

With regard to legal interpretation, Lee and Mouritsen (2018, p. 795) note that "when we speak of *ordinary* meaning, we are asking an empirical question—about the sense of a word or phrase that is most likely implicated in a given linguistic context." And they argue that the tools of corpus linguistics—focusing on the tools briefly introduced earlier (frequency counts, collocation data, and concordance lines)—can help answer such questions. With regard to our target example of "vehicle," for instance, they argue that "corpus data can tell us the relative frequency of different senses of *vehicle* . . . in naturally occurring language" (829).

The different senses of "vehicle" that they have in mind here, however, are *not* the broad senses that standard dictionaries aim to provide. Their concern is with ordinances such as "no vehicles in the park," which provide a context that rather clearly excludes three of the four senses suggested by one online dictionary:

[1] A thing used for transporting people or goods, especially on land, such as a car, lorry, or cart.

[2] A thing used to express, embody, or fulfil something.

[3] A film, television programme, song, etc., that is intended to display the leading performer to the best advantage.

[4] A privately controlled company through which an individual or organization conducts a particular kind of business, especially investment. (Lexico.com, April 26, 2021)

The linguistic context of the ordinance makes clear that we're concerned with something like the first sense. Correspondingly, Lee and Mouritsen's concern in asking about the "relative frequency of different senses of *vehicle*" is with the range of things—the range of potential vehicles—that might reasonably be taken to fall under the broad "transporting" sense of the term and, relatedly, how well this extension is captured by standard dictionary definitions like [1]. Thus, Lee and Mouritsen (2018, p. 788) note, "when judges speak of ordinary meaning, they often seem to be speaking to a question of relative frequency," where this is taken to fall along a continuum: "Whether we regard the ordinary meaning of a given word to be the *possible*, *common*, or the *most common* sense of that word in a given context, linguistic corpora allows us to determine empirically where a contested sense of a term falls" (831–2).

In other words, what seems to be at issue with regard to "sense" in Lee and Mouritsen's discussion is just how broad the range of conveyances at issue is ordinarily taken to be in a given context. And while I believe that linguistic corpora can *help* with this task, I'm skeptical that corpus tools will provide a convincing answer on their own. One major reason for this is that assessing the use of a word "in a given context" can be difficult with corpora, although the extent of the difficulty depends on just how finely grained we take the context to be. For instance, with regard to the ordinance "no vehicles in the park," we might wonder whether the relevant context is discussions of parks, or prohibitions against vehicles, or prohibitions against vehicles in parks, or a specific prohibition against vehicles in a specific park. The more finely grained the context, the less likely there are to be a suitable number of examples in a corpus to warrant drawing conclusions about typicality from an investigation of the corpus.

7.2 Corpus Analyses

Let's turn to the specifics of Lee and Mouritsen's illustrative corpus analysis for the contemporary usage of the term "vehicle." As we've seen, they hold that "corpus data can tell us the relative frequency of different senses of *vehicle*" and they contend that "if the search for ordinary meaning entails analyzing the relative frequency of competing senses of a given term, then corpus linguistics seems the most promising tool" (829). To do this for contemporary usage, Lee and Mouritsen begin by presenting the fifty most common collocates of "vehicle" in the News on the Web (NOW) corpus.[5]

Lee and Mouritsen find that the most common terms occurring in the vicinity of "vehicle" in the corpus include "electric," "motor," "cars," "traffic," and so on. They reasonably conclude that many of the collocates "strongly indicate *automobile* as a likely candidate for the most common use of the term." They then go on to note that two types of conveyances that might plausibly be thought to fall under the category of "vehicle" are not found in the top collocates: "airplane does not appear, though two particular types of aircraft are attested in the collocates—unmanned aerial vehicles (drones) and spacecraft" and, similarly, that "*bicycle* does not appear among the collocates of *vehicle* in contemporary usage" (838). Lee and Mouritsen then suggest that this finding raises an important question: "if *vehicle* is never used to refer to *bicycle* or *airplane* in the corpus data, then we may end up with an even further extension of our frequency continuum from *possible but rare* to *possible but unattested*" (840).

Lee and Mouritsen note, however, that before concluding that the use of "vehicle" to refer to bicycles or airplanes is unattested, we should also evaluate the KWIC data for the term. To do this, they reviewed a random sample of 100 concordance lines for "vehicle" from the same corpus. What they found is that the vast majority of these were referring to automobiles (91%) and that "the NOW Corpus data included no *airplanes, bicycles, tricycles, skateboards, roller-skates, toy cars,* or any of what Hart and others have characterized as penumbral, disputed cases" (842). While Lee and Mouritsen do not draw the strong conclusion that current usage of "vehicle" does not include such penumbral cases, they do take the corpus results to be suggestive of that conclusion, writing that "some seemingly *possible* meanings are unattested and may not be current" (842).

This motivates Lee and Mouritsen to look further, searching for concordance lines including both "vehicle" and one or the other of two disputed terms—"bicycle" or "airplane." They find a few texts in which bicycles are counted as vehicles, but report that they "were unable to find a single collocation or concordance line that reflected the use of *vehicle* to mean *airplane*" (844). And they take this to further raise the question of whether "*airplane* is even a possible sense of *vehicle*" (844).

One lesson to draw from Lee and Mouritsen's results with regard to "bicycle" is that we should be quite cautious about drawing a strong conclusion concerning absence from limited searches of a corpus. Finding that the top 50 collocates and a random sample of 100 concordance lines for "vehicle" does not indicate the use of the term to include bicycles provides reasonably compelling evidence that this is not an especially common use. But it does not provide compelling evidence that this use is *not* current or even that this use is *not* to be found in the corpus. Drawing this type of conclusion would require a more extensive analysis.

To illustrate, I will extend Lee and Mouritsen's analysis concerning bicycles and airplanes (and to further "disputed cases" later). To do so, I'll switch from the NOW corpus, which comprises texts from web-based newspapers and magazines, to COCA, which provides a more balanced corpus being drawn from wider range of sources.

A search for collocates of "vehicle" on COCA provides a similar list to that reported by Lee and Mouritsen. Here are the top 50 in order of decreasing frequency:

> motor, electric, drive, fuel, utility, driver, road, armored, st, sport, operate, steal, emergency, truck, unmanned, passenger, launch, emission, park, us, traffic, speed, hybrid, commercial, autonomous, aerial, accident, fleet, sport-utility, tank, stolen, investment, sales, strike, engine, used, all-terrain, average, recreational, ford, equipment, registration, oct, crash, license, bradley, approach, fighting, theft, off-road[6]

As with the list produced by Lee and Mouritsen, the most frequent collocates are suggestive of the hypothesis that "vehicle" is most commonly used with regard to automobiles. And, again, we find that "airplane" and "bicycle" do not occur in the top 50 collocates. We should be hesitant to draw a strong conclusion from this, however. For one, we might also note that "automobile" does not occur in either the previous list or Lee and Mouritsen's (although "cars" did occur in their list). Further, for purposes of assessing whether "vehicle" is ever used in the corpus to refer to such conveyances, as opposed to whether it is commonly used in this way, there is little reason to restrict ourselves to the top 50 collocates. In fact, expanding the list, we find that "bicycle" occurs in the top 150 collocates, appearing ahead of "automobile"; and, while "airplane" does not occur, "aircraft" is in the top 100 collocates and "helicopter" in the top 150.

Further, searching instead for collocates of "vehicle" *and* "bicycle," including their plurals, gives eighty-three instances on COCA (which is comparable to "vehicle(s)" and "automobile(s)" with fifty-five instances and "vehicle(s)" and "airplane(s)" with twenty-five instances). While many of these co-occurrences do not reflect that bicycles are being described as vehicles, looking at the concordance lines we find that some of them are. For instance, we find texts such as "his bicycle is his only vehicle" and "remember that a bicycle is a legal vehicle and always ride with the traffic, not against it." Similarly, looking at the co-occurrences of "vehicle(s)" and "airplane(s)," we find a number of texts where airplanes are being described as vehicles, including "it looks like according to the chatter, the airplane is the preferred vehicle as a weapon" and "I discovered a large, flat expanse named O'Hare Airport, to and from which great winged vehicles called airplanes somehow flew." Thus, with regard to the question of whether "*airplane* is even a possible sense of *vehicle*," we can offer a clear affirmative answer: "vehicle" is sometimes used in American English to refer to airplanes, even if this does not appear to be a common use.

While we do find concordance lines where "vehicle" is used to refer to a bicycle or airplane, we also find texts that suggest a contrast such as "services to reduce or eliminate your need to own your own vehicle or bicycle" or "patrol in vehicles or occasionally in airplanes." Often, the contrast is with the phrase "motor vehicle," such as in "open to bicycle travel and motor vehicle use." In fact, "motor vehicle" is the most common bigram for "vehicle" and a look through concordance lines suggests that this is, in fact, what is often meant by generic uses of the term.

A potential worry, here, is that the frequency of collocates in the corpus are likely to in part reflect how frequently we talk about different types of conveyances, and this will be influenced by the prevalence of these conveyances and how newsworthy they are (Herenstein, 2017).[7] Plausibly, we might expect to see more references to automobiles than bicycles or airplanes in a standard corpus given the relative frequency of these conveyances. In fact, frequency counts from COCA suggest that this is the case, with "automobile(s)" or the more common "car(s)" occurring 324,960 times compared to 51,848 times for "bicycle(s)" or "bike(s)" and 86,794 times for "airplane(s)" or "plane(s)." The worry, of course, is that accepting that people talk about cars more frequently than bikes or planes, then even if "vehicle" could be applied equally to each, we would still expect the most frequent collocates to be suggestive of automobiles.

7.3 The Nonappearance Fallacy

Tobia (2020) seeks to assess the reliability of corpus methods for purposes of legal interpretation. He calls on the results of a series of questionnaire studies to conclude that "the way people understand ordinary terms and phrases (for example, 'vehicle' or 'carrying a firearm') varies systematically from what a dictionary definition or relevant legal corpus linguistics' usage data would indicate about the meaning" (734). This leads to a striking philosophical conclusion—that "*ordinary meaning diverges from ordinary use*" (735).

At the heart of this critique is the claim that advocates of the use of corpus methods in legal interpretation, most prominently including Lee and Mouritsen, employ fallacious reasoning, generating instances of what Tobia terms *The Nonappearance Fallacy*. This is "the mistaken assumption that the nonappearance of some use in a corpus indicates that this use is outside of ordinary meaning" (789). This is illustrated with an argument based on the conclusion suggested by Lee and Mouritsen earlier: "*across thousands of sources in our corpus, we could not find even one example of an airplane referred to as a 'vehicle'; therefore the ordinary meaning of 'vehicle' does not include airplanes*" (789–90). It is important to note, here, that Lee and Mouritsen do not actually put forward such an argument; rather, they take the nonappearance of "airplane" to *raise the question* of whether this is a possible current use of "vehicle" (see also Lee and Mouritsen, 2021).

Is the nonappearance fallacy actually a fallacy? A first thing to point out is that we should distinguish this "fallacy" from drawing a hasty conclusion based on a given corpus analysis. Tobia can be read as primarily critiquing how corpus methods have *typically* been used in the law, while allowing that more careful analyses might play an important role. Read in this way, Tobia's critique is not at odds with the methodological points I am attempting to draw out here. Nonetheless, the description given for the nonappearance fallacy is suggestive of a stronger claim—one concerning what we can conclude from nonappearance in a *corpus* rather than the failure to find appearances in a limited *analysis* using that corpus.

As already noted, it is *not* the case that the use of "vehicle" to include airplanes does not occur in standard corpora. In fact, although I employed COCA, instances of such a use are also to be found in NOW, even when restricting to sources from the United States and in the timeframe employed by Lee and Mouritsen (e.g., "few commercial airplanes—the preferred vehicle for moving gold—have been flying in recent months"). The point is that it is hasty to conclude that a particular use does not occur in a corpus from an analysis based, for instance, on the top 50 collocates of the term of interest and a random sample of 100 concordance lines (although it is fair to take such findings to raise the question). Further, we should be cautious about drawing such a conclusion from even a more detailed look at a corpus, or a range of corpora, *if* one of the terms of interest is uncommon, as will be illustrated in the following.

If we were to find (against the actual facts) that in large corpora like NOW and COCA there are *no* instances of a reasonably common term like "vehicle" being used to refer to a relatively common type of conveyance like an airplane, this would certainly be suggestive that the term is not currently used in this way (although it might have been in a past, which might be assessed by turning to historical corpora). And if we further found that (against the actual facts) "vehicle" was never used to refer to similar aerial conveyances, such as aircraft or helicopters, this would at the very least seriously raise the question of whether such conveyances fall under the contemporary, ordinary meaning of "vehicle." At this point, strong alternative evidence would be called for if we were to conclude that despite the lack of corpus evidence, the ordinary meaning nonetheless still includes such conveyances.

The primary evidence that Tobia provides with regard to the ordinary meaning of "vehicle" today comes from the "concept conditions" in the questionnaire studies he presents. In his first study, lay participants in the concept condition were asked to consider the noun "vehicle" and then to answer if each of ten potential types of vehicles is a vehicle, selecting either "Yes" or "No" for each. In addition to asking about "vehicle" itself, this list included both what we might consider central cases (automobile, car, bus, and truck) and disputed cases (bicycle, airplane, ambulance, golf cart, and toy car). Tobia found that over 90 percent of participants judged that an automobile is a vehicle, and similarly for car, bus, truck, and golf cart. Roughly 85 percent made the same judgment about an ambulance, roughly 75 percent for an airplane, and roughly 65 percent for a bicycle. By contrast, over 75 percent of participants judged that a toy car is *not* a vehicle.

Similar results were found for lay participants in a subsequent study with an expanded range of potential vehicles. Participants first evaluated the ten entities from the previous study and then a further set of fifteen potential vehicles. Based on the results reported in Figure 5 of Tobia's article, for "automobile," "car," "bus," "truck," "bicycle," "airplane," "ambulance," and "golf cart" a clear majority of lay participants gave an affirmative response. And a clear majority gave a negative response for "toy car." Turning to the new items, for "moped," "helicopter," "horse-drawn carriage," and "a nonfunctioning commemorative truck (e.g., a World War II Truck that has been decorated as a World War II monument)" a clear majority of lay participants gave an affirmative response. In contrast, for "a drone," "skateboard," "pair of roller skates," "baby stroller," "pair of crutches," "pogo stick," "baby shoulder-carrier," "life raft," and "zip line" a clear majority gave negative responses. Finally, participants were split with regard to an "electric wheelchair," with a slight majority affirming, and with regard to a "wooden canoe," with a slight majority denying.

As Lee and Mouritsen (2021) point out, Tobia treats these results as speaking directly to the ordinary meaning of "vehicle." But, as we'll return to later, this requires some interpretation that goes beyond the results, both with regard to how participants understood the task presented to them and how this bears on ordinary meaning. Setting this aside for the time being, however, it is worth noting that each of the potential types of vehicles that a majority of lay people affirmed as vehicles in Tobia's studies can be rather quickly found to be attested in COCA. In fact, using the labels reported in Figure 5 (e.g., "wheelchair" instead of "electric wheelchair" and "WWII Truck" instead of the longer description), and setting aside "airplane" and "bicycle" which were discussed previously, I was able to record an instance of each being described as a vehicle in COCA, with the exception of "WWII truck," in roughly fifteen minutes of total search time. Texts reflecting this usage include the following (emphasis added):

Thursday during his arraignment on charges of repeatedly stabbing a 60-year-old tow **truck** driver whose vehicle had somehow crushed Horner's mother

Petzel drove his pickup truck into the back of a **car** and sent the vehicle into the path of a motorcycle coming the other way

Several people were injured in a crash involving a charter **bus** and another vehicle in Baltimore County

Jones faces lesser criminal charges of second-degree vehicle tampering in the **automobile** theft

Perhaps in an **ambulance**, certainly a vehicle of some kind

Abrams tried to impress the fact that the **golf cart** is a vehicle and safety is of the utmost importance

people need to be re-educated so they look at mass transit or light vehicle (bicycles, **mopeds**, scooters or motorcycles) before they jump in their car

he will get into a vehicle, perhaps a **helicopter**, and he will swing by the White House

in loan from the school's **carriage** shop, vehicles ranging from a phaeton to a farm wagon sat side by side[8]

interest by elite athletes, despite the high cost, since racing **wheelchairs** are special purpose vehicles[9]

An initial search for "WWII truck" yielded no instances, although for a rather clear reason: neither "WWII truck," "World War II truck," nor their plurals appear in COCA. This illustrates the worry raised above concerning drawing a conclusion from the nonappearance of a particular use of a word or phrase that does not occur frequently. That said, there are certainly instances of trucks being referred to as vehicles in the corpus. Further, a bit more digging reveals instances of a WWII truck being described as a vehicle, such as "the old World War II vehicle jerked forward," where the expanded context describes the vehicle at issue as a Jeep (for WWII this would most likely be the Willys MB/Ford GPW, which is also known as the ¼-ton 4×4 Command Reconnaissance Truck).

In contrast, I was able to find instances for only two of the remaining items from Tobia's list being referred to as vehicles in COCA—drones (e.g., "a new brand of unmanned aerial vehicle, or drone"), as noted by Lee and Mouritsen (2018), and canoes (e.g., "our vehicle was the voyaging canoe Hokule'a").[10] Thus, while there are attested instances of "vehicle" being used to refer to drones and canoes in the corpus, a majority of the lay participants in Tobia's study denied that canoes are vehicles (roughly 55%) and a large majority denied that drones are vehicles (just over 80%). As such, while Tobia (2020, p. 727) holds that "ordinary meaning exceeds datasets of common usage—even very large ones," even if we were to accept that majority opinion on the conceptual judgments he elicited is the definitive measure of ordinary meaning, it is simply not clear that this is the case.

Tobia (2020, p. 795) notes that "it is tempting to think that any acceptable use must be found *somewhere* in a large corpus, and any use that is not reflected is therefore not part of the ordinary meaning." He then takes the results of his study to suggest against this tempting thought:

> However, as the experimental results indicate, ordinary meaning sometimes diverges from ordinary use: people's understanding of language is not always reflected in recorded speech and writing, especially their understanding concerning nonprototypical category membership. (790)

While it is certainly correct that we should not expect every possible use of a term to appear in even large corpora, especially if one of the target terms is infrequent, Tobia's claim undersells their power. In fact, each of the conveyances that his experimental results suggest as an acceptable reference for "vehicle" is attested in COCA. And this should not be overly surprising for exactly the reason Tobia gestures at in noting that this thought is tempting: we are dealing with large collections of utterances, and generally expect meaning to be reflected in use.

In fact, that the readily attested uses in COCA so closely correspond with the judgments of the majority or near-majority of Tobia's participants offers supportive evidence for these being acceptable uses. That is, rather than finding that the corpus results and experimental results conflict with one another, they provide a consilience of evidence: all of the items that a majority of Tobia's participants affirmed I was able to find in the corpus, and all but two of the items that a majority denied I was unable to find in the corpus. As already noted, these two items were "wooden canoe," where participants were split, and "drone," where a large percentage of Tobia's participants judged are not vehicles. There are a number of possible explanations of this divergence for "drone." It might be that we should treat the phrase "unmanned aerial vehicle"—or even uses of "vehicle" alone that are related to this phrase—as using the term in a different sense than the one of interest, such that occurrences in the corpus should be discounted. Relatedly, the divergence might reflect differences in presumed context, with "unmanned aerial vehicle" being used more commonly in a military context, including to refer to drones *transporting* munitions or cargo, while "drone" in Tobia's studies might have instead suggested consumer drones that might be treated as more of a toy (and hence garner ratings more similar to those found for "toy car").

This raises a larger issue with regard to the assumption that questionnaire studies like those employed by Tobia in his concept conditions can cleanly deliver the ordinary meaning of a term like "vehicle." Lee and Mouritsen (2021) raise a number of potential concerns about this assumption, including worries about how readily we can infer natural linguistic behaviors from a survey instrument like that employed by Tobia. A general worry here is that studies like those reported by Tobia are not free from context but instead provide an artificial context: participants know that they are taking part in a study and are being observed, and the judgments they give can reflect this (see Sytsma & Livengood 2016, Chapter 9, for discussion). Participants' responses are elicited in an experimental context that might affect the judgments that they make.

A number of choices go into designing questionnaire studies, including the wording of the materials and the types of examples used. Focusing on the example of "drone," we can note that the question in Tobia's studies occurred with fourteen other examples and that these were given after ten prior questions. The range of entities included in these questions might reasonably be expected to set the context for how "drone" would be understood, and it seems plausible that in a context including questions about a toy car, baby stroller, horse-drawn carriage, pogo stick, skateboard, and so on, the notion of "drone" that would occur to participants would correspond more with toys flown in a park than combat vehicles. Further, we might worry that the first ten items leaned toward more clear examples of vehicles, with the exception of "toy car," while the fifteen items presented after this focused on less clear cases. That "drone" occurred alongside unattested examples like "baby stroller" and "pogo stick" might have encouraged skepticism with regard to whether drones are vehicles. The point here is not to discount questionnaire studies, or even the specific types of questions used by Tobia, but instead to note that they aren't free from problems.

In Tobia's second study, participants were asked to consider the noun "vehicle," then made judgments about each of the ten entities from his first study with regard to whether it is a *prototypical* vehicle and whether it is *technically* a vehicle. While Tobia primarily discusses the results with regard to two further conditions in his first study not discussed previously, the results are also potentially telling with regard to his concept condition.[11] What Tobia finds is that the mean rating for all of the entities in the "technically" condition was notably above the midpoint on his scale, with the exception of "toy car" and with "bicycle" receiving the lowest rating of the other items. This coincides with the majority responses for his concept condition, as discussed earlier, suggesting the possibility that Tobia's concept condition tended to elicit judgments about what is *technically* a vehicle. In contrast, judgments of prototypicality reflected the expected central cases, with only "automobile," "car," "bus," and "truck" showing mean ratings notably above the midpoint (followed by "ambulance" with a mean just above the midpoint).

With regard to "ordinary meaning," it is a matter of interpretation whether what we're after is something more like prototypical examples of vehicles or a broader range of entities that might technically be counted as falling under the concept. The key point I want to draw out here, however, is that the data from Tobia's second study is also consistent with the corpus analyses we have seen. The prototypical judgments coincide with the most common use of "vehicle" suggested by the analyses, while the "technically" judgments coincide with the less frequent but attested uses in the corpora. Again, what we find is a convergence between the questionnaire studies and the corpus analyses.

7.4 Providing Context

Klapper, Schmidt, and Tarantola (ms) are also critical of the use of corpus methods in assessing ordinary meaning for purposes of legal interpretation, but they advocate for a different type of questionnaire method from those already discussed from Tobia.[12] As noted, the ordinary use of a term will vary with context. And one worry about questionnaire studies is that they might inadvertently provide a context that biases participants' responses. As Lee and Mouritsen (2018, p. 861) state, "survey data is notoriously susceptible to context effects and response bias." One benefit of corpus methods, then, and one prominent reason that has been offered for their use in experimental philosophy, is that they provide a view of "words in the wild," outside of experimental contexts.[13] This is a key part of recent claims that corpus methods can fruitfully complement the questionnaire studies run by experimental philosophers.

The flip side of this coin is that corpus methods are not so well suited to telling us about the use of a term or phrase in a given context, especially if the context is highly specific. As noted earlier, if the context of interest is specific enough, it is unlikely that there will be sufficient instances of the term or phrase being used in that context in standard corpora to warrant reasonable inferences. Questionnaire studies, on the other hand, can provide a specific context. This is of clear relevance in legal interpretation, where a statute provides a context of interest. To illustrate, we've already seen that the corpus evidence suggests that "vehicle" is used with reference to a number of different types of transportation—most commonly cars, but also other types of motor vehicles, as well as (less frequently) bicycles, helicopters and other aircraft, carriages, and so on. And this is, in fact, in line with the data Tobia reports for conceptual judgments. That the term is used to refer to this range of types of transportation, however, does not necessarily mean that people will typically interpret "vehicle" this broadly in a specific context, such as when presented with the rule "no vehicles in the park." As Klapper, Schmidt, and Tarantola (ms, p. 22) note, "surveys, unlike any other methods, can provide respondents with a whole statutory provision," allowing researchers to "test a term's ordinary meaning as part of a statute and not simply isolated words."

Klapper et al. demonstrate by providing the results of a questionnaire study where participants were provided with a legal context for their conceptual judgments. In the first part of their study, participants were given a brief description of three out of five statutes involved in actual legal cases. More importantly for our purposes, in the second part participants were then given one of six vignettes describing a prohibition on vehicles in a public space. They then rated their approval of the ordinance and were asked to judge whether they thought the ordinance prohibited a series of potential vehicles: "Cars," "Bicycles," "Mopeds," "Baby carriages (strollers)," "Tobboggans," "Skateboards," "Drones," "Motorized wheelchairs," "Ambulances (even in cases of emergencies)," "Shopping carts," and "Tricycles." The vignettes varied in terms of the background motivation provided for the ordinance—including the harm it was in response to (injury, property damage, and nuisance) and the conveyance involved in the harm (go-kart or skateboard)—and the setting for the ordinance (park or college campus). A control condition simply told participants: "A local city ordinance prohibits 'vehicles in the park.'"

Based on the corpus and questionnaire studies discussed earlier, what results would we expect to find here? We've seen that "vehicle" is most commonly used to pick out cars and other motor vehicles, and that this is in line with the empirical results for prototypicality judgments. But the term is also sometimes used more broadly to include other conveyances such as bicycles, with this being in line with the empirical results for judgments about what technically counts as a vehicle. Focusing on Klapper et al.'s control condition, the presumed setting for a prohibition against vehicles in the park would be a natural, public area focused on recreation, suggesting an area largely set apart from motor vehicle traffic.[14] And the lack of further specification with regard to "vehicle," coupled with the evidence surveyed earlier with regard to the most common use of the term, would reinforce this contrast. That is, it seems reasonable to expect that people would tend to focus on the most common and prototypical examples here. Based on the previous evidence, we would then expect a large majority of participants to judge that the ordinance prohibits cars and a weaker majority to judge that it prohibits mopeds (sharing features of both motorcycles and bicycles). Similar considerations would suggest some uncertainty with regard to ambulances, while predicting that the majority would deny that the ordinance applies to the remaining items. With regard to ambulances, however, the phrasing of the item deliberately emphasizes their use as emergency vehicles, and common sense would suggest that they should *not* be prohibited from responding to emergencies in a park.

These predictions are closely in line with Klapper et al.'s results. While they do not provide the percentages for each item in the control condition alone, across the conditions they report finding that the top 4 items in decreasing percentage of agreement were cars (80%), mopeds (66%), bicycles (31%), and skateboards (29%). Further, the percentages for bicycles and skateboards, here, appear to be elevated somewhat by a notable increase in agreement for the condition in which the motivation for the prohibition involves a skateboarder crashing into a family: in this condition 60 percent answered that the prohibition applied to bicycles and 59 percent that it applied to skateboards.

As this illustrates, Klapper et al. found that the information provided about the motivation for the prohibition notably affected participants' responses. Similarly, they found that how expansive participants took the prohibition to be was negatively related to their attitudes toward the prohibition. In line with the foregoing discussion, we might take this to highlight concerns with questionnaire methods, suggesting that participants' attitudes and the specific context provided are impacting their judgments, potentially compromising what we should derive from these results with regard to ordinary meaning.

While Klapper et al. acknowledge this worry, they argue that this does not undermine the value of questionnaire methods, noting that surveys can include evaluative questions about statutes that "can allow interpreters to isolate the effects of respondents' normative preferences . . . and to control for it in some degree when estimating ordinary meaning" (37). I fully agree; but, I also hold that it is important to clearly note the hedge here ("in some degree"), since it raises questions about how fully factors like this have been controlled for. Such concerns bring us back to the methodological point I've been stressing, highlighting the value of calling on distinct sources of evidence. Since the use of questionnaire methods does not preclude the use of corpus methods, and vice versa, we can further check worries about one type of method by employing another.

7.5 Conclusion

While recent methodological debates in experimental jurisprudence have suggested an adversarial relationship between advocates of corpus methods and advocates of questionnaire methods, the situation is rather different in experimental philosophy, where a number of practitioners have been pushing for the use of corpus methods as a complement to questionnaire methods, with the hope that by calling on distinct sources of evidence potential issues with each can be controlled for, ultimately providing a consilience of evidence. I believe this is the right approach. Methods are not Highlanders where there can be only one. Researchers can (and I think should) use both questionnaire methods and corpus methods in investigating the ordinary meaning of words or phrases of interest. This has been illustrated by taking a new look at the legal hypothetical of a prohibition on vehicles in the park. Despite three sets of authors advocating for different methods, and the suggestion that these methods are at odds, I believe that the results are instead remarkably consistent and together paint a fuller picture of the "ordinary meaning" of the term "vehicle," both with regard to its most common or prototypical use and with regard to its broader extension or the range of conveyances that it might technically be applied to.

Acknowledgments

I want to thank Eugen Fischer, Kevin Tobia, and Pascale Willemsen for their extremely helpful suggestions.

Notes

1 This is not to say that researchers in these areas are after exactly the same thing, and indeed legal interpretation typically focuses on the ordinary or public meaning of a term given the context of some legal text, while philosophers tend to focus on

analyzing ordinary concepts more generally, even if this is sometimes restricted to certain contexts (such as that provided by a given thought experiment).

2 And philosophers have increasingly been calling on corpus methods, ranging from targeted web searches, to the tools I'll focus on here (frequency counts, collocates, and concordance lines), to the creation of corpora and employment of sophisticated computational approaches. While the use of corpus methods in philosophy dates back to at least the 1970s—for example, Meuiner, Rolland, and Daoust (1976) and McKinnon (1970); thanks to Louis Chartrand for making me aware of this work— their use has expanded in recent years. A non-exhaustive list of recent, English-language work in philosophy employing or discussing corpus methods broadly construed includes the following: Ludlow (2005); Meunier, Forest, and Biskri (2005); de Villiers, Stainton, and Szatmari (2007); Knobe and Prinz (2008); Wright and Bartsch (2008); Reuter (2011); Sainte-Marie, Meunier, Payette, and Chartier (2011); Slingerland and Chudek (2011); Herbelot, von Redecker, and Müller (2012); Bluhm (2013, 2016); Nagel (2013, 2021); Overton (2013); Tallant (2013); Vetter (2014); Andow (2015a, 2015b); Fischer, Engelhardt, and Herbelot (2015); Liao, McNally, and Meskin (2016); Nichols, Kuman, Lopez, Ayars, and Chan (2016); Wright, Sedlock, West, Saulpaugh, and Hopkins (2016); Pence (2016, 2022); Ramsey and Pence (2016); Allen et al. (2017); Fischer and Engelhardt (2017); Hahn, Zenker, and Bluhm (2017); Murdock, Allen, and DeDeo (2017); Schwitzgebel and Dicey Jennings (2017); Sytsma and Reuter (2017); Alfano, Higgins, and Levernier (2018); Alfano (2018); Nichols and Pinillos (2018); van Wierst et al. (2018); Pence and Ramsey (2018); Alfano and Cheong (2019); Betti, van den Berg, Oortwijn, and Treijtel (2019); Malaterre, Chartier, and Pulizzotto (2019); Mejía-Ramos et al. (2019); Pease, Aberdein, and Martin (2019); Sytsma, Bluhm, Willemsen, and Reuter (2019); Caton (2020); Mizrahi (2020a, 2020b, 2021, forthcoming); Weatherson (2020); Hinton (2021); Sytsma (2021); Mizrahi and Dickinson (2021); Gastaldi (2021); Nichols (2021); Fischer and Sytsma (2021); Fischer, Engelhardt, and Sytsma (2021); Hansen, Porter, and Francis (2021); Malaterre and Chartier (2021); Malaterre, Lareau, Pulizzotto, and St-Onge (2021); Bonino, Maffezioli, and Tripodi (2021); Allen and Murdock (2022); Ginammi, Bloem, Koopman, Wang, and Betti (2022); Sytsma (2022); Zahorec, Bishop, Hansen, Schwenkler, and Sytsma (2022); Nie (forthcoming); Tsugita, Izumi, and Mizumoto (forthcoming); Lean, Rivelli, and Pence (forthcoming); Willemsen, Baumgartner, Frohofer, and Reuter (this volume); Sytsma and Snater (forthcoming).

3 https://www.english-corpora.org/coca/

4 When encountering words, language users infer that their referents have the features stereotypically associated with the word (e.g., the "secretary" will be female), unless inferences are canceled by the context (Levinson, 2000). Use frequencies influence what inferences are made, at different levels. Stereotypical associations are built up not only through observation of co-occurrence frequencies in the physical environment but also through exposure to co-occurrence patterns in linguistic usage (McRae & Jones, 2013). Moreover, about 40 percent of English words have several distinct, but related senses (Byrd et al., 1987), and the inferences people draw from such polysemes are influenced by the relative use frequencies of their different senses. Where one sense is clearly dominant, comprehenders are liable to make inferences licensed only by that dominant sense also from subordinate uses (Fischer & Engelhardt, 2017, 2020; Fischer, Engelhardt, & Sytsma, 2021).

5 https://www.english-corpora.org/now/

6 All searches were conducted April 2021. An examination of the context for occurrences of "vehicle" and "st" reveals that this includes both "st" as an abbreviation for "Saint" (as in "all this took place a block away from Boulevard St. Laurent and the vehicle involved was a white grocery van") and as an abbreviation for "Street" (as in "a key was used to damage a vehicle [on] King St., 4300 block"). Similarly, "us" includes both entries like "there were three of us in the vehicle" and "the company passed 200,000 in U.S. sales of electric vehicles last quarter." Finally, context indicates that "bradley" is overwhelmingly referring to a type of military vehicle.

7 The latter issue might be compounded by the type of sources used to produce a corpus, which often include magazines and newspapers.

8 A phaeton being a type of horse-drawn carriage.

9 While racing wheelchairs are not electric wheelchairs—the specific phrase tested by Tobia—another concordance line is at least consistent with treating electric wheelchairs as vehicles: "All feature at least one continuous mile of wide (12 to 14 feet), paved path of secure, scenic footing, where no cars or motorized vehicles are allowed (wheelchairs are OK)."

10 Hōkūleʻa is a replica of a traditional Polynesian voyaging canoe, and while such canoes were traditional built with koa wood hulls, due to time constraints the hulls of Hōkūleʻa were built of plywood, fiberglass, and resin (archive.hokulea.com/build .html).

11 In the other two conditions, participants were given either details about a dictionary definition of "vehicle" or basic corpus results (the top 50 collocates from Lee and Mouritsen along with nine concordance lines), with these being phrased in terms of a fictional type of entity—an "ailac." Participants were then asked to make judgments about the same ten entities as in the concept condition, but now answering, for example, "Is a car an ailac?" Tobia takes these results to speak to the use of dictionaries and corpus linguistics in the law. As noted earlier, here it is important to distinguish between how corpus linguistics have been used in the law and how they might be used to give a more careful analysis. Tobia's results arguably speak to the former, but not the latter. Thus, while the information Tobia provided to participants "is *precisely* what recent advocates of legal corpus linguistics recommend" (2020, p. 756), this information does *not* represent a careful corpus analysis of "vehicle" for the reasons discussed earlier, such that the relevance to assessing the *careful* use of corpus tools in legal interpretation is highly doubtful (see Lee and Mouritsen, 2021 for further discussion of this point).

12 See, however, Experiments 1A and 1B reported in the appendices to Tobia (2020). These studies included a description of an ordinance, similar to the context provided in the control condition of Klapper et al.'s study described later. In the concept condition of 1A, this was "Now imagine that a town passes an ordinance that says 'no vehicles in the park.'" Participants then rated whether each of the same ten potential vehicles used in Tobia's first study was allowed in the park. Results were similar, except that now only a slight minority treated bicycles as falling under the ordinance.

13 Often questionnaires are used to elicit conceptual judgments with regard to specific vignettes, typically drawn from thought experiments in the literature. This can then raise the question, however, of whether the results tell us something interesting about the lay concept at issue or whether the results are specific to the context provided by the vignette. For an example of relevance to the law (Tobia, 2021; Knobe & Shapiro, 2021), consider the large body of work indicating that norm violations impact people's causal judgments (e.g., Knobe & Fraser, 2008; Hitchcock & Knobe, 2009; Sytsma,

Livengood, & Rose, 2012; Kominsky, Phillips, Gerstenberg, Lagnado, & Knobe, 2015; Henne, Pinillos, & De Brigard, 2017; Livengood, Sytsma, & Rose, 2017; Kominsky & Phillips, 2019; Sytsma, 2021). One prominent response to this work has been to argue that this "norm effect" simply reflects experimental pragmatics, with participants inferring that the experimenters meant something like responsibility when they asked about causation (Samland & Waldmann, 2016). In response, Sytsma et al. (2019) turn to corpus methods to make the case that the similarity between the use of "caused the" and "responsible for the" is found in ordinary English, outside of the experimental setting.

14 If there were doubts here, this could be addressed with further empirical work, including a corpus analysis focused on the noun "park."

References

Alfano, M. (2018). Digital humanities for history of philosophy: A case study on Nietzche. In L. Levenberg, T. Neilson, & D. Rheams (Eds.), *Research methods for the digital humanities* (pp. 85–101). Cham, Switzerland: Palgrave Macmillan.

Alfano, M., & Cheong, M. (2019). Examining moral emotions in Nietzsche with the semantic web exploration tool: Nietzsche. *Journal of Nietzsche Studies, 50*(1), 1–10.

Alfano, M., Higgins, A., & Levernier, J. (2018). Identifying virtues and values through obituary data-mining. *The Journal of Value Inquiry, 52*, 59–79.

Allen, C., Luo, H., Murdock, J., Pu, J., Wang, X., Zhai, Y., & Zhao, K. (2017). Topic modeling the Hàn diǎn ancient classics. *Journal of Cultural Analytics, 2*(1), online.

Allen, C., & Murdock, J. (2022). LDA topic modelling: Contexts for the history and philosophy of science. In G. Ramsey & A. De Block (Eds.), *The dynamics of science: Computational frontiers in history and philosophy of science*. Pittsburgh: Pittsburgh University Press.

Andow, J. (2015a). How distinctive is philosophers' intuition talk? *Metaphilosophy, 46*(4–5), 515–38.

Andow, J. (2015b). How 'Intuition' exploded. *Metaphilosophy, 46*(2), 189–212.

Betti, A., van den Berg, H., Oortwijn, Y., & Treijtel, C. (2019). History of philosophy in ones and zeros. In E. Fischer & M. Curtis (Eds.), *Methodological advances in experimental philosophy* (pp. 295–332). London: Bloomsbury Academic.

Bluhm, R. (2013). Don't ask, look! Linguistic corpora as a tool for conceptual analysis. In M. Hoeltje, T. Spitzley, & W. Spohn (Eds.), *Was dürfen wir glauben? Was sollen wir tun? Sektionsbeiträge des achten internationalen Kongresses der Gesellschaft für Analytische Philosophie e.V.* (pp. 7–15). Duisburg-Essen, Germany: DuEPublico.

Bluhm, R. (2016). Corpus analysis in philosophy. In M. Hinton (Ed.), *Evidence, experiment, and argument in linguistics and the philosophy of language* (pp. 91–109). New York: Peter Lang.

Bonino, G., Maffezioli, P., & Tripodi, P. (2021). Logic in analytic philosophy: A quantitative analysis. *Synthese, 198*, 10991–1028.

Byrd, R., Calzolari, N., Chodorow, M., Klavans, J., Neff, M., & Rizk, O. (1987). Tools and methods for computational lexicology. *Computational Linguistics, 13*, 219–40.

Caton, J. (2020). Using linguistic corpora as a philosophical tool. *Metaphilosophy, 51*(1), 51–70.

de Villiers, J., Stainton, R., & Szatmari, P. (2007). Pragmatic abilities in autism spectrum disorder: A case study in philosophy and the empirical. *Midwest Studies in Philosophy, 31*(1), 292–317.

Fischer, E., & Engelhardt, P. (2017). Diagnostic experimental philosophy. *Teorema: International Journal of Philosophy, 36*(3), 117–37.

Fischer, E., & Engelhardt, P. (2020). Lingering stereotypes: Salience bias in philosophical argument. *Mind and Language, 35*, 415–39.

Fischer, E., Engelhardt, P., & Herbelot, A. (2015). Intuitions and illusions: From explanation and experiment to assessment. In E. Fischer & J. Collins (Eds.), *Experimental philosophy, rationalism, and naturalism: Rethinking philosophical method* (pp. 259–92). London: Routledge.

Fischer, E., Engelhardt, P., & Sytsma, J. (2021). Inappropriate stereotypical inferences? An adversarial collaboration in experimental ordinary language philosophy. *Synthese, 198*(11), 10127–68.

Fischer, E., & Sytsma, J. (2021). Zombie intuitions. *Cognition, 215*, 104807.

Gastaldi, J. (2021). Why can computers understand natural language? The structuralist image of language behind word embeddings. *Philosophy & Technology, 34*, 149–214.

Ginammi, A., Bloem, J., Koopman, R., Wang, S., & Betti, A. (2022). Bolzano, Kant and the traditional theory of concepts. In A. de Block & G. Ramsey (Eds.), *The dynamics of science: Computational frontiers in history and philosophy of science*. Pittsburgh: Pittsburgh University Press.

Hahn, U., Zenker, F., & Bluhm, R. (2017). Causal argument. In M. R. Waldmann (Ed.), *The Oxford handbook of causal reasoning* (pp. 475–94). Oxford: Oxford University Press.

Hansen, N., Porter, J., & Francis, K. (2021). A corpus study of 'Know': On the verification of philosophers' frequency claims about language. *Episteme, 18*, 242–68.

Hart, H. L. A. (1958). Positivism and the separation of law and morals. *Harvard Law Review, 71*(4), 593–629.

Henne, P., Pinillos, Á., & De Brigard, F. (2017). Cause by omission and norm: Not watering plants. *Australasian Journal of Philosophy, 95*(2), 270–83.

Herbelot, A., von Redecker, E., & Müller, J. (2012). Distributional techniques for philosophical enquiry. In *Proceedings of the 6th Workshop on Language Technology for Cultural Heritage, Social Sciences, and Humanities* (pp. 45–54). Avignon, France: Association for Computational Linguistics.

Herenstein, E. (2017). The faulty frequency hypothesis: Difficulties in operationalizing ordinary meaning through corpus linguistics. *Standford Law Review Online, 70*, 112–22.

Hinton, M. (2021). Corpus linguistics methods in the study of (meta)argumentation. *Argumentation, 35*, 435–55.

Hitchcock, C., & Knobe, J. (2009). Cause and norm. *The Journal of Philosophy, 106*, 587–612.

Klapper, S., Schmidt, S., & Tarantola (unpublished manuscript). *Ordinary meaning from ordinary people*.

Knobe, J., & Fraser, B. (2008). Causal judgments and moral judgment: Two experiments. In W. Sinnott-Armstrong (Ed.), *Moral psychology, volume 2: The cognitive science of morality* (pp. 441–7). Cambridge, MA: MIT Press.

Knobe, J., & Prinz, J. (2008). Intuitions about consciousness: Experimental studies. *Phenomenology and the Cognitive Sciences, 7*, 67–85.

Knobe, J., & Shapiro, S. (2021). Proximate cause explained: An essay in experimental jurisprudence. *University of Chicago Law Review, 88*, 165–236.

Kominsky, J., & Phillips, J. (2019). Immoral professors and malfunctioning tools: Counterfactual relevance accounts explain the effect of norm violations on causal selection. *Cognitive Science, 43*(11), e12792.

Kominsky, J., Phillips, J., Gerstenberg, T., Lagnado, D., & Knobe, J. (2015). Causal superseding. *Cognition, 137*, 196–209.

Lean, O., Rivelli, L., & Pence, C. (forthcoming). Digital literature analysis for empirical philosophy of science. *British Journal for the Philosophy of Science*.

Lee, T., & Mouritsen, S. (2018). Judging ordinary meaning. *The Yale Law Journal, 127*(4), 788–879.

Lee, T., & Mouritsen, S. (2021). The corpus and the critics. *The University of Chicago Law Review, 88*, 275–366.

Levinson, S. (2000). *Presumptive meanings: The theory of generalized conversational implicature*. Cambridge, MA: MIT Press.

Liao, S., McNally, L., & Meskin, A. (2016). Aesthetic adjectives lack uniform behavior. *Inquiry: An Interdisciplinary Journal of Philosophy, 59*(6), 618–31.

Livengood, J., Sytsma, J., & Rose, D. (2017). Following the FAD: Folk attributions and theories of actual causation. *Review of Philosophy and Psychology, 8*(2), 274–94.

Ludlow, P. (2005). Contextualism and the new linguistic turn in epistemology. In G. Preyer & G. Peter (Eds.), *Contextualism in philosophy: Knowledge, meaning, and truth* (pp. 11–51). Oxford: Oxford University Press.

Malaterre, C., & Chartier, J. (2021). Beyond categorical definitions of life: A data-driven approach to assessing lifeness. *Synthese, 198*, 4543–72.

Malaterre, C., Chartier, J., & Pulizzotto, D. (2019). What is this thing called *Philosophy of Science*? A computational topic-modeling perspective, 1934–2015. *HOPOS: The Journal of the International Society for the History of Philosophy of Science, 9*(2), 215–49.

Malaterre, C., Lareau, F., Pulizzotto, D., & St-Onge, J. (2021). Eight journals over eight decades: A computational topic-modeling approach to contemporary philosophy of science. *Synthese, 199*, 2883–923.

Malaterre, C., Pulizzotto, D., & Lareau, F. (2020). Revisiting three decades of biology and philosophy: A computational topic-modeling perspective. *Biology & Philosophy, 35*(5).

McKinnon, A. (1970). *The kierkegaard indices*. Leiden: Brill.

McRae, K., & Jones, M. (2013). Semantic memory. In D. Reisberg (Ed.), *Oxford handbook of cognitive psychology*. Oxford: Oxford University Press.

Mejía-Ramos, J., Alcock, L., Lew, K., Rago, P., Sangwin, C., & Inglis, M. (2019). Using corpus linguistics to investigate mathematical explanation. In E. Fischer & M. Curtis (Eds.), *Methodological advances in experimental philosophy* (pp. 239–63). London: Bloomsbury Academic.

Meunier, J., Forest, D., & Biskri, I. (2005). Classification and categorization in computer-assisted reading and text analysis. In H. Cohen & C. Lefebvre (Eds.), *Handbook of categorization in cognitive science* (pp. 955–78). Amsterdam: Elsevier.

Meunier, J., Rolland, S., & Daoust, F. (1976). A system for text and content analysis. *Computers and the Humanities, 10*(5), 281–6.

Mizrahi, M. (2021). Conceptions of scientific progress in scientific practice: An empirical study. *Synthese, 199*, 2375–94.

Mizrahi, M. (forthcoming). Theoretical virtues in scientific practice: An empirical study. *British Journal for the Philosophy of Science*.

Mizraha, M. (2020a). The case study method in philosophy of science: An Empirical study. *Perspectives on Science, 28*(1), 63–88.

Mizrahi, M. (2020b). Hypothesis testing in scientific practice: An empirical study. *International Studies in the Philosophy of Science, 33*(1), 1–21.

Mizrahi, M., & Dickinson, M. (2021). The analytic—Continental divide in philosophical practice: An empirical study. *Metaphilosophy, 52*(5), 668–80.

Murdock, J., Allen, C., & DeDeo, S. (2017). Exploration and exploitation of victorian science in Darwin's reading notebooks. *Cognition, 159,* 117–26.

Nagel, J. (2013). Knowledge as a mental state. *Oxford Studies in Epistemology, 4,* 275–310.

Nagel, J. (2021). The psychological dimension of the lottery paradox. In I. Douven (Ed.), *Lotteries, knowledge, and rational belief: Essays on the lottery paradox* (pp. 48–73). Cambridge: Cambridge University Press.

Nichols, S. (2021). *Rational rules: Towards a theory of moral learning.* Oxford: Oxford University Press.

Nichols, S., Kuman, S., Lopez, T., Ayars, A., & Chan, H. (2016). Rational learners and moral rules. *Mind & Language, 31*(5), 530–54.

Nichols, S., & Pinillos, Á. (2018). Skepticism and the acquisition of "Knowledge." *Mind & Language, 33*(4), 397–414.

Nie, Chenwei (forthcoming). Can a bodily theorist of pain speak Mandarin? *Philosophia.*

Overton, J. (2013). "Explain" in scientific discourse. *Synthese, 190*(8), 1383–405.

Pease, A., Aberdein, A., & Martin, U. (2019). Explanation in mathematical conversations: An empirical investigation. *Philosophical Transactions of the Royal Society A, 377,* 20180159.

Pence, C. (2016). RLetters: A web-based application for text analysis of journal articles. *PLoS ONE, 11*(1), e0146004.

Pence, C. (2022). How not to fight about theory: The debate between biometry and mendelism in nature, 1890–1915. In A. de Block and G. Ramsey (Eds.), *The dynamics of science: Computational frontiers in history and philosophy of science.* Pittsburgh: Pittsburgh University Press.

Pence, C., & Ramsey, G. (2018). How to do digital philosophy of science. *Philosophy of Science, 85*(5), 930–41.

Ramsey, G., & Pence, C. (2016). evoText: A new tool for analyzing the biological sciences. *Studies in History and Philosophy of Science Part C, 57,* 83–7.

Reuter, K. (2011). Distinguishing the appearance from the reality of pain. *Journal of Consciousness Studies, 18*(9–10), 94–109.

Sainte-Marie, M., Meunier, J., Payette, N., & Chartier, J. (2011). The concept of evolution in the *Origin of Species*: a computer-assisted analysis. *Literary and Linguistic Computing, 26*(3), 329–34.

Samland, J., & Waldmann, M. (2016). How prescriptive norms influence causal inferences. *Cognition, 156,* 164–76.

Schwitzgebel, E., & Dicey Jennings, C. (2017). Women in philosophy: Quantitative analyses of specialization, prevalence, visibility, and generational change. *Public Affairs Quarterly, 31*(2), 83–105.

Slingerland, E., & Chudek, M. (2011). The prevalence of mind–body dualism in early China. *Cognitive Science, 35*(5), 997–1007.

Sytsma, J. (2021). Causation, responsibility, and typicality. *Review of Philosophy and Psychology, 12,* 699–719.

Sytsma, J. (2022). Crossed wires: Blaming artifacts for bad outcomes. *The Journal of Philosophy, 119*(9), 489–516.

Sytsma, J., Bluhm, R., Willemsen, P., & Reuter, K. (2019). Causal attributions and corpus analysis. In E. Fischer and M. Curtis (Eds.), *Methodological advances in experimental philosophy* (pp. 209–38). London: Bloomsbury Academic.

Sytsma, J., & Livengood, J. (2016). *The theory and practice of experimental philosophy.* Peterborough: Broadview Press.

Sytsma, J., Livengood, J., & Rose, D. (2012). Two types of typicality: Rethinking the role of statistical typicality in ordinary causal attribution. *Studies in History and Philosophy of Biological and Biomedical Sciences, 43*, 814–20.

Sytsma, J., & Reuter, K. (2017). Experimental philosophy of pain. *Journal of Indian Council of Philosophical Research, 34*(3), 611–28.

Sytsma, J., & Snater, M. (2023). Consciousness, phenomenal consciousness, and free will. In P. Henne & S. Murray (Eds.), *Advances in experimental philosophy of action*. London: Bloomsbury Academic.

Tallant, J. (2013). Intuitions in physics. *Synthese, 190*, 2959–80.

Tobia, K. (2020). Testing ordinary meaning. *Harvard Law Review, 134*(2), 726–806.

Tobia, K. (2021). Law and the cognitive science of ordinary concepts. In B. Brożek, J. Hage, & N. Vincent (Eds.), *Law and mind: A survey of law and the cognitive sciences* (pp. 86–96). Cambridge: Cambridge University Press.

Tsugita, S., Izumi, Y., & Mizumoto, M. (forthcoming). Knowledge-how attribution in English and Japanese. In *Epistemic agency and epistemic environments in East-West philosophy—extending knowledge*. Palgrave.

Ulatowski, J., Weijers, D., & Sytsma, J. (2020). Corpus methods in philosophy. *The Brains Blog*. https://philosophyofbrains.com/2020/12/15/cognitive-science-ofphilosophy-symposium-corpus-analysis.aspx

van Wierst, P., Hofstede, S., Oortwijn, Y., Castermans, T., Koopman, R., Wang, S.,Westenberg, M. A., & Betti, A. (2018). BolVis: Visualization for text-based research in philosophy. In *Proceedings of the 3rd Workshop on Visualization for the Digital Humanities*.

Vetter, B. (2014). Dispositions without conditions. *Mind, 123*, 129–56.

Weatherson, B. (2020). *A history of philosophy journals, volume 1: Evidence from topic modeling, 1876–2013*. http://www-personal.umich.edu/~weath/lda/

Willemsen, P., Baumgartner, L., Frohofer, S., & Reuter, K. (2023). Examining evaluativity in legal discourse: A comparative corpus-linguistic study of thick concepts. In K. Prochownik and S. Magen (Eds.), *Advances in experimental philosophy of law*. (pp. 192–214). London: Bloomsbury Academic.

Wright, J., & Bartsch, K. (2008). Portraits of early moral sensibility in two children's everyday conversations. *Merrill-Palmer Quarterly, 54*(1), 56–85.

Wright, J., Sedlock, T., West, J., Saulpaugh, K., & Hopkins, M. (2016). Located in the think of it: Young children's use of thin moral concepts. *Journal of Moral Education, 45*, 308–23.

Zahorec, M., Bishop, R., Hansen, N., Schwenkler, J., & Sytsma, J. (forthcoming). Linguistic corpora and ordinary language: On the dispute between Ryle and Austin about the use of "Voluntary," "Involuntary," "Voluntarily," and "Involuntarily." In D. Bordonaba (Ed.), *Experimental philosophy of language: Perspectives, methods and prospects*. Springer.

Examining Evaluativity in Legal Discourse:
A Comparative Corpus-Linguistic Study of Thick Concepts

Pascale Willemsen, Lucien Baumgartner, Severin Frohofer and
Kevin Reuter

8.1 Introduction

Legal professionals need to be objective in many respects. For instance, each defendant has a constitutional right to be given a fair trial, independent of any personal liking or disliking that the legal professionals involved might have for the defendant. This involves an objective, unbiased treatment of the available evidence, and, especially on the side of the defense, a fair representation of the defendant. Legal professionals must only follow the law and cannot allow their own norms and ideals to affect their legal judgments. Because of this particularly high need for objectivity, one might suspect that the legal discourse is devoid of verbally expressed evaluations. The legal system is there to reveal the truth and, relatedly, legal processes should be characterized by a strictly regulated, objective, impersonal, and unbiased adjudication to not distort the quested facts. Accordingly, so one might assume, this must also be reflected in the language of legal professionals.

However, consider the following case. In 1978, Ted Bundy was convicted of murder, attempted murder, and burglary and sentenced to death. In his statement, Judge Edward Cowart said:

> The court finds that of both these killings were indeed heinous, atrocious, and cruel, and that they were extremely wicked, shockingly evil, vile, and the product of a design to inflict a high degree of pain and utter indifference to human life.

While the statement does not appear to be particularly unusual and many people might sympathize with its general message, the statement demonstrates a very explicit display of, arguably, the judge's contempt of the defendant and, so one might think, reflects the judge's very personal opinion. Given a statement like this, we might wonder whether the legal system is that non-evaluative after all.

The Ted Bundy trial was special not just because of the seriousness of the allegations. It was also the first trial in which a dental impression was used as evidence. One of the victims showed a bite wound on her body, and it was argued by forensic odontologists that the particularities of Ted Bundy's teeth matched the wound. The defense attorney John Henry Browne objected to the acceptability of this evidence by saying:

> The evidence in this case presents many reasonable doubts. It is a sad day for our system of justice that can put a man's life on the line because they say he has crooked teeth. How tragic it would be if a man's life were to be taken from him because 12 people *thought* that he was probably guilty, but they were *not sure*.

Should we take issue with this statement? If the legal system understands itself as a non-evaluative business in which personal approval and disapproval should have no place, should phrases like "a sad day for our system of justice," and "how tragic it would be" not make us rather uncomfortable?

Perhaps, you might say, we cherry-picked the Ted Bundy case in which Judge Cowart was a bit over the line, and the defense lawyer desperately tried to avoid the inevitable. Perhaps, you might think, evaluative statements in extreme cases like the Ted Bundy trial are hardly avoidable but are less common in more mundane cases.

If these points are correct, we should be able to find evidence that legal discourse is indeed more descriptive and less evaluative than public discourse. Surprisingly, little evidence has been collected in support of that view. Several studies have investigated evaluativity in legal texts (e.g., Heffer, 2007; Finegan, 2010; Mazzi, 2010; Goźdź-Roszkowski & Pontrandolfo, 2012). However, there are two reasons for why these studies do not allow us to answer our main question directly. First, previous research has so far mostly addressed very particular ways of being evaluative and the linguistic phenomena under investigation are rather limited for drawing more general conclusions. Second, almost all previous studies lack a direct comparison between legal and some form of baseline or control discourse, such as the ordinary public discourse. As a consequence, it is very hard to determine how evaluative legal discourse is and if it is more or less evaluative than other conversational contexts.

The aim of this chapter is to provide an analysis of the evaluativity of legal discourse. However, in doing so, we need to avoid both these shortcomings. First, we compared legal texts with public discussions in terms of the evaluative extent and intensity of their contents. For this purpose, we created two corpora. Our *legal professional corpus* is based on court opinions from the US Courts of Appeals; the *public corpus* is based on blog discussions on the internet forum Reddit and serves as our control discourse. Second, in order to reach a rather general and robust conclusion about the evaluativity of legal discourse, we focused on a linguistic phenomenon that is broad, frequent, and at the heart of evaluative judgments: the use of thick adjectives. While thin terms like "good" and "bad" merely express approval or disapproval, thick terms combine evaluative and descriptive content. For instance, "generous" combines a positive evaluation with the descriptive feature "willingness to share limited resources with others," and "rude" combines a negative evaluation with the descriptive features "causing offense by violating rules of good manner." Thin concepts are not ideal items to measure the evaluativity of a text because writers often try to avoid plain terms like "good" and "bad." Thick concepts, in contrast, are more subtle ways of being evaluative. In addition, thick concepts come in a much greater variety due to their descriptive components. While there is only a limited number of terms to express one's approval or disapproval using a thin term, there are plenty of thick terms that all express (dis-) approval, but are different with respect to their descriptive elements. Consequently, thick concepts are the perfect items to examine the evaluative extent and intensity of legal contexts.

Here is how we will proceed. In Section 8.2, we review the current state of the literature and develop our own "thick concepts" approach. Section 8.3 describes the generation of the legal and ordinary discourse corpora and the selection of suitable terms for the corpus analysis. Section 8.4 contains the actual corpus study, which consists of a global descriptive analysis of the two corpora (Section 8.4.1) and hypothesis-driven inferential analyses (Section 8.4.2). We discuss the limitations of our study, possible alternative interpretations, and the philosophical importance of our findings in the General Discussion (Section 8.5).

8.2 Evaluative Language—What Should We Be Looking for?

Evaluations play an important part in communicative interactions. As members of social groups, we are not merely interested in exchanging factual information with one another, but we also have various normative interests. We wish to establish normative standards for how to behave and try to reinforce or alter one another's behavior to meet these standards (e.g., Sripada, 2007; Schmidt & Tomasello, 2012; Rakoczy & Schmidt, 2012; Feldmann Hall, Son, & Heffner, 2018). Evaluative language contributes to this goal in a unique way (e.g., Hare, 1952, Stevenson, 1937, Williams, 1985).

Philosophers have been interested in evaluative language as part of a larger, metaethical project that aims to understand the meaning of ethical terms, such as "good" or "bad." Also, in the last thirty years, a wider circle of cognitive scientists has become involved in studying evaluative language, including experimental and theoretical linguists, developmental and behavioral psychologists, and experimental philosophers (e.g., Cepollaro, Sulpizio, & Bianchi, 2019; Del Pinal & Reuter, 2017; Reuter, Löschke, & Betzler, 2020; Willemsen & Reuter, 2020, 2021; Baumgartner, Willemsen, & Reuter, 2022). The identification of evaluativity is yet difficult, as evaluation can be realized in various ways. Bednarek (2008) offers an extensive overview of the different approaches to evaluativity, including eight different perspectives that are each connected to various cognitive scientific sub-disciplines.

Given the complexity of evaluation as a linguistic phenomenon and the variety of approaches one could take, examining evaluative language in the legal discourse requires serious pragmatic decisions on where and how to start. In this section, we lay out the decisions we made for this chapter, and we further elaborate on why we believe that they provide a promising starting point.

8.2.1 Previous Empirical Studies

Several corpus studies have investigated evaluative language in the courtroom by focusing on different linguistic devices by which legal professionals express their stance. Some focus on linguistic patterns rather than particular words (e.g., Mazzi, 2010;[1] Goźdź-Roszkowski & Pontrandolfo, 2012[2]). There are also several studies focusing on individual words (e.g., Heffer, 2007;[3] Finegan, 2010;[4] Goźdź-Roszkowski, 2018[5]). These studies strongly suggest that, thanks to numerous linguistic devices, legal speech, especially in court, is indeed evaluative—although often more subtly. Moreover, a few studies compare the legal discourse with ordinary language (e.g., Marín & Rea, 2014;[6] Wang & Yin, 2020[7]). These studies indicate that the legal discourse is less evaluative than ordinary discourses.

Two features of these studies stand out. First, the empirical evidence is generated by analyzing linguistic corpora consisting of legal texts and by applying corpus-linguistic tools to detect evaluations. Given the insights this method has already provided, we aim to extend this method further. Second, while these studies do provide fascinating insights into the evaluativity of legal language, only very few compare the legal corpus to some form of baseline corpus, thus making it difficult to evaluate *how* evaluative the legal discourse actually is. Such a comparison is one of the main goals we set ourselves in this chapter.

Going beyond the extant empirical studies, we believe that other linguistic devices might be able to shed light on how evaluative the legal discourse is as well. We suggest the investigation of what philosophers have called thick concepts and, more specifically, the use of thick adjectives.

8.2.2 Thick Concepts

Thick concepts, so philosophers argue, are special in expressing evaluative and descriptive content at the same time. Although different kinds of thick concepts are discussed in the literature, such as ethical, epistemic, and aesthetic thick concepts, most attention has been given to thick *ethical* concepts (see, e.g., Eklund, 2011; Roberts, 2013; Väyrynen, 2021). Typical examples are virtue concepts, such as *rude, friendly, cruel, compassionate*, and, as Williams (1985, p. 144) claims, "*treachery* and *promise* and *brutality* and *courage*."[8]

Some legal scholars have already highlighted the importance of thick concepts for various debates in the legal domain as well. Feldman (1997), for example, in discussing Williams (1995), presupposes the existence of thick *legal* concepts and stresses their significance for common-law reasoning. She claims that not only can the philosophical debate about thick concepts shed light on the mechanisms of legal language, but, conversely, philosophy can "learn more about the nature and workings of thick concepts" (p. 180) by paying closer attention to the way "judges and lawyers apply, deploy, manipulate, exploit, and engineer" (p. 185) thick terms. David Enoch and Kevin Toh (2013, p. 264) seem to agree with Feldman when arguing that "many of the crucial legal concepts that our legal judgments deploy are thick concepts." However,

Enoch and Toh do not provide an exemplary list of legal concepts they believe to be thick. Instead, they focus on the notion of legality itself and elaborate on why "legal" communicates both descriptive and evaluative content. In a recent study, Flanagan and Hannikainen (2020) provide empirical data on the evaluative dimension of the folk concept of law. Flanagan and Hannikainen find that a rule's legal character depends heavily on whether the rule is in alignment with what is considered morally acceptable and that "wickedness diminishes lawfulness" (2020, p. 11). Recently, Almeida, Struchiner, and Hannikainen (2021) empirically demonstrated that "rule" has a dual-character structure with two distinct sets of criteria, each sufficient to determine one sense in which the concept applies. One of the criteria is descriptive, while the other is normative.[9]

Chris Heffer (2007) has provided more extensive empirical evidence on the role that thick concepts play in legal discourse—even though he does not use the label "thick concepts" and does not link his findings to the philosophical debate. He finds that in the legal discourse, evaluative judgments are often conveyed not only by "the use of attitudinal lexis, particularly adjectival epithets (*normal, capable, reliable*) but also through attitudinal nouns (*liar, thief, saint*) and verbs (*lie, steal*)" (Heffer, 2007, p. 154). Heffer has identified an excellent starting point for a systematic investigation of evaluative language in legal discourse. We aim to build on this research and connect it more systematically with the philosophical debate on thick concepts.

Thick ethical concepts strike us as particularly relevant in the legal domain. First, the source of the criminal system is the moral convictions of the people within the criminal legal system (e.g., Hart, 1963; Devlin, 1965; for a discussion see Edwards, 2021). Second, conversely, the criminal system can also change our moral views, "such that neglected values come to be taken seriously by community members" (e.g., Green, 2013). Thus, while certainly not all moral matters are also legally relevant, we should expect at least a significant overlap in the terms that are used.

In addition to thick *ethical* concepts, thick *epistemic* concepts[10] are highly relevant for legal arguments. One of the central features of the law is to determine whether a crime has been committed. This involves, among other things, the evaluation of whether a piece of evidence can be legally "admissible" in a trial (as the dental imprint in the Bundy trial), whether it can "prove" the defendant's guilt or innocence "beyond reasonable doubt," whether a witness's testimony is "credible" or "trustworthy," and whether or not an action was "justified" or "careless."

Given the importance of thick ethical, legal, and epistemic concepts, we decided to investigate the evaluativity of legal discourse by studying the use of a wide selection of thick ethical, epistemic, and legal adjectives.[11]

8.2.3 Conjunctions of Adjectives and Sentiment Analysis

Having selected thick adjectives as our linguistic phenomena to study evaluative language, we still lack a way to determine how legal professionals and ordinary people use these terms. Simply counting the number of thick terms in both corpora will, of course, not do. We are not interested in how often people use thick terms but instead we want to know how evaluative these terms are *when* they are used.

We decided to investigate the extent to which thick terms are used evaluatively by looking at those occurrences in which thick terms are conjoined with adjectives through the connective "and." The connective "and" is a simple means to connect two adjectives, and its use is restricted in that the two conjoined adjectives usually share the same polarity (Elhadad & McKeown, 1990; Hatzivassiloglou & McKeown, 1997). Thus, while "dishonest and unfair" seems to be a standard way to use the connective "and," "dishonest and fair" seems to be very unusual and requiring a specific context, as we would expect a person to rather say "dishonest *but* fair" to highlight the different polarities that are conjoined together.[12]

Given the way the "and" connective works, we propose a rather simple operationalization to measure the extent to which thick adjectives are used evaluatively. If a thick term like "unfair" is conjoined with another evaluative term like "deplorable" or "rude," we can infer that the term is used evaluatively. In contrast, if "unfair" is conjoined with more descriptive adjectives like "difficult" or "ambiguous," then the term is also used more descriptively. Such an interpretation of the use of thick terms is not deductively valid but an inference to the best explanation. In the General Discussion section (Section 8.5), we will discuss other possible interpretations of our data. Importantly, we cannot make any inferences from a single or a small number of occurrences. Thus, we need to analyze a huge number of uses of a term like "unfair" to determine whether that term is used more descriptively or more strongly evaluatively. In other words, we need large corpora.

An important question remains: How do we *measure* the evaluative intensity of the conjoined adjective like "rude" or "ambiguous" to determine the way the target adjective like "unfair" is used? Due to the absence of a good metric of evaluativeness, we worked with a proxy, namely *sentiment values*. Sentiment dictionaries, such as SentiWords, encode both the polarity (positive vs. negative) and the intensity for an enormous number of adjectives. These sentiment values range from "–1" meaning highly negative to "+1" meaning highly positive. In order to give our readers a better feel for the sentiment values that are attributed to terms in SentiWords, Figure 8.1 shows some exemplary adjectives for various different sentiment scores.

Unfortunately, sentiment values not only represent the level of evaluativeness but also encode other aspects like subjectivity, emotion, and value association (for discussions of what sentiment represents in lexical sentiment analysis, see, e.g., Benamara, Chardon, Mathieu, Popescu, & Asher, 2012; Mohammad, 2020; Taboada, Brooke, Tofiloski, Voll, & Stede, 2011). However, recording the sentiment values of

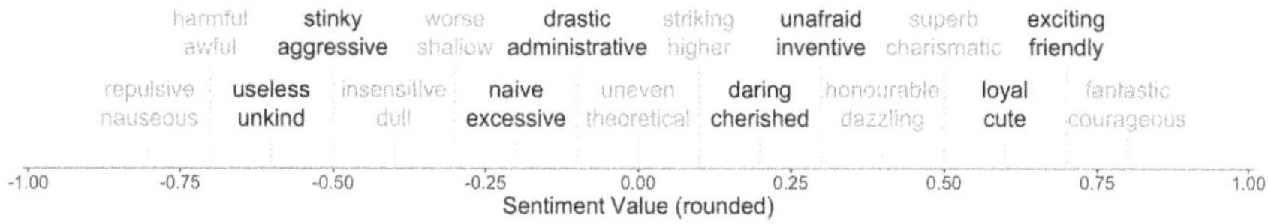

Figure 8.1 Sentiment values of various adjectives from the dictionary SentiWords. © Pascale Willemsen, Lucien Baumgartner, Severin Frohofer, and Kevin Reuter.

hundreds of conjoined adjectives and subsequently calculating the average of those sentiment values gives us a reliable picture of the way the target adjective, for example, "unfair," is used, especially given the high number of occurrences we aimed to collect and analyze. Having described our approach to examine the evaluativity of both legal and ordinary discourse, we are now ready to discuss and analyze the data of our empirical study.[13]

8.3 Data

To address the question of how evaluative the legal discourse is in comparison to everyday talk and writing, we created two new text corpora. In this section, we describe the generation of the corpora and the selection of terms we used for our analysis.

8.3.1 Data Sources

Two corpora were generated. First, we created a corpus with legal documents (henceforth, "legal corpus" or LC), based on the Free Law Project 2020, which provides open data from court opinions of the US Courts of Appeals for the first to eleventh regional circuit (without Washington DC and the federal court).[14] The courts of appeals are considered among the most powerful and influential courts in the United States, as they often set a legal precedent that guides subsequent legal rulings. Court opinions—our text data—are announced after the case is tried. They usually include a summary of facts, the applicable law and how it relates to the facts, the rationale for the decision, and a judgment.

Second, we created a corpus that includes non-legal language, based on comments on the world's largest online forum Reddit (henceforth, "Reddit Corpus" or RC).[15] Reddit seems to be a suitable control corpus for contrasting legal writings with ordinary texts.[16] Other corpora, for example, corpora containing newspaper articles, would certainly allow us to make further interesting comparisons. Unfortunately, the inclusion of further corpora is beyond the scope of this chapter.

8.3.2 Corpus Generation and Adjective Selection

Both the court opinions from the Free Law Project 2020 and the Pushshift Reddit Data Set (Baumgartner et al., 2020) contain a wealth of information, not all of which are necessary for our purposes. As a first step, we needed to select adjectives that are suitable to measure the evaluativeness of the two corpora. We started with those thick adjectives that are often discussed in the philosophical literature as prototypical, agreed-upon thick terms, such as "cruel" or "honest." We further required that all thick terms be regularly used in ordinary conversations. For instance, the terms "lewd" or "chaste" belong to some of the paradigmatic examples of thick terms, but we did not expect these terms to be part and parcel of the vocabulary of most laypeople or relevant in the legal context.

Within the group of thick terms, we created three sub-groups. The first group comprised thick *ethical* terms that are related to issues of moral relevance, such as "honest" and "rude." We expected thick *ethical* terms to show up frequently in the legal discourse, as offenses in the criminal law are not merely legal offenses but transgress moral norms, too. Good candidates seemed to be terms related to physical harm, violations of someone else's property or dignity, and terms with which we may describe the defendant's character.[17]

The legal system operates within a set of epistemic norms—norms of what we should believe and may conclude from a given set of premises. Therefore, we created a second group consisting of thick *epistemic* concepts, including, among others, terms like "logical" or "reasonable." Finally, it is plausible to believe that some terms are used predominantly in the legal context and are likely to be thick, such as the term "legal" itself, but also "legitimate" or "unlawful." Thus, the third group comprised such thick *legal* terms. While the philosophical literature hardly discusses thick legal terms, we selected legal terms based on Merriam-Webster's Law Dictionary as well as the authors' intuitions on which of the adjectives in the dictionary provide good examples of thick concepts.

In a second step, we examined the validity of our selection of terms based on our legal corpus. Since the legal corpus did not provide enough occurrences of all the terms we had initially selected in order to run a sufficiently robust analysis, we had to adapt our list (e.g., the adjectives "brutal" and "crude" are rarely used in legal contexts).[18] Other terms like "cruel" occur frequently, yet are often part of legal phrases, for example, "cruel and unusual punishment." Infrequently occurring adjectives and those with a predominantly phrasal use were subsequently dropped.[19] The final list contained the following twenty-four target adjectives:

- *Descriptive*: "active," "ambiguous," "complex," "explicit," "limited," "practical"
- *Negative thick ethical*: "dishonest," "improper," "unfair"
- *Positive thick ethical*: "careful," "honest," "proper"
- *Negative thick epistemic*: "illogical," "inappropriate," "inconsistent"
- *Positive thick epistemic*: "consistent," "logical," "reasonable"
- *Negative thick legal*: "illegal," "unjust," "unlawful"
- *Positive thick legal*: "lawful," "legal," "legitimate"

In a third step, we reduced the legal and Reddit corpus to conjunctions that contain our target adjectives. All observations in the respective corpora were "and"-conjunctions of two adjectives, one of which was the predefined *target adjective* while the other was what we henceforth call the *conjoined adjective*. The final LC contains 49,199 entries, whereas RC has 69,211. Both corpora were cleaned, PoS tagged, and lemmatized, and the conjoined adjectives were annotated with sentiment values from the SentiWords dictionary (Baccianella, Esuli, & Sebastiani, 2010; Esuli & Sebastiani, 2006; Gatti, Guerini, & Turchi, 2016; Guerini & Turchi, 2013).

8.4 Empirical Study

The goal of our corpus study was to measure the use of evaluative language by legal professionals. A rather straightforward approach would be to simply measure the overall sentiment score of the two corpora. Therefore, we did this for both the legal and the public corpus. In other words, we calculated the average sentiment score of the 49,199 entries of LC as well as of the 69,211 entries of RC. The legal corpus has an average absolute sentiment value of 0.2569, whereas the Reddit corpus is significantly higher with 0.3083. From this, one might infer that legal texts are less evaluative compared to ordinary discussions. This conclusion would yet be premature. Legal texts are different from ordinary writing, as they are often more technical and their claims are often more specific. Let us illustrate this with an example: while the sentence "Voting is important" has a sentiment score of 0.28 (average sentiment value of "voting" [0.12] and "important" [0.45]), "Cats are important" has a SentiScore of 0.44 (average sentiment value of "cat" [0.43] and "important" [0.45]). However, just because legal professionals are more likely to talk about voting and laypeople more about cats, this does not mean that legal scholars speak and write less evaluatively.

As we have argued earlier, to investigate whether legal language is indeed more descriptive than everyday conversations, we need to focus on the very use of evaluative terms (that legal scholars undoubtedly use a lot) even if looking at conjoined adjectives presents a much more limited phenomenon to study evaluative language. Hence, we deem this more limited approach to yield much more promising results.

We start by providing the basic descriptive statistics for our corpora, to gain insights into the data distributions (Section 8.4.1). We then present the main results of our comparative analysis between legal language and public discourse (Section 8.4.2).

8.4.1 Summary Statistics

In the following, we present the summary statistics for the key variables in each corpus: the sentiment values of conjoined adjectives (on a [−1,1] interval-scale), the sentiment polarity of the target adjective (pos/neg/neutral), and the concept classes of the target adjectives (Descriptive/Epistemic/Ethical/Legal). Table 8.1 shows the average sentiment dispersion and lexical diversity (*K* values) by class and polarity for the legal as well as the Reddit corpus.[20]

Let us look at the *legal corpus* first. There are two main takeaways. First, we have more extreme sentiment values for negative target adjectives than for positive or neutral ones. Negative conjuncts also have a higher diversity than positive target adjectives (the lower the *K*, the more diverse). Second, irrespective of the concept class, positive target adjectives are conjoined with other positive adjectives, on average. Negative target adjectives, on the other hand, have a distinctly negative average, and the ones have a more neutral average. At first glance, the average observed sentiment seems consistent with our assumption that "and"-conjunctions pair adjectives of the same polarity.

Table 8.1 Summary statistics comparing the Legal Corpus with the Reddit Corpus for three Classes of Concepts (descriptive, epistemic, legal, and ethical) as well as their Polarity (neutral, negative, or positive). The higher the lexical diversity of the conjuncts, the lower the *K*-value. © Pascale Willemsen, Lucien Baumgartner, Severin Frohofer, and Kevin Reuter.

Class	Polarity	Legal Corpus		Reddit Corpus	
		Avg.	K	Avg.	K
Descriptive	Neutral	0.05	102.40	–	–
Epistemic	Negative	−0.26	124.78	−0.34	73.19
	Positive	0.17	342.11	0.30	94.69
Legal	Negative	−0.19	249.80	−0.38	198.62
	Positive	0.17	1530.47	0.21	132.81
Ethical	Negative	−0.30	507.77	−0.39	80.10
	Positive	0.21	640.33	0.31	125.27

Compared to the legal corpus, the *Reddit corpus* shows a far more polar sentiment dispersion, which indicates that laypeople use the same adjectives more evaluatively than legal professionals. Lexical diversity is also a lot higher in RC than in LC. The difference is most acute for legal and ethical thick concepts and less so for thick epistemic concepts. Otherwise, RC exhibits the same patterns we noted earlier for LC.

Figure 8.2 shows the sentiment dispersion on the level of the target adjectives shared by LC and RC (excl. descriptive concepts). The polarity of the target adjective indeed looks like a good indicator for the polarity of the conjoined adjective and vice versa: the sentiment spread (i.e., the whiskers) is mostly limited to either the positive or the negative region of the scale. In addition, the differences between the corpora we noted earlier are also present at the level of the target adjectives: LC has lower averages (i.e., dots) than RC across the board, except for "dishonest" and "improper."

8.4.2 Comparing the Use of Evaluative Adjectives by Legal Professionals and Laypeople

In our comparative analysis, we assess the average context effects for both corpora. First, we are interested in whether there is a *difference in intensity* of evaluative language between legal professionals and laypeople. If the legal context is indeed less evaluative, we should find that those potentially evaluative terms that do appear in legal conversations are communicated with less evaluative intensity compared to ordinary conversations.

8.4.2.1 Hypotheses

Our main hypotheses concern differences in sentiment intensity of conjoined adjectives between both corpora:

(H₁): The legal corpus contains conjunctions with more neutral sentiment values than the Reddit-based corpus.

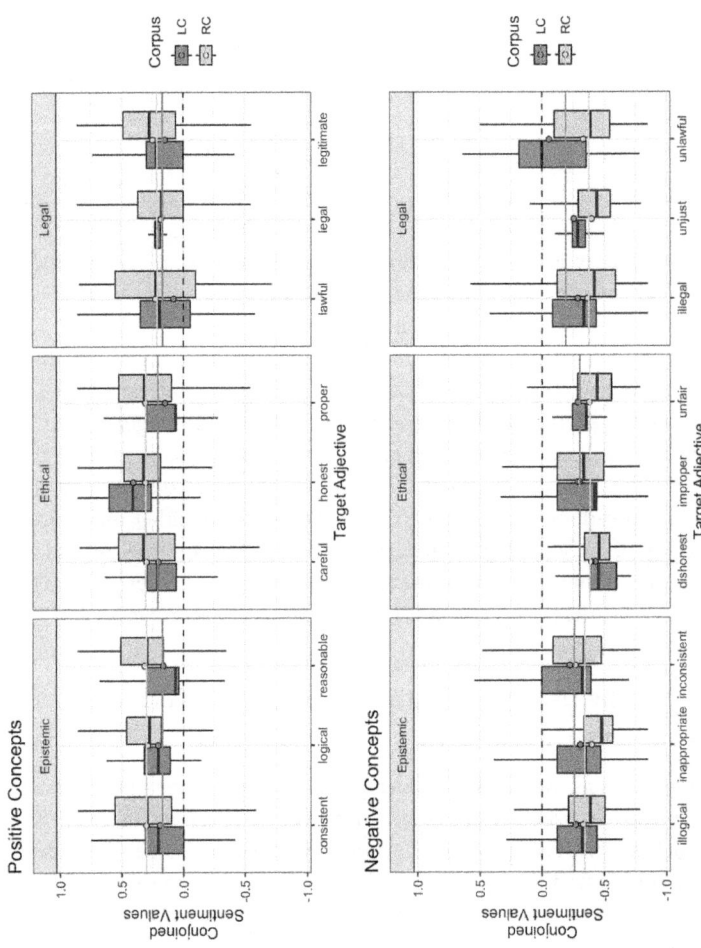

Figure 8.2 Sentiment dispersion by target adjectives. The upper part of the figure displays sentiment dispersion of positive concepts in the three concept classes (epistemic, ethical, and legal) for three target items per class. The lower part of the figure displays the same for negative concepts. Example: the average conjoined sentiment for "careful" is 0.297 in RC and 0.201 in LC; the lower and upper quantiles are both above zero, indicating a generally positive distribution. © Pascale Willemsen, Lucien Baumgartner, Severin Frohofer, and Kevin Reuter.

(**H₂**): The legal corpus has more neutral conjoined sentiment values than the Reddit-based corpus for both positive and negative target adjectives.

(**H₃**): Differences in sentiment values between both corpora persist across all concept classes.

We also aimed to measure whether our concept classes, that is, thick ethical versus thick epistemic versus thick legal, are distinguishable in legal language, that is, whether they form distinct strata along the evaluative sentiment continuum. Hence, we also investigated the following hypothesis:

(**H₄**): All concept classes have significantly different sentiment averages for their respective adjective conjunctions in the legal corpus.

8.4.2.2 Results

To assess the overall evaluative intensity of the target adjective, we disregarded the polarity of the sentiment scores. To test **H₁**, we used a linear model with the absolute sentiment values as dependent variable (DV) and the corpora (LC vs. RC) as independent variable (IV). Based on this model, we computed the estimated marginal means (EMMs) for both corpora. The EMM for RC is 0.3622 (95% CI: 0.3607/0.3637), and the one for LC is 0.2360 (95% CI: 0.2341/0.2380) on the absolute sentiment scale. LC has an average context effect of β = –0.1262 compared to RC, t-value: –99.63, $Pr(>|t|) =< 2e^{-16}$, all other things equal. Hence, the sentiment values of the conjoined adjectives are significantly less intense for LC than for RC.

To test **H₂**, we further discriminated the *polarity* of the target adjectives. We, therefore, used the polarity discriminator (positive vs. negative) as part of an interaction term (IV) with the corpus dummy (LC vs. RC) and performed pairwise contrasts between the EMMs of the sentiment values for each corpus by target polarity. The effect of positive polarity compared to negative polarity was $\beta_1 = 0.6456$, t-value: 324.43, whereas the effect of LC compared to RC dropped slightly to $\beta_2 = 0.1085$, t-value: 35.31. The interaction of positive polarity and LC compared to the intercept has an effect of $\beta_3 = -0.2130$, t-value: – 58.68. All effects were highly significant ($Pr(>|t|) =< 2e^{-16}$). The pairwise contrasts are all significant, which supports that LC has more neutral values than RC on both sides of the sentiment scale.[21] In other words, the difference between both corpora persisted when we took polarity into account.

Our last comparative hypothesis concerns the question of whether different *concept classes* yield different results in their legal use compared to their everyday use. To test **H₃**, we again used absolute sentiment values as DV. As IV, we used an interaction term between the corpus dummy (LC vs. RC) and the concept class factor (ethical vs. epistemic vs. legal). Subsequently, we used pairwise contrasts (on the absolute scale) between LC and RC for the EMMs of each concept class. For epistemic concepts, the difference between RC and LC is 0.1426 (t-ratio = 71.640, p-value < 0.0001); for legal concept, the difference is 0.0985 (t-ratio = 42.669, p-value < 0.0001); and for ethical concepts, it is 0.1153 (t-ratio = 48.231, p-value < 0.0001). In sum, the differences show significantly higher estimated values for RC compared to LC across all classes, which is consistent with the findings of the previous models.

Table 8.2 Pairwise contrasts between Concept Classes of the same polarity within Legal Corpus. *P*-value adjustment: Tukey method for comparing a family of four estimates.

Contrast	Estimate	SE	df	t-ratio	p-value
Polarity = negative					
Desc. – Epistemic	0.1784	0.0058	49191	30.613	<.0001
Desc. – Legal	0.1073	0.0059	49191	18.032	<.0001
Desc. – Ethical	0.2204	0.0054	49191	41.052	<.0001
Epistemic – Legal	−0.0712	0.0061	49191	−11.653	<.0001
Epistemic – Ethical	0.0420	0.0055	49191	7.574	<.0001
Legal – Ethical	0.1132	0.0057	49191	19.956	<.0001
Polarity = positive					
Desc. – Epistemic	−0.0467	0.0037	49191	−12.792	<.0001
Desc. – Legal	−0.0459	0.0037	49191	−12.495	<.0001
Desc. – Ethical	−0.0838	0.0042	49191	−20.118	<.0001
Epistemic – Legal	0.0009	0.0028	49191	0.316	0.9891
Epistemic – Ethical	−0.0371	0.0035	49191	−10.739	<.0001
Legal – Ethical	−0.0383	0.0035	49191	−10.948	<.0001

Besides analyzing differences between both corpora, we were interested to find out whether different concept classes can be distinguished in LC (H_4). As it is not possible to perform polarity contrasts for descriptive concepts, we dropped the descriptive concept class to investigate H_4. The linear model contains untransformed sentiment values as DV and an interaction of polarity (positive vs. negative) and concept class (ethical vs. epistemic vs. legal) as IV. We further conducted pairwise contrast between concept classes of the same polarity. Table 8.2 shows the contrasts for all evaluative concept classes as a function of polarity. Among negative concepts, all classes have significantly distinct sentiment averages. The same was true for positive concepts, with the following exception: the difference between epistemic concepts ("consistent," "logical," "reasonable") and legal concepts ("lawful," "legal," "legitimate") was *not* significant. The estimated between-class differences are overall much smaller for positive than for negative target adjectives.

The results support our hypothesis (H_4) that legal professionals use certain concept classes in a more evaluative manner than others. On average, ethical concepts are much thicker (i.e., more evaluative) than epistemic concepts, and epistemic concepts are thicker than legal concepts. It is important to stress, however, that the differences are overall very small and that their significance is positively impacted by the high number of observations. We are nonetheless confident that the comparative design and the within-context design establish a precedent for a sentiment-based analysis of concepts' thickness.

8.5 General Discussion

In recent years, evaluative language has attracted much attention from a variety of scholars in philosophy, linguistics, psychology, and other domains. There has also been significant progress in examining various aspects of evaluative language in the *legal domain* using corpus analytic tools. However, we have also observed that those previous studies are not sufficiently general and usually not comparative, which makes it difficult to address the question of how evaluative legal texts are.

Building on these two observations, the first step in our research was the identification of a linguistic approach to examine evaluative language in the legal domain more generally. We decided to investigate the arguably largest class of evaluative terms, namely thick terms. Thick terms are ubiquitous and highly frequent vehicles to make evaluative claims. Of course, by focusing on thick terms, we are not able to provide a complete picture of the evaluativity of legal discourse, but our approach allows for a *more* comprehensive view than any of the approaches we have found in the literature. The second step was to build corpora that allow for a comparative investigation of evaluative language. Thus, we decided to investigate both a legal corpus and an ordinary discourse corpus that includes comments and discussions drawn from Reddit. Our main empirical study was then guided by two questions:

1. How *strongly* evaluative do legal scholars use thick terms like "illegal" and "dishonest"?
2. Are there differences between legal and ordinary discourse in terms of how those terms are used?

To answer these questions, we investigated the sentiment values of adjectives that are conjoined with our target thick terms through the modifier "and." If legal discourse is indeed less evaluative, claims such as "cruel and calculating" (SentiScore of "calculating" is 0.15793) should be more representative of legal discussions, and claims such as "cruel and mean" (SentiScore of "mean" is −0.66570) more representative of ordinary discussions.

Examining the use of 49,199 occurrences of thick adjectives in the legal corpus and 69,211 occurrences of thick adjectives in the Reddit corpus, we were able to provide evidence for the claim that legal texts are less evaluative than ordinary writing. For all six different classes of thick terms that we investigated (negative epistemic, positive epistemic, negative legal, positive legal, negative ethical, and positive ethical), legal scholars use thick terms more often in conjunction with adjectives that are more descriptive according to their sentiment values from the dictionary SentiWords.

In the remaining parts of this chapter, we first tackle two objections against our interpretation of the empirical results (Section 8.5.1) and then discuss some philosophical implications in regard to the evaluative variability of thick concepts (Section 8.5.2).

8.5.1 Two Objections

In this chapter, we have made the following inference:

1. Our empirical studies show that thick terms are conjoined more often with descriptive terms in legal texts compared to ordinary texts.

2. Thus, thick terms are used more descriptively in legal discourse compared to ordinary discourse.

Obviously, this inference is not deductively valid but what we take to be an inference to the best explanation. However, other explanations for the empirical results are possible. Let us now discuss what we consider to be the two most plausible objections to our studies and our interpretation.

8.5.1.1 *The "Technical and Sophisticated Use" Objection*

We justified our focus on thick terms instead of doing a global sentiment analysis of the two corpora by arguing that legal statements and conversations are often very technical, leading to the use of terms that are likely to be less evaluative. However, it seems a similar objection can be made against the approach we used in this chapter: legal scholars often need to engage with more technical matters and, additionally, are trained to use vocabulary that is especially suited to engage with those matters. We can distinguish two versions of this objection. First, legal discourse is shaped by language games that distort the aggregated sentiment values of the target adjectives. Second, legal scholars may use less common and, hence, less evaluative words—be they technical terms or more sophisticated Latin or Greek-based vocabulary—in conjunction with thick adjectives, for example, a legal professional might say things like "honest and pellucid." Such uses would similarly push down the sentiment scores for the selected terms.

In response to the first objection, let us repeat once more that we only selected adjectives for our study that are not parts of common legal phrases, which indicate a different semantic embedding. Of course, the technical uses of thick terms might be more widespread and harder to detect, and, as such, would continue to influence our results. Nonetheless, we believe we took reasonable precautionary measures to escape this objection.

To tackle the second strand of the objection, we computed the lexical diversity of the legal corpus in relation to the Reddit corpus, that is, we calculated, how many conjoined adjectives appeared in LC but not in RC, and vice versa. The results reveal that for all six different classes examined, the percentage of adjectives that are used in LC but not in RC is relatively low (see Table 8.3). Perhaps not surprisingly, the percentage of adjectives found in LC but not in RC that are combined with our target *legal* terms is the highest. Table 8.3 also lists the average sentiment values for those adjectives that appear in both corpora and only one of them. The average sentiment values are consistently more polar in the intersection than in the complementary sets.

While we need to be cautious in not overinterpreting these results, we can fairly safely conclude that legal professionals, by and large, do not conjoin a great number of adjectives with our target terms that laypeople would not also use. In other words, they speak the "same" language.

8.5.1.2 *The "Two Scales" Objection*

Our task at hand was to measure the evaluativeness of our thick *target* adjectives. The central auxiliary tool for this task is the SentiWords dictionary, which assigns each *conjoined* adjective a sentiment value on a scale $[-1,1]$. Using the power of high

Table 8.3 Overlap between corpora. The different measures of Jaccard's Distance show the overlap ratio between RC and LC (RC ∩ LC), the ratio of unique tokens in RC (RC \ LC), and the ratio of unique tokens in LC (LC \ RC). The right-hand side of the table contains the average sentiment within the subsets.

Class	Polarity	Jaccard's Distance			Avg. Sentiment		
		RC ∩ LC	RC \ LC	LC \ RC	RC ∩ LC	RC \ LC	LC \ RC
Epistemic	Negative	0.177	0.705	0.117	−0.278	−0.181	−0.1150
	Positive	0.226	0.663	0.110	0.213	0.133	0.0369
Legal	Negative	0.179	0.586	0.236	−0.286	−0.214	−0.0968
	Positive	0.223	0.565	0.211	0.195	0.113	0.0876
Ethical	Negative	0.144	0.579	0.277	−0.327	−0.235	−0.1230
	Positive	0.198	0.700	0.102	0.258	0.137	0.0744

numbers (almost 120,000 uses of thick adjectives in total), we believe we get a robust and representative estimate of the evaluative force of our target adjectives. Crucially, we use the same sentiment values of the SentiWords dictionary for both corpora LC and RC. One might object, however, that such a general application of SentiWords to different corpora is not warranted. To illustrate the potential problem, consider how differently the term "good" is used in various contexts. On the one hand, imagine a piano teacher who seldom makes a positive comment about the skills of her students. Then, one day, she listens to one of her students and states, "That was good." Well, you bet this was not just good, but most likely excellent. On the other hand, imagine you read a reference letter, in which the referee writes that her student's "analytic skills are good." This is a damning verdict: the student almost certainly will not get the job.

Applied to our case at hand, it seems we would need two different sentiment dictionaries for both contexts that reflect the true nature of the evaluative force of words. In the piano teacher context, the term "good" would be assigned a sentiment value that is much higher compared to the referee context. If legal discourse is more like the piano teacher context and ordinary discourse is more like the referee context, then it seems that we cannot conclude that legal scholars use thick terms more descriptively, because we did not use sentiment scores for the value assignment that are suited to the respective corpora.

An important thing to note is that SentiWords contains prior polarities, that is, the sentiment values of words out of context. In that respect, SentiScores are indicative of evaluativeness, regardless of context, and provide a measure of lexical evaluativeness. According to this measure, our study suggests that legal professionals use adjectives more neutrally than laypeople. Importantly, our approach does indeed take context into account, insofar as we assume that sentiment propagation patterns in conjunctions are a better estimate of evaluativeness than raw SentiScores. The objection, however, states that this is not yet sufficient: not only should context matter for measuring but also for the basis of measurement. In response to this objection, we believe our method can account for context-dependent scaling. Instead of generating two different scales before measurement, we can model shifts in evaluativeness as part of the measurement itself.

To do so, we would need to consider the corpus as a set of variables that are specified in the broader embedding of our conjunctions. Such variables include negation, conditionals, modifiers, intensifiers, animacy, etc. Taking into account these variables would allow us to rescale the lexical SentiScore-values. In a perfect world, these variables account for the totality of contextual differences between legal and public discourse. In other words, we can operate with a single scale, while still accounting for pragmatic shifts in scale.

While we believe the objection does not undermine our approach to measuring the evaluativity of thick terms, we have not yet determined how those variables like negation, intensifier, and animacy vary across the two corpora. So, why have we not done so yet? The short answer is: because it is a lot of work. Our long-term goal is to build a classifier for evaluative concept classes. Such a classifier will ultimately tell us, how the results of our study shift with a more fine-grained evaluative looking-glass. While we are already underway to address pragmatic mechanisms of evaluation by studying propagation patterns of evaluative information across conjunctions, presenting a more comprehensive picture will take some time.

8.5.2 Philosophical Implications

A central project in moral philosophy is to provide an adequate characterization and, eventually, a definition of thick ethical concepts. As we have already argued elsewhere (Willemsen & Reuter, 2020, 2021; Baumgartner, Willemsen, & Reuter, 2022), we believe that this philosophical project can benefit greatly from empirical research on how thick concepts are used in different discourses. We, therefore, strongly agree with Feldman that by investigating and understanding the use of thick concepts in the legal domain, philosophers will be able to understand thick concepts more generally. Based on the empirical study presented in this chapter, what philosophical conclusions can we draw?

A major point of disagreement in the philosophical debate concerns the question of whether and to what extent thick concepts are variable in their evaluative content. Does a thick concept like *dishonest* always communicate an evaluative attitude with a fixed polarity and robust intensity, or are thick terms variable in their intensity and may even change their polarity? (Blackburn, 1992; Hare, 1952; Väyrynen, 2021).

Our results suggest that thick concepts can indeed vary in their evaluative intensity in two ways. First, our data indicate that the evaluative dimension of a thick term is more intense in ordinary conversational contexts compared to the legal context. Thus, thick concepts are variable depending on the conversational domain in which they are used. Second, even within a conversational domain, thick concepts can be more or less evaluatively intense. This is demonstrated by the relatively large variance we found when recording uses of thick adjectives in our corpora. However, looking more closely at the ratings for all eighteen adjectives we studied, our data does not suggest that the polarity of a thick concept is likely to be very flexible: almost all thick adjectives ("lawful" and "unlawful" being the only exceptions) predominantly co-occur with adjectives of the same polarity.

We would like to emphasize that these results are at best indicative and cannot suffice to decide the variability question. Our selection of terms is limited and a more comprehensive list of terms needs to be tested to allow for any general claims. Nevertheless, the methodological approach we presented in this chapter motivates such follow-up studies to give a more precise picture of the variability of thick terms.

8.6 Conclusion

This chapter provides a novel approach to the question of whether and how evaluative legal language is, using the tools from corpus linguistics. We created a legal corpus as well as an ordinary, Reddit-based corpus to examine thick adjectives as they are a frequently used linguistic means to communicate evaluation. Our analysis revealed that legal professionals use thick terms more often in conjunction with descriptive terms, suggesting that legal texts are less evaluative than ordinary discussions.

Funding Information and Acknowledgment

This research was funded by the Swiss National Science Foundation (SNSF), grant numbers PZ00P1_201737 and PCEFP1_181082. We would like to express our gratitude to Davide Mazzi and Justin Sytsma for providing feedback on an earlier draft of this manuscript. Correspondence concerning this chapter should be addressed to Pascale Willemsen.

Notes

1 Mazzi examines the most striking linguistic tools underlying judges' evaluative statements, including straightforwardly evaluative verbal and adjectival items (like "disagree" and "incorrect"), and he analyzes the pattern "this/these/that/those + labelling noun." He finds that this pattern "is characterized by the occurrence of inherently evaluative elements as labelling nouns" (e.g., "distortion," "misapplication," "omission," and "nonsense banner"), while the negative semantic prosody is predominant.

2 Goźdź-Roszkowski and Pontrandolfo's research focuses on the pattern "noun + that" (e.g., "fact that"). They find that certain nouns tend to entail negative polarity in their collocational environment (e.g., "fact that"), while others are used primarily with terms of positive polarity (e.g., "view that").

3 Heffer finds that "the figures [of evaluative terms] on the whole are comparatively low, as would be expected of genres where explicit construal of judgement is proscribed" (Heffer, 2007, p. 159). He also reveals that the intensity of the inscription of judgment in sentencing seems to match the severity of the respective crime.

4 Finegan investigates the use of stance adverbials, such as "properly," "improperly," "appropriately," and "correctly."

5 Goźdź-Roszkowski argues that "liberty" and "dignity" are keywords in the majority and dissenting opinions of two landmark civil rights cases concerning same-sex marriage given by the Supreme Court of the United States. Goźdź-Roszkowski

sees these keywords as manifestations of a superordinate (ethical) value—that is, respect—toward which the judges' argumentation is oriented; and Goźdź-Roszkowski highlights the "central importance" of the related evaluative language for legal argumentation.

6 Marín and Rea examine the so-called sub-technical terms of the legal discourse, that is, terms that are shared by the general and the legal field. They either denote the same (legal) concept in both fields (like "judge" or "court") or have a special meaning in the legal field that differs from its use in everyday language (like "trial" or "relief"). Marín and Rea provide both qualitative and corpus-based approaches to the process of specialization of such sub-technical legal terms.

7 Wang and Yin compare the top 50 keywords of a legislative Chinese corpus and a general Chinese corpus, respectively, and assign them to different semantic categories to work out the linguistic features of legislative Chinese. They find that politics and economy are the predominant semantic categories and that the keywords "show strong professionalism" (p. 651).

8 For an introduction to and discussion of thick ethical concepts, see Väyrynen (2021).

9 For discussions on dual-character concepts, see, for example, Knobe, Prasada, and Newman (2013), Del Pinal and Reuter (2017), Reuter (2019).

10 For a discussion of thick epistemic concepts, see Väyrynen (2021) and the special issue in Philosophical Papers, edited by Kotzee and Wanderer (2008).

11 Thick concepts can be nouns (such as "liar," "traitor," "honesty," or "brutality"), adverbs ("shamelessly," "rudely," or "bravely"), verbs ("to lie," "to torture," or "to care"), and adjectives ("cruel," "friendly," etc.). While all of these word classes would be interesting to investigate, adjectives provide the most straightforward starting point. First, philosophers usually discuss thick nouns or adjectives, with verbs and adverbs hardly ever being mentioned. Second, the use of thick nouns seems rather uncommon in ordinary conversations—we hardly ever speak of an "act of kindness" or "cruelty being inflicted on a person," but we would rather express the same thought by using the corresponding adjective.

12 Focusing on conjunctions allows us to hold pragmatic effects constant (i.e., to connective-based effects), and, as a consequence, to use sentiment propagation patterns within connectives as a metric for evaluativeness.

13 In Reuter, Baumgartner, and Willemsen (ms), we use the "and" connective to determine the evaluative extent of thick concepts with the goal to differentiate thick adjectives from thin, descriptive, and value-associated adjectives.

14 The courts of appeals are the intermediate appellate courts of the federal judiciary of the United States. Their task is to determine whether the law was applied correctly in the actual trial court. The courts of appeals sit below the Supreme Court, which is the last judicial instance to be consulted. In the vast majority of federal cases, these courts of appeals constitute the final legal instance.

15 For the Reddit corpus (RC), we gathered data using the API for the Pushshift Reddit Data Set provided by Baumgartner, Zannettou, Keegan, Squire, and Blackburn (2020).

16 See also Napolitano & Reuter (2021) for a recent corpus study on "conspiracy theory" using Reddit as a suitable corpus for investigating laypeople's language.

17 Examples were selected based on the vast literature on thick ethical concepts. We specifically selected terms that seem to be relevant for the legal domain as well, excluding archaic terms or those connected to objectionable moral values. Again, "blasphemy," "lewdness," and "chastity" might play no or at least a negligible role in legal discourses.

18 In order for a term to be analyzable, we needed a sufficiently high number of occurrences of that term in both corpora. As LC is a much smaller corpus, the number of occurrences within LC was therefore our main limiting factor.

19 To avoid selection bias, we inductively selected a second battery of adjectives. We computed the co-occurrences of all adjectives and ranked each adjective based on their frequency and lexical diversity. We then selected promising adjectives that also matched our predefined concept classes. This inductive selection process was based on an analysis of part of speech tags (PoS tags) in the legal corpus. PoS tagging is an unsupervised method to annotate the syntactic structure of text data. For each of the legal corpus' sub-corpora (first to eleventh court circuits), we first drew a random sample of 2000 documents which were subsequently PoS tagged using UDPipe (Straka & Strakovà, 2017; Straka & Strakovà, 2020). Based on these PoS tags, we isolated all adjective pairs in "and" conjunctions. As a measure for lexical diversity, we used Yule's K (Yule, 1944; Tweedie & Baayen, 1998).

20 A more detailed version including the sentiment dispersion of the concept classes of Table 8.1 can be found at https://osf.io/8vx29/?view_only=336a7d04340a4c62a00a2f9 bf4c2a44a.

21 For negative terms, the mean sentiment in RC is 0.3659 (95% CI: −0.3689/−0.3629), whereas it is −0.2574 (95% CI: −0.2627/−0.2522). For positive terms, RC has an average sentiment of 0.2797 (95% CI: 0.2772/0.2822), while the one for LC is 0.1751 (95% CI: 0.1723/0.1780). In both cases, confidence intervals do not overlap, which indicates that LC has significantly lower average sentiment values on both sides of the sentiment spectrum.

References

Almeida, G., Struchiner, N., & Hannikainen, I. (2021). Rule is a dual character concept. Available at SSRN 4018823.

Baccianella, S., Esuli, A., & Sebastiani, F. (2010). SENTIWORDNET 3.0: An enhanced lexical resource for sentiment analysis and opinion mining. *Proceedings of the 7th International Conference on Language Resources and Evaluation, 10*, 2200–4. https://www.aclweb.org/anthology/L10-1531/.

Baumgartner, J., Zannettou, S., Keegan, B., Squire, M., & Blackburn, J. (2020). The pushshift reddit dataset. *Proceedings of the International AAAI Conference on Web and Social Media, 14*(1), 830–9. https://ojs.aaai.org//index.php/ICWSM/article/view/7347.

Baumgartner, L., Willemsen, P., & Reuter, K. (2022). The polarity effect of evaluative language. *Philosophical Psychology*, https://doi.org/10.1080/09515089.2022.2123311.

Bednarek, M. (2008). *Emotion talk across corpora*. New York: Palgrave Macmillan. doi: https://doi.org/10.1057/9780230285712.

Benamara, F., Chardon, B., Mathieu, Y., Popescu, V., & Asher, N. (2012). How do negation and modality impact on opinions? *Proceedings of the ACL-2012 workshop on extra-propositional aspects of meaning in computational linguistics (ExProM-2012)*, 10–18. https://halshs.archives-ouvertes.fr/halshs-00751065.

Blackburn, S. (1992). Through thick and thin. *Proceedings of the Aristotelian Society, 66*, 284–99.

Cepollaro, B., Sulpizio, S., & Bianchi, C. (2019). How bad is it to report a slur? An empirical investigation. *Journal of Pragmatics, 146*, 32–42. doi: doi.org/10.1016/j.pragma.2019.03.012.

Del Pinal, G., & Reuter, K. (2017). Concepts in social cognition: Commitments and the normative dimension of conceptual representation. *Cognitive Science, 41*, 477–501. https://doi.org/10.1111/cogs.12456.

Devlin, P. (1965). *The enforcement of morals.* Oxford: Oxford University Press.

Edwards, J. (2021). Theories of criminal law. *The stanford encyclopedia of philosophy* (Fall 2021 Edition), edited by Edward N. Zalta. https://plato.stanford.edu/archives/fall2021/entries/criminal-law/.

Eklund, M. (2011). What are thick concepts?. *Canadian Journal of Philosophy, 41*(1), 25–49. doi: https://doi.org/10.1353/cjp.2011.0007.

Elhadad, M., & McKeown, K. (1990). Generating connectives. *Proceedings of the 13th conference on computational linguistics, 3*, 97–101. https://doi.org/10.3115/991146.991164.

Enoch, D., & Toh, K. (2013). *Legal* as a thick concept. In W. Waluchow & S. Sciaraffa (Eds.), *Philosophical foundations of the nature of law* (pp. 257–78). Oxford: Oxford University Press. doi: 10.1093/acprof:oso/9780199675517.001.0001.

Esuli, A., & Sebastiani, F. (2006). SENTIWORDNET: A publicly available lexical re-source for opinion mining. In *Proceedings of the student research workshop at the 14th conference of the european chapter of the association for computational linguistics* (pp. 417–22). https://www.aclweb.org/anthology/L06-1225/.

Feldman, H. L. (1997). Blending fields: Tort law, philosophy, and legal theory. *South Carolina Law Review, 49*(1), 167–85.

FeldmanHall, O., Son, J., & Heffner, J. (2018). Norms and the flexibility of moral action. *Personality Neuroscience, 1*, E15. https://doi.org/10.1017/pen.2018.13.

Finegan, E. (2010). Corpus linguistic approaches to "legal language": Adverbial expression of attitude and emphasis in Supreme Court opinions. In M. Coulthard & A. Johnson (Eds.), *The Routledge handbook of forensic linguistics* (1st ed., pp. 65–77). London: Routledge.

Flanagan, B., & Hannikainen, I. R. (2020). The folk concept of law: Law is intrinsically moral. *Australasian Journal of Philosophy*, 1–15. doi:10.1080/00048402.2020.1833953.

Free Law Project (2020). Court listener: Bulk data. https://www.CourtListener.com.

Gatti, L., Guerini, M., & Turchi, M. (2016). SentiWords: Deriving a high precision and high coverage lexicon for sentiment analysis. *IEEE Transactions on Affective Computing, 7*(4), 409–21. doi: https://doi.org/10.1109/TAFFC.2015.2476456.

Goźdź-Roszkowski, S. (2018). Values and valuations in judicial discourse: A corpus-assisted study of (dis)respect in US supreme court decisions on same-sex marriage. *Studies in Logic, Grammar and Rhetoric, 53*, no. 1(66), 61–79. doi: https://doi.org/10.2478/slgr-2018-0004.

Goźdź-Roszkowski, S., & Pontrandolfo, G. (2012). Evaluative patterns in judicial discourse: A corpus-based phraseological perspective on American and Italian criminal judgments. *International Journal of Law, Language & Discourse, 3*(2), 9–69.

Green, L. (2013). Should law improve morality?. *Criminal Law and Philosophy, 7*, 473–94. doi: https://doi.org/10.1007/s11572-013-9248-3.

Guerini, M., Gatti, L., & Turchi, M. (2013). Sentiment analysis: How to derive prior polarities from SentiWordNet. In *Proceedings in EMNLP 2013 –2013 conference on empirical methods in natural language processing*, 1259–69. https://www.aclweb.org/anthology/D13-1125.

Hare, R. M. (1952), *The language of morals.* Oxford: Clarendon Press. ISBN: 9780198810773.

Hart, H. L. A. (1963). *Law, liberty and morality.* New York: Random House.

Hatzivassiloglou, V., & McKeown, K. (1997). Predicting the semantic orientation of adjectives. In *35th annual meeting of the association for computational linguistics and eighth conference of the European chapter of the association for computational linguistics* (pp. 174–81). doi: https://doi.org/10.3115/976909.979640.

Heffer, C. (2007). Judgment in court: Evaluating participants in courtroom discourse. In K. Kredens & S. Goźdź-Roszkowski (Eds.), *Language and the law: International outlooks* (pp. 145–79). Frankfurt am Main: Peter Lang. ISBN: 9783631574478.

Knobe, J., Prasada, S., & Newman, G. E. (2013). Dual character concepts and the normative dimension of conceptual representation. *Cognition*, *127*(2), 242–57.

Kotzee, B. & Wanderer, J. (Eds.) (2008). Epistemology through thick and thin. *Philosophical Papers*, *37*(3).

Marin, M. J., & Rea, C. (2014). Researching legal terminology: A corpus-based proposal for the analysis of sub-technical legal terms. Asp. *La revue du GERAS*, *66*, 61–82. doi: 10.4000/asp.4572.

Mazzi, D. (2010). "This argument fails for two reasons . . .": A linguistic analysis of judicial evaluation strategies in US supreme court judgments. *International Journal for the Semiotics of Law*, *23*, 373–85. doi: https://doi.org/10.1007/s11196-010-9162-0.

Mohammad, S. M. (2020). Sentiment analysis: Detecting valence, emotions, and other affectual states from text. *Emotion Measurement*, 201–37. doi: https://doi.org/10.1016/B978-0-08-100508-8.00009-6.

Napolitano, M. G., & Reuter, K. (2021). What is a conspiracy theory?. *Erkenntnis*, 1–28. https://link.springer.com/article/10.1007/s10670-021-00441-6.

Rakoczy, H., & Schmidt, M. F. H. (2012). The early ontogeny of social norms. *Child Development Perspectives*, *7*(1), 17–21. https://doi.org/10.1111/cdep.12010.

Reuter, K. (2019). Dual character concepts. *Philosophy Compass*, *14*(1), e12557.

Reuter, K., Baumgartner, L., & Willemsen, P. (ms). Tracing thick and thin concepts through corpora.

Reuter, K., Löschke, J., & Betzler, M. (2020). What is a colleague? The descriptive and normative dimension of a dual character concept. *Philosophical Psychology*, *33*(7), 997–1017.

Roberts, D. (2013). Thick concepts. *Philosophy Compass*, *8*(8), 677–88. doi: https://doi.org/10.1111/phc3.12055.

Schmidt, M. F. H., & Tomasello, M. (2012). Young children enforce social norms. *Current Directions in Psychological Science*, *21*(4), 232–6. https://doi.org/10.1177/0963721412448659.

Sripada, C. S. (2007). Nativism and moral psychology: Three models of the innate structure that shapes the contents of moral norms. In W. Sinnott-Armstrong (Ed.), *Moral psychology: The evolution of morality: Adaptations and innateness*, (pp. 319–44). Cambridge, MA: Bradford Books (MIT Press).

Stevenson, C. L. (1937). The emotive meaning of ethical terms. *Mind*, *46*(181), 14–31. https://doi.org/10.1093/mind/XLVI.181.14.

Straka, M., & Strakovà, J. (2020). UDPipe at EvaLatin 2020: Contextualized embeddings and treebank embeddings. *Proceedings of Language Resources and Evaluation*. https://arxiv.org/abs/2006.03687.

Straka, M., & Straková, J. (2017). Tokenizing, POS tagging, lemmatizing and parsing UD 2.0 with UDPipe. In *Proceedings of the CoNLL 2017 shared task: Multilingual parsing from raw text to universal dependencies*. doi: https://doi.org/10.18653/v1/K17-3009.

Taboada, M., Brooke, J., Tofiloski, M., Voll, K., & Stede, M. (2011). Lexicon-based methods for sentiment analysis. *Computational Linguistics*, *37*(2), 267–307. doi: https://doi.org/10.1162/COLI_a_00049.

Tweedie, F. J., & Baayen, R. H. (1998). How variable may a constant be? Measures of lexical richness in perspective. *Computers and the Humanities, 32,* 323–52. doi: https://doi.org/10.1023/A:1001749303137.

Väyrynen, P. (2021). Thick ethical concepts. In *The stanford encyclopedia of philosophy* (Spring 2021 Edition), Edward N. Zalta (ed.). https://plato.stanford.edu/archives/spr2021/entries/thick-ethical-concepts/.

Wang, S., & Yin, J. (2020). A corpus-based study of keywords in legislative Chinese and general Chinese. In *Workshop* on *Chinese lexical semantics* (pp. 639–53). Cham: Springer. doi: 10.1007/978-3-030-38189-9_65.

Willemsen, P., & Reuter, K. (2020). Separability and the effect of valence. In Stephanie Denison, Michael Mack, Yang Xu, & Blair Armstrong (Eds.), *Proceedings of the 42th annual conference of the cognitive science society 2020* (pp. 794–800).

Willemsen, P., & Reuter, K. (2021). Separating the evaluative from the descriptive: An empirical study of thick concepts. *Thought: A Journal of Philosophy.* doi: https://doi.org/10.1002/tht3.488.

Williams, B. (1985). *Ethics and the limits of philosophy.* Cambridge, MA: Harvard University Press. ISBN: 9780674268586.

Williams, B (1995). What has philosophy to learn from tort law? In D. G. Owen (Ed.), *Philosophical foundations of tort law* (pp. 487–97). Oxford: Oxford University Press. ISBN: 9780198265795.

Yule, G. U. (1944). *The statistical study of literary vocabulary.* Cambridge University Press. ISBN: 9781107633711.

A Case for Behavioral Studies in Experimental Jurisprudence

Leonard Hoeft

9.1 Introduction

While both experimental philosophy and empirical legal studies have become a staple of their respective disciplines, legal philosophy has remained indifferent or even antagonistic to empirical approaches. From an outside perspective this seems surprising. After all, most legal philosophers agree that law or at least legal systems are social constructs, yet few seem to welcome the methods of social science. This resistance continues despite established research programs regarding law—among others—in psychology (Mueller & Nadler, 2017; Bartol & Bartol, 2015; Brewer & Williams, 2005; Kapardis, 2014; Zamir, 2015), economics (Zamir & Teichman, 2018; Parisi, 2017, 2019a, 2019b; Cooter & Ulen, 2014) and sociology (Pribán, 2020; Deflem, 2008; Trevino, 2017; Black, 2010). Many consider empirical legal studies (ELS)[1] to be the dominant trend in legal research (George, 2006; Ulen, 2008) and expect it to grow (Lindgren, 2006), others even see an empirical revolution in law (Ho & Kramer, 2013).[2]

Experimental jurisprudence (X-Jur) may change legal philosophy's isolation. As a young discipline, it has yet to define a distinctive canon of methods and goals. Only recently a series of excellent reviews have summarized the research in X-Jur so far (Tobia, 2022; Prochownik, 2021; Sommers, 2021) and helped to gain an understanding of the status quo of (as well as dispel some recurring myths regarding) the field. Therefore, they present an opportunity to take stock and suggest some modifications for the future.

In this chapter, I will argue that the strong focus of X-Jur on vignette studies targeting the ordinary meaning of language restricts the theoretical scope of the field and faces the drawbacks inherent to any single empirical methodology. I propose to supplement vignette studies with behavioral studies, both to address a different set of questions in legal theory and to make existing results more methodologically robust.

In the next section, I will sketch potential reasons of why legal philosophy has resisted empirical approaches so far. The following section draws on the aforementioned literature reviews to illustrate how X-Jur has set out to diversify jurisprudence. Then, I will illustrate some of the limitations of the currently predominant method targeting ordinary concepts related to law via vignette studies. In the section "Why Behavior," I will argue that behavioral studies can address some of those theoretical and methodological concerns and provide a richer empirical background for the X-Jur research program. Finally, some examples of behavioral studies are introduced to demonstrate how prototypical legal institutions can be reconstructed and investigated in behavioral laboratory experiments.

9.2 Legal Philosophy and Empirical Methods

Jurisprudence has certainly not followed suit in what some describe to be a naturalistic turn (Hacker, 2006; Maddy, 2007) in philosophy itself (Coleman, 2001b).

This skepticism about empirical methodology can be traced back to H. L. A. Hart, arguably the most renowned legal philosopher of the twentieth century. He famously derided empirical methods as "useless" and "questionable, indeed blinding" (Hart, 1983, p. 162). Instead, he proposed that "longstanding philosophical perplexities could often be resolved . . . by sensitive piecemeal discrimination and characterization of the different ways . . . in which human language is used" (Hart, 1983, p. 2). (Anglo-American) Jurisprudence has since focused mainly on this linguistic version of conceptual analysis (Twining, 2007, p. 36), in which the knowledge of both how human language is used and how law operates was often taken from folk and philosophers' intuitions (Galligan, 2010).

This methodology has been subject to criticism: for one it is unclear whether the careful deconstruction of legal concepts in (mostly Western) societies will tell us much about law in any given society in general (Twining, 2007, p. 43). More importantly, the value of a priori reasoning come in doubt. Quine showed that adjusting a web of beliefs to new evidence is an indeterminate process that cannot be fixed by a set of a priori norms (Quine, 1976, p. 60). Therefore, no strict boundary between synthetic statements and analytic statements can be drawn, and all are subject to confirmation by evidence (Coleman, 2004). Without analytic truths, no concepts bear meaning irrespective of their context. Therefore, Quine suggested to empirically investigate how actors adjust their web of beliefs in their respective fields.

Although some legal philosophers now believe old-fashioned conceptual analysis to be obsolete, they typically exempt twenty-first-century analytical jurisprudence from this criticism and remain skeptical of the merit of empirical approaches (Coleman, 2001b). And even those who acknowledge the idea of interdisciplinary work usually do so with qualifications (Dickson, 2015; Green, 2008; Coleman, 2004). One of the criticisms of empirical work with respect to law is that legal philosophy is not about any legal system specifically, or human law, generally. As Shapiro (2011, p. 407) pointed out, non-human societies could have law, and therefore social science as the study of human societies was of no relevance to the philosophers. Another argument goes that conceptual analysis will remain important for jurisprudence as even a naturalist perspective will presuppose some of it, perhaps even a positivist conception of legality (Coleman, 2001b, p. 121; Twining, 2007, p. 56).[3] After all, without conceptual analysis, social science may inadvertently study something other than law itself (Green, 2012).

To what extent this is true, remains subject to debate. Many legal philosophers today believe that law is a social construct and phenomenon (Schauer, 2005; Green, 2012; Coleman, 2009; Marmor, 2007, p. 36). If it is conceptually true that law is a social construct (like any other), conclusions about law based of conceptual analysis would be valid of all other social constructs (Priel, 2019): any necessary feature of law (as a social construct) would be shared with all other social constructs. Those contingent features that differentiate it from other social constructs, on the other hand, would have to be studied empirically, as they are not part of the concept of social constructs, and one would have to turn to social-scientific methods that are used for the study of most other social phenomena.

As a consequence of these criticisms, naturalistic approaches to jurisprudence have gained some traction (Leiter, 2007; Twining, 2007; Schauer, 2015; Priel, 2011; Lacey, 2006). For instance, Leiter argues that analytical reflection on concepts of law and adjudication cannot reveal how legal norms exert control in specific instances. Instead, the patterns of reasoning of legal officials should be analyzed (Leiter, 1997, 2001). Apart from the application of law, its social function of guiding or coercing behavior may be a target for empirical analysis (Hoeft, 2019).

Importantly, such empirical approaches to jurisprudence can be seen as consistent with parts of Scandinavian and American legal realism (Holtermann, 2016) or perhaps as a form of "new legal realism" in opposition to neoclassical law and economics that may have emerged with legal realism in mind, but turned out to be formalistic and analytically oriented as well (Nourse & Shaffer, 2009). Advocates of "new legal realism" believe it transcends empirical legal studies in the breath of social science included and in extending the focus beyond questions of legal doctrine (Talesh, Mertz, & Klug, 2021). However, even these naturalistic legal philosophers rarely engage with social-scientific findings (with some notable exceptions: Tamanaha, 1997; Lyons, 2008; Schauer, 2015; Mikhail, 2009), let alone work empirically themselves.

9.3 X-Jur: The Status Quo

X-Jur challenges the antagonisms toward empirical approaches in jurisprudence. Although providing a precise definition of this young and dynamic field seems premature, as the name suggests, experimental jurisprudence addresses jurisprudential questions with empirical—namely experimental—data.[4] Understood as a "broad church" (Dickson, 2015), this would encompass the whole variety of experimental methods.

Yet the research in X-Jur has a clear focus regarding the choice of methods and topics. Most studies so far experimentally target the ordinary counterparts of legal concepts in laypeople (Prochownik, 2021; Sommers, 2021). While some of the recent research investigate how laypeople understand law in general (see Prochownik, 2021 for a review), the majority contributes to understanding lay concepts corresponding to central legal terms such as causality, intent, knowledge, and reasonableness in close connection to movements such as "new private law" or "ordinary meaning" (Tobia, 2022). Moreover, ordinary language counterparts of legal terms have been widely studied with a methodology that targets the use and understanding of language, such as vignette studies.

Vignette studies present participants with written scenarios and ask them to evaluate different statements or answer questions with regard to the said scenario. As such they have been very popular in experimental philosophy in general. Especially, through these evaluations experimental philosophers aim to understand the cognitive processes behind ordinary concepts (Knobe, 2016, p. 37). Typically, people's answers to such questions are interpreted as intuitions that provide information about their concepts (e.g., Stich & Tobia, 2016, p. 9). Similarly, much of X-Jur employs vignettes to understand the intuitions underpinning legal concepts in laypeople (Tobia, 2022; Sommers, 2021). Even though, proponents of the field welcome diversification (Tobia, 2022; Sommers, 2021), there are currently few studies featuring other methods such as neuroimaging and computational and corpus linguistics (Sommers, 2021; but see Willemsen et al., this volume; Sytsma, this volume). Notably absent are behavioral studies (for my attempt to utilize experimental economics with respect to H. L. A. Hart's internal point of view, see Hoeft, 2019). One reason for the popularity of the vignette methodology over others may be that testing the intuitions involved in conceptual analysis is seen as a form of cognitive scientific experimentation that targets ordinary cognition and not necessarily behavior (Tobia, 2022; Prochownik, 2021).

9.4 Limitations

This section will argue that the current focus of X-Jur on extending conceptual analysis via vignette studies limits the field in both scope and robustness. On the one hand, an empirical approach to jurisprudence should not be limited to extended conceptual analysis. On the other hand, each empirical approach comes with a set of drawbacks that can be best addressed by using a plethora of different methods.

9.4.1 Conceptual Analysis

At first glance, vignette studies targeting ordinary meaning seem to fit naturally into linguistic conceptual analysis as it was employed by legal philosophers in the twentieth century. After all, if concepts are grounded in the use of language by laypeople, then empirical methods allow to go beyond the intuitions of the theorists regarding what the folk use of language might look like. As mentioned in the section on traditional legal philosophy, H. L. A. Hart, who is credited with the linguistic turn of jurisprudence in the twentieth century, thought philosophical issues could be resolved by paying attention to the use of language. He believed "the diverse and complex ways in which words work . . . would serve to dispel confusion . . . which had helped to generate vague inconclusive and conflicting theories of the nature of corporate bodies or of . . . legal rights . . ." (Hart, 1983, p. 3). Even today, proponents of conceptual analysis argue that understanding concepts may lead to a better understanding of the phenomenon concepts are about (Knobe, 2016, pp. 37, 40).

Unsurprisingly, this view of ordinary language analysis has engendered a lot of criticism, simply because social phenomena are not necessarily illuminated by a priori intuitions, whether they are shared or not. Concepts may not be a good description of the phenomenon they are about (Weinberg, Nichols, & Stich, 2001): "Thought . . . even if it is collective and public, as revealed by language use—is never a guarantee of truth. The fact that we collectively think about something in a certain way does not mean that things are that way" (Marmor, 2013; Knobe, 2016, pp. 37, 40). Social practices and institutions can function without their participants having a conscious or articulable grasp of them (Searle, 1997, p. 47; Schauer, 2004; Jackson, 2000, p. 44).

Therefore, experimental philosophers are typically wary of such strong claims and aim at the concept's themselves, not the phenomenon they (may) describe. They rather understand concepts as psychological entities (Knobe, 2016, p. 37), and, accordingly, try to understand "not . . . the world, but . . . people's concept of the world" (Machery, 2017, p. 212). However, what concepts are and their importance in experimental philosophy remains subject to debate, and empirical studies can be seen as examining (naturalized) concepts as psychological entities (Machery, 2017, p. 209). Alternatively, these studies may be perceived not as a form of conceptual analysis but simply an investigation of the cognitive processes behind intuitions (Knobe, 2016, p. 50). In any case, X-Phi has been mainly concerned with the cognitive processes behind concepts, a commitment that X-Jur seems to share so far (Tobia, 2022). Certainly, testing the way ordinary concepts are reflected in the use of language led to surprising and interesting findings, examples being research on the concept of law (Hannikainen et al., 2021; Flanagan & Hannikainen, 2020; Donelson & Hannikainen, 2020) or legal decision-making (Struchiner, Almeida, & Hannikainen, 2020; Bystranowski et al., 2021; 55Kneer & Bourgeois-Gironde, 2017; Macleod, 2019).

Still, I believe adopting the cognitive perspective from experimental philosophy and restricting the providence of (experimental) jurisprudence to the ordinary concepts (i.e., legally important concepts of laypeople) would be a mistake. Law is, perhaps more so than other topics of philosophical interest, not just a phenomenon of language and cognition but a set of real-world institutions and behaviors. The concepts employed by legal professionals and laypeople aim at understanding and navigating that shared social practice.

Previously, legal philosophers understood ordinary language analysis as their best bet to understand law as a social practice at a time when social-scientific methods seemed ill-suited to analyze normative behavior (Mikhail, 2007). As empirical methods have diversified recently, now would be the chance to provide an account of law as it is, not merely as it is seen. An empirical research program regarding social norms or racism, for example, would care not only about the folk theory of social norms or racism but also about how the norm-compliant or racist behavior actually works in practice.

Even if X-Jur is understood to be mainly about (conceptual) cognition, its current focus on vignette studies seems problematic. As an experimental psychologist without formal training in philosophy, I find it hard to comment on the understanding of concepts in X-Phi in the first place. This may be in part due to a different view of "cognitive processes" (Alexander, Mallon, & Weinberg, 2010) and "intuition" held by experimental philosophers compared to other psychologists or cognitive scientists (Kauppinen, 2015, p. 169). For example, in the research program on moral judgment and decision-making, people's answers to moral dilemmas are typically seen as a result of a cognitive process, not an illustration of the process itself. While in X-Phi, judgments about hypothetical cases are generally interpreted as intuitions (Knobe, 2016, p. 40), in psychological research they are understood as answers that could have been the result of either a deliberative or an intuitive decision process. Intuitions and underpinning cognitive processes are then either unobtrusively observed (via FMRI and Eye- or Mousetracking) or manipulated (via cognitive load, etc.) (Greene, 2014; for methods of inducing intuitive processing modes, see Horstmann, Hausmann, & Ryf, 2009, p. 219). Vignette studies, on the other hand, play only a small role in experimental psychology in general (Alexander, Mallon, & Weinberg, 2010). Their methodological effectiveness is doubted by many psychologists and behavioral scientists (Woolfolk, 2011, 2013), as people are often not competent in their self-assessment of cognition and behavior (Wilson & Dunn, 2004; Poon, Koehler, & Buehler, 2014). This concern seems especially virulent for intuitions and other cognitive processes that work fast, automatically and context-independent (Machery, 2017, p. 211).

Experimental philosophers seem to sympathize with this concern. In their vignettes and associated questions they rather ask participants to use a concept instead of asking about its content directly (Machery, 2017, p. 210). But by doing so they still seem to presuppose that there is a clear way to infer cognitive processes from vignette data (this concern will be addressed in the next section) and that the use of a concept happens mainly through the use of language in abstract classification tasks such as vignettes. If concepts are best illustrated by empirical studies on their use (Machery, 2017, p. 210), then one may ask why these studies are exclusively focused on the concepts' linguistic applications. For example, my concept of fairness may as well be inferred from my behavior in a situation where fairness norms apply and whether my concept of dog includes the property "dangerous" may be revealed by my behavior around dogs. In other words, if people can indeed have mistaken views of their own concepts (Machery, 2017, pp. 210, 220), it begs the question as to why vignettes would be a more credible way to elicit them.

Another limitation of conceptual analysis in its current form is the difficulty to select and improve upon them. In case the concept describes an external phenomenon, one job of naturalized conceptual analysis would be to assess the empirical validity of concepts (Machery, 2017, p. 223). This would assume—in the case of the concept of law—that we have empirical knowledge of how law works in general. But even fundamental questions in jurisprudence such as "can law be reduced to formal sanctions" are still far from settled (for completely different accounts on this question, see Schauer, 2015 and Hoeft, 2019). So even if we were to elucidate the (folk) concept of law, it would difficult to improve upon it without understanding how a legal system actually functions. Why should this precondition (an empirical account of what a concept describes) not fall under the umbrella of X-Jur?

Finally, I agree that understanding the ordinary counterparts of legal concepts may be relevant to "ordinary meaning interpretation" and "new private law" (Tobia, 2022). In this vein, there has been indeed a plethora of fascinating work on causation, intent, knowledge, and reasonableness (Tobia, 2022). However, it should be noted that other legal systems may not place the same weight on ordinary meaning interpretation as the judicial system in the United States does and consider some of the X-Jur topics as questions of legal dogma instead. Therefore, it is not straightforward what is the significance of the ordinary meaning interpretations for such countries. Thus, even though I find the idea of returning these questions to the core of jurisprudence appealing, they are not necessary conditions of legal systems and do not directly speak to the issues in general jurisprudence that have dominated the jurisprudential discourse in the last century. Vignette studies on questions of general jurisprudence could be worthwhile (see Hannikainen et al. (2021) and Donelson and Hannikainen (2020)), but studying such abstract concepts with vignettes brings its own issues, some of which are described later.

9.4.2 Experimental Control

Vignettes have a salient advantage in their degree of freedom to vary the scenarios: One can construct a fictional society and legal system, or one can ask about any given change or aspect of a real legal system. There is, however, a price tag.

The freedom in design implies the loss of experimental control by invoking moral, legal, and social concepts, whose understanding by the participants may be variable and idiosyncratic. This may pose a problem, especially if the researcher investigates a concept of which he has a different understanding from the participants and thus misinterprets the evidence. But it could also mean that participants give answers based on entirely unanticipated and unobserved concepts. Experimentalists are usually quick to add that unobserved variables are "constant over treatments." Therefore, due to randomization into a control group and a treatment group, such unobserved variables should be similarly distributed in both and therefore not muddy the identification of a causal factor for a difference between the treatment and control group. But this is only the case if none of the unobserved variables interacts with or changes as a reaction to the treatment itself. Such interaction can be hard to control for in vignettes (or even behavioral studies[5]): imagine presenting participants with a vignette where a person performs an act whose legality is varied across treatments. In this case, some participants in a treatment where the illegality would seem counterintuitive (e.g., a fictive society that passed a law where citizens aged thirty to forty are not allowed to drive bicycles) may understand legality as "temporary legality": the law may be passed but is probably unconstitutional and will therefore be shot down eventually. Others may assume that a society which allows such behavior must have a corrupt government or deeply immoral citizens and voice their protest by thinking, "well, I do not see this as real law." Another subset may interpret questions about legality as questions about the likelihood something will be treated or enforced by the state. While the causal effect of varying legality is still identified (participants think about sanctions due to illegality), one cannot specify the mechanism by which that effect comes to pass. This will make inferring conclusions for the real world difficult (any social sanction may have the same effect in the real world, while illegality with poor enforcement may have not). In order to maximize experimental control, vignettes would have to be short and devoid of context, which in turn may change the elicited intuition from the intuition that is supposed to be studied (Wang, 2018).

Problems of experimental control will be heightened with vignette studies targeting concepts with judgments on fictional scenarios. This presupposes that there is a way to invoke specific concepts through language (e.g., the concept of intent may be investigated by describing a fictional scenario and asking participants whether person X acted intentionally). But words are not necessarily the "atoms" of linguistic structure (Jackendorff, 2012, p. 179) and can refer to different (or no) concepts in different contexts (Marmor, 2013; Moore, 1989). Moreover, drawing conclusions from linguistic behavior to cognitive states of subjects is not easy. Subjects will answer even if they have no intuition either way and their answers may reflect something other than their intuitions (Bengson, 2013). Besides, differences in responses may reflect differences in performance errors or how task is understood (Ludwig, 2010). Even in those cases when we are certain the answers reflect concepts, distinguishing between disagreement on one concept, the use of different concepts by participants or just noise is difficult (Kauppinen, 2007), especially if the content of the concept itself is to be filled empirically (Alexander, Mallon, & Weinberg, 2010): if we are studying what the concept of intent entails, how can we know whether variance in the participants answers are due to the variability of the concept, disagreement on the concept or some participants applying the concept "knowingly" instead. Finally, much will hinge on the operationalization of the vignette itself and contextual circumstances (Cullen, 2010; Wang, 2018; DeRose, 2011), such as competence of the participants, conditions that avoid performance errors by otherwise competent participants, and focus on semantic considerations, (Kauppinen, 2007), as opposed to speaker's reference or pragmatic meaning (Deutsch, 2009). While the researcher may be interested in whether a specific concept technically applies to a situation, participants may instead use language pragmatically. For instance, when asked if I ate my lunch voluntarily yesterday, I may disagree not because I believe it not to be technically true but because it would be inappropriate to use the term "voluntarily" in this context. A broader notion would be that participants may engage in "loose talk" (Kauppinen, 2014; Talbot, 2012). Take as an example questions on the intelligibility, enforcement, or consistency of law (Hannikainen et al., 2021): in this study, the authors test whether the mandatory procedural principles of a legal system put forth by Lon Fuller (e.g., intelligibility and consistency) are shared among laypeople across different countries. For each of the principles, participants are asked whether "Some laws are . . ." or "There could be laws that . . . ." For example, the questions on intelligibility read: "Some laws are not understandable to most of those subject to them" and "There could be laws that are not understandable to most of those subject to them." Those on Consistency read: "In a single jurisdiction, there are sometimes laws that contradict one another" and "In a single jurisdiction, there could be laws that contradict one another." One interesting finding is the heterogeneity in the answers, both for each question itself and between the two questions concerning the same principle. The substantial disagreement between participants observed in this study may reflect genuine disagreement over the nature of law, mistakes in the application of their own concept of law they would correct after further reflection, or simply different concepts of intelligibility or consistency. Differences in answers to "Some laws are" and "There could be laws" questions may be due to different concepts of law held by the study participants, one being "norms that people have called law," another "law as an abstract ideal." Participants may also try to voice their ad hoc and personal opinions instead of specifying their actual concept of legality (e.g., saying no to "There are sometimes laws that contradict one another" could actually mean "I believe there should be no laws that contradict one another"; much in the same way one might exclaim "You can't be serious" knowing full well the opposite is true). Additionally, vignettes typically allow participants to infer from context what is being researched (Schwarz, 2007, 1995), which makes participants likely to conform to an experimental demand effect. If the goal remains unclear to participants, the resulting confusion may make the data even harder to interpret (Cullen, 2010; DeRose, 2011). In any case, the concept in question may interact with other concepts evoked by answering a vignette (DeRose, 2011). For instance, people's disagreement about the intelligibility of law (i.e., whether the law can or should be intelligible) may not reflect differences in the concept of law, but differences in the concept of intelligibility.

On top of the aforementioned problems with vignette studies in general, vignette studies in X-Jur face an additional issue of separating legal and extralegal concepts. One may assume that laypeople apply ordinary concepts and (legal) experts apply their legal concept. Yet it seems like a strong assumption that both always and only apply one concept. As a trained lawyer I have a legal concept of reasonableness but also an ordinary one, and laypeople know of some legal counterparts to their ordinary concepts and may try to apply those despite their imperfect legal knowledge if a vignette consists of a legal problem. For instance, consider giving laypeople vignettes on a driver causing a car accident and asking whether the driver behaved negligently. Which concept of negligence, legal or ordinary, would their answer reveal? What if the participants answer differently when handed traffic law's that stipulate reasonable driving. One may intuit that they are now applying a legal concept. But it is also possible that they are flexible regarding their extralegal concept of negligence (i.e., there is no fixed, context-independent lay concept of negligence).

9.4.3 Point of View

Closely related to the concern about the interpretation of laypeople's answers is a jurisprudential issue: Hart pointed out that accepting legal norms or a legal system may entail different attitudes and activities for citizens and legal officials who are professionally concerned with them. However, many contemporary legal philosophers agree that a legal system entails that at least some part of its population takes an internal point of view (Hart, Green, Raz, & Bulloch, 2012) toward it. What role this "self-perception" of a legal system plays in jurisprudence remains subject to debate

(Coleman, 2004), with some even believing jurisprudence should consist purely in extending and developing the self-perception of a given legal system (Dworkin, 1986).

This debate has implications for experimental jurisprudence. Those who argue legal philosophy has to build on the internal point of view of citizens or legal officials may object to empirical evidence that asks participants to judge issues in fictional or foreign legal system, precisely because the participants do not have an internal, but an external point of view. For instance, when judging whether a duly issued but deeply immoral norm is indeed a law (Flanagan & Hannikainen, 2020), participants' answers may vary depending on whether they take an external point of view or an internal point of view (i.e., are socialized in a legal system in which this kind of law would be unconstitutional).[6] The different perspective may have repercussions for the experimental evidence: Legal theory may stipulate that law has to converge with moral or social norms from the internal point of view of its citizens without implying that this is evident from an external point of view. Participants may argue that a law violating moral norms in a fictional legal system is not "truly" law, but may perceive it otherwise if this were the case in their own legal system. On the other hand, in vignettes concerning their own legal system, the answers of participants will depend on their idiosyncratic knowledge of and experience with their own legal system.

9.5 Why Behavior?

It is easy enough to criticize empirical work, as every methodology has its limitations and drawbacks. The point of this chapter is not to suggest abandoning vignette studies: understanding the folk theory of law and of related legal concepts is important, but not the only potential domain of X-Jur. In this section, I will show how behavioral experiments could supplement vignette studies to address both new theoretical questions and the limitations mentioned in the previous sections.

9.5.1 Methodological Diversification

Behavioral studies are the preferred method of behavioral economist precisely for avoiding some of the methodological issues of vignette studies discussed in the previous section. They differ from the latter in a number of respects. First, instead of asking for opinions or judgments about hypothetical scenarios, participants are requested to make choices that have real consequences for themselves and others. Typically, the experimenter creates a "microeconomic system" in which participants interact with each other, with each choice having monetary consequences for themselves and others (Smith, 1976). For example, instead of asking participants whether they should or would share resources with others, they are tasked to split a real amount of money between themselves and another participant. The idea behind this procedure is to induce a valuation to choices, as otherwise subjects have no incentive to reveal their true preferences.[7]

As to the second point of difference, behavioral designs are usually based on game-theoretical decision tasks. In X-Jur, they could be used to understand how law exerts social control by modifying the behavior and beliefs of citizens. They can also be used to make existing X-Jur findings more robust, for instance, with respect to cognitive processes that are often the target of the vignette studies. While in its inception, game theory may have purposely abstracted from studying cognitive mechanisms, behavioral studies now often use games to illuminate those mechanisms (the subfield sometimes referred to as psychological game theory, see Camerer, 2003; Wagner, 2013; Battigalli & Dufwenberg, 2009, 2020). This has been mainly done by eliciting and manipulating beliefs or changing context of a decision to understand what factors (e.g., social preferences) drive human behavior. For example, a series of studies on "guilt aversion" disentangled whether the act of making a promise or just the expectations created thereby lead to reciprocating trust by randomly reallocating the promiser to a different promisee in the treatment condition (Vanberg, 2008).

Such an approach could be relevant to X-Jur. In particular, behavioral experiments could expand on the work by Hannikainen et al. (2021) and Donelson & Hannikainen (2020) by testing whether subjects punish others for violating legal norms that satisfy Fuller's principles of inner morality or not. Since an experimenter cannot ask subjects to violate laws, one can combine vignettes with behavioral experiments by asking subjects to indicate how willing they would be to break a fictional law and then have them play a behavioral game that allows for punishment.[8] Alternatively, one could create a "toy society" (the typical approach for behavioral economics, as detailed later) in a lab where participants play a game allowing for both cooperative and egocentric behavior. Then, one could introduce to these societies norms and sanctioning institutions that would either satisfy Fuller's criteria of inner morality of law or not and see whether they manage to sustain cooperative behavior inside the group.[9] This would allow a different empirical angle at Fuller's theory. After all, a legal system violating Fuller's criteria could exist and be effective even if citizens do not believe this to be possible. Additionally, participants in these "toy societies" come closer to taking an internal point of view with regard to their group standards and behavior than in abstract individual evaluation tasks like those in vignette studies.

Third difference to vignette studies is that behavioral economists typically use neutral language to describe their games to avoid the identification problems posed by activating a host of different concepts through contextually rich vignettes mentioned earlier. Even if a behavior modeled in an economic game amounts to punishment, it will be described by an experimenter as "point-reduction" to avoid participants' potential idiosyncratic understandings of terms such as "punishment" or "fairness" which are hard to control for (Rubin, Cailin, & Bruner, 2019, p. 175). However, a strict adherence to this standard may not be advisable for X-Jur as law trades in meaningful language. There is no such thing as "neutral" law, as normative language is one of the defining features of any legal system. Even behavioral economists have deviated from neutral language in part, usually by selectively and cautiously adding specific terms in behavioral studies and comparing them to a neutral frame (examples are found in the subsection on framing). This may be appealing for X-Jur too, as I will discuss in the section on prototypical legal institutions later.

9.5.2 Expanding Legal Theory

Others have already argued that not only concepts but also actions and behaviors are of interest for (experimental) philosophy in general (Rose & Danks, 2013). This seems especially true for X-Jur. The section on conceptual analysis already pointed out that many proponents of the method believed they could use concepts to study the phenomenon concepts were about. Even experimental philosophers opting for a purely cognitive understanding of concepts would eventually be interested in comparing those concepts to their real-world counterparts (Machery, 2017). But how can one answer the question concerning whether the ordinary concept of law (in general) is accurate? One of the issues X-Jur could address is precisely the problem that an empirically validated real-world account of law in general does not exist. As Lewis Kornhauser pointed out: "No one . . . advocates a social-scientific concept of law . . ." (Kornhauser, 2004). It would be a missed opportunity for X-Jur to forgo creating such an account of law and focus on cognition alone. Most legal philosophers today believe law to be a social construct. Then, they require some descriptive information about the phenomenon they theorize about (Galligan, 2010). X-Jur could therefore offer a source of such descriptive information that would go beyond simply providing the naturalized conceptual analysis of law. For instance, its potential further questions of interest could include the following: Do legal systems have to converge with morality to be effective? Can a legal system only persist if its norms satisfy specific formal requirements, such as articulated by Fuller? Do legal norms function in the same way social norms in general do? Can legal compliance be reduced to formal sanctions? Do citizens treat legal norms like other moral or social norms or do they enjoy a special status? How does law exert social control: only via modifying behavior or by also expressing public attitudes, providing information, changing beliefs, and so on?

Addressing these questions empirically may not always provide a strict test of jurisprudential theories, as they were usually not designed to be empirically tested. Nonetheless, they can still show areas of interest for empirical work, such that a social-scientific concept of law would not be untethered from the existing jurisprudential discussions. As an example, in his seminal book H. L. A. Hart identified three main jurisprudential questions (Hart et al., 2012, p. 13): How does law differ from or is related to orders backed by threats? What are rules and how is law an affair of rules? How does legal obligation differ from, and how is it related to, moral obligations? Since Hart perceived law to be a system of social control, and grounded parts of his legal theory in social practice (Hart et al., 2012, pp. 39f, 55, 58, 255f), one may argue that these questions have an outright empirical content.

Crucially, what is needed is a social-scientific concept of "law as it is," not "law as it is perceived by laypeople." Even H. L. A. Hart, who initiated the linguistic turn of legal philosophy in the twentieth century, was ultimately interested in offering a descriptively accurate account of law as an actual social practice based on social facts, conduct, and beliefs (Marmor, 2013; Hoeft, 2019). Surely, a social-scientific concept of law will have to account for the cognition and "folk theories" held by people but is by no means restricted to these components. The same holds for the ordinary counterparts of legal concepts such as intent or causation. For example, a naturalistic concept of law could detail when and why people act intentionally, and why sanctioning intentional actions more severely (a cross-cultural legal phenomenon) leads to less overall harm.

9.5.3 Legal Compliance and Application

Finally, a mix of behavioral and vignette studies would help distinguish between how law regulates conduct by modifying the behavior of citizens and how law is applied by legal professionals using legal concepts. Compliance is more concerned with behavior, application more with cognition. Both are important jurisprudential topics.

At least for laypeople, law overwhelmingly regulates behavior, seldomly only the use of thought or its linguistic expressions. With the exception of legal officials, most citizens are concerned with legal compliance. Legal compliance usually does not require citizens to have a clear understanding of the underlying legal concepts. And correspondingly, many or even most legal norms do not (directly) address citizens at all, as administrative law has grown substantially over the last decades. Legal professionals, on the other hand, are also tasked with applying legal concepts in a correct manner. Here, cognition matters to law greatly, as their understanding of a legal concept will inevitably be reflected in the efficacy and application of law.

Naturally, both legal compliance and application require a mix of behavior and cognition. Abiding by the law requires some understanding of which behavior is pro- and prescribed, which may (or may not) require an understanding of the underlying legal concepts. And applying the law usually requires not only cognition but a complex set of judgment and decision-making regarding its applicability, interpretation, and enforcement. This interaction should not distract from the difference of legal compliance and application. Complying with norms prohibiting theft will in many cases neither be a conscious decision nor involve applying a lay concept of ownership. Even if it does, most citizens comply with the norm without knowing the differences between the legal concept of ownership and possession. Especially in complex modern legal systems, a sophisticated understanding of the legal concepts by laypeople is neither necessary nor expected by law itself. When faced with complex borderline cases, people may look to social norms, principles of fairness, gut feelings, or other cues to gauge whether this could be a legal violation. Surely, in some cases people will try to apply their ordinary counterpart of a legal concept. But even then, applying a concept in a decision-making scenario with personal stakes and limited options ("maybe" will typically not be available) differs from applying it with respect to written sentences in a survey study. The latter is much more similar to the work of legal professionals, who read case files and wonder if a legal concept applies in this scenario.

At least for a large part of law's function—regulating the behavior of citizens, behavioral studies are therefore needed. Ideally, they would allow the researchers to investigate how norms induce the kind of socially desirable behavior legal norms often proscribe: cooperation, trust, honesty, and so on. The following section will briefly overview how economists have implemented prototypical legal features in contexts that study these behaviors.

9.6 Testing (Prototypical) Legal Institutions in the Lab

The foregoing remarks suggest that experimental jurisprudence should diversify to include behavioral studies. A typical behavioral design to study cooperation would employ a Public Good Game, in which participants play in groups of four people. Each participant has an experimental financial endowment they can either invest in their private or in a group account. The money in their private account is theirs to keep, while the money in the group account is doubled and split among all group members. This setting constitutes a social dilemma, as for the group, full investment in the group account is best as all participants end up with twice their initial endowment. Yet for each individual, investing in their private account is best as for each dollar they give to the group account, they will only receive 0.5 dollars back for themselves.

A methodological drawback for the study of law in behavioral experiments is that the researcher cannot implement a legal norm in this scenario: she can neither assign the status of real valid norm in a jurisdiction, nor can she create a setting in which participants are able to do so. Behavioral economists have found clever work-arounds to test what I would describe as prototypical legal institutions in the laboratory. In the following, I will introduce some of them to illustrate how behavioral studies in X-Jur could look like. To be clear, behavioral experiments in this vein do not pretend to implement real law in a laboratory. In that respect, they trade some external validity for internal validity, as all experiments do. The idea is to test hypotheses not about the law itself but about features of law that can actually be implemented in a laboratory. For example, while one cannot recreate law in the laboratory, one can do so with norms in general. That legal systems feature norms and that norms do not work entirely differently in that system is a part of any legal theory only field studies or other empirical work could test. Then again, this objection can always be leveraged against all experimental work: people may use different concepts or use concepts differently in a survey setting then in the real world. By design, such objections will not be answered by vignettes themselves.

9.6.1 Framing

Understood in the tradition of Kahneman and Tversky's pioneering study (Tversky & Kahneman, 1981), framing constitutes a change in the description of a decision scenario, while the material outcomes and choices remain the same.[10] In a standard behavioral economic study design, instructions are worded with ostensibly neutral terms, such as "decision task," "place tokens in account A or B," and so on. As mentioned, this is done to avoid unobservable variables. For example, if the game were described as a "Public Good Game," participants may have different concepts of the term which are hard to control for. It may also invite moral reasoning or reflection on why the decision task represents a public good at all. Framing in this context of neutral instructions means to introduce "rich" concepts in a controlled manner. For example, the neutral instructions can be changed in only one aspect by adjusting the description of the Public Good Game to a "community game" (Dufwenberg, Gächter, & Hennig-

Schmidt, 2011) and investigating how this affects cooperation rates and beliefs about what other group members will do.

This methodology can be used to study law: one of the main features of law is assigning the status of illegality to an action. Since this is not possible in the laboratory, one can instead frame a choice in legal terms. For instance, Blaufus, Hundsdoerfer, Jacob, and Sünwoldt (2016) asked participants to complete a real effort task where they could earn money by keying multiple-choice test sheets into a computer. At the end of the experiment, the income was subject to a tax reduction. Participants could choose to try and avoid some of the tax which would be discovered with some probability. This choice was either framed as legal tax loophole or illegal tax evasion. In another experiment, Engel and Kurschilgen (2013) let participants play multiple rounds of the aforementioned Public Good Game. In between each round, they asked participants if they believed a general contribution norm (to the public account) in their group exists, and what contribution level it stipulated. In one treatment, the instructions included a paragraph that described how customary law can come into being, the idea being to frame emerging norms in the Public Good Game as customary law.

Framing may be of particular interest to X-Jur, as it allows one to test the influence of specific concepts on behavior and beliefs about the behavior or beliefs of others. While methodologically more conservative than traditional vignette studies, it would allow testing the influence of introducing concepts of interest against a wide range of previous experimental results in a "neutral" frame. This is harder to do with vignette studies that often differ in more than one aspect.

9.6.2 Institutionalized Sanctions/Restricting Choices

One typical feature of law is employing a sanctioning system that is executed by courts of law and differs from informal punishment by peers. Economists have introduced sanctioning mechanisms in different games (Bohnet & Cooper, 2003; Tyran & Feld, 2006; Putterman, Tyran, & Kamei, 2011; Houser, Xiao, McCabe, & Smith, 2008). An example of such a sanctioning system would be a mechanism that reduces the payoff of the lowest contributor in a Public Good Game (Andreoni, 2012). Typically, the sanctioning mechanism is specified to be non-deterrent to see how the presence of the mechanism itself (apart from the created incentives) influences players' behavior. An even stronger way to model this feature of law would be to restrict the choice set of participants: Instead of sanctioning specific behavior, the researcher could exclude the "illegal" action from the choice set in a treatment condition. For instance, in this vein, Falk, Fehr, and Zehnder (2006) had participants play a game that modeled how firms hire workers. By introducing a "minimum wage" and thereby restricting the choice set of the wage offers, the researchers showed how the minimum wage led to higher reservation wages of the workers even after the choice restriction was removed.

9.6.3 Normative Concepts

Most legal philosophers believe that legal systems have to reference some normative institution for their legitimacy. In democracies, this is typically voting and representation, but it may also refer to legitimacy conferred by a higher power or a power exerting some kind of authority. Previous research has given subjects who played a repeated Public Good Game the opportunity to vote for implementing a formal sanctioning system and showed that the act of voting itself (irrespective of the implemented policy) influences cooperation (Markussen, Putterman, & Tyran, 2013; Bó, Foster, & Putterman, 2010).

Other researchers investigated the power of authoritative norms on behavior. For example, in a complex non-linear Public Good Game (in which the social optimum is not a full contribution), Silverman Slemrod, and Uler (2014) requested participants to contribute a specific amount of money that was determined by authorities (i.e., faculty members). In other treatments, they combined the request with sanctions to enhance cooperation. Only a combination of authority and sanctions could raise cooperation levels. Even a simple request by the researcher was enough to motivate destructive behavior in a game where the participants' only choice was to invest their own resources to destroy those of others (Karakostas & Zizzo, 2016).

An integral part of law is its ability to create obligations. Experimental behavioral studies can use the position of the experimenter as somebody who—similar to a governing body—creates incentives, norms, or obligations and affects how these rules affect the judgment or behavior of participants. For example, Galbiati and Vertova (2008) ran a Public Good Game with a treatment in which the instructions stipulated an obligation concerning a minimum contribution requirement that was, however, unenforced by experimenters. The presence of the obligation initially raised players' contributions (Galbiati & Vertova, 2008) even when the obligations were imposed asymmetrically on different players (and therefore could be considered unfair) (Riedel & Schildberg-Hörisch, 2013). Moreover, when combined with non-deterrent sanctions, such obligations also prevented the (typical) decline in contributions over time (Galbiati & Vertova, 2014), although this combination could also crowd out the intrinsic motivation to contribute (Bernasconi, Corazzini, & Marenzi, 2013).

9.6.4 Signaling

Legal norms are endogenous to society. Their existence and enforcement are not random exogenous events but endogenous choices by members of that society that may signal something about their society. In this section, I will examine some examples of signaling that have been studied by behavioral experiments.

Violating a norm is often not observable to others. When an institution punishes a norm transgressor, that may signal their guilt and communicate that the respective norm exists and is enforced. In a Public Good Game, a punishment mechanism that punishes a transgressor in public is, therefore, more effective than one whose punishment is carried out without the ability of other group members to observe it (Xiao & Houser, 2011). However, punishment can only signal normative transgression if its only motive is the violation of a norm itself. Xiao (2013) modeled this mechanism by allowing third parties to punish two participants playing the so-called sender-receiver game. In this game, the receiver has to make a pay-off-relevant decision for both players based on the information provided by the sender, who may try to deceive the receiver. Punishment of the sender by a third party was taken to be indicative of wrongful information, but only if the third party could not profit from the act of punishing. However, this corrupting effect of profit-seeking punishment was mitigated if the punishers were asked to justify their decision (Xiao & Tan, 2014).

Law can also help people coordinate their actions with other members of society by signaling what others may and may not do.[11] McAdams and Nadler (2005) had participants play a Hawk/Dove game, in which their payoff depended on their ability to coordinate with others. They showed that even random spinner which highlights one equilibrium strategy in a two-player game where participants can choose between either an aggressive or a passive option enabled participants to coordinate more successfully on one equilibrium. The effect was stronger for a suggestion by a third party selected on merits. Moreover, this result was replicated in a version of the game that was framed as a legal conflict to the participants, with the third party's suggestion being described as a mandatory legal rule (McAdams & Nadlers, 2008). Interestingly, the effect could only be seen in a game where participants actually had an incentive to coordinate their actions with others. Similar results were found in vignette studies. For instance, providing default contract terms influenced how much participants were willing to negotiate in a fictional legal bargaining scenario (Korobkin, 1998). An initial contract influenced how participants negotiated in an (strategically identical) economic bargaining game (Bartling & Schmidt, 2015).

Finally, a legal norm or its absence can signal its own necessity. Namely, if a law was put in place, this might mean that enough people had engaged in an undesirable activity to motivate outlawing it. This mechanism was tested by studies based on a "minimum effort" game. In this game, two players can independently choose effort levels that are costly. The lowest effort level among them determines the payoff of both, minus the personal cost of their exerted effort. Galbiati, Schlag, and van der Weele (2013), repeated this game for two rounds, with both players learning the effort of the other only at the end of round two. Between the two rounds, either a third party informed of the effort levels in round one and could decide to punish both players or sanctions were meted out automatically independently of the first-round behavior. Only when the sanctions could be administered by the third party and only for those players who had high effort levels in the first round, the effort levels were adjusted as a reaction to the sanction (Galbiati, Schlag, & van der Weele, 2013). That was because only in these cases the players understood that the third party's choice to sanction signaled that their counterparts chose a low effort level in the first round. Danilov and Sliwka (2016) found a similar effect in a principal-agent game. In this game, the principal can offer fixed wages or performance-contingent wages to the agent. Then, the agent chooses an effort level at a private cost that determines the payoff of the principal. A fixed wage signals trust, as the wage of the agent is independent of his later chosen effort level. The researchers found that if the principal was informed of behavior by previous participants before offering a fixed wage, they were less likely to exploit his trust than when an uninformed principal offered the same fixed wage. They understood that an informed principal may have chosen the fixed wage when previous participants repaid trust and, therefore, wanted to comply with the signaled social norm.

9.7 Conclusion

Experimental jurisprudence should avoid focusing too heavily on one empirical and philosophical methodology, namely vignettes and empirical conceptual analysis. Behavioral studies are an especially pertinent addition to the X-Jur because they can make existing findings more robust and help create an empirically validated account of law as a social practice.

As an extension of experimental philosophy, X-Jur currently focuses on analyzing the cognition involved in laypeople's concepts of legal relevance. Since people may not have a conscious grasp of their concepts, vignette studies are employed to see how people use concepts. But judging the applicability of a concept through language in written scenarios is only one potential use of concepts. People may also use concepts to guide their behavior or form beliefs about the actions and beliefs of others and so on. Behavioral studies can therefore supplement the investigation of concepts in X-Jur. Additionally, methodological diversification would allow X-Jur to avoid some of the general criticism leveraged against vignette studies, which experimental psychologists and economists often see unfavorably (and for good reasons).

Behavioral studies would also open avenues to new questions of jurisprudential interest. Law is not just a set of cognitive concepts but a social practice consisting of institutions, behavior, and beliefs. Many hypotheses in legal philosophy aim to explain how this social practice works as it is, not just as it is seen. A large part of this social practice is exerting social control by modifying the behavior of citizens. Often, legal systems remain agnostic as to the cognition involved in compliance, but it is unlikely legal compliance would be well addressed through vignette studies. Vignettes are closer to the kind of evaluation that legal officials such as judges are tasked with. Behavioral studies can fill the gap by showing how law exerts social control.

Such studies implement economic games studying behavior law typically tries to encourage, such as cooperation and trust. While it is impossible to manipulate real law in a laboratory setting, behavioral studies can implement prototypical legal features, such as introducing institutionalized sanctions, signaling, or normative concepts such as voting or authority. Combining behavioral studies with empirical conceptual analysis via framing seems especially promising. It would allow for deviating from neutral instructions by introducing specific concepts in the instructions for the participants. This would, in turn, enable studying how participants use concepts not just in verbal classification but also to guide behavior and form beliefs about what others think and do.

Notes

1 The use of this term seems to vary considerably, and sometimes excludes sociology as well as law and economics (Eisenberg, 2011). Here, I use it inclusively referring to empirical work in law from any social science.

2 Although this has mostly been an American phenomenon, for the divergence with respect to German legal scholarship (see Grechenig & Gelter, 2008).

3   Quine's argument mainly questions a priori conceptual analysis. In practice, even empirical researchers presuppose concepts such as "norms" and "law," meaning their content must be elucidated for empirical work to be meaningful.

4   Some proponents of X-Jur have suggested that the name is a misnomer, and the field should welcome any empirical approach to jurisprudence (Tobia, 2022).

5   As behavioral studies try to use neutral instructions and present decision scenarios that are new to participants, importing unobserved concepts should be less of a concern. Avoiding terms such as "sanctions" or "society" means that the corresponding concepts, which are unknown to the researcher and may vary individually for each participant, are less likely to determine the participants decisions.

6   Note that this internalization does not depend on the scenario itself. Even when asked to take the perspective of members of a different legal norm system, this will hardly be enough to recreate the experience of normativity of people who actually live in that society. Behavioral studies can avoid this problem to some degree by creating "toy societies" in which one can implement norms that participants identify with. This will, of course, not amount to the kind of internalization legal philosophers talk about. Still, the norms and behavior that groups develop show substantial heterogeneity (Reuben & Riedl, 2013).

7   Incentives are relevant even outside of behavioral studies as subjects may skimp on the cognitive effort required to give meaningful answers in a vignette (Pölzler, 2021). They could be shown to influence some results in X-Phi even in vignette studies (Schoenegger, 2021; but see de Bruin, 2021 for an example in which incentivization had no impact).

8   I have used a similar design to test whether breaking a legal norm leads to loss of reputation.

9   Of course, such norms would not have a legal status. But if one were to find that norms in general are incapable of guiding behavior absent specific minimalistic criteria, it would beg the question how legal norms should accomplish the same. It could also help pinpoint why these criteria are necessary conditions for norms to be effective.

10 In this sense, vignettes may be considered studies in framing altogether since there is no choice that has (material or other) consequences for themselves or other participants. Economists tend to refer to this judgments or opinions without cost or consequences as "cheap talk."

11 The paradigmatic example is which side of the road to drive on. Without previous experience, I may expect people to drive on the side of the road the law stipulates.

References

Alexander, J., Mallon, R., & Weinberg, J. M. (2010). Accentuate the negative. *Review of Philosophy and Psychology, 1*(2), 297–314. https://doi.org/10.1007/s13164-009-0015-2.

Andreoni, J., & Gee, L. K. (2012). Gun for hire: Delegated enforcement and peer punishment in public goods provision. *Journal of Public Economics, 96*(11–12), 1036–46. https://doi.org/10.1016/j.jpubeco.2012.08.003.

Bartling, B., & Schmidt, K. M. (2015). Reference points, social norms, and fairness in contract renegotiations. *Journal of the European Economic Association, 13*(1), 98–129. https://doi.org/10.1111/jeea.12109.

Bartol, C. R., & Bartol, A. M. (2015). *Psychology and law: Research and practice.* Los Angeles: SAGE Publications.

Battigalli, P., & Dufwenberg, M. (2009). Dynamic psychological games. *Journal of Economic Theory, 144*(1), 1–35. https://doi.org/10.1016/j.jet.2008.01.004.

Bengson, J. (2013). Experimental attacks on intuitions and answers. *Philosophy and Phenomenological Research, 86*(3), 495–532. https://doi.org/10.1111/j.1933-1592.2012 .00578.x.

Bernasconi, M., Corazzini, L., & Marenzi, A. (2013). "Expressive" obligations in public good games: Crowding-in and crowding-out effects. *Research in Economics, 67*(1), 13–24. https://doi.org/10.1016/j.rie.2012.09.004.

Black, D. (2010). *The behavior of law*. Bingley: Emerald Group Publishing.

Blaufus, K., Hundsdoerfer, J., Jacob, M., & Sünwoldt, M. (2016). Does legality matter? The case of tax avoidance and evasion. *Journal of Economic Behavior & Organization, 127*, 182–206. https://doi.org/10.1016/j.jebo.2016.04.002.

Bó, P. D., Foster, A., & Putterman, L. (2010). Institutions and behavior: Experimental evidence on the effects of Democracy. *The American Economic Review, 100*(5), 2205–29. https://doi.org/10.1257/aer.100.5.2205.

Bohnet, I., & Cooter, R. D. (2003). *Expressive law: Framing or equilibrium selection?* (SSRN Scholarly Paper ID 452420). Social Science Research Network. https://papers.ssrn.com /abstract=452420.

Brewer, N., & Williams, K. D. (2005). *Psychology and law: An empirical perspective*. New York: Guilford Publications.

Bystranowski, P., Janik, B., Próchnicki, M., Hannikainen, I. R., da Franca Couto Fernandes de Almeida, G., & Struchiner, N. (2022). Do formalist judges abide by their abstract principles? A two-country study in adjudication. *International Journal for the Semiotics of Law - Revue Internationale de Sémiotique Juridique, 35*(5), 1903–35. https://doi.org /10.1007/s11196-021-09846-6.

Camerer, C. (2003). *Behavioral game theory: Experiments in strategic interaction*. New York: Princeton University Press.

Coleman, J. (2009). Beyond inclusive legal positivism*. *Ratio Juris, 22*, 359–94. https://doi .org/10.1111/j.1467-9337.2009.00430.x.

Coleman, J. L. (2001a). *Hart's postscript: Essays on the postscript to "The Concept of Law."* Oxford University Press.

Coleman, J. L. (2001b). Naturalized jurisprudence and naturalized epistemology. *Philosophical Topics, 29*(1/2), 113–26. https://doi.org/10.5840/philtopics2001291/211.

Coleman, J. L. (2004). Methodology. In J. L. Coleman, S. J. Shapiro, & K. E. Himma (Eds.), *The Oxford handbook of jurisprudence and philosophy of law* (pp. 311–51). Oxford University Press.

Cooter, R., & Ulen, T. S. (2014). *Law and economics* (6th ed.). Boston: Pearson Education.

Cullen, S. (2010). Survey-driven romanticism. *Review of Philosophy and Psychology, 1*(2), 275–96. https://doi.org/10.1007/s13164-009-0016-1.

Danilov, A., & Sliwka, D. (2016). Can contracts signal social norms? Experimental evidence. *Management Science*. https://doi.org/10.1287/mnsc.2015.2336.

de Bruin, B. (2021). Saving the armchair by experiment: What works in economics doesn't work in philosophy. *Philosophical Studies, 178*(8), 2483–508. https://doi.org/10.1007/ s11098-020-01559-z.

Deflem, M. (2008). *Sociology of law: Visions of a scholarly tradition*. Cambridge: Cambridge University Press. https://doi.org/10.1017/CBO9780511815546.

DeRose, K. (2011). Contextualism, contrastivism, and X-Phi surveys. *Philosophical Studies, 156*(1), 81–110. https://doi.org/10.1007/s11098-011-9799-x.

Deutsch, M. (2009). Experimental philosophy and the theory of reference. *Mind & Language*, 24(4), 445–66. https://doi.org/10.1111/j.1468-0017.2009.01370.x.

Dickson, J. (2015). Ours is a broad church: Indirectly evaluative legal philosophy as a facet of jurisprudential inquiry. *Jurisprudence*, 6(2), 207–30. https://doi.org/10.1080/20403313.2015.1044310.

Donelson, R., & Hannikainen, I. R. (2020). Fuller and the folk, The inner morality of law revisited. In T. Lombrozo, J. Knobe, & S. Nichols (Eds.), *Oxford studies in experimental philosophy volume 3* (pp. 6–28). Oxford: Oxford University Press.

Dufwenberg, M., Gächter, S., & Hennig-Schmidt, H. (2011). The framing of games and the psychology of play. *Games and Economic Behavior*, 73(2), 459–78. https://doi.org/10.1016/j.geb.2011.02.003.

Dworkin, R. (1986). *Law's empire*. Cambridge, MA: Harvard University Press.

Eisenberg, T. (2011). THE origins, nature, and promise of empirical legal studies and a response to concerns. *University of Illinois Law Review*, 2011, 1713–38.

Engel, C., & Kurschilgen, M. (2013). The coevolution of behavior and normative expectations: An experiment. *American Law and Economics Review*, 15(2), 578–609. https://doi.org/10.1093/aler/aht010.

Falk, A., Fehr, E., & Zehnder, C. (2006). Fairness perceptions and reservation wages: The behavioral effects of minimum wage laws. *The Quarterly Journal of Economics*, 121(4), 1347–1381.

Flanagan, B., & Hannikainen, I. R. (2020). The folk concept of law: Law is intrinsically moral. *Australasian Journal of Philosophy*, 1–15. https://doi.org/10.1080/00048402.2020.1833953.

Galbiati, R., Schlag, K. H., & van der Weele, J. J. (2013). Sanctions that signal: An experiment. *Journal of Economic Behavior & Organization*, 94, 34–51. https://doi.org/10.1016/j.jebo.2013.08.002.

Galbiati, R., & Vertova, P. (2008). Obligations and cooperative behaviour in public good games. *Games and Economic Behavior*, 64(1), 146–70. https://doi.org/10.1016/j.geb.2007.09.004.

Galbiati, R., & Vertova, P. (2014). How laws affect behavior: Obligations, incentives and cooperative behavior. *International Review of Law and Economics*, 38, 48–57. https://doi.org/10.1016/j.irle.2014.03.001.

Galligan, D. T. (2010). Legal theory and empirical research. In P. Cane & H. Kritzer (Eds.), *Oxford handbook of empirical legal research* (pp. 977–1002). Oxford: Oxford University Press.

George, T. E. (2006). An empirical study of empirical legal scholarship: The top law schools symposium: The next generation of law school rankings: Ranking methodologies. *Indiana Law Journal*, 81(1), 141–62.

Grechenig, K., & Gelter, M. (2008). The transatlantic divergence in legal thought: American Law and Economics vs. German Doctrinalism. *Hastings International and Comparative Law Review*, 31(1), 295–360.

Green, L. (2008). Positivism and the inseparability of law and morals. *New York University Law Review*, 83, 1035–58.

Green, L. (2012). Introduction. In H. Hart, L. Green, J. Raz, & P. A. Bulloch (Eds.), *The concept of law* (3 ed., pp. xv–lii). Oxford University Press.

Greene, J. D. (2014). Beyond point-and-shoot morality: Why cognitive (neuro)science matters for ethics. *Ethics*, 124(4), 695–726. https://doi.org/10.1086/675875.

Hacker, P. M. S. (2006). Passing by the naturalistic turn: On Quine's Cul-de-Sac. *Philosophy*, 81(02), 231–53. https://doi.org/10.1017/S003181910631604X.

Hannikainen, I. R., Tobia, K. P., de Almeida, G. da F. C. F., Donelson, R., Dranseika, V., Kneer, M., . . . Struchiner, N. (2021). Are there cross-cultural legal principles? Modal reasoning uncovers procedural constraints on law. *Cognitive Science, 45*(8), e13024. https://doi.org/10.1111/cogs.13024.

Hart, H., Green, L., Raz, J., & Bulloch, P. A. (2012). *The concept of law* (3. Auflage.). Oxford: Oxford University Press.

Hart, H. L. A. (1983). *Essays in jurisprudence and philosophy*. Oxford: Oxford University Press.

Ho, D. E., & Kramer, L. (2013). Introduction: The empirical revolution in law. *Stanford Law Review, 65*(6), 1195–202.

Hoeft, L. (2019). The force of norms? The internal point of view in light of experimental economics. *Ratio Juris, 32*(3), 339–62. https://doi.org/10.1111/raju.12250.

Holtermann, J. v H. (2016). Getting real or staying positive: Legal realism(s), legal positivism and the prospects of naturalism in jurisprudence. *Ratio Juris, 29*(4), 535–55. https://doi.org/10.1111/raju.12071.

Horstmann, N., Hausmann, D., & Ryf, S. (2009). Methods for inducing intuitive and rational decision making. In A. Glöckner & C. Witteman (Eds.), *Foundations for tracing intuition: Challenges and methods* (pp. 219–37). Psychology Press.

Houser, D., Xiao, E., McCabe, K., & Smith, V. (2008). When punishment fails: Research on sanctions, intentions and non-cooperation. *Games and Economic Behavior, 62*(2), 509–32. https://doi.org/10.1016/j.geb.2007.05.001.

Jackendorff, R. (2012). Language. In K. Frankish & W. M. Ramsey (Eds.), *The Cambridge handbook of cognitive science* (pp. 171–92). Cambridge: Cambridge University Press.

Jackson, F. (2000). *From metaphysics to ethics: A defence of conceptual analysis*. Oxford: Oxford University Press.

Kapardis, A. (2014). *Psychology and law: A critical introduction* (4th ed.). Cambridge: Cambridge University Press.

Karakostas, A., & Zizzo, D. J. (2016). Compliance and the power of authority. *Journal of Economic Behavior & Organization, 124*, 67–80. https://doi.org/10.1016/j.jebo.2015.09.016.

Kauppinen, A. (2007). The rise and fall of experimental philosophy. *Philosophical Explorations, 10*(2), 95–118. https://doi.org/10.1080/13869790701305871.

Kauppinen, A. (2014). Ethics and empirical psychology—Critical remarks to empirically informed ethics. In M. Christen, C. van Schaik, J. Fischer, M. Huppenbauer, & C. Tanner (Eds.), *Empirically informed ethics: Morality between facts and norms* (Vol. 32, pp. 279–306). Springer International Publishing. https://doi.org/10.1007/978-3-319-01369-5.

Kauppinen, A. (2015). Moral intuition in philosophy and psychology. In J. Clausen & N. Levy (Eds.), *Handbook of neuroethics* (pp. 169–83). Dordrecht: Springer Netherlands. https://doi.org/10.1007/978-94-007-4707-4_163.

Kneer, M., & Bourgeois-Gironde, S. (2017). Mens rea ascription, expertise and outcome effects: Professional judges surveyed. *Cognition, 169*, 139–46. https://doi.org/10.1016/j.cognition.2017.08.008.

Knobe, J. (2016). Experimental philosophy is cognitive science. In J. Sytsma & W. Buckwalter (Eds.), *A companion to experimental philosophy* (pp. 37–52). John Wiley & Sons.

Kornhauser, L. A. (2004). Governance structures, legal systems, and the concept of law symposium: Law and economics and legal scholarship. *Chicago-Kent Law Review, 79*(2), 355–82.

Korobkin, R. B. (1998). Inertia and preference in contract negotiation: The psychological power of default rules and form terms. *ResearchGate, 51*(6), 1584–651.

Lacey, N. (2006). Analytical jurisprudence versus descriptive sociology revisited. *Texas Law Review, 89,* 945–82.

Leiter, B. (1997). Rethinking legal realism: Toward a naturalized jurisprudence. *Texas Law Review, 76,* 267–315.

Leiter, B. (2001). Legal realism and legal positivism reconsidered. *Ethics, 111*(2), 278–301. https://doi.org/10.1086/233474.

Leiter, B. (2007). *Naturalizing jurisprudence: Essays on American legal realism and naturalism in legal philosophy.* Oxford: Oxford University Press.

Lindgren, J. T. (2006). Predicting the future of empirical legal studies. *Boston University Law Review, 86*(5), 1447–60.

Ludwig, K. (2010). Intuitions and relativity. *Philosophical Psychology, 23*(4), 427–45. https://doi.org/10.1080/09515089.2010.505877.

Lyons, D. (2008). The legal entrenchment of illegality. In M. Kramer, C. Grant, & B. Colburn (Eds.), *The legacy of H.L.A. Hart: Legal, political and moral philosophy* (pp. 29–44). Oxford University Press.

Machery, E. (2017). *Philosophy within its proper bounds* (1st ed.). Oxford: Oxford University Press.

Macleod, J. A. (2019). Ordinary causation: A study in experimental statutory interpretation. *Indiana Law Journal, 94*(3), 957–1030.

Maddy, P. (2007). *Second philosophy: A naturalistic method.* Oxford: Oxford University Press.

Markussen, T., Putterman, L., & Tyran, J.-R. (2013). Self-organization for collective action an experimental study of voting on sanction regimes*. *The Review of Economic Studies,* rdt022. https://doi.org/10.1093/restud/rdt022.

Marmor, A. (2007). *Law in the age of pluralism* (New ed.). Oxford: Oxford University Press.

Marmor, A. (2013). Farewell to conceptual analysis (in jurisprudence). In W. Waluchow & S. Sciaraffa (Eds.), *Philosophical foundations of the nature of law* (pp. 209–29). Oxford: Oxford University Press.

McAdams, R. H., & Nadler, J. (2005). Testing the focal point theory of legal compliance: The effect of third-party expression in an experimental Hawk/Dove game. *Journal of Empirical Legal Studies, 2*(1), 87–123.

McAdams, R. H., & Nadler, J. (2008). Coordinating in the shadow of the law: Two contextualized tests of the focal point theory of legal compliance. *Law & Society Review, 42*(4), 865–98.

Mikhail, J. (2007). "Plucking the Mask of Mystery from its Face": Jurisprudence and HLA Hart. *Georgetown Law Journal, 95,* 733–79.

Mikhail, J. (2009). Moral grammer and intuitive jurisprudence: A formal model of unconscious moral and legal knowledge. In D. Bartels, C. Bauman, L. Skitka, D. L. Medin, & B. H. Ross (Eds.), *Psychology of learning and motivation: Moral judgment and decision making* (pp. 27–100). Academic Press.

Moore, M. S. (1989). The interpretive turn in modern theory: A turn for the worse? *Stanford Law Review, 41*(4), 871–957. https://doi.org/10.2307/1228741.

Mueller, P., & Nadler, J. (2017). Social psychology and the law. In F. Parisi, *Oxford handbook of law and economics: Volume 1: Methodology and concepts* (pp. 124–60). Oxford: Oxford University Press.

Nourse, V., & Shaffer, G. (2009). Varieties of new legal realism: Can a new world order prompt a new legal theory. *Cornell Law Review, 95,* 61–138.

Parisi, F. (2017). *Oxford handbook of law and economics: Volume 1: Methodology and concepts*. Oxford: Oxford University Press.

Parisi, F. (2019a). *Oxford handbook of law and economics: Volume 2: Private and commercial law*. Oxford: Oxford University Press.

Parisi, F. (2019b). *Oxford handbook of law and economics: Volume 3: Public law and legal institutions*. Oxford: Oxford University Press.

Pölzler, T. (2021). Insufficient effort responding in experimental philosophy. In T. Lombrozo, J. Knobe, & S. Nichols (Eds.), *Oxford studies in experimental philosophy volume 4* (pp. 214–56). Oxford: Oxford University Press.

Poon, C. S. K., Koehler, D. J., & Buehler, R. (2014). On the psychology of self-prediction: Consideration of situational barriers to intended actions. *Judgment and Decision Making, 9*(3), 207–25.

Pribán, J. (2020). *Research handbook on the sociology of law*. Cheltenham, Northampton, MA: Edward Elgar Publishing Ltd.

Priel, D. (2011). Jurisprudence and psychology. In M. Del Mar (Ed.), *New waves in philosophy of law* (pp. 77–99). Croydon: Palgrave Macmillan. //www.palgrave.com/gp/book/9780230276598

Priel, D. (2019). Law as a social construction and conceptual legal theory. *Law and Philosophy, 38*(3), 267–87. https://doi.org/10.1007/s10982-019-09349-3.

Prochownik, K. M. (2021). The experimental philosophy of law: New ways, old questions, and how not to get lost. *Philosophy Compass, n/a*(n/a), e12791. https://doi.org/10.1111/phc3.12791.

Putterman, L., Tyran, J.-R., & Kamei, K. (2011). Public goods and voting on formal sanction schemes. *Journal of Public Economics, 95*(9–10), 1213–22. https://doi.org/10.1016/j.jpubeco.2011.05.001.

Quine W. v. O. (1976). Two dogmas of empiricism. In S. G. Harding (Ed.). *Can theories be refuted?: Essays on the Duhem-Quine thesis* (pp. 41–64). Dordrecht: Springer Netherlands. https://doi.org/10.1007/978-94-010-1863-0.

Reuben, E., & Riedl, A. (2013). Enforcement of contribution norms in public good games with heterogeneous populations. *Games and Economic Behavior, 77*(1), 122–37. https://doi.org/10.1016/j.geb.2012.10.001.

Riedel, N., & Schildberg-Hörisch, H. (2013). Asymmetric obligations. *Journal of Economic Psychology, 35*, 67–80. https://doi.org/10.1016/j.joep.2012.12.003.

Rose, D., & Danks, D. (2013). In defense of a broad conception of experimental philosophy: A broad conception of experimental philosophy. *Metaphilosophy, 44*(4), 512–32. https://doi.org/10.1111/meta.12045.

Rubin, H., Cailin, O., & Bruner, J. (2019). Experimental economics for philosophers. In E. Fischer, M. Curtis, & J. Beebe (Eds.), *Methodological advances in experimental philosophy* (pp. 175–208). London: Bloomsbury Publishing.

Schauer, F. (2004). The limited domain of the law. *Virginia Law Review, 90*(7), 1909–56. https://doi.org/10.2307/1515650.

Schauer, F. (2005). The social construction of the concept of law: A reply to Julie Dickson. *Oxford Journal of Legal Studies, 25*(3), 493–501.

Schauer, F. (2015). *The force of law*. Cambridge, MA: Harvard University Press.

Schoenegger, P. (2021). Experimental philosophy and the ncentivization challenge: A Proposed application of the Bayesian truth serum. *Review of Philosophy and Psychology*. https://doi.org/10.1007/s13164-021-00571-4.

Schwarz, N. (2007). Cognitive aspects of survey methodology. *Applied Cognitive Psychology, 21*(2), 277–87. https://doi.org/10.1002/acp.1340.

Searle, J. R. (1997). *The construction of social reality*. New York: Free Press.

Shapiro, S. (2011). *Legality*. Cambridge, MA: Harvard University Press.

Silverman, D., Slemrod, J., & Uler, N. (2014). Distinguishing the role of authority "in." and authority "to." *Journal of Public Economics, 113*, 32–42. https://doi.org/10.1016/j .jpubeco.2014.02.003.

Smith, V. L. (1976). Experimental economics: Induced value theory. *The American Economic Review, 66*(2), 274–9.

Sommers, R. (2021). Experimental jurisprudence. *Science, 373*(6553), 394–5. https://doi .org/10.1126/science.abf0711.

Stich, S., & Tobia, K. P. (2016). Experimental philosophy and the philosophical tradition. In *A companion to experimental philosophy* (pp. 3–21). John Wiley & Sons, Ltd. https:// doi.org/10.1002/9781118661666.ch1.

Struchiner, N., Almeida, G. da F. C. F. de, & Hannikainen, I. R. (2020). Legal decision-making and the abstract/concrete paradox. *Cognition, 205*, 104421. https://doi.org/10 .1016/j.cognition.2020.104421.

Talbot, B. (2012). The irrelevance of folk intuitions to the "hard problem" of consciousness. *Consciousness and Cognition, 21*(2), 644–50. https://doi.org/10.1016/j.concog.2010.12.005.

Talesh, S., Mertz, E., & Klug, H. (2021). Introduction. In S. Talesh, E. Mertz, & H. Klug (Eds.), *Research handbook on modern legal realism* (pp. 1–20). Cheltenham, Northampton, MA: Edward Elgar Publishing.

Tamanaha, B. Z. (1997). *Realistic socio-legal theory: Pragmatism and a social theory of law* (Repr. 2004). Oxford: Oxford University Press.

Tobia, K. P. (2022). Experimental jurisprudence. *University of Chicago Law Review, 89*. https://doi.org/10.2139/ssrn.3680107.

Trevino, A. J. (2017). *The sociology of law: Classical and contemporary perspectives*. New York: Routledge.

Tversky, A., & Kahneman, D. (1981). The framing of decisions and the psychology of choice. *Science, 211*(4481), 453–8. https://doi.org/10.1126/science.7455683.

Twining, W. (2007). *General jurisprudence: Understanding law from a global perspective*. Cambridge University Press. https://doi.org/10.1017/CBO9780511807374.

Tyran, J.-R., & Feld, L. P. (2006). Achieving compliance when legal sanctions are non-deterrent*. *Scandinavian Journal of Economics, 108*(1), 135–56. https://doi.org/10.1111 /j.1467-9442.2006.00444.x.

Ulen, T. S. (2008). The appeal of legal empiricism. In T. Eger, C. Ott, J. Bigus, & G. von Wangenheim (Eds.), *Internationalization of the law and its economic analysis: Festschrift für Hans-Bernd Schäfer zum 65. Geburtstag* (pp. 71–88). Gabler Verlag.

Vanberg, C. (2008). Why do people keep their promises? An experimental test of two explanations. *Econometrica, 76*(6), 1467–80. https://doi.org/10.3982/ECTA7673.

Wagner, P. A. (2013). Game theory as psychological investigation. In H. Hanappi (Ed.). *Game theory relaunched* (pp. 325–44). InTech. https://doi.org/10.5772/2563.

Wang, T. (2018). The experimental critique and philosophical practice. *Philosophical Psychology, 31*(1), 89–109. https://doi.org/10.1080/09515089.2017.1396310.

Weinberg, J. M., Nichols, S., & Stich, S. (2001). Normativity and epistemic intuitions. *Philosophical Topics, 29*(1/2), 429–60.

Wilson, T. D., & Dunn, E. W. (2004). Self-knowledge: Its limits, value, and potential for improvement. *Annual Review of Psychology, 55*, 493–518. https://doi.org/10.1146/ annurev.psych.55.090902.141954.

Woolfolk, R. L. (2011). Empirical tests of philosophical intuitions. *Consciousness and Cognition, 20*(2), 415–16. https://doi.org/10.1016/j.concog.2011.01.013.

Woolfolk, R. L. (2013). Experimental philosophy: A methodological critique: Experimental philosophy. *Metaphilosophy*, 44(1–2), 79–87. https://doi.org/10.1111/meta.12016.

Xiao, E. (2013). Profit-seeking punishment corrupts norm obedience. *Games and Economic Behavior*, 77(1), 321–44. https://doi.org/10.1016/j.geb.2012.10.010.

Xiao, E., & Houser, D. (2011). Punish in public. *Journal of Public Economics*, 95(7–8), 1006–17. https://doi.org/10.1016/j.jpubeco.2010.11.021.

Xiao, E., & Tan, F. (2014). Justification and legitimate punishment. *Journal of Institutional and Theoretical Economics (JITE) / Zeitschrift Für Die Gesamte Staatswissenschaft*, 170(1), 168–88.

Zamir, E. (2015). *Law, psychology, and morality: The role of loss aversion*. Oxford: Oxford University Press.

Zamir, E., & Teichman, D. (2018). *Behavioral law and economics*. Oxford: Oxford University Press.

Experimental Longtermist Jurisprudence

Eric Martínez and Christoph Winter

Recent scholarship has revealed a seemingly stark mismatch between the value of future generations and the lack of protection afforded to them under present legal systems. Although climate change, pandemics, nuclear war, and artificial intelligence impose greater threats to the future of humanity than any previous risk (Ord, 2020), legal systems fail to grant future generations democratic representation in the legislature, standing to bring forth a lawsuit in the judiciary, and serious consideration in cost-benefit analyses in the executive. What is the source of this disconnect, is it justified, and—to the extent that it is not justified—what might one do about it?

Here we discuss how a new research field within experimental jurisprudence— which we refer to as *experimental longtermist jurisprudence*—might help address these questions and in turn help determine the appropriate level and form of legal protection to future generations.

The chapter is divided into three sections. In Section 10.1, we provide an overview of the substantive and methodological underpinnings of experimental longtermist jurisprudence. In Section 10.2, we introduce three research programs within experimental longtermist jurisprudence, and in Section 10.3, we discuss the normative implications of each of these research programs.

10.1 Foundations of Experimental Longtermist Jurisprudence

Experimental longtermist jurisprudence (XLJ) is, in essence, a form of experimental jurisprudence[1] concerned with issues relating to the long-term future. The main substantive and methodological underpinnings of experimental longtermist jurisprudence are

1. the view that one should be particularly concerned with ensuring that the long-run future goes well (*longtermism*);
2. the view that said concern ought to extend to the legal system (*legal longtermism*); and
3. the practice of using experimental methods as a means of evaluating the validity and implications of legal longtermism (*experimental legal longtermism*).

Here, we discuss each of these foundations in turn.

10.1.1 The Philosophical Foundations of Longtermism

The set of philosophical theories associated with the view that one should be particularly concerned with ensuring that the long-run future goes well has been referred to as longtermism (MacAskill, 2022).[2] Longtermism is based on three main assumptions—one normative, two empirical—which we briefly detail here in turn.[3]

The first assumption, often referred to as the normative assumption, is that when assessing the moral value of our actions, all consequences matter equally—independent of when, where, or how they occur.[4] For example, just as many of the most influential thought experiments in contemporary moral philosophy have argued or implied that the welfare of someone living far away geographically ought to be valued the same as the welfare of someone living close by (e.g., Singer, 1972; Rawls, 1971; Pogge, 1989; Beitz, 1983), according to longtermism, so too should the welfare of someone living far away in the future be valued the same as the welfare of someone living right now. Additionally, longtermism also argues (in a similar vein as other mainstream philosophical views (see, e.g., Pettit & Smith, 2000; cf. Parfit, 1984, pp. 24–5)) that, ceteris paribus, indirect consequences ought to be given the same value as direct consequences, and unintended consequences ought to be given the same value as intended consequences (Greaves & MacAskill, 2019, p. 6). For example, a direct consequence of distributing insecticide-treated bed nets in sub-Saharan Africa is a reduction of malaria incidents and child mortality (Pryce, Richardson, & Lengeler, 2018). However, the fact that these consequences are direct does not on its own imply that these consequences "matter" more per se than some of the indirect consequences of distributing insecticide-treated bed nets, such as improved education (Kuecken, Thuilliez, & Valfort, 2014) and increased GDP growth (Gallup & Sachs, 2001; Sachs & Malaney, 2002). Nor does it matter whether said GDP growth or improved education was less intended relative to reducing malaria incidents and child mortality. If this is right, such that all consequences matter equally across time and space, then insofar as future generations exist, it follows that future generations are of equal value in principle as the current generation.[5]

The second assumption states that, *in expectation*, the future is vast in size—that is, it is likely to consist of at least a fairly large number of future generations, each consisting, on average, of a fairly large number of individuals, such that the number of individuals[6] living in the future will collectively be far greater than the number of individuals living in the present. One way to estimate the future lifespan of humans is by extrapolating from the typical lifespan of a mammalian species, estimated to be anywhere from 600,000 years (Barnosky et al., 2011; Ceballos, 2015) to 1.7 million years (Foote & Raup, 1996). Since *Homo sapiens* is estimated to be 300,000 years old (see Galway-Witham & Stringer, 2018; Schlebusch et al., 2017), this would suggest that *Homo sapiens* has 300,000 to 1.4 million years of potential flourishing before extinction. Given that *Homo sapiens* in many ways might be considered more successful than other mammalian species and, in particular, appears less vulnerable to the typical threats of extinction as other mammals,[7] some experts have pointed out that this estimate may be overly conservative (Greaves & MacAskill, 2019). If so, humans might instead be expected to survive for as long as the earth remains habitable (anywhere between

.9 and 1.5 billion years: Caldeira & Kasting, 1992), even setting aside the prospect of leaving earth and colonizing other habitable systems (Beckstead, 2014), in which case the upper bound, however unlikely, would be as high as quintillions of years (the estimated expected end of the universe: Adams & Laughlin, 1997).

In addition to the expected number of future generations, it also stands to reason that for most (if not all) future generations, there will, in expectation, be greater numbers of people living at any given time than there are presently. After all, the number of people who are living now is estimated to be more than ten times higher than the number of people who were living 200 years ago (7 billion versus 600 million, respectively: Roser, Ritchie, & Ortiz-Ospina, 2019), and current projections estimate that future generations will likewise be greater, even if one assumes that global population growth will slow at a certain point in the near future (United Nations, 2019). In combination with the first assumption (i.e., that consequences affecting each of these individuals would, all else equal, matter just as much as those affecting individuals living in the present), this would imply that insofar as we *can* positively influence the experiences of future generations, their sheer size and value dictates that we *ought* to protect them.

The third assumption states that there are feasible and predictable ways to positively influence the experiences of future generations. For example, while this assumption may initially seem less plausible than the previous two assumptions, given the apparent impracticality of influencing the future in ways that are reasonably foreseeable, longtermists have pointed to examples of both (a) historical trends that have had long-lasting effects on the trajectory of human civilization (e.g., religious values and the implementation of certain legal systems)[8] and (b) predictable and feasible ways of influencing the future, particularly with respect to existential risks associated with advanced artificial intelligence, extreme climate change, and synthetic biology (Winter et al., 2021; see also Section 10.2.1 *infra*). Together with the previous assumptions, this implies that not only should we value and protect future generations in *principle*, but that we can—and therefore should—protect their interests in *practice*.[9]

10.1.2 Legal Longtermism

One of the primary means through which we might conceivably protect future generations—and the one with which XLJ is chiefly concerned—is via the legal system. The set of views associated with the claim that law and legal institutions ought to protect those in the far future can be referred to as *legal longtermism*.[10] Normatively, the premises associated with legal longtermism are similar, if not identical, to those of philosophical longtermism (depending on the extent to which one believes that those with moral value warrant legal consideration). Empirically, the assumptions are also similar, with the additional supposition that there are feasible and predictable *legal* mechanisms to protect future generations.

That said, given that many of the examples cited in support of the feasibility assumption of philosophical longtermism relate to the legal system, as a practical matter one who accepts the assumptions of philosophical longtermism may automatically accept the premises of legal longtermism. In particular, some of the long-lasting, intergenerational effects of legal systems cited to by legal longtermists include

(a) the medieval establishment of the common law's continued influence on the laws governing Great Britain and its former colonies (Berman, 1985), (b) the long-lasting influence of Roman law on many civil-code systems (Watson, 1991), and (c) and the persistence of Eastern legal institutions (Kuran, 2011; Cheng, Rosett, & Woo, 2003). Legal longtermists have further argued that legal interventions could play a significant role in mitigating some of the catastrophic risks highlighted earlier and ensuring a more positive long-term trajectory (Winter et al., 2021).

As it currently stands, however, legal systems provide hardly any legal protection to future generations. Legal institutions have been and continue to be very short-term oriented, with policy making geared toward solving contemporary issues and with democratic, legislative, and judicial processes generally reserved exclusively for the current generation (cf. ACE Project, 2021; John & MacAskill, 2020). While a few attempts have been made to provide legal protection to future generations, even fewer legal mechanisms have been successfully implemented as a result, and those implemented so far have been largely ineffectual (see, e.g., Araújo & Koessler, 2021).

The primary substantive aims of XLJ relate largely to (a) understanding the source of this disconnect, such as by studying the nature of people's beliefs regarding legal longtermism, how the theory of longtermism coheres with people's ordinary concept of rights and duties, and what contributes to those beliefs and (b) deriving normative implications based on that understanding. The methodological framework for satisfying these aims is detailed in the next section.

10.1.3 Experimental Legal Longtermism

Like other forms of experimental jurisprudence, XLJ employs methods traditionally associated with the field of experimental psychology to explore substantive questions traditionally associated with the field of jurisprudence.[11] XLJ can be thought of as an experimental branch of longtermist jurisprudence, with the goals of (a) uncovering the cognitive underpinnings of beliefs relevant to the jurisprudential framework laid out in the previous section and (b) advancing legal, philosophical, and policy arguments on the basis of those findings. In the case of XLJ, these methods include both surveys and controlled experiments. Here, we briefly discuss each of these in turn.

Administering surveys in the context of XLJ research, as in other, more traditional forms of empirical legal studies research, involves straightforwardly asking people questions regarding the aspects of legal longtermism or some legal longtermism-relevant issue. Such research may be aimed at either testing a specific hypothesis or merely gathering information. For example, a survey might evaluate the level of acceptance of different aspects of legal longtermism by identifying which arguments in favor of and against legal longtermism resonate with participants and for what reasons. The results may fuel other hypotheses and be used as inputs into other XLJ research.

Controlled experiments, on the other hand, involve indirectly examining people's views regarding legal longtermism by, for example, asking participants questions about carefully controlled stimuli. Such stimuli are often in the form of contrastive vignettes, in which particular aspects of a situation are systematically manipulated to identify the psychological processes underlying certain concepts, intuitions, or judgments relevant to legal longtermism. In contrast to the survey method, the primary descriptive aim of the controlled-experiment technique is to better understand the cause of people's beliefs as opposed to the beliefs themselves.

Unlike conventional surveys and controlled experiments, however, XLJ is concerned not only with descriptive questions of fact but also with normative questions of legal philosophy, doctrine, and policy. Thus, XLJ can be considered a two-step process. In Step 1, a researcher takes the role of a cognitive scientist, trying to gain insight into a legal longtermist-relevant feature of the human mind via an experimental study. In Step 2, a researcher takes the role of a philosopher, legal theorist, lawyer, and/or policy maker, reasoning about the normative implications of the experimental findings uncovered at Step 1.

XLJ can also be conceptualized as containing three separate but interdependent levels of abstraction, corresponding to the three possible sets of normative implications alluded to in the previous paragraph:

1. The *philosophical level*, concerned with determining whether and to what extent future generations ought to be provided legal protection according to an ideal legal system;
2. The *doctrinal level*, concerned with determining to what extent and how future generations ought to be provided legal protection according to the doctrines of the current legal system;
3. The *applied level* (or *policy level*), concerned with determining which legal mechanisms and instruments ought to be prioritized and/or implemented so as to provide the appropriate level of legal protection to future generations.

In the remainder of the chapter, we first provide an overview of Step 1 of XLJ research at each of the three levels (Section 10.2) and then turn to an overview of Step 2 of XLJ research at each of the three levels (Section 10.3). For a concise overview of the different levels of abstraction at each of the two steps, see Table 10.1.

Table 10.1 Experimental Longtermist Jurisprudence at Three Levels of Abstraction. © Eric Martínez and Christoph Winter

	Level I: **Philosophical Level**	**Level II:** **Doctrinal Level**	**Level III:** **Applied Level**
Step 1: **Descriptive Aims**	What are people's general beliefs about the concept of legal longtermism, and why people hold those beliefs?	To what extent does longtermism map onto people's understanding of law, the legal system, and legally relevant concepts?	What are people's intuitions about how more specific areas of law and concrete legal mechanisms could address more concrete long-term challenges?
Step 2: **Normative Aims**	How and to what extent should future generations be provided legal protection (independent of existing legal doctrine)?	How and to what extent should future generations be provided legal protection (according to existing legal doctrine)?	Which legal mechanisms and instruments can and ought to be implemented so as to provide the appropriate level of legal protection to future generations?

10.2 Experimental Longtermist Jurisprudence at Three Levels of Abstraction

As discussed earlier, XLJ can be conceptualized as containing three interrelated levels of abstraction, including what we refer to as the philosophical level, the doctrinal level, and the applied level. Here we discuss each of these levels of abstraction in turn with respect to Step 1 of XLJ research (empirical aims and methodology), while in the final third of the chapter we focus on Step 2 of XLJ research (normative implications).

10.2.1 Philosophical-Level XLJ

Step 1 of XLJ research at the philosophical level involves investigating (a) people's general beliefs about legal longtermism (i.e., the claim that we ought to provide legal protection to those in the far future, as well as the three underlying premises of that claim) and (b) why people[12] hold those beliefs. Here we discuss each of these two types of philosophical-level XLJ methods in turn, in terms of both existing literature and future directions.

With regard to (a) beliefs about legal longtermism, for example, Martínez and Winter (2021a) surveyed a set of over 500 legal academics from around the English-speaking world regarding their views on the desirability and feasibility of using the legal system to protect future generations and influence the long-term future. In terms of desirability, legal academics rated their desired level of legal protection for future generations as several times higher than their perceived current level of legal protection afforded to future generations, and roughly equal to the current level of legal protection afforded to humans living in the present. Moreover, the difference between the desired and current level of legal protection was rated as higher for future generations than for other neglected groups, such as non-human animals. Martínez and Winter (2021b) found similar results in a set of over 1000 US American adults, while Martínez and Winter (in press a) found similar results in a cross-cultural survey of approximately 3000 adults in Australia, Canada, Chile, Japan, Mexico, Spain, South Africa, South Korea, United Kingdom, and the United States (see also Martínez and Winter, in press b).

In terms of feasibility, the vast majority of law professors in Martínez and Winter's (2021a) sample at least somewhat agreed that there were predictable, feasible mechanisms through which the law could influence the long-term future, both in general and with regard to specific risks and via different areas of law. These main findings held true independent of demographic factors such as age, gender, political affiliation, and legal training, strongly suggesting that academic legal experts across the English-speaking world endorse to a surprisingly significant degree the normative and descriptive assumptions of legal longtermism. Investigating this question with regard to experts in other fields as well as a more general audience (e.g., cross-culturally) could give experimental legal philosophers (and legal actors more generally) a better sense of whether people endorse legal longtermism and to what degree.

With regard to (b) why people hold those beliefs, philosophical-level XLJ is concerned with understanding both the *proximate cause* of longtermism-related beliefs (cognitively, what leads people to hold certain longtermist-related beliefs and/ or engage in longtermist-related behavior) and *ultimate cause* of those beliefs (what evolutionary or adaptive forces gave rise to them in the first place).

For example, with respect to the normative assumption, there are many reasons to expect cognitively why people may assign a significantly higher legal-social discount rate to people in the far future than those who have thought more about this issue from a philosophical perspective (i.e., moral philosophers).[13] Decades of work in the fields of behavioral economics and cognitive psychology have demonstrated that human judgment is prone to various sorts of cognitive biases, many of which are believed to influence our thinking about the long-term future (Yudkowsky, 2008; Ord, 2020; see also Schubert, Caviola, & Faber, 2019), including the following:

1. Present bias and hyperbolic discounting, the trend of overvaluing immediate rewards and undervaluing long-term consequences (e.g., Mischel & Ebbesen, 1970; O'Donoghue & Rabin, 1999; O'Donoghue & Rabin, 2015)
2. Scope insensitivity, the inability to value a problem with a multiplicative relationship to its size (e.g., Desvouges, Naughton, & Parsons, 1992; Kahneman, Ritov, Schkade, Sherman, & Varian, 1999; Slovic, 2010)
3. Diminishing marginal utility of life (Greene & Baron, 2001)
4. The availability heuristic, the tendency to heavily weigh judgments based on information that is available and/or can be readily recalled (Tversky & Kahneman, 1973; Schwarz et al., 1991; Gilovich, Griffin, & Kahneman, 2002).

Since work on cognitive biases suggests that experts are often just as susceptible to these biases as non-experts,[14] it stands to reason that there may not be much of a legal expertise effect when assessing group differences in longtermist-related views. Indeed, as mentioned earlier, Martínez and Winter (2021a) found similar levels of endorsement for the normative premise of legal longtermism in legal experts as those observed in lay adults. On the other hand, it is plausible that proximate causes other than expertise could lead to revealed group differences, such as based on political affiliation. For example, recent political psychology literature has revealed ideological differences in the expanse of empathy (Waytz, Iyer, Young, & Graham, 2016), compassion, and moral circle (Waytz, Iyer, Young, Haidt, & Graham, 2019); political conservatives appear to expend their empathy toward more local targets (i.e., smaller, closer, more well-defined, and less encompassing social circles), whereas liberals tend to empathize with more global targets (i.e., larger, farther, less structured, and more encompassing social circles, including nonhumans). Insofar as future generations are considered more "global targets," one would likewise expect ideological differences in the expanse of empathy and compassion toward them, particularly with regard to those in the far future as opposed to the near future.[15]

With regard to the ultimate cause of beliefs toward legal longtermism, there are also plausible evolutionary explanations for why humans would not have developed certain longtermist beliefs. For example, while it is relatively easy to imagine why it would have been useful for humans to develop an inclination toward protecting near-term future generations (e.g., to ensure that one's children and grandchildren survive and flourish), it seems more difficult to imagine how an impulse toward protecting long-term future generations would have developed. After all, there would never be any opportunity in one's lifetime to directly act on this impulse nor any available feedback mechanism to observe the results of acting on this impulse, as far-future descendants would come into existence long after the end of that lifetime. Furthermore, while reciprocal altruism is observed among individuals and groups that are unrelated and sometimes physically distant from one another (e.g., Trivers, 1971), the mechanisms underlying such behavior seem unlikely to lead to prosocial tendencies toward future generations, given the impracticability of reciprocally cooperating with generations not living at the same time.

That said, with respect to both the proximate and ultimate cause of legal longtermist beliefs, many of these hypotheses and predictions have yet to be tested experimentally, leaving them ripe for exploration by XLJ researchers.[16]

10.2.2 Doctrinal-Level XLJ

Step 1 of doctrinal-level XLJ involves investigating the extent to which longtermism maps onto people's understanding of law, the legal system, and legally relevant concepts. As discussed in Tobia (2020a), legally relevant concepts can take various forms and may or may not have both a legal and an ordinary language counterpart. These forms include the following:

1. Legal concepts such as "promissory estoppel" and "subject matter jurisdiction," which do not have an ordinary language counterpart
2. Hybrid concepts such as "rights," "duties," and "person," which exist as legal concepts and are also used by laypeople in an everyday, non-legalistic context
3. Ordinary concepts such as "January," "dollar," and "vegetable," which do not have an explicitly legal counterpart but may nonetheless be legally relevant (see, e.g., Nix *v.* Hedden, 1893).

XLJ is concerned with each of these types of concepts, insofar as one can advance legal arguments on the basis of their experimental investigation.[17]

With regard to legal concepts without an explicit ordinary language counterpart, for example, a recent doctrinal-level project investigated to what degree law professors' understanding of the concept of standing (*locus standi*) extended to future generations.[18] In a set of common-law-trained law professors from around the world, Martínez and Winter (2021) found that a slight majority of respondents leaned toward or accepted the proposition that there was a reasonable legal basis for granting standing to humans living in the near future (understood as up to 100 years from now), while slightly more than one-third of participants leaned toward or accepted the proposition for humans living in the far future (understood as over 100 years from now). The figure for humans living in the near future was slightly higher than that for non-human animals and sentient artificial intelligence but lower than that for groups such as corporations, unions, and, perhaps surprisingly, the environment (understood as rivers, trees, or nature itself).

For *locus standi* and other specialized legal concepts that do not have an explicit ordinary language counterpart and are unfamiliar to those without legal training, surveying legal experts to the exclusion of laypeople (i.e., those unfamiliar with legal doctrine) may make more sense.[19] However, for classes of legally relevant concepts that do have an ordinary language counterpart familiar to laypeople—such as hybrid concepts like personhood, rights, and duties—XLJ is concerned with understanding how ordinary people understand those concepts in relation to longtermism, as well as to what degree this understanding differs from that of legal experts. For example, in Martínez and Winter's (2021b) survey of over 1000 US adults, 64.09 percent of participants considered at least some subset of humans living in the near future to be persons, and 61.75 percent considered at least some subset of humans living in the far future to be persons. Similar results were observed in Martínez and Winter's (in press a) cross-cultural survey of lay adults in ten different countries. In both studies, the percentage was higher than that observed in Martínez and Tobia's (2021) survey of over 500 law professors, in which just over 50 percent of participants considered at least some subset of humans living in the near future to be persons, and fewer than 50 percent considered at least some subset of humans living in the far future to be persons.

As will be further discussed in Section 10.3.2, from a legal perspective much of the emphasis on surveying lay intuitions—either in addition to or in lieu of those of legal experts—is based on the doctrine of ordinary meaning analysis, particularly prominent in the United States and other common-law jurisdictions but relevant to other jurisdictions as well, which states that words in a legal document should be interpreted according to their ordinary meaning.[20] In cases where ordinary meaning analysis does not apply, as well as in jurisdictions that do not have this doctrine or any equivalent to begin with, one might question the utility of surveying laypeople about legal concepts. However, as Tobia (2022) points out, most experimental jurisprudence studies, regardless of the jurisdiction, tend to emphasize laypeople and rarely use legal experts as subjects except in tandem with a lay sample, suggesting a potentially deeper reason for the utility of surveying laypeople.[21]

While one might expect a priori that similar cognitive (and evolutionary) factors would be at play in shaping how and to what extent longtermism fits into both expert and laypeople's understanding of legally relevant concepts, recent evidence suggests that those with legal training (including judges and even law students) interpret ordinary legal concepts (such as intentionality) differently from those without legal training (e.g., elite non-law students and the general public: Tobia, 2020b).

That said, it is unclear how legal training might affect people's judgments. In some cases one might expect legal training to result in a less longtermist-friendly interpretation of certain concepts.[22] For example, when interpreting the concepts of "rights" and "duties," lawyers might be influenced by the fact that most jurisdictions do not currently grant many legal rights to future generations, nor do they impose many legal obligations on current generations to protect future generations, whereas laypeople may simply interpret those concepts in a normative, jurisdiction-independent sense. With regard to personhood, although those with legal training in many respects have a more expansive interpretation of the concept of personhood that extends to corporations and other entities beyond "natural persons," in other respects they have a narrower interpretation of the concept that is detached from the concept of "human," hence explaining the discrepancy between the endorsement rates observed among lay participants (Martínez & Winter, 2021b) (with respect to considering future generations' personhood) relative to expert participants (Martínez & Tobia, 2021).[23]

10.2.3 Applied-Level XLJ

Step 1 of the third level of abstraction, which we refer to as applied-level XLJ, involves examining people's intuitions about how more specific areas of law or even concrete legal mechanisms—such as constitutional provisions, congressional statutes, and agency regulations—could address more concrete long-term challenges, such as existential risks posed by artificial intelligence, extreme climate change, and synthetic biology. Note that while the use of the term *applied* might suggest that this level is dependent on the previous two levels, applied-level XLJ research can be undertaken either independently of or in tandem with research at the previous two levels.[24] Here, we discuss a few examples of applied-level XLJ, as well as their relationship to philosophical-level and doctrinal-level XLJ.

Whereas previously discussed XLJ research at the philosophical level found that the vast majority of law professors surveyed endorse the feasibility assumption of legal longtermism (i.e., that law can predictably and feasibly influence the long-term future), the applied-level research investigated their beliefs regarding how and in what ways the law can influence the long-term future (Martínez & Winter, 2021a). In a set of law professors ($n \approx 170$), subjects were asked whether they believed there were predictable, feasible mechanisms through which different areas of law could influence the long-term future (understood as at least 100 years from now) and very long-term future (understood as at least 1000 years from now). These questions represent applied-level research, as the different areas of law would be the means of influencing the long-term future. For each area of law surveyed, the majority of participants endorsed[25] the proposition that there were predictable, feasible mechanisms through which to influence the long-term future, though the percentage of those who agreed was significantly higher for some areas (environmental law, constitutional law, and property law) than for others (contract law and criminal law). Participants were also asked whether they believed there were predictable, feasible mechanisms through which law as a whole could influence the (very) long-term future with regard to different real-world issues. As with the areas of law, for each of the issues surveyed, the majority of participants at least somewhat agreed with the proposition that there were feasible, predictable legal mechanisms that could influence the long-term future, while the mean level of agreement was significantly higher for some areas (e.g., climate change) than for others (e.g., artificial intelligence) (Martínez & Winter, 2021a).

In addition to investigating the long-term predictability and feasibility of general areas of law, two other approaches to applied-level research include investigating existing and/or proposed legal instruments with potential longtermist implications and assessing subjects' intuitions regarding (a) normatively, whether they would be in favor of implementing said instruments and/or (b) descriptively, how they would interpret the said instrument—once implemented—in various longtermism-relevant scenarios.

With regard to the first approach, on normative intuitions, a researcher might investigate—either directly, through survey methods, or indirectly, through a series of contrastive vignettes—expert and/or lay[26] intuitions regarding, for example, statutorily mandated budgets to reduce existential risk. Are most people in favor of implementing the said budgets? If so, how much of their jurisdiction's total spending do they think should be allocated to the said budgets (both overall and relative to other types of spending, such as military expenditures)? Are people's judgments influenced by cognitive factors such as scope neglect, thus causing those who might otherwise endorse longtermist legal protection to disregard the potential necessity or benefit of existential-risk-related legal mechanisms? These types of questions, as well as the methodological techniques to answer them, closely resemble those asked at the philosophical level, the main difference being that both the longtermist scenarios and the legal mechanisms related to those scenarios are much more specific at the applied level than at the philosophical level.

With regard to the second approach, a researcher might investigate people's intuitions regarding a constitutional provision stating that the government "should protect current and future generations against existential threats." Does this constitutional provision require the government to implement budgets to reduce existential risks? Who has standing to sue on future generations' behalf if such protection is not provided? What counts as an existential threat according to this provision? How might one's interpretation of this provision differ for a constitutional provision compared to a statutory or regulatory provision? With regard to the latter question, pilot evidence from Martínez and Winter (2021) suggests that various sorts of hypothetical constitutional provisions (such as a commitment to spend 1 percent of GDP toward protection against existential risk, or a provision granting standing to future generations), are interpreted by legal experts as granting similar levels of protection to future generations. Further work is needed to confirm this finding as well as to investigate the other questions posed here.

It also remains unclear under what circumstances longtermists might prefer a precise or vaguely worded provision. On the one hand, for similar reasons discussed with regard to the philosophical and doctrinal level, one might expect a priori that more specific provisions (whether constitutional, statutory, or regulatory in nature) would tend to be interpreted more favorably toward future generations than would vaguer ones. First, if the judge (or other interpreter) does not endorse legal longtermism, then to the extent that they do not want to protect future generations, the language in a legal instrument must be sufficiently specific so as to ensure a longtermism-friendly interpretation. Second, even if a judge does endorse legal longtermism, they may not decide in a way that is longtermism-friendly in cases where human reasoning is especially prone to faulty statistical intuitions or biases (cf. Schubert, Caviola, & Faber, 2019). This may be an issue specifically with regard to existential risks, which require reasoning based on very small probability scenarios of enormous magnitude and therefore might be influenced by factors such as scope neglect.

On the other hand, there are other reasons to expect that vague *standard*-like provisions might lead to broader protection of future generations in certain circumstances over more precisely drafted *rule*-like provisions. First, in cases where a judge wants to help future generations, a vague or abstract provision will allow the said judge to choose the broadest interpretation possible, whereas a precisely worded provision would constrain them to wording chosen by a particular legislator. Second, vague norms also allow for potentially increasingly longtermism-friendly interpretations over time, as future judges (and laypeople) might well extend their moral circle over time[27] and, by extension, be more likely to adopt a longtermism-friendly interpretation.[28]

In terms of specific types of legal instruments and mechanisms, since constitutional provisions are generally more vague and broad than statutes, then insofar as vague provisions tend to lead to more longtermism-friendly interpretations, so too would one expect constitutional mechanisms to be more longtermism-friendly than statutory mechanisms, particularly since the former, ceteris paribus, constitutes higher and more powerful law.[29] Conversely, insofar as more specific provisions seem friendlier to future generations, then one would expect statutory mechanisms to likewise be friendlier toward future generations, as well. Moreover, depending on the jurisdiction, one would also expect in this regard that regulations, whose provisions are generally even more fleshed out than statutes and are often just as binding on the judge as legislation-passed statutes, to be longtermism-friendly, as well.[30]

With regard to the second approach on descriptive intuitions, it seems reasonable to expect that there would be significant differences between experts and non-experts in their interpretations of specific longtermist legal mechanisms. Given the aims of applied-level XLJ, it seems reasonable here to focus on expert intuitions as opposed to lay intuitions (since the former will be more representative of the ultimate decision maker when the instrument is to be applied), unless there is reason to believe that expert and non-expert intuitions do not significantly deviate in certain cases at hand. Furthermore, given the large inter-jurisdictional variation in both the design and interpretation/application of legal instruments, it is important to ensure that findings of one jurisdiction are shown to be replicable in other jurisdictions before generalizing results.[31]

Taking into account these and other relevant methodological considerations, applied-level XLJ would help provide insight into which sorts of prospective legal instruments are most likely to promote longtermist goals and which are more likely to be ineffectual or harmful toward longtermist goals. We discuss these normative implications (as well as those with regard to the philosophical and doctrinal levels) in the next section.

10.3 Normative Implications of Experimental Longtermist Jurisprudence

While Section 10.2 focused on the empirical aims of experimental longtermist jurisprudence research at three levels of abstraction, here we discuss whether and how those empirical findings might inform normative discussions. This section is likewise split up into three subsections and covers philosophical implications (10.3.1), legal implications (10.3.2), and policy implications (10.3.3). Note that while each of these types of implications generally maps on to a distinct level of abstraction covered in the previous section, there is also a significant degree of overlap, which we acknowledge when relevant.

10.3.1 Philosophical Implications

Philosophically, XLJ is concerned with determining whether and to what extent future generations ought to be provided legal protection (independent of existing legal doctrine). Here, we outline three general approaches similar to other forms of experimental philosophy: (a) the *if-then* approach, (b) the *debunking* approach(es), and (c) the *pluralism* approach.[32] Note that these relate mostly to philosophical-level XLJ, though the doctrinal level and applied level may often be relevant, as well.

The if-then approach is the most straightforward and essentially states that if relevant participants consistently make a judgment in favor of a particular moral (or legal) claim, then that claim has prima facie normative weight. Note that "relevant participants" here is potentially open to interpretation and may refer to laypeople or certain types of experts, depending on one's normative lens. Here we may distinguish between *democratic if-then* approaches to XLJ, which involve drawing normative inferences based on the judgments of laypeople, and *technocratic if-then* approaches, which involve drawing normative inferences based on the judgments of experts. With regard to both democratic and technocratic if-then approaches, the normative import provided by participants' judgments alone seems quite limited due to classic is-ought concerns (i.e., just because most people believe X does not mean that most people should believe X, nor does it mean that X is true[33]), and the said judgments will never be enough on their own to deliver an "all-things-considered" normative conclusion, even in cases where all actors agree.[34] However, if one either assumes or makes additional arguments in favor of the reliability and trustworthiness of laypeople's or experts' intuitions in relevant contexts, then the if-then approach may help deliver valuable philosophical insights.

While the limitations of the if-then approach seem to apply to its use in justifying the normative premise of XLJ (all consequences matter equally), this approach (particularly the technocratic if-then approach) seems more promising as a way of justifying the empirical premises of legal longtermism, particularly the feasibility assumption. For example, to the extent that legal academics are experts on the potential long-term effects of law,[35] it follows that their endorsement of the claim that there are feasible, predictable mechanisms through which the law can influence the long-term future would strengthen the same empirical premise underlying legal longtermism (i.e. that there are feasible, predictable mechanisms through which the law can influence the long-term future), which in turn would provide some evidentiary and normative weight to legal longtermism.

The second set of approaches to drawing normative philosophical inferences from XLJ is known as *debunking*. Whereas the if-then approach assigns normative weight to relevant participant judgments outright, debunking approaches argue against assigning normative weight to judgments that are unreliable. Here again, "unreliable" can be open to interpretation and is essentially a catchall term for morally irrelevant factors or processes. According to one prevalent version of this approach, often referred to as *cognitive debunking*,[36] a judgment is considered to be unreliable if the underlying psychological process giving rise to that judgment—or, to use the terminology used in Section 10.2, the proximate cause of that judgment— does not reliably "get to the truth" (Wedgwood, 2007) or "track the truth" (Andow, 2016), or it cannot be classified as a "truth-tracking process" (Greene, 2013, 2014; Winter, in press).

The debunking approach is perhaps the most formalized of the philosophical approaches covered in this section and can be represented as follows:

(P1) Judgment p is the output of a psychological process that is substantially influenced by factor F. (Empirical premise)

(P2) If a judgment is the output of a psychological process that is substantially influenced by factor F, then it is pro tanto unreliable. (Normative premise)

(C) Judgment p is pro tanto unreliable.

With regard to legal longtermism, for example, let us say that p is the judgment that future generations must not be protected under the law to the same degree as the current generation, and F is one of the cognitive biases laid out in Section 10.2. According to the debunking approach, to the extent that the underlying cognitive processes of this judgment are influenced by these cognitive biases, this judgment is unreliable.

While the debunking approach is often used to lower the normative weight of one judgment, one might instead decide to assign different normative weight to the judgments of laypeople and experts depending on the context. This approach, sometimes referred to as pluralism (Earp et al., 2021), might particularly apply at the doctrinal level, where laypeople and legal experts might both have reliable but competing judgments of longtermist-relevant ordinary legal concepts, such as *person(hood)*. In these cases, one might assign normative weight to the lay judgments in cases where the word is used in its "ordinary" sense and to expert judgments in cases where the word appears to be a "term of art." This distinction will be further explored in the next section as we discuss the legal implications of XLJ.

10.3.2 Legal Implications

In addition to providing philosophical arguments for why and to what extent future generations ought to be provided legal protection in an ideal legal system, XLJ might also be used to advance *legal* arguments regarding the extent to which future generations ought to be provided legal protection according to the doctrines of current legal systems. Here we discuss how doctrinal-level XLJ might be utilized to advance such normative legal arguments, using as illustration two principles of legal interpretation: ordinary meaning and terms of art.

Legal interpretation is ubiquitous to legal argumentation and decision-making, and in many jurisdictions, ordinary meaning analysis has been referred to as "the most fundamental principle" of legal interpretation (Slocum, 2015).[37] According to the ordinary meaning rule, words in a statute (see, e.g., Moskal *v.* United States, 1990; United States *v.* Turkette, 1981; Richards *v.* United States, 1962), treaty (see, e.g., Vienna Convention on the Law of Treaties art. 31, 1969; Slocum & Wong, 2021), contract (California Civil Code, 2018; Jowett, Inc. *v.* United States, 2000; Harris *v.* Dep't of Veterans Affairs, 2015) or other legal document should generally be interpreted according to their ordinary meaning or usage (as opposed to their technical definition, for example).[38] Although there is debate as to what "ordinary meaning" itself means, most jurists seem to agree that it, to some extent, encompasses how a typical or reasonable person generally understands and uses a given word or concept (see, e.g., Tobia, 2020b; Lee & Mouritsen, 2018; Klapper, Schmidt, & Tarantola, 2020).[39] Since one of the goals of XLJ at the doctrinal level is to discover how the typical person understands and interprets longtermism-relevant words and concepts, the findings of doctrinal-level XLJ could plausibly be used to advance ordinary-meaning-related legal arguments (see, e.g., Martínez & Winter, 2022, investigating the ordinary meaning of existential risk).

Of course, not all cases of interpretation involve ordinary meaning analysis, particularly in cases involving terms of art—that is, words that have a particular meaning in a field (such as law, science, or business) that deviates from that word's ordinary meaning or usage (see, e.g., Corning Glass Works *v.* Brennan, 1974; Housey Pharm., Inc. *v.* Astrazeneca U.K. Ltd., 2004; Occidental Life Ins. Co. of Cal. *v.* United States, 1965). In such cases, where the terms are to be given their *technical* as opposed to *ordinary* meaning (e.g., Frankfurter, 1947), XLJ could be useful in terms of (a) identifying terms of art (cf. Nix *v.* Hedden, 1893) and (b) interpreting terms of art, once identified. For example, in cases where it is unclear whether a given longtermism-relevant word is a term of art, one could compare the interpretations of ordinary people and legal experts (or experts in the relevant field) to verify whether the two interpretations tend to deviate significantly from one another. If they do, one could advance a legal argument in favor of interpreting the word as a term of art as opposed to performing ordinary meaning analysis.[40] Furthermore, in cases where a longtermism-relevant term has already been identified as a term of art, one could use the judgments of experts gathered through XLJ research to advance legal arguments in favor of using those judgments to interpret the term of art in question.

Note that these approaches to advancing legal arguments are similar but not identical to the pluralistic approaches to advancing philosophical arguments identified in the previous section. While the pluralistic approach could be used to identify how the law should conceptualize longtermism-relevant concepts, independent of current legal doctrine, the approaches outlined here could be used to determine and convince legal actors—such as judges—how longtermism-relevant concepts should be interpreted according to existing legal doctrine. In other words, whereas the normative legal arguments discussed in this section could plausibly be used in the courtroom to address questions of law,[41] many of the normative philosophical arguments could not.

10.3.3 Policy Implications

In addition to the aforementioned philosophical and legal normative implications, at the policy level XLJ is concerned with determining which legal mechanisms can and ought to be implemented so as to provide the appropriate level of legal protection to future generations. Two ways of doing so include (a) identifying the most implementable longtermist policies and legal instruments in a given jurisdiction and (b) identifying legal instruments that, once implemented, would most effectively protect the interests of future generations. Here we discuss each of these approaches in turn.

The first approach to drawing policy implications involves using XLJ findings—particularly at the applied level, though to some extent at the philosophical and doctrinal levels, as well—to identify longtermism-relevant policies that would be more feasibly implemented. For example, suppose that an applied-level XLJ research project finds that the vast majority of citizens in a democratic jurisdiction are in favor of implementing mandatory federal budgets for protection against existential threats but are not in favor of granting future generations personhood status. To the extent that legislative decision makers are receptive to the popular will of their constituents, this would imply that implementing mandatory federal budgets for existential threats would be more feasible than granting future generations personhood status, and further that, from a legal longtermist perspective, ceteris paribus, one should prefer to attempt to implement the former as opposed to the latter.[42]

The second approach to drawing policy implications involves using XLJ findings to identify legal instruments that, once implemented, would be most favorably interpreted from a longtermist perspective. For example, suppose that an applied-level XLJ research project investigating two versions of a longtermism-relevant provision finds that the vast majority of legal experts interpret version A of the provision much more favorably toward future generations in most relevant scenarios than version B of the provision. Insofar as legal experts' interpretations are reflective of that of the judge tasked with applying the provision in a longtermism-relevant case, it would follow that from a longtermist perspective, ceteris paribus, one should prefer to implement version A of the provision as opposed to version B.

Although these might seem like overly specific policy implications, at a general level one might also be able to draw policy implications regarding the relative feasibility and desirability of (a) broad versus narrow provisions; (b) constitutions versus statutes, regulations, and other legal instruments; and (c) rights versus privileges, duties, and other legal concepts within longtermism-relevant legal instruments. For example, as briefly discussed in Section 10.2.3, there are a priori reasons to believe that both broad standards and narrow rules might be preferable from a longtermist perspective in various scenarios. Applied-level XLJ research could test these predictions and provide general policy guidance to those hoping to implement longtermism-relevant legal mechanisms.

Note that while this approach of drawing normative policy implications from interpretive intuitions may seem superficially similar to the approach for drawing normative *legal* implications from such intuitions, the two differ in subtle yet important respects. For example, consider a proposed longtermism-relevant piece of legislation that is found to be interpreted by the majority of laypeople to offer legal protection to future generations, while the majority of legal experts interpret it as not offering legal protection to future generations. In this case, one might argue from a longtermist policy perspective that it should not be implemented due to the fact that since legal experts interpret it as not offering legal protection to future generations, that the deciding judge will likewise interpret it as not offering legal protection to future generations. However, supposing that this legislation were in fact implemented, then one might make the normative *legal* argument that the ordinary meaning of the text implies legal protection to future generations, since the majority of laypeople—whose intuitions are arguably a better reflection of ordinary meaning than those of a legal expert—interpret the statute in that manner and that consequently the judge similarly ought to interpret the text in this manner.[43]

10.4 Conclusion

This chapter has presented a new research area within the burgeoning field of experimental jurisprudence aimed at informing philosophical, legal, and political debates related to the long-term future. As alluded to in Section 10.1, longtermism is a comparatively new research area in the realm of philosophy and has even more recently made its way into the realm of law and jurisprudence. Whereas many areas of study within experimental philosophy and experimental jurisprudence focus on issues of long-standing discussion within general philosophical literature, XLJ offers the rare opportunity within these fields to apply cutting-edge methodological approaches to cutting-edge substantive issues relevant to philosophers, lawyers, and policy makers. Indeed, XLJ research has already shown that the vast majority of legal scholars consider the protection of the long-term future of utmost importance (Martínez & Winter, 2021a).

At the same time, much of the early work in XLJ, though promising, has only scratched the surface in terms of answering both the empirical questions posed in Section 10.2 and the normative debates of Section 10.3, and we encourage both experimentalists familiar with the methods outlined in Section 10.1.3 as well as theorists familiar with the substantive questions outlined in Sections 10.1.1 and 10.1.2 to work on advancing XLJ research at each of the three levels of abstraction introduced in this chapter. Furthermore, this levels of abstraction framework not only serves to lay out the diverse set of empirical and normative aims within XLJ but also contributes to a more general conceptualization within experimental and theoretical jurisprudence, and we invite researchers within the broader sphere of legal philosophy to incorporate this framework into future projects when useful.

Acknowledgments

For comments, discussion, and critique, we are grateful to Kevin Tobia, Sean Richardson, and Piotr Bystranowski, as well as our editor and reviewer. We also want to thank Suzanne Van Arsdale in particular for help with the manuscript and many useful suggestions.

Notes

1 Note that experimental jurisprudence may also be referred to as *experimental legal philosophy*, though for the sake of simplicity we will use the terminology experimental jurisprudence throughout the chapter.

2 However, there is not yet a widely accepted definition of longtermism (see, e.g., MacAskill, 2019). Also note that there are several different versions of longtermism. The version that we lay out here is most similar to "weak longtermism," which holds merely that we should be particularly concerned with ensuring that the long-run future goes well, as opposed to "strong longtermism," which holds that impacts on the long-run future are the most important feature of our actions. For more information on further distinctions within strong longtermism, see Greaves and MacAskill (2021). For more information on the philosophical foundations of longtermism more generally, see Parfit (1984); Beckstead (2013, 2019); and Greaves and MacAskill (2021).

3 Note that our presentation of the case for longtermism deviates slightly from the presentation in the formal longtermist literature in that (a) we provide three assumptions instead of two (the feasibility argument is not presented as an "assumption" in longtermist literature), and (b) we do not explicitly discuss any of the objections to longtermism. These deviations are largely for the purpose of brevity and readability; for a more thorough discussion of the objections, see Greaves and MacAskill (2021) and Tarsney (2020). For a concise overview of these objections that is tailored to a legal audience, see Winter et al. (2021).

4 An alternative framing of this assumption would be to state that (a) all consequences matter equally insofar as they affect welfare, and (b) the welfare of those living in the future matters equally as the welfare of those living today. Note, however, that the use of the term "consequences" does not necessarily imply that longtermism is an inherently consequentialist theory, as consequentialism is just one approach to justifying longtermism. For example, one might alternatively argue (from a deontological perspective) that we owe a duty to future generations, independent of what a consequentialist/utilitarian calculus might demand, or (from a virtue ethics perspective) that it is a virtue to act in a way that protects future generations by exercising patience, self-discipline, benevolence, and taking responsibility for our actions (Gaba, 1999, pp. 283–7; cf. also Ord, 2020). One might also conceivably value future generations from a purely aesthetic or intellectual achievement standpoint (Todd, 2017). Our apparent focus on consequences in

discussing the assumptions of longtermism stems from the fact that most non-consequentialist ethical theories maintain that, ceteris paribus, consequences matter to some degree.

5   While it may still seem counterintuitive that we should not adopt a "social discount rate" (as we do for money, for example), this view seems to be shared by most, if not all, moral philosophers that have written about the issue (Parfit, 1984; Cowen & Parfit, 1992; Broome, 1994; Mogensen, 2019), as well as by many theoretical economists (38 percent according to a survey performed by Drupp, Freeman, Groom, & Nesje, 2018). As we outline later on, XLJ research has uncovered that legal scholars also seem to broadly share this view (or at least a much smaller discount rate than is currently being applied).

6   Note that although the paragraph argues mostly from the perspective of humans, "individuals" here can refer not only to humans but to potentially all other forms of sentience, as well (e.g., non-human animals and sentient artificial intelligence [assuming its existence]). Indeed, there appear to be very compelling arguments for including this broader set of sentient beings within a moral calculus, and, by extension, within the definition of individuals as presented above (Bentham, 1789; Singer, 1973; Gruen, 2017). That said, independent of how one defines individuals here, the associated arguments—both for this assumption and for longtermism as a whole—would proceed similarly as presented in the main body text.

7   The usual threats of extinction faced by species include environmental, demographic, and genetic factors (Benson et al., 2016).

8   See generally the emerging field of persistence studies, for example, Giuliano and Nunn (2021) with further references therein; see also Pirie (2021).

9   Note that in terms of justifying longtermism, the extent to which premise three (feasible and predictable) must be true arguably depends in part on the extent to which premise two (future is vast in size) turns out to be true (and vice versa). For example, the greater in size the future turns out to be, the more one can be confident in longtermism despite less feasible, predictable ways of influencing the long-term future. Conversely, the more feasible and predictable one believes it is to influence the long-term future, the smaller the number of future individuals must be for one to conclude that longtermism is true. To some extent, this is also the case with regard to premise one (all consequences matter equally); even if, in spite of the reasons laid out above, one does not believe the future is worth valuing *to the same degree* as the present, and thus discounts the value of future generations as discussed in note 5, one could still conclude that longtermism is true depending on the expected size of future generations, feasibility and predictability of influence, and degree of discounting. Note that the interrelation of these premises/assumptions influences not only confidence in longtermism but also confidence in weak longtermism versus strong longtermism discussed in note 2; that is, depending on such calculations, one might not only conclude that we should be "particularly" but rather "primarily" concerned with ensuring that the long-run future goes well (cf. Greaves & MacAskill, 2021).

10 As with philosophical longtermism, there are several possible versions of legal longtermism. For example, analogous to *strong philosophical longtermism*, we may define *strong legal longtermism* as the view that "the primary determinant of the value of a legal mechanism is the effect of that mechanism on the far future."

11 For an overview of experimental jurisprudence, see Tobia (2022). For an overview of experimental philosophy more generally, see Knobe et al. (2012).

12 As we clarify further, note that "people" here can refer not only to laypeople but also to legal experts, within or across different jurisdictions depending on the study.

13 See *supra* note 5. See also Greaves (2017) for a survey of discounting in public policy, including a survey of the arguments for and against a positive rate of pure time preference. Among moral philosophers, a zero rate of pure time preference is endorsed by, among others, Broome (2008), Buchholz and Schumacher (2010), Cline (1992), Cowen and Parfit (1992), Dasgupta (2008), Dietz, Hepburn, and Hope (2008), Gollier (2012), Harrod (1948), Pigou (1932), Ramsey (1928), Sidgwick (1907), Solow (1974), and Stern (2008). Other related philosophical works include Cowen and Parfit (1992), Mogensen (2019), and Parfit (1984). In a survey of experts on social discounting, 38 percent accepted a zero rate of pure time preference (Drupp et al., 2018).

14 For a comprehensive list of relevant studies on expert intuition, see Guthrie, Rachlinski, and Wistrich (2000); see also Winter (2020, p. 249).

15 That said, the results from Martínez and Winter (2021) indicate that conservatives and liberals alike endorse greater levels of legal protection for future generations than those granted to future generations under current legal institutions, suggesting that future generations may be within the moral circle of both liberals and conservatives.

16 Note that with regard to the ultimate cause, computational approaches—such as game-theoretic modeling—may be a more promising means for uncovering legal longtermism-relevant insight than experimental approaches. In other words, this might be better suited for the realm of what we might label as *computational longtermist jurisprudence* as opposed to experimental longtermist jurisprudence, though the two approaches are, of course, by no means mutually exclusive.

17 Connecting the second level more explicitly with the first level, one might also ask to what extent people's endorsement (or lack thereof) of legal longtermism is a result of or relates to their conception of ordinary legal concepts.

18 Standing (*locus standi*) in many jurisdictions refers to the legal right of one to bring forth a lawsuit.

19 As will be discussed further in Section 10.3, note that surveying laypeople on issues *underlying* specialized concepts (e.g., should future generations be represented in court) may still make sense at the philosophical or applied level as opposed to the doctrinal level.

20 Examples of jurisdictions that explicitly employ some version of ordinary meaning analysis include Australia (e.g., Electricity Generation Corporation *v* Woodside Energy, 2014), the United Kingdom (River Wear Commissioners *v*. Adamson, 1877), South Africa (Venter *v*. R, 1907; Carney, 2016), the United States (see generally Slocum, 2015), and Singapore (Interpretation Act Sec. 9A, 1993), as well as international law (Vienna Convention on the Law of Treaties art. 31, 1969). Ordinary meaning has also been found to be relevant in civil-code jurisdictions, as well, including Argentina, Finland, France, Germany, Italy, Poland, and Sweden (see generally MacCormick & Summers, 2016).

21 Alternatively, one may argue that the use of lay people reflects a bias for convenience, as it is much easier to recruit lay subjects than legal professionals. We further discuss these issues in Section 10.3, *infra*.

22 Compare this to the effect of philosophical training on people's judgments of philosophical-based legal longtermism, discussed in note 5 and accompanying text.

23 For example, whereas laypeople may be more inclined to associate the concept of "person" with the concept of "human," which would presumably lead to a relatively high degree of endorsement of the view of future humans as "persons," lawyers may be more reticent to do so given that (a) future humans are not commonly thought of as legal persons, and (b) it might seem counterintuitive that future humans could do things that legal persons are commonly thought to be able to do (e.g., enter into contracts, sue and be sued, own property, etc.). On the other hand, it is also counterintuitive that corporations and other juridical persons could do these things, so perhaps the latter may not be so much of an impediment to a lawyer's ability to consider future generations as legal persons (just as it may not impede consideration of non-human animals, for example), hence explaining why a slight majority still endorsed personhood for humans living in the near future.

24 In practice, however, research that investigates more concrete legal mechanisms is most likely carried out for instrumental purposes—that is, not for the purposes of determining (or even arguing) whether longtermism fits or ought to fit the goals of the current legal system, but rather how a longtermism-friendly policy maker might design legal instruments that will ultimately be interpreted in a longtermism-friendly way.

25 For each area of law, participants were asked, on a scale of 1–7 (1 being "strongly disagree, 4 being "neutral, and 7 being "strongly agree"), to rate their level of agreement with the following statement: "There are feasible, predictable mechanisms through which the law can influence the long-term future (understood as at least 100 years from now) via . . ." followed by the relevant area of law. For each area, the majority of participants responded 5 or higher (indicating at least "somewhat agree").

26 For further discussion on the relative normative implications of using expert versus lay intuitions in this context, see Section 10.3.

27 Anthis & Paez (2021); Singer ([1981] 2011).

28 For example, the eighth amendment to the US Constitution (1791) prohibits "cruel and unusual punishment." In the mid-twentieth century judges began to interpret this phrase as an "evolving standard" (Trop *v.* Dulles, 1958) with more progressive judges eventually interpreting it as including capital punishment despite the original interpretation of this provision not including capital punishment (Furman *v.* Georgia, 1972; Stinneford, 2019).

29 On the other hand, constitutions are surprisingly short-lived; Elkins, Ginsburg, and Melton (2007) found that (a) the average lifespan of a constitution is just seventeen years, and (b) the probability of a constitution lasting at least fifty years is just 19 percent. Although systematic data with regard to statutes appears unavailable, there are many cases of legislation outlasting several iterations of a nation's constitution (e.g., the German Penal Code of 1871: Mueller, 1961).

30 Other potential reasons dictating in favor of regulatory mechanisms (particularly in the United States) are that they are more easily passed than statutes, can be updated more easily based on new information, and tend to be implemented by those with expert knowledge of the material in question.

31 It also seems likely that many of the legal mechanisms evaluated at the applied level are jurisdiction-specific; accordingly, in some cases it may make less sense to attempt to replicate some of the exact findings of one experiment in another jurisdiction and instead investigate these differences to understand what makes a particular jurisdiction have more longtermism-friendly interpretations.

32 Note that the labels for these approaches are not yet very well-established. We have adapted the terminology from Earp, Lewis, Dranseika, and Hannikainen (2021)

regarding approaches to drawing normative implications in experimental bioethics, as we find this to be a useful taxonomy.

33 Despite the is-ought concerns, many have argued that moral philosophers are, in fact, moral experts (Singer, 1972).

34 Although cases where all potentially relevant participants converge toward one view might provide normative weight toward that view, one would still need to rule out the possibility that the said actors are all systematically biased (see debunking approach later).

35 It remains an open question to what extent legal academics (or legal experts in general) are the relevant experts here, as opposed to, say, superforecasters (cf. Tetlock & Gardner, 2016).

36 Note that cognitive debunking is just one type of debunking approach. Another common debunking approach is evolutionary debunking, which involves assessing whether the evolutionary process that gave rise to a particular belief or judgment is unreliable (see generally Mogensen, 2016).

37 See *supra* note 19.

38 For an overview of the ordinary meaning analysis doctrine, see generally Slocum (2015).

39 For example, in Addison *v.* Holly Hill Fruit Products, Inc. (1944), the court stated, "Legislation when not expressed in technical terms is addressed to the common run of men and is therefore to be understood according to the sense of the thing, as the ordinary man has a right to rely on ordinary words addressed to him" (p. 618).

40 Note that at the philosophical level, one could make an argument for why the law *should* use the lay definition (independent of ordinary meaning analysis or any other doctrine) using the democratic if-then approach. Conversely, one could use a technocratic if-then approach to argue in favor of the interpretation of a legal expert (even for cases currently governed by ordinary meaning analysis).

41 Note that legal interpretation is generally considered a question of law. For example, with regard to the United States, see, e.g., United States *v.* Moore (2009); United States *v.* Shafer (2009).

42 Of course, the assumption that lawmakers are receptive to the interests of the public is not always warranted. For example, in the United States, the majority of Americans believe that the government has a responsibility to provide health care for all (Pew, 2020), yet the United States famously does not provide health care to all of its citizens.

43 This hypothetical scenario, of course, assumes that ordinary meaning analysis would apply to this case, and that the relevant sections of the text would not be interpreted as terms of art (in which case the relevant experts' intuitions would apply to any normative legal-interpretive argument as well).

References

ACE Project (2021). *Comparative data.* https://aceproject.org/epic-en.

Adams, F. C., & Laughlin, G. (1997). A dying universe: The long-term fate and evolution of astrophysical objects. *Reviews of Modern Physics, 69*(2), 337–72. https://link.aps.org/doi/10.1103/RevModPhys.69.337.

Andow, J. (2016, June 7). Reliable but not home free? What framing effects mean for moral intuitions. *Philosophical Psychology, 29*(6), 904–11. https://doi.org/10.1080/09515089.2016.1168794.

Anthis, J. R., & Paez, E. (2021, June). Moral circle expansion: A promising strategy to impact the far future. *Futures, 130*: 102756. https://doi.org/10.1016/j.futures.2021.102756.

Araújo, R., & Koessler, L. (2021, September 30). *The rise of the constitutional protection of future generations* (Legal Priorities Project Working Paper Series No. 7-2021). Legal Priorities Project. https://www.legalpriorities.org/research/constitutional-protection-future-generations.html.

Barnosky, A. D., Matzke, N., Tomiya, S., Wogan, G. O., Swartz, B., Quental, T. B., Ferrer, E. A. (2011, March 2). Has the earth's sixth mass extinction already arrived? *Nature*, *471*(7336), 51–57. https://doi.org/10.1038/nature09678.

Beckstead, N. (2013, May). *On the overwhelming importance of shaping the far future* [Unpublished doctoral dissertation]. Rutgers University. https://doi.org/10.7282/T35M649T.

Beckstead, N. (2014, June 22). *Will we eventually be able to colonize other stars? Notes from a preliminary review*. Future of Humanity Institute, University of Oxford. https://www.fhi.ox.ac.uk/will-we-eventually-be-able-to-colonize-other-stars-notes-from-a-preliminary-review/.

Beckstead, N. (2019). A brief argument for the overwhelming importance of shaping the far future. In H. Greaves & T. Pummer (Eds.), *Effective altruism: Philosophical issues*, (pp. 80–98). Oxford University Press. https://doi.org/10.1093/oso/9780198841364.001.0001.

Beitz, C. R. (1983, October). Cosmopolitan ideals and national sentiment. *The Journal of Philosophy*, *80*(10), 591–600. https://doi.org/10.2307/2026155.

Benson, J. F., Mahoney, P. J., Sikich, J. A., Serieys, L. E., Pollinger, J. P., Ernest, H. B., & Riley, S. P. (2016, August 31). Interactions between demography, genetics, and landscape connectivity increase extinction probability for a small population of large carnivores in a major metropolitan area. *Proceedings of the Royal Society B: Biological Sciences*, *283*(1837), 20160957. https://doi.org/10.1098/rspb.2016.0957.

Bentham, J. (1789), *An introduction to the principles of morals and legislation*. Clarendon Press. http://dx.doi.org/10.1093/oseo/instance.00077240.

Berman, H. J. (1985), *Law and revolution: The formation of the western legal tradition*. Cambridge, MA: Harvard University Press.

Broome, J. (1994, April). Discounting the future. *Philosophy & Public Affairs*, *23*(2), 128–56. https://doi.org/10.1111/j.1088-4963.1994.tb00008.x.

Broome, J. (2008, June). The ethics of climate change: Pay now or pay more later?. *Scientific American*, *298*(6), 96–102. https://www.scientificamerican.com/article/the-ethics-of-climate-change/.

Buchholz, W., & Schumacher, J. (2010, September). Discounting and welfare analysis over time: Choosing the η. *European Journal of Political Economy*, *26*(3), 372–85. https://doi.org/10.1016/j.ejpoleco.2009.11.011.

Caldeira, K., & Kasting, J. F. (1992, December 31). The life span of the biosphere revisited. *Nature*, *360*(6406), 721–3. https://doi.org/10.1038/360721a0.

California Civil Code, Part 2. Contracts, § 1549–1701 (2018). https://leginfo.legislature.ca.gov/faces/codesTOCSelected.xhtml?tocCode=CIV.

Carney, T. R. (2016, May 31). Using frames to determine ordinary meaning in court cases: the case of "plant" and "vermin." *Stellenbosch Papers in Linguistics*, *45*, 31–48. https://doi.org/10.5774/45-0-209.

Ceballos, G., Ehrlich, P. R., Barnosky, A. D., García, A., Pringle, R. M., & Palmer, T. M. (2015, June 19). Accelerated modern human–induced species losses: Entering the sixth mass extinction. *Science Advances*, *1*(5), e1400253. https://doi.org/10.1126/sciadv.1400253.

Cheng, L., Rosett, A., & Woo, M. (Eds.). (2003). *East Asian law: Universal norms and local cultures*. London & New York: Routledge.

Cline, W. R. (1992), *The economics of global warming*. Washington, DC: Institute for International Economics.

Corning Glass Works v. Brennan, 417 U.S. 188 (1974).

Cowen, T., & Parfit, D. (1992). Against the social discount rate. In P. Laslett & J. S. Fishkin (Eds.), *Justice between age groups and generations* (pp. 144–61). New Haven: Yale University Press.

Dasgupta, P. (2008, September 4). Discounting climate change. *Journal of Risk & Uncertainty*, 37(2), 141–69. https://doi.org/10.1007/s11166-008-9049-6.

Desvousges, W. H., Naughton, M. C., & Parsons, G. R. (1992, March). Benefit transfer: Conceptual problems in estimating water quality benefits using existing studies. *Water Resources Research*, 28(3), 675–683. https://doi.org/10.1029/91WR02592.

Dietz, S., Hepburn, C., & Hope, C. (2008, March 28), Discounting and climate change: a non-marginal policy choice [Unpublished manuscript]. https://www.researchgate.net/publication/254809091_Discounting_and_climate_change_a_non-marginal_policy_choice.

Drupp, M. A., Freeman, M. C., Groom, B., & Nesje, F. (2018, November). Discounting disentangled. *American Economic Journal: Economic Policy*, 10(4), 109–34.

Earp, B. D., Lewis, J., Dranseika, V., & Hannikainen, I. (2021), Experimental philosophical bioethics and normative inference. *Theoretical Medicine & Bioethics*. https://doi.org/10.1007/s11017-021-09546-z.

Electricity Generation Corporation v. Woodside Energy Ltd., 7 HCA (2014).

Elkins, Z., Ginsburg, T., & Melton, J. (2007, December 26). *The lifespan of written constitutions* [Unpublished manuscript]. College of Law & Department of Political Science, University of Illinois. https://jenni.uchicago.edu/WJP/Vienna_2008/Ginsburg-Lifespans-California.pdf.

Foote, M., & Raup, D. M. (1996). Fossil preservation and the stratigraphic ranges of taxa. *Paleobiology*, 22(2), 121–40. https://doi.org/10.1017/s0094837300016134.

Frankfurter, F. (1947, May). Some reflections on the reading of statutes. *Columbia Law Review*, 47(4), 527–46.

Gaba, J. (1999). Environmental ethics and our moral relationship to future generations: Future rights and present virtue. *Columbia Journal of Environmental Law*, 24(2), 249–88.

Gallup, J. L., & Sachs, J. D. (2001, January–February). The economic burden of malaria. *American Journal of Tropical Medicine and Hygiene*, 64(1–2 Suppl), 85–96. https://doi.org/10.4269/ajtmh.2001.64.85.

Galway-Witham, J., & Stringer, C. (2018, June 22). How did *Homo sapiens* evolve? *Science*, 360(6395), 1296–8. https://doi.org/10.1126/science.aat6659.

Gilovich, T., Griffin, D., & Kahneman, D. (Eds.) (2002), *Heuristics and biases: The psychology of intuitive judgment*. Cambridge, UK: Cambridge University Press.

Giuliano, P., & Nunn, N. (2021, July). Understanding cultural persistence and change. *The Review of Economic Studies*, 88(4), 1541–81. https://doi.org/10.1093/restud/rdaa074.

Gollier, C. (2012). *Pricing the planet's future: The economics of discounting in an uncertain world*. Princeton: Princeton University Press.

Greaves, H. (2017, November), Discounting for public policy: A survey. *Economics & Philosophy*, 33(3), 391–439. https://doi.org/10.1017/S0266267117000062.

Greaves, H., & MacAskill, W. (2019, September). *The case for strong longtermism* (GPI Working Paper No. 7-2019). Global Priorities Institute. https://globalprioritiesinstitute.org/wp-content/uploads/2020/Greaves_MacAskill_strong_longtermism.pdf.

Greaves, H., & MacAskill, W. (2021, June), *The case for strong longtermism* (GPI Working Paper No. 5-2021). Global Priorities Institute. https://globalprioritiesinstitute.org/wp

-content/uploads/The-Case-for-Strong-Longtermism-GPI-Working-Paper-June-2021 -2.pdf.

Greene, J., & Baron, J. (2001, June 29). Intuitions about declining marginal utility. *Journal of Behavioral Decision Making, 14*(3), 243–55. https://doi.org/10.1002/bdm.375.

Greene, J. D. (2013). *Moral tribes: Emotion, reason, and the gap between us and them.* New York: Penguin Press.

Greene, J. D. (2014). Beyond point-and-shoot morality: Why cognitive (neuro) science matters for ethics. *Ethics, 124*(4), 695–726. https://www.journals.uchicago.edu/doi/abs /10.1086/675875.

Gruen, L. (2017, August 23). The moral status of animals. In E. N. Zalta (Ed.), *Stanford encyclopedia of philosophy.* https://plato.stanford.edu/entries/moral-animal/.

Guthrie, C., Rachlinski, J. J., & Wistrich, A. J. (2000). Inside the judicial mind. *Cornell Law Review, 86*(4), 777–830.

Harris v. U.S. Dep't of Veterans Affairs, 776 F.3d 907 (2015).

Harrod, R. F. (1948). *Towards a dynamic economics: Some recent developments of economic theory and their application to policy.* London: MacMillan and Company.

Housey Pharmaceuticals, Inc. v. Astrazeneca UK Ltd., No. 03–1193 (Fed. Cir. May 7, 2004).

Interpretation Act (Cap 1) s 9A (1993).

John, T., & MacAskill, W. (2020, October). *Longtermist institutional reform* (GPI Working Paper No. 14-2020). Global Priorities Institute. https://globalprioritiesinstitute.org/wp -content/uploads/Tyler-M-John-and-William-MacAskill_Longtermist-institutional -reform.pdf.

Jowett, Inc. v. United States, 234 F.3d 1365 (2000).

Kahneman, D., Ritov, I., Schkade, D., Sherman, S. J., & Varian, H. R. (1999). Economic preferences or attitude expressions? An analysis of dollar responses to public issues. In B. Fischhoff & B. Manski (Eds.), *Elicitation of preferences* (pp. 203–42). New York: Springer.

Klapper, S., Schmidt, S., & Tarantola, T. (2020). Ordinary Meaning from Ordinary People [Unpublished manuscript].

Knobe, J., Buckwalter, W., Nichols, S., Robbins, P., Sarkissian, H., & Sommers, T. (2012). Experimental philosophy. *Annual Review of Psychology, 63*(1): 81–99. https://doi.org /10.1146/annurev-psych-120710-100350.

Kuecken, M., Thuilliez, J., & Valfort, M. A. (2014, December). *Does malaria control impact education? Evidence from Roll Back Malaria in Africa* (Les Notes du G-MonD, Note 12). Paris School of Economics. https://www.parisschoolofeconomics.eu/IMG/pdf/ note12-gmond-malaria-education-africa-pse-december2014.pdf.

Kuran, T. (2011, February–March). Legal roots of economic underdevelopment in the Middle East. *The European Financial Review,* February – March 2011, 10–11.

Lee, T. R. & Mouritsen, S. C. (2018). Judging Ordinary Meaning. *Yale Law Journal, 127*(4), 788–879. https://www.yalelawjournal.org/article/judging-ordinary-meaning.

MacAskill, W. (2019). The definition of effective altruism. In H. Greaves & T. Pummer (Eds.), *Effective altruism: Philosophical Issues* (pp. 10–28). New York: Oxford University Press. https://doi.org/10.1093/oso/9780198841364.001.0001.

MacAskill, W. (2022). *What we owe the future.* New York: Basic Books.

MacCormick, D. N., & Summers, R. S. (Eds.). (2016). *Interpreting statutes: A comparative study.* New York: Routledge.

Martínez, E., & Tobia, K. P. (2022). *What do law professors believe about law and the legal academy? An empirical inquiry* https://papers.ssrn.com/sol3/papers.cfm?abstract_id =4182521.

Martínez, E., & Winter, C. K. (2021a, August 20). *Protecting future generations: A global survey of legal academics* (LPP Working Paper Series No. 1). Legal Priorities Project. https://papers.ssrn.com/sol3/papers.cfm?abstract_id=3931304.

Martínez, E., & Winter, C. (2021b, November 26). Protecting sentient artificial intelligence: A survey of lay intuitions on standing, personhood, and general legal protection. *Frontiers in Robotics and AI: Ethics in Robotics and Artificial Intelligence, 8,* 788355. https://doi.org/10.3389/frobt.2021.788355.

Martínez, E., & Winter, C. (2022). *The ordinary meaning of existential risk* [unpublished manuscript].

Martínez, E., & Winter, C. (in press a). Cross-cultural perceptions of rights for future generations. In K. Tobia (Ed.), *Cambridge handbook of experimental jurisprudence.* https://papers.ssrn.com/sol3/papers.cfm?abstract_id=4262891.

Martínez, E., & Winter, C. (in press b). The intuitive appeal of legal longtermism. In J. Barrett, D. Thorstad, & H. Greaves (Eds.), *Essays on longtermism.* Oxford: Oxford University Press.

Mischel, W., & Ebbesen, E. B. (1970). Attention in delay of gratification. *Journal of Personality & Social Psychology, 16*(2), 329–37. https://doi.org/10.1037/h0029815.

Mogensen, A. (2019, September). *Maximal cluelessness* (GPI Working Paper No. 2-2019). Global Priorities Institute. https://globalprioritiesinstitute.org/wp-content/uploads/2020/Andreas_Mogensen_maximal_cluelessness.pdf.

Mogensen, A. L. (2016). Contingency anxiety and the epistemology of disagreement. *Pacific Philosophical Quarterly, 97*(4), 590–611. https://doi.org/10.1111/papq.12099.

Moskal v. United States, 498 U.S. 103 (1990).

Mueller, G. O., trans. (1961), *The German Penal Code of 1871*, 107, South Hackensack, NJ: Rothman.

Nix v. Hedden, 149 U.S. 304 (1893).

Occidental Life Insurance Co. of Cal. v. United States, 250 F. Supp. 130 (S.D. Cal. 1965).

O'Donoghue, T., & Rabin, M. (1999, March). Doing it now or later. *American Economic Review, 89*(1), 103–24. https://doi.org/10.1257/aer.89.1.103.

O'Donoghue, T., & Rabin, M. (2015, May). Present bias: Lessons learned and to be learned. *American Economic Review, 105*(5), 273–9. https://doi.org/10.1257/aer.p20151085.

Ord, T. (2020). *The precipice: Existential risk and the future of humanity.* New York: Hachette Books.

Parfit, D. (1984). *Reasons and persons.* Oxford: Oxford University Press.

Pettit, P., & Smith, M. (2000, June). Global consequentialism. In B. Hooker, E. Mason, & D. E. Miller (Eds.), *Morality, rules, and consequences: A critical reader* (pp. 121–33). Edinburgh: Edinburgh University Press.

Pigou, A. C. (1932, December 1). The effect of reparations on the ratio of international interchange. *The Economic Journal, 42*(168): 532–43. https://doi.org/10.2307/2223778.

Pirie, F. (2021). *The rule of laws: A 4,000-year quest to order the world.* New York: Basic Books.

Pogge, T. (1989). *Realizing Rawls.* Ithaca: Cornell University Press.

Pryce, J., Richardson, M., & Lengeler, C. (2018). Insecticide-treated nets for preventing malaria. *Cochrane Database of Systematic Reviews,* 11. https://doi.org/10.1002/14651858.CD000363.pub3.

Ramsey, F. P. (1928, December). A mathematical theory of saving. *The Economic Journal, 38*(152), 543–59. https://doi.org/10.2307/2224098.

Rawls, J. (1971). *A theory of justice.* Cambridge, MA: Harvard University Press.

Richards v. United States, 369 U.S. 1 (1962).

River Wear Commissioners v Adamson, 2 App Cas 743 (1877).

Roser, M., Ritchie, H., & Ortiz-Ospina, E. (2019, May). *World population growth*. Our World in Data. https://ourworldindata.org/world-population-growth.

Sachs, J., & Malaney, P. (2002). The economic and social burden of malaria. *Nature, 415*(6872), 680–5. https://doi.org/10.1038/415680a.

Schlebusch, C. M., Malmström, H., Günther, T., Sjödin, P., Coutinho, A., Edlund, H., Jakobsson, M. (2017, November 3). Southern African ancient genomes estimate modern human divergence to 350,000 to 260,000 years ago. *Science, 358*(6363), 652–5. https://doi.org/10.1126/science.aao6266.

Schubert, S., Caviola, L., & Faber, N. S. (2019). The psychology of existential risk: Moral judgments about human extinction. *Scientific Reports, 9*(1), 1–8. https://doi.org/10.1038/s41598-019-50145-9.

Schwarz, N., Bless, H., Strack, F., Klumpp, G., Rittenauer-Schatka, H., & Simons, A. (1991). Ease of retrieval as information: Another look at the availability heuristic. *Journal of Personality & Social Psychology, 61*(2), 195–202. https://doi.org/10.1037/0022-3514.61.2.195.

Sidgwick, H. (1907), *The methods of ethics* (7th ed.). London: Macmillan.

Singer, P. (1972). *Famine, affluence, and morality*. Oxford: Oxford University Press.

Singer, P. (1973). Animal liberation. In R. Garner (Ed.), *Animal rights* (pp. 7–18). London: Palgrave Macmillan. https://doi.org/10.1007/978-1-349-25176-6_1.

Singer, P. ([1981] 2011). *The expanding circle: Ethics, evolution, and moral progress*. Princeton & Oxford: Princeton University Press.

Slocum, B. G. (2015). *Ordinary meaning: A theory of the most fundamental principle of legal interpretation*. Chicago: University of Chicago Press. https://doi.org/10.7208/chicago/9780226304991.001.0001.

Slocum, B. G., & Wong, J. (2021). The Vienna Convention and the ordinary meaning of international law. *Yale Journal of International Law, 46*(2), 192–239. https://papers.ssrn.com/sol3/papers.cfm?abstract_id=3556892.

Slovic, P. (2010), The more who die, the less we care. In P. Slovic (Ed.), *The feeling of risk: New perspectives on risk perception* (pp. 97–106). New York: Routledge.

Solow, R. M. (1974). The economics of resources or the resources of economics. In C. Gopalakrishnan (Ed.), *Classic papers in natural resource economics* (pp. 257–76). London: Palgrave MacMillan. https://doi.org/10.1057/9780230523210_13.

Stern, N. (2008). The economics of climate change. *American Economic Review, 98*(2), 1–37. https://doi.org/10.1257/aer.98.2.1.

Tarsney, C. (2020, May). *The epistemic challenge to longtermism* (GPI Working Paper No. 10-2019). Global Priorities Institute. https://globalprioritiesinstitute.org/wp-content/uploads/Working-paper-10-Christian-Tarsney.pdf.

Tetlock, P. E., & Gardner, D. (2016), *Superforecasting: The art and science of prediction*. New York: Crown Publishers.

Tobia, K. P. (2020a, February 10). *Legal concepts and legal expertise* [Unpublished manuscript]. https://privpapers.ssrn.com/sol3/papers.cfm?abstract_id=3536564.

Tobia, K. P. (2020b). Testing ordinary meaning. *Harvard Law Review, 134*(2), 726–806. https://harvardlawreview.org/2020/12/testing-ordinary-meaning/.

Tobia, K. P. (2022). Experimental jurisprudence. *University of Chicago Law Review, 89*(3), 735–802. https://lawreview.uchicago.edu/publication/experimental-jurisprudence.

Todd, B. (2017, October). Why your impact in millions of years could be what most matters. 80,000 Hours. https://80000hours.org/articles/future-generations/.

Trivers, R. L. (1971). The evolution of reciprocal altruism. *The Quarterly Review of Biology, 46*(1), 35–57. https://www.journals.uchicago.edu/doi/10.1086/406755.

Tversky, A., & Kahneman, D. (1973, September). Availability: A heuristic for judging frequency and probability. *Cognitive Psychology, 5*(2): 207–232. https://doi.org/10.1016/0010-0285(73)90033-9.

United Nations (2019). 2019 Revision of World Population Prospects. https://population.un.org/wpp/.

United States v. Moore, 572 F.3d 489 (2009).

United States v. Shafer, 573 F.3d 267 (2009).

United States v. Turkette, 452 U.S. 576 (1981).

Venter v. R, TS 910 (1907).

Vienna Convention on the Law of Treaties art. 31, opened for signature May 23, 1969, 1155 U.N.T.S. 331.

Watson, A. (1991), *Roman Law and comparative law.* Athens: University of Georgia Press.

Waytz, A., Iyer, R., Young, L., & Graham, J. (2016, February 17). Ideological differences in the expanse of empathy. In P. Valdesolo & J. Graham (Eds.), *Social psychology of political polarization* (pp. 61–77). New York: Routledge.

Waytz, A., Iyer, R., Young, L., Haidt, J., & Graham, J. (2019, September 26). Ideological differences in the expanse of the moral circle. *Nature Communications, 10*(1), 4389. https://www.nature.com/articles/s41467-019-12227-0.

Wedgwood, R. (2007, October). Normativism defended. In B. P. McLaughlin & J. Cohen (Eds.), *Contemporary debates in philosophy of mind* (pp. 85–101). Blackwell Publishing.

Winter, C. K. (2020, February 10). The value of behavioral economics for EU judicial decision-making. *German Law Journal, 21*(2), 240–64. https://doi.org/10.1017/glj.2020.3.

Winter, C. K. (in press). The challenges of artificial judicial decision-making for liberal democracy. In Bystranowski, P., Janik, B., & Próchnicki, M. (Eds.), *Judicial decision-making: Integrating empirical and theoretical perspectives.* https://papers.ssrn.com/sol3/papers.cfm?abstract_id=3933648.

Winter, C. K., Schuett, J., Martínez, E., Van Arsdale, S., Araújo, R., Hollman, N., Rotola, G. (2021, January). Legal priorities research: A research agenda. Legal Priorities Project. https://www.legalpriorities.org/research_agenda.pdf.

Yudkowsky, E. (2008). Cognitive biases potentially affecting judgment of global risks. In *Global catastrophic risks* (pp. 91–119). Oxford: Oxford University Press. https://doi.org/10.1093/oso/9780198570509.001.0001.

Contributors

Guilherme da F. C. F. de Almeida has completed his PhD in legal philosophy at PUC-Rio. He is an assistant professor at The Insper Institute of Education and Research in São Paulo, Brazil.

Lucien Baumgartner is a PhD student at the Institute of Philosophy, University of Zurich, and part of the Eccellenza team of Professor Kevin Reuter. He works primarily in experimental and theoretical philosophy of language. His research focuses on normative expressions in natural language, such as thick concepts, dual-character concepts, and normative generics. He also works on integrating computational corpus analysis into experimental philosophy.

Raff Donelson is an associate professor at the Chicago-Kent College of Law. His research focuses on metaethics, American criminal justice, and methodological questions about legal philosophy. Donelson has published widely in peer-reviewed journals such as *Philosophia*, *Philosophical Issues*, *Metaphilosophy*, *Cognitive Science*, and *Contemporary Pragmatism*. Donelson has also published in a number of American law reviews such as the *North Carolina Law Review*, the *Oklahoma Law Review*, and the *Saint Louis University Law Journal*. Donelson holds a JD and a PhD in philosophy from Northwestern University, an MA from the University of Chicago, and a BA from Williams College.

Severin Frohofer is a PhD student at the Institute of Philosophy, University of Zurich. His research interests lie in the philosophy of language and social epistemology. He currently works on the epistemology and normativity of trust, dual-character concepts, and media ethics, using both theoretical and experimental methods.

Levin Güver is a PhD student at the Faculty of Law, University College London, and a member of the Guilty Minds Lab. His research lies at the intersection of law, philosophy, and psychology, with a special focus on criminal jurisprudence.

Ivar R. Hannikainen is a Ramon y Cajal fellow in the Department of Philosophy I at the University of Granada.

Leonard Hoeft is a PostDoc at the Chair for Public Law, Constitutional Law and Legal Philosophy at the Humboldt University Berlin. He holds a PhD in law and a PhD in economics. His research interests are behavioral economics, jurisprudence, moral psychology and legal decision-making.

Lara Kirfel is a postdoctoral researcher at Stanford University.

Markus Kneer (BA Oxford, PhD ENS/EHESS Paris) is a senior research associate at the Philosophy Department of the University of Zurich, where he leads the Guilty Minds Lab. He works on experimental jurisprudence, philosophy of mind, and philosophy of language. His work has appeared in journals such as *Proceedings of the National Academy of Sciences*, *Cognition Cognitive Science* and *Linguistics and Philosophy*.

Gary Lavery is a postdoctoral researcher associated with the Institute of Cognition and Culture, Queen's University Belfast, Belfast, UK. His research interests are varied, focusing on folk psychology, evolved social contract algorithms, morality, and the development of deontic reasoning

Stefan Magen is Director of the Center for Law, Behavior, and Cognition at Ruhr University Bochum and Full Professor at the Faculty of Law. Magen clerked for Judge Hassemer at the German Federal Constitutional Court and works on Constitutional Law, the Behavioral Analysis of Law, and Naturalistic Legal Philosophy.

Eric Martínez is a PhD candidate at Massachusetts Institute of Technology in the Department of Brain and Cognitive Sciences and a research fellow at the Legal Priorities Project. His research interests lie at the intersection of cognitive science and law—particularly with regard to legal design and decision-making–using both experimental and computational methods. Eric also holds a JD from Harvard Law School and is a licensed attorney in the Commonwealth of Massachusetts.

Karolina Prochownik is a senior researcher at the Center for Law, Behavior, and Cognition, Faculty of Law, Ruhr University Bochum. She holds a PhD in philosophy and a PhD in law. Her research interests are in experimental philosophy, ethics, moral psychology, and the cognitive science of religion.

Kevin Reuter is an SNSF Eccellenza Professor at the Institute of Philosophy, University of Zurich. His research interests are in the philosophy of mind, language, cognitive, social sciences, and experimental philosophy. Currently, he studies evaluative concepts, the nature and concepts of pains and emotions, and (ir)rational decision-making processes.

Paulo Sousa is Director of the Institute of Cognition and Culture and Senior Lecturer in Cognitive Anthropology at the School of History, Anthropology, Philosophy, and Politics, Queen's University Belfast, Belfast, UK. His current research interests focus on lay views of intentional action, agency, and morality, as well as their relationship with legal systems.

Noel Struchiner is Professor of Law and Philosophy at the Pontifical Catholic University of Rio de Janeiro, "Research Productivity Fellow" at CNPq (National

Council for Scientific and Technological Development), and "Scientist of the State of Rio de Janeiro Fellow" at FAPERJ (Carlos Chagas Filho Foundation of Research Support of the State of Rio de Janeiro).

Justin Sytsma is an associate professor in the philosophy program at Victoria University of Wellington. Justin's research focuses on issues in philosophy of psychology and philosophy of mind. As a practitioner of experimental philosophy, Justin's research into these areas often involves the use of empirical methods.

Kevin Tobia is an associate professor of Law and Philosophy (by courtesy) at Georgetown University.

Pascale Willemsen is a postdoctoral researcher at the Institute of Philosophy, University of Zurich, and Principle Investigator of the SNSF-funded research group, Investigating Think Ethical Concepts. Her research interests are in causal cognition, philosophical moral psychology, metaethics, philosophy action, normativity in language, and experimental philosophy. She is further involved in projects concerning the relationship between agency, moral responsibility, and free will; the folk concept of lying; the ethics of omissions; and the relationship between moral responsibility and causal responsibility.

Christoph Winter is Assistant Professor of Law at the Instituto Tecnológico Autónomo de México (ITAM), Research Associate in Psychology at Harvard University, and Director of the Legal Priorities Project.

Index